AMERICAN POLITICAL, ECONOMIC, AND SECURITY ISSUES

NORTH AMERICAN FREE TRADE AGREEMENT AFTER FIVE YEARS

AMERICAN POLITICAL, ECONOMIC, AND SECURITY ISSUES

Additional books in this series can be found on Nova's website
under the Series tab.

Additional E-books in this series can be found on Nova's website
under the E-book tab.

TRADE ISSUES, POLICIES AND LAWS

Additional books in this series can be found on Nova's website
under the Series tab.

Additional E-books in this series can be found on Nova's website
under the E-books tab.

AMERICAN POLITICAL, ECONOMIC, AND SECURITY ISSUES

NORTH AMERICAN FREE TRADE AGREEMENT AFTER FIVE YEARS

MARY E. BERGMANN
EDITOR

Nova Science Publishers, Inc.
New York

LIBRARY OF CONGRESS CATALOGING-IN-PUBLICATION DATA

North American Free Trade Agreement after five years / editor, Mary E. Bergmann.
p. cm.
Includes index.
ISBN 978-1-61122-359-0 (hardcover)
1. Free trade--North America. 2. North America--Economic integration. 3. North America--Economic policy. 4. Canada. Treaties, etc. 1992 Oct. 7 I. Bergmann, Mary E.
HF1746.N57 2010
382'.917--dc22
2010038652

Published by Nova Science Publishers, Inc. † New York

CONTENTS

PREFACE

Economic motivations are generally the major driving force for the formation of free trade agreements among countries, but there are other reasons countries enter into FTAs, including political and security factors. Trade agreements were also expected to improve investor confidence, attract foreign investment, and create jobs. Mexico may have other reasons for entering into FTAs, such as expanding market access and decreasing its reliance on the United States as an export market. This book provides an overview of the North American Free Trade Agreement, the current functions of the free trade agreement, and the effects of this agreement which have affected both countries over the last five years.

Chapter 1 - Mexico has had a growing commitment to trade integration through the formation of free trade agreements (FTAs) since the 1990s and its trade policy is among the most open in the world. Mexico's pursuit of FTAs with other countries not only provides economic benefits, but could also potentially reduce its economic dependence on the United States. The United States is, by far, Mexico's most significant trading partner. About 80% of Mexico's exports go to the United States and 49% of Mexico's imports come from the United States. Mexico's second largest trading partner is China, accounting for approximately 6% of Mexico's exports and imports. In an effort to increase trade with other countries, Mexico has a total of 11 trade agreements involving 41 countries. These include agreements with most countries in the Western Hemisphere including the United States and Canada, Chile, Costa Rica, Nicaragua, Guatemala, El Salvador, and Honduras. In addition, Mexico has negotiated FTAs outside of the Western Hemisphere and entered into agreements with Israel and the European Union in July 2000. Mexico also has an FTA with Japan. The large number of trade agreements, however, has not yet been successful in decreasing Mexico's dependence on trade with the United States.

Chapter 2 - The Government of Canada, the Government of the United Mexican States and the Government of the United States of America, resolved to:

STRENGTHEN the special bonds of friendship and cooperation among their nations;

CONTRIBUTE to the harmonious development and expansion of world trade and provide a catalyst to broader international cooperation;

CREATE an expanded and secure market for the goods and services produced in their territories;

REDUCE distortions to trade;

ESTABLISH clear and mutually advantageous rules governing their trade;

ENSURE a predictable commercial framework for business planning and investment;

BUILD on their respective rights and obligations under the General Agreement on Tariffs and Trade and other multilateral and bilateral instruments of cooperation;

ENHANCE the competitiveness of their firms in global markets;

FOSTER creativity and innovation, and promote trade in goods and services that are the subject of intellectual property rights;

CREATE new employment opportunities and improve working conditions and living standards in their respective territories;

UNDERTAKE each of the preceding in a manner consistent with environmental protection and conservation;

PRESERVE their flexibility to safeguard the public welfare;

PROMOTE sustainable development;

STRENGTHEN the development and enforcement of environmental laws and regulations; and

PROTECT, enhance and enforce basic workers' rights;

In: North American Free Trade Agreement after Five Years   ISBN: 978-1-61122-359-0
Editor: Mary E. Bergmann   © 2011 Nova Science Publishers, Inc.

Chapter 1

MEXICO'S FREE TRADE AGREEMENTS

M. Angeles Villarreal

SUMMARY

Mexico has had a growing commitment to trade integration through the formation of free trade agreements (FTAs) since the 1990s and its trade policy is among the most open in the world. Mexico's pursuit of FTAs with other countries not only provides economic benefits, but could also potentially reduce its economic dependence on the United States. The United States is, by far, Mexico's most significant trading partner. About 80% of Mexico's exports go to the United States and 49% of Mexico's imports come from the United States. Mexico's second largest trading partner is China, accounting for approximately 6% of Mexico's exports and imports. In an effort to increase trade with other countries, Mexico has a total of 11 trade agreements involving 41 countries. These include agreements with most countries in the Western Hemisphere including the United States and Canada, Chile, Costa Rica, Nicaragua, Guatemala, El Salvador, and Honduras. In addition, Mexico has negotiated FTAs outside of the Western Hemisphere and entered into agreements with Israel and the European Union in July 2000. Mexico also has an FTA with Japan. The large number of trade agreements, however, has not yet been successful in decreasing Mexico's dependence on trade with the United States.

Economic motivations are generally the major driving force for the formation of free trade agreements among countries, but there are other reasons countries enter into FTAs, including political and security factors. One of Mexico's primary motivations for the unilateral trade liberalization efforts of the late 1980s and early 1990s was to improve economic conditions in the country, which policymakers hoped would lead to greater investor confidence and attract more foreign investment. Trade agreements were also expected to improve investor confidence, attract foreign investment, and create jobs. Mexico may have other reasons for entering into FTAs, such as expanding market access and decreasing its reliance on the United States as an export market. The slow progress in multilateral negotiations may also contribute to the increasing interest throughout the world in regional trade blocs. Some countries may see smaller trade arrangements as "building blocks" for multilateral agreements.

Since Mexico began trade liberalization in the early 1990s, its trade with the world has risen rapidly, with exports increasing more rapidly than imports. Mexico's trade balance with all countries went from a deficit of $13.5 billion in 1993 to surpluses of $7.1 billion in 1995 and $6.5 billion in 1996. Since 1998, Mexico's trade balance has remained in deficit, reaching $17.5 billion in 2008. The trade balance with the United States went from a deficit of $2.4 billion in 1993 to a surplus of $82.0 billion in 2008. Exports to the United States increased 447% between 1993 and 2008, from $42.9 billion to $292.6 billion. Mexico's imports from the United States increased 237% during the same time period, from $45.3 billion to $152.6 billion.

In the 110th Congress, issues of concern related to the trade and economic relationship with Mexico involved mostly economic conditions in Mexico, issues related to the North American Free Trade Agreement (NAFTA), the effect of NAFTA on Mexico, and Mexican migrant workers in the United States. The 111th Congress will likely maintain an active interest concerning Mexico on these issues. This report provides an overview of Mexico's free trade agreements, its motivations for trade liberalization and entering into free trade agreements, and some of the issues Mexico faces in addressing its economic challenges. This report will be updated as events warrant.

INTRODUCTION

The number of regional trade agreements (RTAs) throughout the world has grown steadily since the early 1990s. One of the reasons for the increasing interest in bilateral or regional trade agreements is the impasse of the Doha Development Agenda (DDA). Many members of the World Trade Organization (WTO) are focusing on regional or bilateral free trade agreements as a key component of their foreign and commercial policy.[1] This interest is evident among industrialized and developing countries, and throughout various world regions, including numerous countries in the Americas, Europe, and Asia. Mexico is a member of the WTO, which permits members to enter into regional trade integration arrangements under certain conditions that are defined within specific WTO rules.[2]

Since the early 1990s, Mexico has had a growing commitment to trade liberalizations and its trade policy is among the most open in the world. Mexico has been actively pursuing free trade agreements with other countries to help promote economic growth, but also to reduce its economic dependence on the United States. The United States is, by far, Mexico's most significant trading partner. Over 80% of Mexico's exports are destined for the United States. In an effort to increase trade with other countries, Mexico has entered into eleven free trade agreements with 41 countries.[3] Mexico has used trade liberalization as one of a number of policy tools to improve economic growth. The government has other programs to promote economic development and to address the issue of poverty.

In the 110th Congress, issues of concern related to the trade and economic relationship with Mexico involved mostly economic conditions in Mexico, issues related to the North American Free Trade Agreement (NAFTA), the effect of NAFTA on Mexico, and Mexican migrant workers in the United States. The 111th Congress will likely maintain an active interest concerning Mexico on these issues. This report provides an overview of Mexico's free trade agreements, its motivations for trade liberalization and entering into free trade agreements, and some of the issues Mexico faces in addressing its economic challenges. This report will be updated as events warrant.

MOTIVATIONS FOR TRADE INTEGRATION

Economic motivations are generally the major driving force for the formation of free trade agreements (FTAs) among countries, but there are other reasons countries enter into FTAs, including political and security factors. One of Mexico's primary motivations for the unilateral trade liberalization efforts of the late 1980s and early 1990s was to improve economic conditions in the country, which policymakers hoped would lead to greater investor confidence and attract more foreign investment. This motivation was a major factor in negotiating NAFTA with the United States and Canada. The permanent lowering of trade and investment barriers and predictable trade rules provided by FTAs can improve investor confidence in a country, which helps attract foreign direct investment (FDI). Multinational firms invest in countries to gain access to markets, but they also do it to lower production costs.

Mexico has other motivations for continuing trade liberalization with other countries, such as expanding market access for its exports and decreasing its reliance on the United States as an export market. By entering into trade agreements with other countries, Mexico also may be seeking to achieve economies of scale in certain sectors of the economy and expand its export market. Free trade agreements provide partners with broader market access for their goods and services. Countries can benefit from trade agreements because producers are able to lower their unit costs by producing larger volumes for regional markets in addition to their own domestic markets.[4] When more units of a good or a service can be produced on a larger scale, companies are able to decrease cost of production.

The slow progress in multilateral negotiations in the World Trade Organization (WTO) may also be a factor in Mexico's motivations to enter into FTAs. Some countries see smaller trade arrangements as "building blocks" for multilateral agreements. Other motivations are political. It is possible that Mexico may be seeking to demonstrate good governance by locking in political and economic reforms through trading partnerships. Trade agreements could forge geopolitical alliances and strengthen diplomatic ties. Some analysts believe that the choice of RTA partners is increasingly based on political and security concerns and not so much on economic rationale.[5]

MEXICAN TRADE LIBERALIZATION

From the 1930s through part of the 1980s, Mexico maintained a strong protectionist trade policy in an effort to be independent of any foreign power and as a means to promote domestic-led industrialization. Mexico established a policy of import substitution in the 1930s, consisting of a broad, general protection of the entire industrial sector. Mexico placed tight restrictions on foreign investment and controlled the exchange rate to encourage domestic industrial growth. Mexico also nationalized the oil industry during this time. These protectionist economic policies remained in effect until the country began to experience a series of economic challenges caused by a number of factors.

The 1980s in Mexico were marked by inflation and a declining standard of living. The 1982 debt crisis in which the Mexican government was unable to meet its foreign debt obligations caused an economic collapse in the mid-1980s. Much of the government's efforts in these addressing challenges were placed on privatizing state industries and moving toward trade liberalization. In the late 1980s and early into the 1990s, the Mexican government implemented a series of measures to restructure the economy that included unilateral trade liberalization, replacing import substitution policies with others aimed at attracting foreign investment, lowering trade barriers and making the country competitive in non-oil exports. Mexico had few options but to open its economy through trade liberalization after the debt crisis. In 1986, Mexico acceded to the General Agreement on Tariffs and Trade (GATT), assuring further trade liberalization measures that led to closer ties with the United States.

In 1990, President Carlos Salinas de Gortari approached then-U.S. President George H.W. Bush with the idea of forming an FTA. In 1992, Mexico's first agreement for free trade in goods, the Mexico-Chile FTA, came into force. The NAFTA, an FTA that includes Canada, as well as the United States and Mexico, entered into force two years later in 1994. It contained much broader provisions that included trade in services, government procurement, dispute settlement procedures, and intellectual property rights protection. In 1999, the original text of the Mexico-Chile FTA was later complemented with broader provisions, similar to those under NAFTA. Mexico's main motivation in pursuing FTAs with the United States and other countries was to stabilize the Mexican economy, which had experienced many difficulties throughout most of the 1980s with a significant deepening of poverty, by attracting foreign direct investment. The expectation in Mexico was that FTAs would increase export diversification and help create jobs, increase wage rates, and reduce poverty. At the time NAFTA went into effect, some studies predicted that the agreement to have an overall positive impact on the U.S. and Mexican economies though there would be some adjustment costs.[6]

MEXICO'S TRADE AGREEMENTS

Mexico's pursuit of free trade agreements with other countries is a way to bring benefits to the economy, but also to reduce its economic dependence on the United States. The United States is, by far, Mexico's most significant trading partner. About 82% of Mexico's exports go to the United States and 50% of Mexico's imports come from the United States. Mexico's second largest trading partner is China, accounting for approximately 6% of Mexico's exports and imports.[7] In an effort to increase trade with other countries, Mexico has a total of 11 trade agreements involving 41 countries (see Table 1). These include agreements with many countries in the Western Hemisphere including the United States and Canada, Chile, Bolivia, Costa Rica, Nicaragua, Uruguay, Guatemala, El Salvador, and Honduras.

Mexico has also negotiated free trade agreements outside of the Western Hemisphere and, in July 2000, entered into agreements with Israel and the European Union. Mexico became the first Latin American country to have preferred access to these two markets.

Mexico has completed a trade agreement with the European Free Trade Association of Iceland, Liechtenstein, Norway, and Switzerland. The Mexican government expanded its outreach to Asia in 2000 by entering into negotiations with Singapore, Korea, and Japan. In 2004, Japan and Mexico signed the Economic Partnership Agreement, the first comprehensive trade agreement that Japan signed with any country.[8] However, the large number of trade agreements has not yet been successful in decreasing Mexico's dependence on trade with the United States.

Table 1. Mexico's Free Trade Agreements

Agreement	Agreement Type	Coverage	Date of Signature	Entry into Force	WTO Legal Cover
North American Free Trade Agreement	FTA and EIA[a]	Goods and Services	December 17, 1992	January 1, 1994	GATT Art. XXIV and GATS V
Costa Rica – Mexico	FTA and EIA	Goods and Services	April 5, 1994	January 1, 1995	GATT Art. XXIV and GATS V
Nicaragua – Mexico	FTA and EIA	Goods and Services	December 18, 1997	July 1, 1998	GATT Art. XXIV and GATS V
Chile – Mexico	FTA and EIA	Goods and Services	April 17, 1998	August 1, 1999	GATTS Art. XXIV and GATS V
European Union[b] –Mexico	FTA and EIA	Goods and Services	December 8, 1997	July 1, 2000 (goods)	GATT Art. XXIV and GATS V
				October 1, 2000 (services)	
Israel – Mexico	FTA	Goods	April 10, 2000	July 1, 2000	GATT Art. XXIV
El Salvador – Mexico	FTA and EIA	Goods and Services	June 29, 2000	March 15, 2001	GATT Art. XXIV and GATSV
Guatemala – Mexico	FTA and EIA	Goods and Services	June 29, 2000	March 15, 2001	GATT Art. XXIV and GATS V
Honduras – Mexico	FTA and EIA	Goods and Services	June 29, 2000	June 1, 2001	GATT Art. XXIV and GATS V
EFTA[c] – Mexico	FTA and EIA	Goods and Services	November 27, 2000	July 1, 2001	GATT Art. XXIV and GATS V
Japan – Mexico	FTA and EIA	Goods and Services	September 17, 2004	April 1, 2005	GATT Art. XXIV and GATS V

Source: World Trade Organization, Regional Trade Agreement Database, see http://www.wto.org/. Notes: The WTO definition of a free-trade area is a group of two or more customs territories in which the duties and other restrictive regulations of commerce (except, where necessary, those permitted under Articles XI, XII, XIII, XIV, XV, and XX of the GATT) are eliminated on substantially all the trade between the constituent territories in products originating in such territories.

a. Economic Integration Agreement (EIA) as defined by the World Trade Organization.

b. Includes Austria, Belgium, Bulgaria, Cyprus, Czech Republic, Denmark, Estonia, Finland, France, Germany, Greece, Hungary, Ireland, Italy, Latvia, Lithuania, Luxembourg, Malta, Netherlands, Poland, Portugal, Romania, Slovak Republic, Slovenia, Spain, Sweden, and United Kingdom.

c. Includes Iceland, Liechtenstein, Norway, and Switzerland.

NAFTA

In 1990, Mexico approached the United States with the idea of forming a free trade agreement. Mexico's main motivation in pursuing an FTA with the United States was to help stabilize the Mexican economy and attract foreign direct investment.[9] The Mexican economy had experienced many difficulties throughout most of the 1980s with a significant deepening of poverty. NAFTA is a free trade agreement that eliminated trade and investment barriers among Canada, Mexico, and the United States. Mexico's intention in entering NAFTA was to increase export diversification by attracting FDI, which would help create jobs, increase wage rates, and reduce poverty.

Upon implementation, almost 70% of U.S. imports from Mexico and 50% of U.S. exports to Mexico received duty-free treatment. The remainder of duties were eliminated over a period of 15 years after the agreement was in effect. The agreement also contains provisions for market access to U.S. firms in most service sectors; protection of U.S. foreign direct investment in Mexico; and intellectual property rights protection for U.S. companies. NAFTA is the first U.S. agreement that addressed environmental and labor concerns by including related provision in separate side agreements to NAFTA. At the time the agreement went into effect, a number of economic studies predicted that the trade agreement would have a positive overall effect on the Mexican economy, narrowing the U.S.-Mexico gap in prices of goods and services and the differential in real wages.

Mexico-Costa Rica

The Mexico-Costa Rica FTA was signed on April 5, 1994, in Mexico City and entered into force on January 1, 1995. It was the first in a series of FTAs negotiated by Mexico loosely based on the NAFTA model of trade agreements. This agreement had been preceded by a partial scope agreement signed by the two countries on July 22, 1982 in which Mexico accorded preferential access to some Costa Rican products. The FTA with Costa Rica phased out tariffs in four stages over a fifteen-year time period. Upon implementation of the agreement, approximately 70% of Mexican goods entered Costa Rica and 80% of Costa Rican goods entered Mexico duty free. By January 1, 2004, almost 97% of trade between the two countries was duty free and by 2009, virtually all tariffs had been eliminated.[10]

In addition to the provisions on national treatment and market access for goods, the agreement contains provisions on agriculture, sanitary and phytosanitary measures, rules of origin, customs procedures, safeguards, standards, cross-border trade in services, investment, government procurement, intellectual property rights protection (IPR), and dispute resolution. Items that are not included in the agreement include energy and basic petrochemicals, telecommunications, financial services, and competition policy. The IPR chapter does not cover patents, industrial designs, and layout designs of integrated circuits.[11]

Mexico-Nicaragua

The FTA with Nicaragua was Mexico's second treaty with a country in Central America, also loosely based on the NAFTA model. It was signed on December 18, 1997, and entered into force on July 1, 1998. Upon implementation, 76% of tariffs on Nicaraguan exports to Mexico and 45% of tariffs on Mexican exports to Nicaragua were eliminated. The remaining tariffs are being phased out in four stages over a fifteen-year period. The agreement is similar to NAFTA and includes provisions on national treatment and market access for goods and services; rules of origin; agriculture; sanitary and phytosanitary measures; telecommunications; financial services; government procurement; investment; IPT; dispute resolution; customs procedures; safeguards; unfair trade practices; standards; and other provisions. It does not include a chapter on competition policy, energy, environment, labor, or transportation.[12] The IPR provisions do not cover patents, industrial designs, and layout designs of integrated circuits.[13]

Mexico-Chile

The Mexico-Chile FTA, completed in 1998, was enacted in Chile on July 7, 1999, and in Mexico on August 1, 1999. Mexico and Chile signed the expanded FTA at the 1998 Summit of the Americas in Santiago, Chile on April 17, 1998. The FTA was expected to deepen the growing trade relationship between the two countries and improve bilateral investment opportunities in both countries. The 1998 agreement replaced an earlier FTA that was reached between the two countries in 1991. It removed tariffs on almost all merchandise trade between the two countries.

The Mexico-Chile FTA includes provisions on national treatment and market access for goods and services; rules of origin; customs procedures; safeguards; standards; agriculture; sanitary and phytosanitary measures; investment; air transportation; telecommunications; temporary entry for business persons; IPR; dispute resolution; and other provisions. It does not include a chapter on energy, environment, or labor.[14] A separate agreement, which was signed simultaneously, includes provisions to avoid double taxation for companies doing business in both countries. The FTA provisions are similar to those under NAFTA, but with no labor and environmental provisions in separate side agreements. Other areas that were not included in the 1998 FTA were financial services, patents, or government procurement.[15]

Mexico-European Union

Negotiations for a free trade agreement between Mexico and the European Union (EU) began in October 1996. The agreement, formally called the Economic Partnership Political Co-ordination and Co-operation Agreement (also known as the Global Agreement), was signed in March 2000 and came into force on July 1, 2000. It was the first transatlantic FTA for the EU. The motivations for the agreement were to expand market access for exports from the EU to Mexico and attract more FDI from the EU to Mexico.[16] On May 17, 2008, Mexico and the European Union agreed on a "strategic association" to further advance trade liberalization and to address climate change issues.[17]

The agreement includes provisions on national treatment and market access for goods and services; government procurement; IPR; investment; financial services; standards; telecommunications and information services; agriculture; dispute settlement; and other provisions. The agreement also includes chapters in which the parties agree to increase cooperation in a number of areas, including mining, energy, transportation, tourism, statistics, science and technology, environment, and other areas.[18] On industrial goods, the EU agreed to eliminate tariffs on 82% of imports by value coming from Mexico on the date of entry into the agreement and to phase out remaining tariffs by January 1, 2003. Mexico agreed to eliminate tariffs on 47% of imports by value from the EU upon implementation of the agreement and to phase out the remaining tariffs by January 1, 2007. In agricultural products and fisheries, signatories agreed to phase out tariffs on 62% of trade within ten years.[19] Tariff negotiations were deferred on certain sensitive products, including meat, dairy products, cereals, and bananas. Most non-tariff barriers, such as quotas and import/export licenses, were removed upon implementation of the agreement. Mexico agreed to phase out import restrictions of new automobiles from the EU by 2007. In government procurement, Mexico agreed to follow provisions similar to those under NAFTA to allow the EU to enter the Mexican market while the EU agreed to follow WTO rules.[20] In services trade, the agreement goes beyond the WTO General Agreement on Trade in Services (GATS). It immediately provided European service operators "NAFTA-equivalent" access to Mexico in a number of areas, including financial services, energy, telecommunications, and tourism.[21]

Mexico-Israel

After two years of negotiations, Mexico and Israel signed a free trade agreement on April 10, 2000 and implemented it on July 1, 2000. The agreement immediately eliminated tariffs on most products traded between Mexico and Israel at the time of the agreement with full tariff elimination scheduled by 2005. Policymakers expected the agreement to provide Mexico with more export access to the Israeli market, increased FDI from Israel to Mexico, and result in increased technology transfer from Israel to Mexico.

The agreement includes provisions on national treatment and market access for goods, rules of origin, customs procedures, emergency actions, competition policy, government procurement, dispute resolution, dispute resolution, and WTO rights and obligations.[22] The agreement covers 98.6% of agricultural goods and 100% of industrial goods. Mexico received immediate duty-free access on 50% of its exports and tariff reductions on 12% of its exports to Israel. Tariff-rate quotas were applied on 25% of Mexican exports to Israel. Most remaining tariff barriers on Mexican exports had a five-year phase out schedule. Israel received immediate duty-free access on about 72% of its exports to Mexico. Another 22.8% of tariffs on Israel exports to Mexico were withdrawn in 2003 and another 4.4% were withdrawn in 2005.[23]

Mexico-El Salvador, Guatemala, and Honduras

Mexico and El Salvador, Guatemala, and Honduras (Northern Triangle) signed a free trade agreement on June 29, 2000. The agreement is often referred to as the Mexico-Northern Triangle FTA, but the WTO has it listed as three separate agreements between Mexico and El Salvador, Guatemala, and Honduras. The agreements with El Salvador and Guatemala entered into force on March 15, 2001, while the agreement with Honduras entered into force on June 1, 2001. Negotiations for the FTA with all three countries began in 1992, stalled for four years, and resumed at the second Tuxtla Summit in 1996. Negotiations ended on May 10, 2000. This agreement was the final of Mexico's NAFTA-type agreements with all Central American countries. Prior to the conclusion of the Mexico-Northern Triangle FTA, Mexico had held separate partial scope agreements with each of the three countries, granting some products preferential access to the Mexican market.

The agreement includes provisions on national treatment and market access for goods and services, the agreement has similar provisions to other Mexican FTAs on agriculture; sanitary and phytosanitary measures; rules of origin; financial services; telecommunications services; temporary entry of business persons; investment; IPR; standards; dispute resolution; safeguards; and unfair trade practices.[24] Upon entry into force of the FTA, approximately 57% of Mexico's exports to the three countries received duty-free treatment. Tariffs on an additional 15% of goods were phased out over a period of three to five years. Mexico eliminated tariffs on 65% of imports from the Northern Triangle countries upon implementation and phased out tariffs on 24% of imports over a three to five year period. Thirty percent of Mexico's agricultural exports received duty-free treatment upon the entry into force of the agreement, another 12% were liberalized over a five-year period, and 41% were liberalized over a period of five to eleven years.[25]

Mexico-European Free Trade Association

Mexico and the European Free Trade Association (EFTA), composed of Iceland, Lichtenstein, Norway, and Switzerland, signed a free trade agreement on November 27, 2000. The agreement entered into force on July 1, 2001. This was the first FTA that the EFTA had concluded with an overseas partner country. Since the agreement entered into force, Mexico and the EFTA have met at least four times to explore possibilities of further trade integration, including agricultural and services trade. In September 2008, the two parties agreed to adopt an amendment on transportation to the agreement to help facilitate trade. They also discussed possibilities of further amendments, such as banning export duties and extending the coverage of trade in processed agricultural products.[26]

The agreement includes provisions on national treatment and market access for goods; agriculture; rules of origin; safeguards; and other provisions.[27] During the first six years, the FTA reduced the average Mexican tariff on EFTA industrial goods from 8% to zero. Mexican industrial exports to the EFTA have been free of duty since the entry into force of the FTA.[28]

Mexico-Japan

Mexico and Japan signed a free trade agreement, formally called an Economic Partnership Agreement (EPA) in September 2004. The EPA was Japan's second free trade agreement, but its most comprehensive bilateral agreement at that time. It was Japan's first agreement to include agricultural products, a factor that resulted in initial opposition in Japan. In addition to the removal of tariff barriers, it includes regulations in other areas, including labor mobility and investment.[29] One of the goals of the Mexico-Japan EPA was to restore the competitiveness of Japanese companies in the Mexican market. Mexico already had free trade with the United States and Canada under NAFTA and with the European Union through an FTA that went into force in July 2000. These two agreements had placed Japanese companies at a disadvantage due to differences in tariff rates and exclusion of Japanese companies from public-works projects in Mexico. Mexico entered the agreement to increase Japanese investment in Mexico, and, thus, create jobs, expand Mexican exports to Japan, expand technology transfer from Japan, and strengthen Mexican industrial competitiveness.[30]

The agreement includes provisions on national treatment and market access for goods; sanitary and phytosanitary measures; standards; rules of origin; customs procedures; safeguards; IPR; dispute settlement; financial services; and government procurement. The agreement also includes chapters in which the two countries agreed to increase cooperation in a number of areas, including vocational education and training, agriculture, tourism, and the environment.[31] The two countries agreed to eliminate tariffs on almost all industrial products within ten years. Tariffs were eliminated immediately in the following areas: electronics, household electric appliances, capital goods, and automobiles. By the year 2015, tariffs will be eliminated on 90% of goods that accounted for 96% in total trade value between the two countries. Prior to the EPA, only 16% of Japanese exports to Mexico entered duty free into the Mexican market, while 70% of Mexican exports to Japan entered duty free. In agriculture, Mexican officials initially called for trade concessions in beef, oranges, pineapples, and leather products, but later agreed to an expansion of Japanese import quotas over a five-year period for pork, beef, chicken, oranges, and orange juice.

These are scheduled to be revised in 2010, the fifth year of the agreement. The value of Mexico's agricultural products exempt from import tariffs was reportedly expected to be less than 50% of its total agricultural exports to Japan.[32] The agreement also allowed for a duty-free quota for motor vehicles and steel upon implementation, with a phase-out scheduled over time. Japan's auto and steel companies were expected to benefit the most from these provisions.[33]

Partial Scope Agreements

Mexico also has a number of partial scope agreements, which are integration agreements with more limited free trade coverage than a free trade agreement. Mexico is a party to the Agreement on the Global System of Trade Preferences Among Developing Countries (GSTP). The GSTP was established in 1988 as a framework for the exchange of trade preferences among developing countries to promote trade among developing countries. The agreement provides tariff preferences on merchandise trade among member countries. It is a treaty to which only Group of 77 member countries may enter.[34] The text of the agreement was adopted after a round of negotiations that was concluded in Belgrade in 1988. The agreement, which entered into force on April 19, 1989, was envisaged as being a dynamic instrument which would be expanded in successive stages in additional rounds of negotiations and reviewed periodically. [35] A second round of negotiations was proposed in the early 1990s to expand trade preferences, but negotiations faltered as members failed to ratify the agreement. In June 2004, GSTP participants launched a third round of negotiations. Forty-four countries have acceded to the agreement.[36]

Mexico is a signatory to the Latin American Integration Association (ALADI), which was established by the Treaty of Montevideo in August 1980 and entered into force on March 18, 1981. ALADI replaced the Latin American Free Trade Association established in 1960 with the goal of developing a common market in Latin America. ALADI members include Argentina, Bolivia, Brazil, Chile, Colombia, Cuba, Ecuador, Mexico, Paraguay, Peru, Uruguay, and Venezuela. Signatory countries have sought economic cooperation amongst each other but have made little progress toward forming a common market. They maintain a flexible goal of encouraging free trade without a timetable for instituting a common market. Members approved a regional tariff preference arrangement in 1984 and expanded it in 1987 and 1990.[37]

Mexico is also a member of the Protocol Relating to Trade Negotiations among Developing Countries (PTN). The PTN is a preferential arrangement involving Bangladesh, Brazil, Chile, Egypt, Israel, Mexico, Pakistan, Paraguay, Peru, Philippines, Republic of Korea, Serbia, Tunisia, Turkey, and Uruguay. It was signed in December 1971 and became effective on February 11, 1973.

Table 2. Mexico's Partial Scope Agreements

Agreement	Coverage	Date of Signature	Entry into Force	WTO Legal Cover
Global System of Trade Preferences Among Developing Countries (GSTP)[a]	Goods	April 13, 1988	April 19, 1989	Enabling Clause
Latin American Integration Association (ALADI)[b]	Goods	August 12, 1980	March 18, 1981	Enabling Clause
Protocol on Trade Negotiations (PTN)[c]	Goods	December 8, 1971	February 11, 1973	Enabling Clause

Source: World Trade Organization, Regional Trade Agreement Database, see http://www.wto.org/.

a. Includes Algeria, Argentina, Bangladesh, Benin, Venezuela, Bolivia, Brazil, Cameroon, Chile, Colombia, Cuba, Ecuador, Egypt, Former Yugoslav Republic of Macedonia, Ghana, Guinea, Guyana, India, Indonesia, Islamic Republic of Iran, Iraq, Republic of Korea, Democratic People's Republic of Korea, Libyan Arab Jamahirlya, Malaysia, Mexico, Morocco, Mozambique, Myanmar, Nicaragua, Nigeria, Pakistan, Peru, Philippines, Singapore, Sri Lanka, Sudan, Tanzania, Thailand, Trinidad and Tobago, Tunisia, Vietnam, and Zimbabwe.

b. Includes Argentina, Venezuela, Bolivia, Brazil, Chile, Colombia, Cuba, Ecuador, Mexico, Paraguay, Peru, and Uruguay.

c. Includes Bangladesh, Brazil, Chile, Egypt, Israel, Republic of Korea, Mexico, Pakistan, Paraguay, Peru, Philippines, Serbia, Tunisia, Turkey, Uruguay.

MEXICO'S MERCHANDISE TRADE

Since the early 1990s, Mexico's trade with the world has risen rapidly, with exports increasing more rapidly than imports. Mexico's exports to all countries increased 465% between 1993 and 2008, from $51.8 billion to $292.6 billion (see Figure 1). Mexico's imports from all countries increased 374% during the same time period from $65.4 billion to $310.1 billion. Mexico's trade balance went from a deficit of $13.5 billion in 1993 to surpluses of $7.1 billion in 1995 and $6.5 billion in 1996. Since 1998, Mexico's trade balance has remained in deficit, reaching $17.5 billion in 2008.

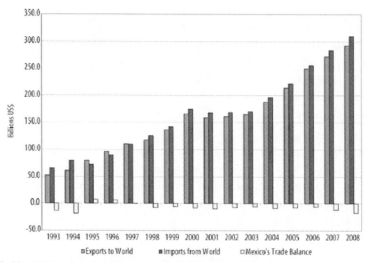

Source: Compiled by CRS using data from Mexico's Ministry of Economy.

Figure 1. Mexico's Merchandise Trade with All Countries.

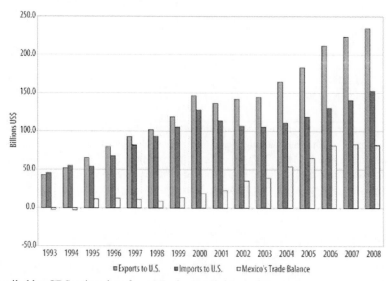

Source: Compiled by CRS using data from Mexico's Ministry of Economy.

Figure 2. Mexico's Merchandise Trade with the United States.

Trade with the United States

Mexico's trade with the United States has increased rapidly since the early 1990s, with exports increasing more rapidly than imports. Mexico's exports to the United States increased 447% between 1993 and 2008, from $42.9 billion to $234.6 billion (see Figure 2). Mexico's imports from the United States increased by 237% during the same time period, from $45.3 billion to $152.6 billion. Mexico's trade balance with the United States went from a deficit of $2.4 billion in 1993 to a surplus of $82.0 billion in 2008.

Trade Trends Since Liberalization

One of Mexico's primary motivations in seeking free trade agreements with other countries after NAFTA took effect was to decrease its dependence on the United States as a trading partner. However, the share of Mexico's exports going to the United States has remained consistently high since NAFTA and the rest of Mexico's FTAs took effect. Over 80% of Mexico's exports are destined for the United States and approximately half of Mexico's imports come from the United States. In 1995, the year after NAFTA took effect, 82.0% of Mexico's exports went to the United States. The U.S. market share of exports rose to 87.0% in 1999 and remained at about the same level until 2005 when it declined to 84.7%. In 2008, the U.S. share decreased to 80.1%. Between 1996 and 2008, Mexico's total exports doubled from $96.0 billion to $292.7 billion (see Table 3). Exports to countries that have FTAs with Mexico increased considerably during this time period, with exports to Israel experiencing the highest percentage increase (1,592%). NAFTA partners (Canada and the United States) ranked first among Mexico's export markets in 2008, followed by the European Union, Japan, and Chile.

Table 3. Composition of Trade: 2008

Mexico's Exports		Mexico's Imports	
Product (HTS 8-digit level)	Value (Billions US$)	Product (HTS 8-digit level)	Value (Billions US$)
Crude Petroleum Oil	43.6	Gasoline	14.6
Color TV Apparatus	18.1	Liquid Crystal Devices NESOI[a]	4.7
Automobiles	16.1	Automobiles (between 1500 and 3000 cm$^{3)}$	4.3
Mobile Telephones	8.6	Processors and Controllers NESOI[a]	4.1
Wire Harnesses for Automobiles	4.3	Automobiles (larger than 3,000 cm$^{3)}$	3.3
Total	292.6	Total	310.1

Source: Mexico's Subsecretaría de Negociaciones Comerciales Internacionales. Compiled by CRS.
a. NESOI is defined as not elsewhere specified or indicated.

Mexico's total imports increased 247% between 1996 and 2008. Imports from NAFTA trading partners increased by 134% during this time period (see Table 4). Imports from its other FTA trading partners increased more rapidly during these years, with imports from Honduras and Chile experiencing the highest rates of growth (increases of 5,000% and 1,416%, respectively). In 2008, NAFTA countries ranked first as sources of imports ($162.1 billion), followed by the European Union ($39.2 billion), and Japan ($16.3 billion). Mexico's imports from countries with which it has not entered into FTAs increased by over 1000% between 1996 and 2008, from $7.3 billion to $86.0 billion, as shown in Table 4.

Eighty-three percent of Mexico's exports are destined for NAFTA trading partners, with the United States accounting for 80% of these exports. The percentage of exports going to the United States and Canada increased from 85% in 1996 to 90% in 2002, and then decreased in the following years, as shown in Table 5. Exports to the European Union accounted for 6% of Mexico's total exports in 2008. The share of Mexico's imports from NAFTA trading partners decreased from 77% in 1996 to 52% in 2008 (see Table 5). The share of Mexico's imports from the European Union increased from 9% in 1996 to 13% in 2008, while the share from non-FTA countries increased from 8% to 28%. Imports from Japan accounted for 5% of Mexico's imports in 2008, while imports from Chile and other FTA partners accounted for 3%. Although Mexico does not have an FTA with China, Mexico's imports from China increased considerably during this period. Imports from China increased from $760 million in 1996 to $34.8 billion in 2008, an increase of over 4000%.

Table 4. Mexico's Exports by FTA Partners (Millions US$)

Partners	1996	1998	2000	2002	2004	2006	2008	% Change 1996-2008
NAFTA	82,017	103,668	149,784	144,889	167,814	216,976	241,687	195%
Costa Rica	209	290	354	373	387	522	922	341%
Nicaragua	61	65	123	93	151	522	371	508%
Chile	781	736	549	323	443	905	1,589	104%
European Union	3,555	3,988	5,799	5,626	6,818	10,967	17,080	381%
Israel	13	24	67	56	62	91	220	1,592%
El Salvador	177	246	307	292	317	497	772	336%
Guatemala	375	623	574	548	673	935	1,388	270%
Honduras	107	146	149	156	182	285	459	329%
EFTA	200	132	131	172	119	154	643	222%
Japan	1,251	552	1,115	1,194	1,191	1,594	2,068	65%
Rest of World	7,258	7,123	7,169	7,324	9,842	16,477	25,467	251%
Total	96,004	117,593	166,121	161,046	187,999	249,925	292,666	205%

Source: Mexico's Ministry of Economy with data from *Banco de México*. Compiled by CRS.

Table 5. Mexico's Imports from FTA Partners (Millions US$)

FTA Partners	1996	1998	2000	2002	2004	2006	2008	% Change 1996-2008
NAFTA	69,280	95,549	131,551	111,037	116,154	137,687	162,066	134%
Costa Rica	58	87	180	416	852	789	777	1,240%
Nicaragua	12	14	27	27	52	78	119	892%
Chile	171	552	894	1,010	1,464	2,470	2,593	1,416%
European Union	7,800	11,846	15,057	16,950	21,657	28,938	39,160	402%
Israel	79	137	297	250	402	429	524	563%
El Salvador	19	25	20	36	50	59	71	274%
Guatemala	77	81	91	117	230	356	501	551%
Honduras	5	12	13	25	66	123	255	5,000%
EFTA	484	648	851	872	1,074	1,386	1,693	250%
Japan	4,132	4,537	6,466	9,349	10,583	15,295	16,326	295%
Rest of World	7,352	11,885	19,011	28,590	44,226	68,442	86,047	1,070%
Total	89,469	125,373	174,458	168,679	186,810	256,052	310,132	247%

Source: Mexico's Ministry of Economy with data from *Banco de México*. Compiled by CRS.

ECONOMIC POLICY CHALLENGES FOR MEXICO

One of Mexico's primary motivations in seeking FTAs with other countries has been to decrease its reliance on the United States as an export market. Though Mexico's total exports have increased substantially since it began trade liberalization, the United States continues to be the dominant export market for Mexican goods. Over 80% of Mexico's exports were destined for the U.S. market in 2007. The reliance of Mexico on the United States as an export market makes the country more susceptible to economic conditions in the United States. The adverse effects of the financial crisis on the U.S. economy have negatively affected economic growth in Mexico. After years of economic stability, Mexico's real gross domestic product (GDP) is forecast to contract 5.8% or more in 2009 and unemployment is expected to rise considerably. In addition, the slowdown in the U.S. economy has resulted in lower demand for Mexican goods in the United States which has an adverse effect on industrial production in Mexico.[38]

Mexico is facing increasing challenges in addressing issues related to productivity and the competitiveness of its exports. Some economists believe that countries in Latin America need to become more competitive in the global economy in order to promote economic growth and reduce poverty. They argue that if Latin American countries are going to prosper, they must improve labor skills and technology to be more competitive in the global economy.[39] Over the past several years, Mexico has been facing increasing competition from China and other Asian economies in the manufacturing sector. In 2003, China replaced Mexico as the second-highest source of U.S. imports. This has presented challenges to Mexico's manufacturing sector and some economists argue that Mexico has fallen behind in its comparative advantage in exporting in industries with intermediate wages and technological sophistication.[40] They argue that Mexico must invest more in education and telecommunications infrastructure to increase productivity and remain competitive.

The emergence of China in the global marketplace has drawn comparisons between the industrial policies of China and Mexico. Some analysts believe that Mexico should make more progress in scientific research to attract and create high-tech industries, such as China has done. They argue that China's policy to help attract foreign direct investment, which initially consisted of special zones with preferential fiscal and customs policies and later modified to establish scientific and technical research facilities, should serve as an example to Mexico's industrial policy. They believe that Mexico's approach has been a combination of fiscal and customs policies to enhance its comparative advantage of sharing a 2000-mile border with the United States, but that Mexico did little to promote scientific and technical research. They add that Mexican programs have not fostered or encouraged research and development activities to facilitate the creation of technological enterprises.[41]

A primary motivation for entering into free trade agreements is to improve economic conditions and create jobs. In the case of Mexico, an additional key motivation has been to address the issue of poverty by creating jobs for the poor. Mexico has made an effort to make trade agreements a tool for promoting economic development and combating poverty, but it is only part of the overall effort of the Mexican government to address these issues. Mexico has implemented a compensatory policy to address poverty through its *Oportunidades* program (formerly known as Progresa). This program provides cash transfers to families in poverty who demonstrate that they regularly attend medical appointments and can certify that children are attending school.[42] The program has been successful in bringing more economic stability to the country and reducing poverty but it has not helped the country's productivity and may not be a long-term solution. Some argue that such programs result in a dependence for cash transfers and do not help poor workers obtain formal sector jobs with prospects for increasing productivity.[43]

Table 6. Market Share of Exports and Imports by FTA Partner

	1996	1998	2000	2002	2004	2006	2008
Market Share of Mexico's Exports[a]							
NAFTA	85%	88%	90%	90%	89%	87%	83%
EU	4%	3%	3%	3%	4%	4%	6%
Japan	1%	0%	1%	1%	1%	1%	1%
Chile	1%	1%	0%	0%	0%	0%	1%
Other FTA Partners	1%	1%	1%	1%	1%	1%	1%
Rest of World	8%	6%	4%	5%	5%	7%	9%
Market Share of Mexico's Imports[a]							
NAFTA	77%	76%	75%	66%	62%	54%	52%
EU	9%	9%	9%	10%	12%	11%	13%
Japan	5%	4%	4%	6%	6%	6%	5%
Chile	0%	0%	1%	1%	1%	1%	1%
Other FTA Partners	1%	1%	0%	2%	2%	2%	2%
Rest of World	8%	9%	11%	17%	24%	27%	28%

Source: Compiled by CRS using data from Mexico's Ministry of Economy.

a. Totals may not add due to rounding.

IMPLICATIONS FOR U.S. INTERESTS

Mexico's numerous free trade agreements and its trade liberalization policy are of interest to U.S. policymakers because of the implications for U.S.-Mexico trade and the overall relationship of the two countries. There is an interdependent relationship between the two countries, as highlighted by the recent slowdown in the U.S. economy and the adverse effects on the Mexican economy. Economic conditions in Mexico are important to the United States because of the proximity of Mexico to the United States, the close trade and investment interactions, and other social and political issues. Another implication for the United States is the effect of Mexico's FTAs on U.S. exports to Mexico. The liberalization of Mexico's trade and investment barriers to other countries has resulted in increasing competition for U.S. goods and services in the Mexican market. However, trade flows are also affected by other factors such as exchange rates, economic growth, and investor confidence, and it is difficult to isolate these effects.

A number of studies suggest that while Mexico's trade liberalization policy, mainly NAFTA, may have brought economic and social benefits to the Mexican economy as a whole, the benefits have not been evenly distributed throughout the country. Wages and employment tend to be higher in states experiencing higher levels of FDI and trade. In terms of regional effects, initial conditions in Mexico determined which Mexican states experienced stronger economic growth as a result of trade liberalization. States with higher levels of telecommunications and transportation infrastructure gained more benefits than poorer states with lower levels of education, infrastructure, and institutional capacity. This affects the United States because Mexican workers who have lost their job due to trade liberalization may migrate to other areas in Mexico or to the United States to seek jobs.[44]

To address issues affecting trade, U.S. policymakers may consider closer cooperation with Mexico to develop complementary policies to ensure that all segments of the two countries benefit from economic integration. The United States and Mexico, along with Canada, have increased cooperation on economic and security issues through the Security and Prosperity Partnership of North America, but there may be additional options that could be considered by both countries. [45] One issue on which a number of economists and other analysts have agreed upon is that Mexico needs to invest more in education, infrastructure, and institutional strengthening to benefit more fully from freer trade. A possible option to address this issue is to create a bilateral or trilateral fund for development that focuses on building infrastructure, improving education and human capital, and creating more opportunities for research and development. U.S. and Mexican policymakers have informally talked about expanding the mandate of the North American Development Bank (NADBank).[46] A number of Members of the U.S. Congress and elected officials from Mexico have discussed the possibility of expanding the mission of the NADBank to go beyond environmental and border issues and consider creating an infrastructure fund that would be managed by NADBank to provide investment in infrastructure, communications, or education.

End Notes

[1] See CRS Report RL32060, World Trade Organization Negotiations: The Doha Development Agenda, by Ian F. Fergusson, World Trade Organization Negotiations: The Doha Development Agenda, by Ian F. Fergusson.

[2] For more information on the specific sets of rules governing regional trade agreements among WTO members, see Regional Trade Agreements: Rules on the WTO website, see http://www.wto.org.

[3] World Trade Organization (WTO), Regional Trade Agreement Database, see http://www.wto.org/

[4] For more information on the costs and benefits of regional trade agreements, see Cohen, Stephen D., Robert A. Blecker, and Peter D. Whitney, Fundamentals of U.S. Foreign Policy, Westview Press, 2003, pp. 49-79.

[5] Crawford, Jo-Ann and Roberto V. Fiorentino, The Changing Landscape of Regional Trade Agreements, World Trade Organization Discussion Paper No. 8, 2005, p. 16.

[6] United States International Trade Commission (USITC), The Likely Impact on the United States of a Free Trade Agreement with Mexico, USITC Publication 2353, February 1991.

[7] Data compiled by CRS using Global Trade Atlas database.

[8] The Asahi Shimbun, "Japan: Free Trade with Mexico," March 12, 2004.

[9] Hufbauer, Gary Clyde, and Jeffrey J. Schott, NAFTA Revisited, Institute for International Economics, October 2005, p. 3.

[10] Salazar-Xirinachs, José Manuel and Maryse Robert, editors, Toward Free Trade in the Americas, April 2001, p. 98.

[11] Decreto de promulgación del Tratado de Libre Comercio entre los Estados Unidos Mexicanos y la República de Costa Rica. See WTO Regional Trade Agreement Database, see http://www.wto.org.

[12] Tratado de Libre Comercio Chile. See WTO Regional Trade Agreement Database, see http://www.wto.org.

[13] Salazar-Xirinachs, José Manuel and Maryse Robert, editors, Toward Free Trade in the Americas, April 2001, p. 99.

[14] Decreto Promulgatorio del Tratado de Libre Comercio entre el Gobierno de los Estados Unidos Mexicanos y el Gobierno de la República de Nicaragua. See WTO Regional Trade Agreement Database, http://www.wto.org.

[15] Bureau of National Affairs (BNA), International Trade Reporter, "Mexico and Chile Sign Off on Expanded Trade Agreement," April 22, 1998.

[16] Reuters, "Cumbre-México y Unión Europea Acuerdan Acelerar Libre Comercio," May 17, 2008.

[17] Ibid.

[18] Global Agreement, Economic Partnership, Political Coordination and Cooperation Agreement between the European Community and its member States and the United Mexican States. See WTO Regional Trade Agreement Database, see http://www.wto.org.

[19] The Chinese University of Hong Kong, The Mexico-EU Free Trade Agreement, 2000, http://intl.econ. cuhk. edu.hk.

[20] Transnational Institute, Mexican Action Network on Free Trade (RMALC), The EU-Mexico Free Trade Agreement Seven Years On, June 2007.

[21] U.S.-Mexico Chamber of Commerce, The Free Trade Agreement Between Mexico and the European Union, August 2000.

[22] Free Trade Agreement Between the State of Israel and the United Mexican States. See WTO Regional Trade Agreement Database, see http://www.wto.org.

[23] U.S.-Mexico Chamber of Commerce, "History of Mexico-Israel Trade Relations," September 2000.

[24] Tratado de Libre Comercio México-El Salvador, Guatemala y Honduras (Triángulo del Norte). See http://www. sice.oas.org.

[25] Salazar-Xirinachs, José Manuel and Maryse Robert, editors, Toward Free Trade in the Americas, April 2001, p. 99-100.

[26] The European Free Trade Association (EFTA) Secretariat, EFTA and Mexico to Amend Free Trade Agreement, September 2008.

[27] Free Trade Agreement between the EFTA States the United Mexican States. . See WTO Regional Trade Agreement Database, see http://www.wto.org.

[28] Mexico-EU Trade Links, "Mexico-EFTA Free Trade Agreement: After Six Years," July 2007.

[29] The Asahi Shimbun, "Japan, Mexico Ink Landmark Accord," September 20, 2004.

[30] Press Center Japan, "Japan and Mexico Agree on Conclusion of Free-Trade Agreement," March 31, 2004.

[31] Agreement Between Japan the United Mexican States for the Strengthening of the Economic Partnership. See WTO Regional Trade Agreement Database, see http://www.wto.org.

[32] Nikkei Weekly, "FTA with Mexico Paves Way for Talks with Asian Nations," March 15, 2004.

[33] The Asahi Shimbun, "Japan, Mexico Ink Landmark Accord," September 20, 2004.

[34] The Group of 77 (G-77) was established on June 15, 1964 by seventy-seven developing countries, signatories of the "Joint Declaration of the Seventy-Seven Countries," issued at the end of the first session of the United Nations Conference on Trade and Development (UNCTAD) in Geneva.

[35] United Nations Conference on Trade and Development, Press Release, "Global System of Trade Preferences," June 16, 2004.

[36] Ibid.

[37] Latin American Integration Association (ALADI) website, see http://www.aladi.org.

[38] *Latin American Newsletters*, "Latin American Mexico and NAFTA Report," June 2009.

[39] *Miami Herald,* "The Left's Favorite U.S. Nobel May Surprise his Fans," by Andres Oppenheimer, August 16, 2009.

[40] Latin America/Caribbean and Asia/Pacific Economics and Business Association, *Economic Integration and Manufacturing Performance in Mexico: Is Chinese Competition to Blame?,* by Ernesto López-Córdova, Working Paper No. 23, December 2004.

[41] *Mexico Now*, "Mexico's and China's Programs to Attract Foreign Investment," by Ramiro Villega and Migual A. Díaz Marín, pp. 52-55.

[42] Santiago Levy, *Progress against Poverty,* Brookings Institution, 2006.

[43] Levy, Santiago, *Good Intensions, Bad Outcomes: Social Policy, Informality, and Economic Growth in Mexico,* Brookings Institution Press, 2008, pp. 1-6.

[44] For more information, see CRS Report RL34733, *NAFTA and the Mexican Economy,* by M. Angeles Villarreal.

[45] See CRS Report RS22701, *Security and Prosperity Partnership of North America: An Overview and Selected Issues*, by M. Angeles Villarreal and Jennifer E. Lake.

[46] NADBank and its sister institution, the Border Environment Cooperation Commission (BECC), were created under a bilateral side agreement to NAFTA called the Border Environmental Cooperation Agreement (BECC) to address environmental infrastructure problems along the U.S.-Mexican border.

In: North American Free Trade Agreement after Five Years   ISBN: 978-1-61122-359-0
Editor: Mary E. Bergmann   © 2011 Nova Science Publishers, Inc.

Chapter 2

NORTH AMERICAN FREE TRADE AGREEMENT

Mary E. Bergmann

PREAMBLE

The Government of Canada, the Government of the United Mexican States and the Government of the United States of America, resolved to:

STRENGTHEN the special bonds of friendship and cooperation among their nations;

CONTRIBUTE to the harmonious development and expansion of world trade and provide a catalyst to broader international cooperation;

CREATE an expanded and secure market for the goods and services produced in their territories;

REDUCE distortions to trade;

ESTABLISH clear and mutually advantageous rules governing their trade;

ENSURE a predictable commercial framework for business planning and investment;

BUILD on their respective rights and obligations under the General Agreement on Tariffs and Trade and other multilateral and bilateral instruments of cooperation;

ENHANCE the competitiveness of their firms in global markets;

FOSTER creativity and innovation, and promote trade in goods and services that are the subject of intellectual property rights;

CREATE new employment opportunities and improve working conditions and living standards in their respective territories;

UNDERTAKE each of the preceding in a manner consistent with environmental protection and conservation;

PRESERVE their flexibility to safeguard the public welfare;

PROMOTE sustainable development;

STRENGTHEN the development and enforcement of environmental laws and regulations; and

PROTECT, enhance and enforce basic workers' rights;

HAVE AGREED as follows:

PART ONE: GENERAL PART

1. OBJECTIVES

Article 101: Establishment of the Free Trade Area

The Parties to this Agreement, consistent with Article XXIV of the *General Agreement on Tariffs and Trade* , hereby establish a free trade area.

Article 102: Objectives

1. The objectives of this Agreement, as elaborated more specifically through its principles and rules, including national treatment, most-favored-nation treatment and transparency, are to:
   a) eliminate barriers to trade in, and facilitate the cross-border movement of, goods and services between the territories of the Parties;
   b) promote conditions of fair competition in the free trade area;
   c) increase substantially investment opportunities in the territories of the Parties;
   d) provide adequate and effective protection and enforcement of intellectual property rights in each Party's territory;
   e) create effective procedures for the implementation and application of this Agreement, for its joint administration and for the resolution of disputes; and
   f) establish a framework for further trilateral, regional and multilateral cooperation to expand and enhance the benefits of this Agreement.

2. The Parties shall interpret and apply the provisions of this Agreement in the light of its objectives set out in paragraph 1 and in accordance with applicable rules of international law.

Article 103: Relation to other Agreements

1. The Parties affirm their existing rights and obligations with respect to each other under the *General Agreement on Tariffs and Trade* and other agreements to which such Parties are party.
2. In the event of any inconsistency between this Agreement and such other agreements, this Agreement shall prevail to the extent of the inconsistency, except as otherwise provided in this Agreement.

Article 104: Relation to Environmental and Conservation Agreements

1. In the event of any inconsistency between this Agreement and the specific trade obligations set out in:
   a) the Convention on International Trade in Endangered Species of Wild Fauna and Flora , done at Washington, March 3, 1973, as amended June 22, 1979,
   b) the Montreal Protocol on Substances that Deplete the Ozone Layer , done at Montreal, September 16, 1987, as amended June 29, 1990,
   c) the Basel Convention on the Control of Transboundary Movements of Hazardous Wastes and Their Disposal , done at Basel, March 22, 1989, on its entry into force for Canada, Mexico and the United States, or
   d) the agreements set out in Annex 104.1,
   such obligations shall prevail to the extent of the inconsistency, provided that where a Party has a choice among equally effective and reasonably available means of complying with such obligations, the Party chooses the alternative that is the least inconsistent with the other provisions of this Agreement.
2. The Parties may agree in writing to modify Annex 104.1 to include any amendment to an agreement referred to in paragraph 1, and any other environmental or conservation agreement.

Article 105: Extent of Obligations

The Parties shall ensure that all necessary measures are taken in order to give effect to the provisions of this Agreement, including their observance, except as otherwise provided in this Agreement, by state and provincial governments.

ANNEX 104.1. BILATERAL AND OTHER ENVIRONMENTAL AND CONSERVATION AGREEMENTS

1. *The Agreement Between the Government of Canada and the Government of the United States of America Concerning the Transboundary Movement of Hazardous Waste*, signed at Ottawa, October 28, 1986.

2. *The Agreement Between the United States of America and the United Mexican States on Cooperation for the Protection and Improvement of the Environment in the Border Area*, signed at La Paz, Baja California Sur, August 14, 1983.

2. GENERAL DEFINITIONS

Article 201: Definitions of General Application

1. For purposes of this Agreement, unless otherwise specified:

   Commission means the Free Trade Commission established under Article 2001(1) (The Free Trade Commission);

   Customs Valuation Code means the *Agreement on Implementation of Article VII of the General Agreement on Tariffs and Trade,* including its interpretative notes;

   days means calendar days, including weekends and holidays;

   enterprise means any entity constituted or organized under applicable law, whether or not for profit, and whether privately-owned or governmentally-owned, including any corporation, trust, partnership, sole proprietorship, joint venture or other association;

   enterprise of a Party means an enterprise constituted or organized under the law of a Party;

   existing means in effect on the date of entry into force of this Agreement;

   Generally Accepted Accounting Principles means the recognized consensus or substantial authoritative support in the territory of a Party with respect to the recording of revenues, expenses, costs, assets and liabilities, disclosure of information and preparation of financial statements. These standards may be broad guidelines of general application as well as detailed standards, practices and procedures;

   goods of a Party means domestic products as these are understood in the *General Agreement on Tariffs and Trade* or such goods as the Parties may agree, and includes originating goods of that Party;

   Harmonized System (HS) means the *Harmonized Commodity Description and Coding System*, and its legal notes, and rules as adopted and implemented by the Parties in their respective tariff laws;

   measure includes any law, regulation, procedure, requirement or practice;

   national means a natural person who is a citizen or permanent resident of a Party and any other natural person referred to in Annex 201.1;

   originating means qualifying under the rules of origin set out in Chapter Four (Rules of Origin);

person means a natural person or an enterprise;

person of a Party means a national, or an enterprise of a Party;

Secretariat means the Secretariat established under Article 2002(1) (The Secretariat);

state enterprise means an enterprise that is owned, or controlled through ownership interests, by a Party; and

territory means for a Party the territory of that Party as set out in Annex 201.1.

2. For purposes of this Agreement, unless otherwise specified, a reference to a state or province includes local governments of that state or province.

ANNEX 201.1. COUNTRY-SPECIFIC DEFINITIONS

For purposes of this Agreement, unless otherwise specified:

national also includes:

a) with respect to Mexico, a national or a citizen according to Articles 30 and 34, respectively, of the Mexican Constitution; and

b) with respect to the United States, "national of the United States" as defined in the existing provisions of the *Immigration and Nationality Act;*

territory means:

a) with respect to Canada, the territory to which its customs laws apply, including any areas beyond the territorial seas of Canada within which, in accordance with international law and its domestic law, Canada may exercise rights with respect to the seabed and subsoil and their natural resources;

b) with respect to Mexico,
   (i) the states of the Federation and the Federal District,
   (ii) the islands, including the reefs and keys, in adjacent seas,
   (iii) the islands of Guadalupe and Revillagigedo situated in the Pacific Ocean,
   (iv) the continental shelf and the submarine shelf of such islands, keys and reefs,
   (v) the waters of the territorial seas, in accordance with international law, and its interior maritime waters,
   (vi) the space located above the national territory, in accordance with international law, and Annex 201.1
   (vii) any areas beyond the territorial seas of Mexico within which, in accordance with international law, including *the United Nations Convention on the Law of the Sea,* and its domestic law, Mexico may exercise rights with respect to the seabed and subsoil and their natural resources; and

c) with respect to the United States,
   (i) the customs territory of the United States, which includes the 50 states, the District of Columbia and Puerto Rico,
   (ii) the foreign trade zones located in the United States and Puerto Rico, and

(iii) any areas beyond the territorial seas of the United States within which, in accordance with international law and its omestic law, the United States may exercise rights with respect to the seabed and subsoil and their natural resources.

PART TWO: TRADE IN GOODS

3. NATIONAL TREATMENT AND MARKET ACCESS FOR GOODS

Article 300: Scope and Coverage

This Chapter applies to trade in goods of a Party, including:

a) goods covered by Annex 300-A (Trade and Investment in the Automotive Sector),
b) goods covered by Annex 300-B (Textile and Apparel Goods), and
c) goods covered by another Chapter in this Part, except as provided in such Annex or Chapter.

Section A - National Treatment

Article 301: National Treatment

1. Each Party shall accord national treatment to the goods of another Party in accordance with Article III of the *General Agreement on Tariffs and Trade* (GATT), including its interpretative notes, and to this end Article III of the GATT and its interpretative notes, or any equivalent provision of a successor agreement to which all Parties are party, are incorporated into and made part of this Agreement.
2. The provisions of paragraph 1 regarding national treatment shall mean, with respect to a state or province, treatment no less favorable than the most favorable treatment accorded by such state or province to any like, directly competitive or substitutable goods, as the case may be, of the Party of which it forms a part.
3. Paragraphs 1 and 2 do not apply to the measures set out in Annex 301.3.

Section B - Tariffs

Article 302: Tariff Elimination

1. Except as otherwise provided in this Agreement, no Party may increase any existing customs duty, or adopt any customs duty, on an originating good.
2. Except as otherwise provided in this Agreement, each Party shall progressively eliminate its customs duties on originating goods in accordance with its Schedule to Annex 302.2.

3. On the request of any Party, the Parties shall consult to consider accelerating the elimination of customs duties set out in their Schedules. An agreement between two or more Parties to accelerate the elimination of a customs duty on a good shall supersede any duty rate or staging category determined pursuant to their Schedules for such good when approved by each such Party in accordance with its applicable legal procedures.

4. Each Party may adopt or maintain import measures to allocate in-quota imports made pursuant to a tariff rate quota set out in Annex 302.2, provided that such measures do not have trade restrictive effects on imports additional to those caused by the imposition of the tariff rate quota.

5. On written request of any Party, a Party applying or intending to apply measures pursuant to paragraph 4 shall consult to review the administration of those measures.

Article 303: Restriction on Drawback and Duty Deferral Programs

1. Except as otherwise provided in this Article, no Party may refund the amount of customs duties paid, or waive or reduce the amount of customs duties owed, on a good imported into its territory, on condition that the good is:
   a) subsequently exported to the territory of another Party,
   b) used as a material in the production of another good that is subsequently exported to the territory of another Party, or
   c) substituted by an identical or similar good used as a material in the production of another good that is subsequently exported to the territory of another Party, in an amount that exceeds the lesser of the total amount of customs duties paid or owed on the good on importation into its territory and the total amount of customs duties paid to another Party on the good that has been subsequently exported to the territory of that other Party.

2. No Party may, on condition of export, refund, waive or reduce:
   a) an antidumping or countervailing duty that is applied pursuant to a Party's domestic law and that is not applied inconsistently with Chapter Nineteen (Review and Dispute Settlement in Antidumping and Countervailing Duty Matters);
   b) a premium offered or collected on an imported good arising out of any tendering system in respect of the administration of quantitative import restrictions, tariff rate quotas or tariff preference levels;
   c) a fee applied pursuant to section 22 of the U.S. Agricultural Adjustment Act, subject to Chapter Seven (Agriculture and Sanitary and Phytosanitary Measures); or
   d) customs duties paid or owed on a good imported into its territory and substituted by an identical or similar good that is subsequently exported to the territory of another Party.

3. Where a good is imported into the territory of a Party pursuant to a duty deferral program and is subsequently exported to the territory of another Party, or is used as a material in the production of another good that is subsequently exported to the

territory of another Party, or is substituted by an identical or similar good used as a material in the production of another good that is subsequently exported to the territory of another Party, the Party from whose territory the good is exported:

a) shall assess the customs duties as if the exported good had been withdrawn for domestic consumption; and

b) may waive or reduce such customs duties to the extent permitted under paragraph 1.

4. In determining the amount of customs duties that may be refunded, waived or reduced pursuant to paragraph 1 on a good imported into its territory, each Party shall require presentation of satisfactory evidence of the amount of customs duties paid to another Party on the good that has been subsequently exported to the territory of that other Party.

5. Where satisfactory evidence of the customs duties paid to the Party to which a good is subsequently exported under a duty deferral program described in paragraph 3 is not presented within 60 days after the date of exportation, the Party from whose territory the good was exported:

a) shall collect customs duties as if the exported good had been withdrawn for domestic consumption; and

b) may refund such customs duties to the extent permitted under paragraph 1 on the timely presentation of such evidence under its laws and regulations.

6. This Article does not apply to:

a) a good entered under bond for transportation and exportation to the territory of another Party;

b) a good exported to the territory of another Party in the same condition as when imported into the territory of the Party from which the good was exported (processes such as testing, cleaning, repacking or inspecting the good, or preserving it in its same condition, shall not be considered to change a good's condition). Except as provided in Annex 703.2, Section A, paragraph 12, where such a good has been commingled with fungible goods and exported in the same condition, its origin for purposes of this subparagraph, may be determined on the basis of the inventory methods provided for in the Uniform Regulations established under Article 511 (Uniform Regulations);

c) a good imported into the territory of a Party that is deemed to be exported from its territory, or used as a material in the production of another good that is deemed to be exported to the territory of another Party, or is substituted by an identical or similar good used as a material in the production of another good that is deemed to be exported to the territory of another Party, by reason of

(i) delivery to a duty-free shop,

(ii) delivery for ship's stores or supplies for ships or aircraft, or

(iii) delivery for use in joint undertakings of two or more of the Parties and that will subsequently become the property of the Party into whose territory the good was deemed to be imported;

d) a refund of customs duties by a Party on a particular good imported into its territory and subsequently exported to the territory of another Party, where that refund is granted by reason of the failure of such good to conform to sample or specification, or by reason of the shipment of such good without the consent of the consignee;

e)   an originating good that is imported into the territory of a Party and is subsequently exported to the territory of another Party, or used as a material in the production of another good that is subsequently exported to the territory of another Party, or is substituted by an identical or similar good used as a material in the production of another good that is subsequently exported to the territory of another Party; or

f)   a good set out in Annex 303.6.

7.   Except for paragraph 2(d), this Article shall apply as of the date set out in each Party's Section of Annex 303.7.

8.   Notwithstanding any other provision of this Article and except as specifically provided in Annex 303.8, no Party may refund the amount of customs duties paid, or waive or reduce the amount of customs duties owed, on a non-originating good provided for in item 8540.11.aa (color cathode-ray television picture tubes, including video monitor tubes, with a diagonal exceeding 14 inches) or 8540.11.cc (color cathoderay television picture tubes for high definition television, with a diagonal exceeding 14 inches) that is imported into the Party's territory and subsequently exported to the territory of another Party, or is used as a material in the production of another good that is subsequently exported to the territory of another Party, or is substituted by an identical or similar good used as a material in the production of another good that is subsequently exported to the territory of another Party.

9.   For purposes of this Article:

customs duties are the customs duties that would be applicable to a good entered for consumption in the customs territory of a Party if the good were not exported to the territory of another party;

identical or similar goods means "identical or similar goods" as defined in Article 415 (Rules of Origin Definitions);

material means "material" as defined in Article 415;

used means "used" as defined in Article 415.

10. For purposes of the Article:

Where a good referred to by a tariff item number in this Article is described in parentheses following the tariff item number, the description is provided for purposes of reference only.

Article 304: Waiver of Customs Duties

1.   Except as set out in Annex 304.1, no Party may adopt any new waiver of customs duties, or expand with respect to existing recipients or extend to any new recipient the application of an existing waiver of customs duties, where the waiver is conditioned, explicitly or implicitly, on the fulfillment of a performance requirement.

2.   Except as set out in Annex 304.2, no Party may, explicitly or implicitly, condition on the fulfillment of a performance requirement the continuation of any existing waiver of customs duties.

3. If a waiver or a combination of waivers of customs duties granted by a Party with respect to goods for commercial use by a designated person can be shown by another Party to have an adverse impact on the commercial interests of a person of that Party, or of a person owned or controlled by a person of that Party that is located in the territory of the Party granting the waiver, or on the other Party's economy, the Party granting the waiver shall either cease to grant it or make it generally available to any importer.

4. This Article shall not apply to measures subject to Article 303.

Article 305: Temporary Admission of Goods

1. Each Party shall grant duty-free temporary admission for:
    a) professional equipment necessary for carrying out the business activity, trade or profession of a business person who qualifies for temporary entry pursuant to Chapter Sixteen (Temporary Entry for Business Persons),
    b) equipment for the press or for sound or television broadcasting and cinematographic equipment,
    c) goods imported for sports purposes and goods intended for display or demonstration, and
    d) commercial samples and advertising films, imported from the territory of another Party, regardless of their origin and regardless of whether like, directly competitive or substitutable goods are available in the territory of the Party.

2. Except as otherwise provided in this Agreement, no Party may condition the duty-free temporary admission of a good referred to in paragraph 1(a), (b) or (c), other than to require that such good:
    a) be imported by a national or resident of another Party who seeks temporary entry;
    b) be used solely by or under the personal supervision of such person in the exercise of the business activity, trade or profession of that person;
    c) not be sold or leased while in its territory;
    d) be accompanied by a bond in an amount no greater than 110 percent of the charges that would otherwise be owed on entry or final importation, or by another form of security, releasable on exportation of the good, except that a bond for customs duties shall not be required for an originating good;
    e) be capable of identification when exported;
    f) be exported on the departure of that person or within such other period of time as is reasonably related to the purpose of the temporary admission; and
    g) be imported in no greater quantity than is reasonable for its intended use.

3. Except as otherwise provided in this Agreement, no Party may condition the duty-free temporary admission of a good referred to in paragraph 1(d), other than to require that such good:
    a) be imported solely for the solicitation of orders for goods, or services provided from the territory, of another Party or non-Party;

b) not be sold, leased or put to any use other than exhibition or demonstration while in its territory;

c) be capable of identification when exported;

d) be exported within such period as is reasonably related to the purpose of the temporary admission; and

e) be imported in no greater quantity than is reasonable for its intended use.

4. A Party may impose the customs duty and any other charge on a good temporarily admitted duty-free under paragraph 1 that would be owed on entry or final importation of such good if any condition that the Party imposes under paragraph 2 or 3 has not been fulfilled.

5. Subject to Chapters Eleven (Investment) and Twelve (Cross Border Trade in Services):

a) each Party shall allow a vehicle or container used in international traffic that enters its territory from the territory of another Party to exit its territory on any route that is reasonably related to the economic and prompt departure of such vehicle or container;

b) no Party may require any bond or impose any penalty or charge solely by reason of any difference between the port of entry and the port of departure of a vehicle or container;

c) no Party may condition the release of any obligation, including any bond, that it imposes in respect of the entry of a vehicle or container into its territory on its exit through any particular port of departure; and

d) no Party may require that the vehicle or carrier bringing a container from the territory of another Party into its territory be the same vehicle or carrier that takes such container to the territory of another Party.

6. For purposes of paragraph 5, "vehicle" means a truck, a truck tractor, tractor, trailer unit or trailer, a locomotive, or a railway car or other railroad equipment.

Article 306: Duty-Free Entry of Certain Commercial Samples and Printed Advertising Materials

Each Party shall grant duty-free entry to commercial samples of negligible value, and to printed advertising materials, imported from the territory of another Party, regardless of their origin, but may require that:

a) such samples be imported solely for the solicitation of orders for goods, or services provided from the territory, of another Party or non-Party; or

b) such advertising materials be imported in packets that each contain no more than one copy of each such material and that neither such materials nor packets form part of a larger consignment.

Article 307: Goods Re-Entered after Repair or Alteration

1. Except as set out in Annex 307.1, no Party may apply a customs duty to a good, regardless of its origin, that re enters its territory after that good has been exported from its territory to the territory of another Party for repair or alteration, regardless of whether such repair or alteration could be performed in its territory.
2. Notwithstanding Article 303, no Party may apply a customs duty to a good, regardless of its origin, imported temporarily from the territory of another Party for repair or alteration.
3. Annex 307.3 applies to the Parties specified in that Annex respecting the repair and rebuilding of vessels.

Article 308: MostFavoredNation Rates of Duty on Certain Goods

1. Annex 308.1 applies to certain automatic data processing goods and their parts.
2. Annex 308.2 applies to certain color television tubes.
3. Each Party shall accord mostfavorednation duty-free treatment to any local area network apparatus imported into its territory, and shall consult in accordance with Annex 308.3.

Section C - Non-Tariff Measures

Article 309: Import and Export Restrictions

1. Except as otherwise provided in this Agreement, no Party may adopt or maintain any prohibition or restriction on the importation of any good of another Party or on the exportation or sale for export of any good destined for the territory of another Party, except in accordance with Article XI of the GATT, including its interpretative notes, and to this end Article XI of the GATT and its interpretative notes, or any equivalent provision of a successor agreement to which all Parties are party, are incorporated into and made a part of this Agreement.
2. The Parties understand that the GATT rights and obligations incorporated by paragraph 1 prohibit, in any circumstances in which any other form of restriction is prohibited, export price requirements and, except as permitted in enforcement of countervailing and antidumping orders and undertakings, import price requirements.
3. In the event that a Party adopts or maintains a prohibition or restriction on the importation from or exportation to a non-Party of a good, nothing in this Agreement shall be construed to prevent the Party from:
   a) limiting or prohibiting the importation from the territory of another Party of such good of that non- Party; or
   b) requiring as a condition of export of such good of the Party to the territory of another Party, that the good not be re-exported to the non-Party, directly or indirectly, without being consumed in the territory of the other Party.

4. In the event that a Party adopts or maintains a prohibition or restriction on the importation of a good from a non-Party, the Parties, on request of any Party, shall consult with a view to avoiding undue interference with or distortion of pricing, marketing and distribution arrangements in another Party.

5. Paragraphs 1 through 4 shall not apply to the measures set out in Annex 301.3.

Article 310: Customs User Fees

1. No Party may adopt any customs user fee of the type referred to in Annex 310.1 for originating goods.

2. The Parties specified in Annex 310.1 may maintain existing such fees in accordance with that Annex.

Article 311: Country of Origin Marking

Annex 311 applies to measures relating to country of origin marking.

Article 312: Wine and Distilled Spirits

1. No Party may adopt or maintain any measure requiring that distilled spirits imported from the territory of another Party for bottling be blended with any distilled spirits of the Party.

2. Annex 312.2 applies to other measures relating to wine and distilled spirits.

Article 313: Distinctive Products

Annex 313 applies to standards and labelling of the distinctive products set out in that Annex.

Article 314: Export Taxes

Except as set out in Annex 314, no Party may adopt or maintain any duty, tax or other charge on the export of any good to the territory of another Party, unless such duty, tax or charge is adopted or maintained on:

a) exports of any such good to the territory of all other Parties; and

b) any such good when destined for domestic consumption.

Article 315: Other Export Measures

1. Except as set out in Annex 315, a Party may adopt or maintain a restriction otherwise justified under Articles XI:2(a) or XX(g), (i) or (j) of the GATT with respect to the export of a good of the Party to the territory of another Party, only if:
    a) the restriction does not reduce the proportion of the total export shipments of the specific good made available to that other Party relative to the total supply of that good of the Party maintaining the restriction as compared to the proportion prevailing in the most recent 36month period for which data are available prior to the imposition of the measure, or in such other representative period on which the Parties may agree;
    b) the Party does not impose a higher price for exports of a good to that other Party than the price charged for such good when consumed domestically, by means of any measure, such as licenses, fees, taxation and minimum price requirements. The foregoing provision does not apply to a higher price that may result from a measure taken pursuant to subparagraph (a) that only restricts the volume of exports; and
    c) the restriction does not require the disruption of normal channels of supply to that other Party or normal proportions among specific goods or categories of goods supplied to that other Party.
2. The Parties shall cooperate in the maintenance and development of effective controls on the export of each other's goods to a non-Party in implementing this Article.

Section D - Consultations

Article 316: Consultations and Committee on Trade in Goods

1. The Parties hereby establish a Committee on Trade in Goods, comprising representatives of each Party.
2. The Committee shall meet on the request of any Party or the Commission to consider any matter arising under this Chapter.
3. The Parties shall convene at least once each year a meeting of their officials responsible for customs, immigration, inspection of food and agricultural products, border inspection facilities, and regulation of transportation for the purpose of addressing issues related to movement of goods through the Parties' ports of entry.

Article 317: Third Country Dumping

1. The Parties affirm the importance of cooperation with respect to actions under Article 12 of the *Agreement on Implementation of Article VI of the General Agreement on Tariffs and Trade* .

2. Where a Party presents an application to another Party requesting antidumping action on its behalf, those Parties shall consult within 30 days respecting the factual basis of the request, and the requested Party shall give full consideration to the request.

Section E - Definitions

Article 318: Definitions

For purposes of this Chapter:

advertising films means recorded visual media, with or without soundtracks, consisting essentially of images showing the nature or operation of goods or services offered for sale or lease by a person established or resident in the territory of any Party, provided that the films are of a kind suitable for exhibition to prospective customers but not for broadcast to the general public, and provided that they are imported in packets that each contain no more than one copy of each film and that do not form part of a larger consignment;

commercial samples of negligible value means commercial samples having a value, individually or in the aggregate as shipped, of not more than one U.S. dollar, or the equivalent amount in the currency of another Party, or so marked, torn, perforated or otherwise treated that they are unsuitable for sale or for use except as commercial samples;

consumed means:

a) actually consumed; or
b) further processed or manufactured so as to result in a substantial change in value, form or use of the good or in the production of another good;

customs duty includes any customs or import duty and a charge of any kind imposed in connection with the importation of a good, including any form of surtax or surcharge in connection with such importation, but does not include any:

a) charge equivalent to an internal tax imposed consistently with Article III:2 of the GATT, or any equivalent provision of a successor agreement to which all Parties are party, in respect of like, directly competitive or substitutable goods of the Party, or in respect of goods from which the imported good has been manufactured or produced in whole or in part;
b) antidumping or countervailing duty that is applied pursuant to a Party's domestic law and not applied inconsistently with Chapter Nineteen (Review and Dispute Settlement in Antidumping and Countervailing Duty Matters);
c) fee or other charge in connection with importation commensurate with the cost of services rendered;

d)   premium offered or collected on an imported good arising out of any tendering system in respect of the administration of quantitative import restrictions, tariff rate quotas or tariff preference levels; and

e)   fee applied pursuant to section 22 of the U.S. *Agricultural Adjustment Act* , subject to Chapter Seven (Agriculture and Sanitary and Phytosanitary Measures);

distilled spirits include distilled spirits and distilled spiritcontaining beverages;

duty deferral program includes measures such as those governing foreign trade zones, temporary importations under bond, bonded warehouses, "maquiladoras", and inward processing programs;

duty-free means free of customs duty;

goods imported for sports purposes means sports requisites for use in sports contests, demonstrations or training in the territory of the Party into whose territory such goods are imported;

goods intended for display or demonstration includes their component parts, ancillary apparatus and accessories;

item means a tariff classification item at the eight- or 10-digit level set out in a Party's tariff schedule;

local area network apparatus means a good dedicated for use solely or principally to permit the interconnection of automatic data processing machines and units thereof for a network that is used primarily for the sharing of resources such as central processor units, data storage devices and input or output units, including in-line repeaters, converters, concentrators, bridges and routers, and printed circuit assemblies for physical incorporation into automatic data processing machines and units thereof suitable for use solely or principally with a private network, and providing for the transmission, receipt, error-checking, control, signal conversion or correction functions for non-voice data to move through a local area network;

performance requirement means a requirement that:

a)   a given level or percentage of goods or services be exported;

b)   domestic goods or services of the Party granting a waiver of customs duties be substituted for imported goods or services;

c)   a person benefitting from a waiver of customs duties purchase other goods or services in the territory of the Party granting the waiver or accord a preference to domestically produced goods or services;

d)   a person benefitting from a waiver of customs duties produce goods or provide services, in the territory of the Party granting the waiver, with a given level or percentage of domestic content; or

e)   relates in any way the volume or value of imports to the volume or value of exports or to the amount of foreign exchange inflows;

printed advertising materials means those goods classified in Chapter 49 of the Harmonized System, including brochures, pamphlets, leaflets, trade catalogues, yearbooks published by trade associations, tourist promotional materials and posters, that are used to promote, publicize or advertise a good or service, are essentially intended to advertise a good or service, and are supplied free of charge;

repair or alteration does not include an operation or process that either destroys the essential characteristics of a good or creates a new or commercially different good;

satisfactory evidence means:

a) a receipt, or a copy of a receipt, evidencing payment of customs duties on a particular entry;
b) a copy of the entry document with evidence that it was received by a customs administration;
c) a copy of a final customs duty determination by a customs administration respecting the relevant entry;
d) any other evidence of payment of customs duties acceptable under the Uniform Regulations established in accordance with Chapter Five (Customs Procedures);

total export shipments means all shipments from total supply to users located in the territory of another Party;

total supply means all shipments, whether intended for domestic or foreign users, from:

a) domestic production;
b) domestic inventory; and
c) other imports as appropriate; and

waiver of customs duties means a measure that waives otherwise applicable customs duties on any good imported from any country, including the territory of another Party.

ANNEX 301.3. EXCEPTIONS TO ARTICLES 301 AND 309

Section A - Canadian Measures

1. Articles 301 and 309 shall not apply to controls by Canada on the export of logs of all species.
2. Articles 301 and 309 shall not apply to controls by Canada on the export of unprocessed fish pursuant to the following existing statutes, as amended as of August 12, 1992:
    a) *New Brunswick Fish Processing Act* , R.S.N.B. c. F18.01 (1982), and *Fisheries Development* Act, S.N.B. c. F15.1 (1977);
    b) *Newfoundland Fish Inspection Act* , R.S.N. 1990, c. F12;

    c) *Nova Scotia Fisheries Act* , S.N.S. 1977, c. 9;

    d) *Prince Edward Island Fish Inspection Act* , R.S.P.E.I. 1988, c. F13; and

    e) *Quebec Marine Products Processing Act* , No. 38, S.Q. 1987, c. 51.

3.   Articles 301 and 309 shall not apply to:

    a) except as provided in Annex 300-A, Appendix 300-A.1, paragraph 4, measures by Canada respecting the importation of any goods enumerated or referred to in Schedule VII of the *Customs Tariff*, R.S.C. 1985, c. 41 (3rd Supp.), as amended,

    b) measures by Canada respecting the exportation of liquor for delivery into any country into which the importation of liquor is prohibited by law under the existing provisions of the *Export Act* , R.S.C. 1985, c. E18, as amended,

    c) measures by Canada respecting preferential rates for certain freight traffic under the existing provisions of the *Maritime Freight Rate Act* , R.S.C. 1985, c. M-1, as amended,

    d) Canadian excise taxes on absolute alcohol used in manufacturing under the existing provisions of the *Excise Tax Act* , R.S.C. 1985, c. E-14, as amended, and

    e) measures by Canada prohibiting the use of foreign or non-duty paid ships in the coasting trade of Canada unless granted a license under the *Coasting Trade Act* , S.C. 1992, c. 31,

to the extent that such provisions were mandatory legislation at the time of Canada's accession to the GATT and have not been amended so as to decrease their conformity with the GATT.

4.   Articles 301 and 309 shall not apply to quantitative import restrictions on goods that originate in the territory of the United States, considering operations performed in, or materials obtained from, Mexico as if they were performed in, or obtained from, a non-Party, and that are indicated by asterisks in Chapter 89 in Annex 401.2 (Tariff Schedule of Canada) of the *Canada United States Free Trade Agreement* for as long as the measures taken under the Merchant Marine Act of 1920, 46 App. U.S.C. §§ 883, and the *Merchant Marine Act of 1936* , 46 App. U.S.C. §§ 1171, 1176, 1241 and 1241o, apply with quantitative effect to comparable Canadian origin goods sold or offered for sale into the U.S. market.

5.   Articles 301 and 309 shall not apply to:

    a) the continuation or prompt renewal of a non-conforming provision of any statute referred to in paragraph 2 or 3; and

    b) the amendment to a non-conforming provision of any statute referred to in paragraph 2 or 3 to the extent that the amendment does not decrease the conformity of the provision with Articles 301 and 309.

Section B - Mexican Measures

1.   Articles 301 and 309 shall not apply to controls by Mexico on the export of logs of all species.

2.   Articles 301 and 309 shall not apply to:

    a) measures under the existing provisions of Articles 192 through 194 of the *General Ways of Communication Act* ("Ley de Vias Generales de

Comunicación") reserving exclusively to Mexican vessels all services and operations not authorized for foreign vessels and empowering the Mexican Ministry of Communications and Transportation to deny foreign vessels the right to perform authorized services if their country of origin does not grant reciprocal rights to Mexican vessels; and

b) export permit measures applied to goods for exportation to another Party that are subject to quantitative restrictions or tariff rate quotas adopted or maintained by that other Party.

3. Articles 301 and 309 shall not apply to:

a) the continuation or prompt renewal of a non-conforming provision of the statute referred to in paragraph 2(a); and

b) the amendment to a non-conforming provision of the statute referred to in paragraph 2(a) to the extent that the amendment does not decrease the conformity of the provision with Articles 301 and 309.

4.

(a) Notwithstanding Article 309, for the first 10 years after the date of entry into force of this Agreement, Mexico may adopt or maintain prohibitions or restrictions on the importation of used goods provided for in the items, as of August 12, 1992, in the Tariff Schedule of the *General Import Duty Act* (Tarifa de la "Ley del Impuesto General de Importación") set out below:

Note: (For purposes of reference only, descriptions are provided next to the corresponding item.)

Item	Description
8407.34.99	Gasoline engines of more than 1,000 cm3, except for motorcycles
8413.11.01	Distributors fitted with a measuring device even if it includes a totalizing mechanism
8413.40.01	Trailer type, from 36 up to 60 m3/hr capacity; without hydraulic elevator for the discharge hose
8426.12.01	Mobile portals on tires and straddle carriers
8426.19.01	Other (overhead travelling cranes, bridge cranes and straddle carriers)
8426.30.01	Portal cranes
8426.41.01	Cranes with structural iron jib (lattice) with mechanical working, self-propelled, with unit weight up to 55 tons
8426.41.02	Cranes with hydraulically actuated rigid jib, selfpropelled with maximum capacity above 9.9 tons and not exceeding 30 tons
8426.41.99	Other (machinery and apparatus, self propelled, on tires)
8426.49.01	Cranes with structural iron jib (lattice) with mechanical working, with unit weight up to 55 tons
8426.49.02	Cranes with hydraulically actuated rigid jib, selfpropelled, with load capacity above 9.9 tons and not exceeding 30 tons
8426.91.01	Cranes, other than those provided for in items 8426.91.02, 8426.91.03 and 8426.91.04
8426.91.02	Cranes with hydraulic working, with articulated or rigid booms, with capacity up to 9.9 tons at 1 meter radius

(Continued)

Item	Description
8426.91.03	Isolated elevating cranes, basket type, with carrying capacity equal to or less than 1 ton and up to 15 meters lift
8426.91.99	Other (machinery and apparatus; designed for mounting on road vehicles)
8426.99.01	Cranes, other than those provided for in items 8426.91.02
8426.99.02	Swivel cranes
8426.99.99	Other (cranes and air cables ("blondines"); overhead travelling cranes, handling or unloading frames, bridge cranes, straddle carriers and straddle cranes)
8427.10.01	With load capacity up to 3,500 kilograms, measured at 620 millimeters from the frontal surface of the forks, without battery or loader
8427.20.01	With explosion or internal combustion engine, with carrying capacity up to 7,000 kilograms, measured at 620 millimeters from the frontal surface of the forks
8428.40.99	Other (escalators and moving walkways)
8428.90.99	Other (machinery and apparatus for lifting, loading, unloading or handling)
8429.11.01	Caterpillar type
8429.19.01	Other (bulldozers and angledozers)
8429.20.01	Graders
8429.30.01	Scrapers
8429.40.01	Tamping machines
8429.51.02	Frontend loader with hydraulic working, wheeltype, with capacity equal or less than 335 HP
8429.51.03	Mechanical shovels, other than those provided for in item 8429.51.01
8429.51.99	Other (mechanical shovels, excavators, loaders and frontend shovel loaders)
8429.52.02	Draglines or excavators, other than those provided for in item 8429.52.01
8429.52.99	Other (machinery with a 360 revolving superstructure)
8429.59.01	Trenchers
8429.59.02	Draglines, with dragging load capacity up to 4,000 kilograms
8429.59.03	Draglines or excavators, other than those provided for in item 8429.59.04
8429.59.99	Other (selfpropelled bulldozers, angledozers, graders, scrapers, mechanical shovels, excavators, loaders, shovel loaders, tamping machines and road rollers)
8430.31.01	Rotation and/or percussion perforators
8430.31.99	Other (selfpropelled cutters, pullers or wrenchers and machines to open tunnels or galleries)
8430.39.01	Boring shields
8430.39.99	Other (not selfpropelled cutters, pullers or wrenchers and machines to open tunnels or galleries)
8430.41.01	Boring or sinking machinery, other than those provided for in item 8430.41.02
8430.41.99	Other (selfpropelled probing or boring machinery)
8430.49.99	Other (not selfpropelled probing or boring machinery)
8430.50.01	Excavators, frontal carriers with hydraulic mechanism, with capacity equal to or less than 335 h.p
8430.50.02	Scrapers
8430.50.99	Other (selfpropelled machinery and apparatus)
8430.61.01	Graders (pushers)

Item	Description
8430.61.02	Tamping or compacting rollers
8430.61.99	Other (machinery and apparatus, not selfpropelled)
8430.62.01	Scarification machine (ripping machine)
8430.69.01	Scrapers, not selfpropelled
8430.69.02	Trencher machine, other than those provided for in item 8430.69.03
8430.69.99	Other (trenchers, other than those provided for in items 8430.69.01, 8430.69.02 and 8430.69.03)
8452.10.01	Sewing machines of the household type
8452.21.04	Industrial machines, other than those provided for in items 8452.21.02, 8452.21.03 and 8452.21.05
8452.21.99	Other (automatic sewing machines)
8452.29.05	Machines or heads for industrial use, with straight seams, straight needle and a rotating and oscillating thread linking device, double backstitching, flat bed and transportation only
8452.29.06	Industrial machines, other than those provided for in items 8452.29.01, 8452.29.03 and 8452.29.05
8452.29.99	Other (non-automatic sewing machines)
8452.90.99	Other (parts of sewing machines)
8471.10.01	Analogue or hybrid automatic data processing machines
8471.20.01	Digital or numerical automatic data processing machines, containing in the same housing at least a central processing unit and an input and output unit
8471.91.01	Numerical or digital processing units, even if presented with the rest of the system, including one or two of the following types of units contained in the same housing: storage units, input units, output unit
8471.92.99	Other (input or output units whether or not entered with the rest of a system and whether or not containing storage units in the same housing)
8471.93.01	Storage units, including the rest of the system
8471.99.01	Other (automatic data processing machines and units thereof)
8474.20.01	Crushing and grinding with two or more cylinders
8474.20.02	Crushing jawbone and grinding millstone
8474.20.03	Blade crushing machines
8474.20.04	Crushing machines of balls or bars
8474.20.05	Drawer cone crushing, with diameter no more than 1200 millimeters
8474.20.06	Grinding hammer percussion
8474.20.99	Other (machines and apparatus to break, crush or grind or pulverize dirt, stones and other solid mineral materials)
8474.39.99	Other (mixing machines)
8474.80.99	Other (machines and apparatus to classify, sieve, separate, break, crush, grind, mix, or knead dirt, stones and other mineral materials)
8475.10.01	Machines for assembling lamps
8477.10.01	Injectionmolding machines for thermoplastic materials, up to 5 kg capacity for one molding model
8701.30.01	Caterpillar tractors with an engine power at the flywheel equal to or above 105 h.p., but less than 380 h.p. measured at 1,900 rpm, including pushing blade

(Continued)

Item	Description
8701.90.02	Railroad tractors, on tires with mechanical mechanism for pavement
8711.10.01	Motorcycles fitted with an auxiliary motor with reciprocating piston engine not exceeding 50 cm3
8711.20.01	Motorcycles fitted with an auxiliary motor with reciprocating piston engine over 50 cm3 but not over 250 cm3
8711.30.01	Motorcycles fitted with an auxiliary motor with reciprocating piston engine over 250 cm3 but not over 500 cm3
8711.40.01	Motorcycles fitted with an auxiliary motor with reciprocating piston engine over 500 cm3 but less than 550 cm3
8711.90.99	Other (motorcycles, cycles fitted with an auxiliary motor and sidecars without a reciprocating piston engine, and that are not sidecars for motorcycles and velocipedes of any kind presented separately)
8712.00.02	Bicycles, other than of the type for racing
8712.00.99	Other (cycles, not motorized, except bicycles, and tricycles for the transport of merchandise)
8716.10.01	Trailers and semitrailers for housing and camping, of the caravan type
8716.31.02	Steeltank type tankers, including cryogenic or hoppers
8716.31.99	Other (tankers except of the steeltank type, and of the thermal type for the transportation of milk)
8716.39.01	Trailers or semitrailers of the platform type, with or without stakes, including those accepted for the transport of boxes or metal baskets for cans and bottles or container carriers, or low beds, except those with hydraulic or pneumatic suspension and collapsible gooseneck
8716.39.02	Trailers or semitrailers for the transport of vehicles
8716.39.04	Trailers of the modularplatform type with directional axis, including transporter bridge section, hydraulic couplings or gooseneck or motor for hydraulic conditioning of the equipment
8716.39.05	Semitrailers of the lowbed type, with pneumatic or hydraulic suspension and collapsible gooseneck
8716.39.06	Trailers and semitrailers of the closedbox type, including refrigerated
8716.39.07	Trailers and semitrailers of the steeltank type, including cryogenic and hoppers
8716.39.99	Other (trailers and semitrailers for the transportation of goods, other than those provided for in items 8716.39.01, 8716.39.02, 8716.39.04, 8716.39.05, 8716.39.06 and 8716.39.07, and that are not vehicles for the transport of goods, with solid rubber wheels, nor doubledecker trailers or semitrailers of the type recognized as used exclusively for hauling cattle
8716.40.01	Other trailers and semitrailers not used for transporting goods
8716.80.99	Other (non-automotive vehicles except trailers or semitrailers, wheel barrows and handcarts, or wheel barrows of hydraulic operation)

b) Notwithstanding subparagraph (a), Mexico shall not prohibit or restrict the importation, on a temporary basis, of used goods provided for in the items set out in subparagraph (c) for the provision of a crossborder service subject to Chapter Twelve (CrossBorder Trade in Services) or the performance of a contract subject to Chapter Ten (Government Procurement), provided that the imported goods

(i) are necessary to the provision of the cross border service or the performance of the contract awarded to a supplier of another Party,

(ii) are used solely by or under the supervision of the service provider or the supplier performing the contract,

(iii) are not sold, leased or loaned while in the territory of Mexico,

(iv) are imported in no greater quantity than is necessary for the provision of the service or the performance of the contract,

(v) are reexported promptly on completion of the service or the contract, and (vi) comply with other applicable requirements on the importation of such goods to the extent they are not inconsistent with this Agreement.

c) Subparagraph (b) applies to used goods provided for in the following items:

Item	Description
8413.11.01	Distributors fitted with a measuring device even if it includes a totalizing mechanism
8413.40.01	Concrete pumps for liquids, not fitted with a measuring device from 36 up to 60 m3/hr capacity
8426.12.01	Mobile portals on tires and straddle carriers
8426.19.01	Other (overhead travelling cranes, bridge cranes and straddle carriers)
8426.30.01	Portal cranes
8426.41.01	Cranes with hydraulically actuated rigid jib, selfpropelled with maximum capacity above 9.9 tons and not exceeding 30 tons
8426.41.02	Cranes with structural iron jib (lattice) with mechanical working, selfpropelled, with unit weight up to 55 tons
8426.41.99	Other (machinery and apparatus, self propelled, on tires)
8426.49.01	Cranes with structural iron jib (lattice) with mechanical working, with unit weight up to 55 tons
8426.49.02	Cranes with hydraulically actuated rigid jib, selfpropelled, with load capacity above 9.9 tons and not exceeding 30 tons
8426.91.01	Cranes, other than those provided for in items 8426.91.02, 8426.91.03 and 8426.91.04
8426.99.01	Cranes
8426.99.02	Swivel cranes
8426.99.99	Other (cranes and air cables ("blondines"); overhead travelling cranes, handling or unloading frames, bridge cranes, straddle carriers and straddle cranes)
8427.10.01	With load capacity up to 3,500 kilograms, measured at 620 millimeters from the frontal surface of the forks, without battery or loader
8428.40.99	Other (escalators and moving walkways)
8428.90.99	Other (machinery and apparatus for lifting, loading, unloading or handling)
8429.11.01	Caterpillar type
8429.19.01	Other (bulldozers and angledozers)
8429.30.01	Scrapers
8429.40.01	Tamping machines
8429.51.02	Frontend loader with hydraulic working, wheeltype, with capacity equal or less than 335 HP
8429.51.03	Mechanical shovels, other than those provided for in item 8429.51.01
8429.51.99	Other (mechanical shovels, excavators, loaders and frontend shovel loaders)
8429.52.02	Draglines or excavators, other than those provided for in item 8429.52.01
8429.52.99	Other (machinery with a 360 revolving superstructure)

(Continued)

Item	Description
8429.59.01	Trenchers
8429.59.02	Draglines, with dragging load capacity up to 4,000 kilograms
8429.59.03	Draglines or excavators, other than those provided for in item 8429.59.04
8429.59.99	Other (selfpropelled bulldozers, angledozers, graders, scrapers, mechanical shovels, excavators, loaders, shovel loaders, tamping machines and road rollers)
8430.31.01	Rotation and/or percussion perforators
8430.31.99	Other (selfpropelled cutters, pullers or wrenchers and machines to open tunnels or galleries)
8430.39.01	Boring shields
8430.39.99	Other (not selfpropelled cutters, pullers or wrenchers and machines to open tunnels or galleries)
8430.41.01	Boring or sinking machinery, other than those provided for in item 8430.41.02
8430.41.99	Other (selfpropelled probing or boring machinery)
8430.49.99	Other (not selfpropelled probing or boring machinery)
8430.50.01	Excavators, frontal loaders with hydraulic mechanism, with capacity equal to or less than 335 h.p.
8430.50.02	Scrapers
8430.50.99	Other (selfpropelled machinery and apparatus)
8430.61.01	Graders (pushers)
8430.61.02	Tamping or compacting rollers
8430.62.01	Scarification machine (ripping machine)
8430.69.01	Scrapers, not selfpropelled
8430.69.02	Trencher machine, other than those provided for in item 8430.69.03
8430.69.99	Other (trenchers, other than those provided for in items 8430.69.01, 8430.69.02 and 8430.69.03)
8452.10.01	Sewing machines of the household type
8452.21.04	Industrial machines, other than those provided for in items 8452.21.02, 8452.21.03 and 8452.21.05
8452.21.99	Other (automatic sewing machines)
8452.29.06	Industrial machines, other than those provided for in items 8452.29.01, 8452.29.03 and 8452.29.05
8452.29.99	Other (non-automatic sewing machines)
8452.90.99	Other (parts of sewing machines)
8471.10.01	Analogue or hybrid automatic data processing machines
8474.20.01	Crushing and grinding with two or more cylinders
8474.20.03	Blade crushing machines
8474.20.04	Crushing machines of balls or bars
8474.20.99	Other (machines and apparatus to break, crush or grind or pulverize dirt, stones and other solid mineral materials)
8474.39.99	Other (mixing machines)
8474.80.99	Other (machines and apparatus to classify, sieve, separate, break, crush, grind, mix, or knead dirt, stones and other mineral materials)
8477.10.01	Injectionmolding machines for thermoplastic materials, up to 5 kg capacity for one molding model
8701.30.01	Caterpillar tractors with an engine power at the flywheel equal to or above 105 h.p., but less than 380 h.p. measured at 1,900 rpm, including pushing blade

Section C - U.S. Measures

1. Articles 301 and 309 shall not apply to controls by the United States on the export of logs of all species.
2. Articles 301 and 309 shall not apply to:
    a) taxes on imported perfume containing distilled spirits under existing provisions of section 5001(a)(3) and 5007(b)(2) of the Internal Revenue Code of 1986, 26 U.S.C. 5001(a)(3), 5007(b)(2), and
    b) measures under existing provisions of the Merchant Marine Act of 1920, 46 App. U.S.C. 883; the Passenger Vessel Act, 46 App. U.S.C. 289, 292, and 316; and 46 U.S.C. 12108, to the extent that such measures were mandatory legislation at the time of the United States' accession to the GATT and have not been amended so as to decrease their conformity with the GATT.
3. Articles 301 and 309 shall not apply to:
    a) the continuation or prompt renewal of a non-conforming provision of any statute referred to in paragraph 2; and
    b) the amendment to a non-conforming provision of any statute referred to in paragraph 2 to the extent that the amendment does not decrease the conformity of the provision with Articles 301 and 309.

ANNEX 302.2. TARIFF ELIMINATION

1. Except as otherwise provided in a Party's Schedule attached to this Annex, the following staging categories apply to the elimination of customs duties by each Party pursuant to Article 302(2):
    a) duties on goods provided for in the items in staging category A in a Party's Schedule shall be eliminated entirely and such goods shall be duty-free, effective January 1, 1994;
    b) duties on goods provided for in the items in staging category B in a Party's Schedule shall be removed in five equal annual stages beginning on January 1, 1994, and such goods shall be duty-free, effective January 1, 1998;
    c) duties on goods provided for in the items in staging category C in a Party's Schedule shall be removed in 10 equal annual stages beginning on January 1, 1994, and such goods shall be duty-free, effective January 1, 2003;
    d) duties on goods provided for in the items in staging category C+ in a Party's Schedule shall be removed in 15 equal annual stages beginning on January 1, 1994, and such goods shall be duty-free, effective January 1, 2008; and
    e) goods provided for in the items in staging category D in a Party's Schedule shall continue to receive duty-free treatment.
2. The base rate of customs duty and staging category for determining the interim rate of customs duty at each stage of the U.S. Generalized System of Preferences and the General Preferential Tariff of Canada.
3. For the purpose of the elimination of customs duties in accordance with Article 302, interim staged rates shall be rounded down, except as set out in each Party's Schedule

attached to this Annex, at least to the nearest tenth of a percentage point or, if the rate of duty is expressed in monetary units, at least to the nearest .001 of the official monetary unit of the Party.

4. Canada shall apply a rate of customs duty no higher than the rate applicable under the staging category set out for an item in Annex 401.2, as amended, of the *Canada-United States Free Trade Agreement* which Annex is hereby incorporated into and made a part of this Agreement, to an originating good provided that:

    a) notwithstanding any provision in Chapter Four, in determining whether such good is an originating good, operations performed in or materials obtained from Mexico are considered as if they were performed in or obtained from a non-Party; and

    b) any processing that occurs in Mexico after the good would qualify as an originating good in accordance with subparagraph (a) does not increase the transaction value of the good by greater than seven percent.

5. Canada shall apply a rate of customs duty no higher than the rate applicable under the staging category set out for an item in Column I of its Schedule to this Annex to an originating good provided that:

    a) notwithstanding any provision in Chapter Four, in determining whether such good is an originating good, operations performed in or materials obtained from the United States are considered as if they were performed in or obtained from a non-Party; and

    b) any processing that occurs in the United States after subparagraph (a) does not increase the transaction value of the good by greater than seven percent.

6. Canada shall apply to an originating good to which neither paragraph 4 nor 5 applies a rate of customs duty no higher than the rate indicated for its corresponding item in Column II of its Schedule to this Annex. The rate of customs duty in Column II for such good shall be:

    a) in each year of the staging category indicated in Column I, the higher of

        (i) the rate of customs duty under the staging category set out for the item in Annex 401.2, as amended, of the *Canada-United States Free Trade Agreement*, and

        (ii) the General Preferential Tariff rate of customs duty for the item applied on July 1, 1991, reduced in accordance with the applicable staging category set out for the item in Column I of its Schedule to this Annex; or

    b) where specified in Column II of its Schedule to this Annex, the most-favored-nation rate of customs duty for the item applied on July 1, 1991, reduced in accordance with the applicable staging category set out for the item in Column I of its Schedule to this Annex, or reduced in accordance with the applicable staging category otherwise indicated.

7. Paragraphs 4 through 6 and 10 through 13 shall not apply to textile and apparel goods identified in Appendix 1.1 of Annex 300-B (Textiles and Apparel Goods).

8. Paragraphs 4, 5 and 6 shall not apply to agricultural goods as defined in Article 708. For these goods, Canada shall apply the rate applicable under the staging category set out for an item in Annex 401.2, as amended, of the *Canada-United States Free Trade Agreement* to an originating good when the good qualifies to be marked as a good of the United States pursuant to Annex 311, without regard to whether the good is

marked. When an originating good qualifies to be marked as a good of Mexico, pursuant to Annex 311, whether or not the good is marked, Canada shall apply the rate applicable under the staging category set out for an item in Column I of its Schedule to this Annex.

9. As between the United States and Canada, Articles 401(7) and 401(8) of the *Canada-United States Free Trade Agreement* is hereby incorporated and made a part of this Annex. The term "goods originating in the territory of the United States of America" in Article 401(7) of that agreement shall be determined in accordance with paragraph 4 of this Annex. The term "goods originating shall be determined in accordance with paragraph 12 of this Annex.

10. Mexico shall apply a rate of customs duty no higher than the rate applicable under the staging category set out for an item in Column I of its Schedule to this Annex to an originating good when the good qualifies to be marked as a good of the United States, pursuant to Annex 311, without regard to whether the good is marked.

11. Mexico shall apply a rate of customs duty no higher than the rate applicable under the staging category set out for an item in Column II of its Schedule to this Annex to an originating good when the good qualifies to be marked as a good of Canada, pursuant to Annex 311, without regard to whether the good is marked.

12. The United States shall apply a rate of customs duty no higher than the rate applicable under the staging category set out for an item in Annex 401.2, as amended, of the *Canada-United States Free Trade Agreement* to an originating good when the good qualifies to be marked as a good of Canada pursuant to Annex 311, without regard to whether the good is marked.

13. The United States shall apply a rate of customs duty no higher than the rate applicable under the staging category set out for an item in its Schedule to this Annex to an originating good when the good qualifies to be marked as a good of Mexico pursuant to Annex 311, whether or not the good is marked.

Schedule of Canada
(Tariff Schedule Attached as Separate Volume)
Schedule of Mexico
(Tariff Schedule Attached as Separate Volume)
Schedule of the United States
(Tariff Schedule Attached as Separate Volume)

ANNEX 303.6. GOODS NOT SUBJECT TO ARTICLE 303

1. For exports from the territory of the United States to the territory of Canada or Mexico, a good provided for in U.S. tariff item 1701.11.02 that is imported into the territory of the United States and used as a material in the production of, or substituted by an identical or similar good used as a material in the production of, a good provided for in Canadian tariff item 1701.99.00 or Mexican tariff items 1701.99.01 and 1701.99.99 (refined sugar) is not subject to Article 303.

2. For trade between Canada and the United States the following are not subject to Article 303:

a) imported citrus products;

b) an imported good used as a material in the production of, or substituted by an identical or similar good used as a material in the production of, a good provided for in U.S. items 5811.00.20 (quilted cotton piece goods), 5811.00.30 (quilted man-made piece goods) or 6307.90.99 (furniture moving pads), or Canadian items 5811.00.10 (quilted cotton piece goods), 5811.00.20 (quilted man-made piece goods) or 6307.90.30 (furniture moving pads), that are subject to the most-favored-nation rate of duty when exported to the territory of the other Party; and

c) an imported good used as a material in the production in the production of, apparel that is subject to the mostfavorednation rate of duty when exported to the territory of the other Party.

ANNEX 303.7. EFFECTIVE DATES FOR THE APPLICATION OF ARTICLE 303

Section A - Canada

For Canada, Article 303 shall apply to a good imported into the territory of Canada that is:

a) subsequently exported to the territory of the United States on or after January 1, 1996, or subsequently exported to the territory of Mexico on or after January 1, 2001;

b) used as a material in the production of another good that is subsequently exported to the territory of the United States on or after January 1, 1996, or used as a material in the production of another good that is subsequently exported to the territory of Mexico on or after January 1, 2001; or

c) substituted by an identical or similar good used as a material in the production of another good that is subsequently exported to the territory of the United States on or after January 1, 1996, or substituted by an identical or similar good used as a material in the production of another good that is subsequently exported to the territory of Mexico on or after January 1, 2001.

Section B - Mexico

For Mexico, Article 303 shall apply to a good imported into the territory of Mexico that is:

a) subsequently exported to the territory of another Party on or after January 1, 2001;

b) used as a material in the production of another good that is subsequently exported to the territory of another Party on or after January 1, 2001; or

c) substituted by an identical or similar good used as a material in the production of another good that is subsequently exported to the territory of another Party on or after January 1, 2001.

Section C - United States

For the United States, Article 303 shall apply to a good imported into the territory of the United States that is:

a) subsequently exported to the territory of Canada on or after January 1, 1996, or subsequently exported to the territory of Mexico on or after January 1, 2001;

b) used as a material in the production of another good that is subsequently exported to the territory of Canada on or after January 1, 1996, or used as a material in the production of another good that is subsequently exported to the territory of Mexico on or after January 1, 2001; or

c) substituted by an identical or similar good used as a material in the production of another good subsequently exported to the territory of Canada on or after January 1, 1996, or substituted by an identical or similar good used as a material in the production of another good subsequently exported to the territory of Mexico on or after January 1, 2001.

ANNEX 303.8. EXCEPTION TO ARTICLE 303(8) FOR CERTAIN COLOR CATHODE-RAY TELEVISION PICTURE TUBES

Mexico

Mexico may refund customs duties paid, or waive or reduce the amount of customs duties owed, on a good provided for in item 8540.11.aa (color cathode-ray television picture tubes, including video monitor cathode-ray tubes, with a diagonal exceeding 14 inches) or 8540.11.cc (color cathode-ray television picture tubes for high definition television, with a diagonal exceeding 14 inches) for a person who, during the period July 1, 1991 through June 30, 1992, imported into its territory no fewer than 20,000 units of such good that would not have been considered to be an originating good had this Agreement been in force during that period, where the good is:

a) subsequently exported from the territory of Mexico to the territory of the United States, or is used as a material in the production of another good that is subsequently exported from the territory of Mexico to the territory of the United States, or is substituted by an identical or similar good used as a material in the production of another good that is subsequently exported to the territory of the United States, in an amount, for all such persons combined, no greater than
   (i) 1,200,000 units in 1994,
   (ii) 1,000,000 units in 1995,

(iii) 800,000 units in 1996,

(iv) 600,000 units in 1997,

(v) 400,000 units in 1998,

(vi) 200,000 units in 1999, and

(vii) zero units in 2000 and thereafter, provided that the number of units of the good on which such customs duties may be refunded, waived or reduced in any year shall be reduced, with respect to that year, by the number of units of such good that qualifies as an originating good during the year immediately preceding that year, considering operations performed in, or materials obtained from, the territories of Canada and the United States as if they were performed in, or obtained from, a non-Party; or

b) subsequently exported from the territory of Mexico to of another good that is subsequently exported from the territory of Mexico to the territory of Canada, or is substituted by an identical or similar good used as a material in the production of another good that is subsequently exported to the territory of Canada, for all such persons combined, in an amount no greater than

(i) 75,000 units in 1994,

(ii) 50,000 units in 1995, and

(iii) zero units in 1996 and thereafter.

ANNEX 304.1. EXCEPTIONS FOR EXISTING WAIVER MEASURES

Article 304(1) shall not apply in respect of existing Mexican waivers of customs duties, except that Mexico shall not:

a) increase the ratio of customs duties waived to customs duties owed relative to the performance required under any such waiver; or

b) add any type of imported good to those qualifying on July 1, 1991, in respect of any waiver of customs duties in effect on that date.

ANNEX 304.2. CONTINUATION OF EXISTING WAIVERS OF CUSTOMS DUTIES

For purposes of Article 304(2):

a) as between Canada and Mexico, Canada may condition on the fulfillment of a performance requirement the waiver of customs duties under any measure in effect on or before January 1, 1989, on any goods entered or withdrawn from warehouse for consumption before January 1, 1998;

b) as between Canada and the United States, Article 405 of the *Canada-United States Free Trade Agreement* is hereby incorporated and made a part of this Annex solely with respect to measures adopted by Canada or the United States prior to the date of entry into force of this Agreement;

c) Mexico may condition on the fulfillment of a performance requirement the waiver of customs duties under any measure in effect on July 1, 1991, on any goods entered or withdrawn from warehouse for consumption before January 1, 2001; and

d) Canada may grant waivers of customs duties as set out in Annex 300-A (Trade and Investment in the Automotive Sector).

ANNEX 307.1. GOODS RE-ENTERED AFTER REPAIR OR ALTERATION

Section A - Canada

Canada may impose customs duties on goods, regardless of their origin, that re-enter its territory after such goods have been exported from its territory to the territory of another Party for repair or alteration as follows:

a) for goods set out in Section D that re-enter its territory from the territory of Mexico, Canada shall apply to the value of the repair or alteration of such goods the rate of customs duty for such goods applicable under its Schedule to Annex 302.2;

b) for goods other than those set out in Section D that re-enter its territory from the territory of the United States or Mexico, other than goods repaired or altered pursuant to a warranty, Canada shall apply to the value of the repair or alteration of such goods the rate of customs duty for such goods applicable under the Tariff Schedule of Canada attached to Annex 401.2 of the Canada United States Free Trade Agreement, as incorporated into Annex 302.2 of this Agreement; and

c) for goods set out in Section D that re-enter its territory from the territory of the United States, Canada shall apply to the value of the repair or alteration of such goods the rate of customs duty for such goods applicable under its Schedule attached to Annex 401.2 of the *Canada United States Free Trade Agreement* , as incorporated into Annex 302.2 of this Agreement.

Section B - Mexico

Mexico may impose customs duties on goods set out in Section D, regardless of their origin, that re-enter its territory after such goods have been exported from its territory to the territory of another Party for repair or alteration, by applying to the value of the repair or alteration of those goods the rate of customs duty for such goods that would apply if such goods were included in staging category B in Mexico's Schedule to Annex 302.2.

Section C - United States

1. The United States may impose customs duties on:
   a) goods set out in Section D, or

b) goods that are not set out in Section D and that are not repaired or altered pursuant to a warranty,

regardless of their origin, that reenter its territory after such goods have been exported from its territory to the territory of Canada for repair or alteration, by applying to the value of the repair or alteration of such goods the rate of customs duty applicable under the Canada United States Free Trade Agreement, as incorporated into Annex 302.2 of this Agreement.

2. The United States may impose customs duties on goods set out in Section D, regardless of their origin, that reenter its territory after such goods have been exported from its territory to the territory of Mexico for repair or alteration, by applying to the value of the repair or alteration of such goods a rate of customs duty of 50 percent reduced in five equal annual stages beginning on January 1, 1994, and the value of such repair or alteration shall be duty-free on January 1, 1998.

Section D - List of Goods

Any vessel, including the following goods, documented by a Party under its law to engage in foreign or coastwise trade, or a vessel intended to be employed in such trade:

a) cruise ships, excursion boats, ferryboats, cargo ships, barges and similar vessels for the transport of persons or goods, including
    (i)   tankers,
    (ii) refrigerated vessels, other than tankers, and
    (iii) other vessels for the transport of goods and other vessels for the transport of both persons and goods, including open vessels;
b) fishing vessels, including factory ships and other vessels for processing or preserving fishery products of a registered length not exceeding 30.5m;
c) lightvessels, fire-floats, dredgers, floating cranes, and other vessels the navigability of which is subsidiary to their main function, floating docks, floating or submersible drilling or production platforms; and drilling ships, drilling barges and floating drilling rigs; and
d) tugboats.

ANNEX 307.3. REPAIR AND REBUILDING OF VESSELS

United States

For the purpose of increasing transparency regarding the types of repairs that may be performed in shipyards outside the territory of the United States that do not result in any loss of privileges for such vessel to:

(a) remain eligible to engage in coastwise trade or to access U.S. fisheries,
(b) transport U.S. government cargo, or

(c) participate in U.S. assistance programs, including the "operating difference subsidy,"

the United States shall,

(d) provide written clarification no later than July 1, 1993, to the other Parties of current U.S. Customs and Coast Guard practices that constitute, and differentiate between, the repair and the rebuilding of vessels, including clarifications with respect to "jumboizing", vessel conversions and casualty repairs, and

(e) begin a process, no later than the date of entry into force of this Agreement, to define the terms "repairs" and "rebuilding" under U.S. maritime law, including the Merchant Marine Act of 1920, 46 App. U.S.C. 883, and the Merchant Marine Act of 1936, 46 App. U.S.C. 1171, 1176, 1241 and 1241(o).

ANNEX 308.1. MOST-FAVORED-NATION RATES OF DUTY ON CERTAIN AUTOMATIC DATA PROCESSING GOODS AND THEIR PARTS

Section A - General Provisions

1. Each Party shall reduce its most-favored-nation rate of duty applicable to a good provided for under the tariff provisions set out in Tables 308.1.1 and 308.1.2 in Section B to the rate set out therein, to the lowest rate agreed by any Party in the Uruguay Round of Multilateral Trade Negotiations, or to such reduced rate as the Parties may agree, in accordance with the schedule set out in Section B, or with such accelerated schedule as the Parties may agree.

2. Notwithstanding Chapter Four (Rules of Origin), when the most-favored-nation rate of duty applicable to a good provided for under the tariff provisions set out in Table 308.1.1 in Section B conforms with the rate established under paragraph 1, each Party shall consider the good, when imported into its territory from the territory of another Party, to be an originating good.

3. A Party may reduce in advance of the schedule set out in Table 308.1.1 or Table 308.1.2 in Section B, or of such accelerated schedule as the Parties may agree, its most-favored-nation rate of duty applicable to any good provided for under the tariff provisions set out therein, to the lowest rate agreed by any Party in the Uruguay Round of Multilateral Trade Negotiations, or the rate set out in Table 308.1.1 or 308.1.2, or to such reduced rate as the Parties may agree.

4. For greater certainty, most-favored-nation rate of duty does not include any other concessionary rate of duty.

Section B - Rates of Duty and Schedule for Reduction

Table 308.1.1

	Tariff Rate	Schedule [1]
Automatic Data Processing Machines (ADP)		
8471.10	3.9%	S
8471.20	3.9%	S
Digital Processing Units		
8471.91	3.9%	S
Input or Output Units		
Combined Input/Output Units		
Canada:		
8471.92.10	3.7%	S
Mexico:		
8471.92.09	3.7%	S
United States:		
8471.92.10	3.7%	
Display Units:		
Canada:		
8471.92.32	3.7%	
8471.92.33	Free	S
8471.92.34	3.7%	S
8471.92.39	3.7%	S
Mexico:		
8471.92.10	3.7%	S
8471.92.11	Free	S
United States:		
8471.92.30	Free	S
8471.92.40.75	3.7%	S
8471.92.40.85	3.7%	S
Other Input or Output Units:		
Canada:		
8471.92.40	3.7%	S
8471.92.50	Free	S
8471.92.90	Free	S
Mexico:		
8471.92.12	3.7%	S
8471.92.99	Free	S
United States:		
8471.92.20	Free	S
8471.92.80	Free	S
8471.92.90.20	Free	S
8471.92.90.40	3.7%	S

	Tariff Rate	Schedule [1]
8471.92.90.60	Free	S
8471.92.90.80	Free	S
Storage Units		
8471.93	Free	S
Other Units of Automatic Data Processing Machines		
8471.99	Free	S
Parts of Computers		
8473.30	Free	R
Computer Power Supplies		
Canada:		
8504.40.40	Free	S
8504.90.80	Free	S
Mexico:		
8504.40.12	Free	S
8504.90.08	Free	S
United States:		
8504.40.00A	Free	S
8504.40.00B	Free	S
8504.90.00B	Free	S

[1] R on the date of entry into force of this Agreement
S in five equal annual stages commencing January 1, 1999.

Table 308.1.2

	Tariff Rate	Schedule [1]
Metal Oxide Varistors		
Canada:		
8533.40.10	Free	R
Mexico:		
8533.40.07	Free	R
United States:		
8533.40.00A	Free	R
Diodes, Transistors and Similar Semiconductor Devices; Photosensitive Semiconductor Devices; Light Emitting Diodes; Mounted Piezo-electric Crystals		
8541.10	Free	R
8541.21	Free	R
8541.29	Free	R
8541.30	Free	R
8541.50	Free	R
8541.60	Free	R
8541.90	Free	R
Canada:		

Table 308.1.2. (Continued)

	Tariff Rate	Schedule [1]
8541.40	Free	R
Mexico:		
8541.40	Free	R
United States:		
8541.40.20	Free	S
8541.40.60	Free	R
8541.40.70	Free	R
8541.40.80	Free	R
8541.40.95	Free	R
Electronic Integrated Circuits and Microassemblies		
8542	Free	R

[1] R on the date of entry of this Agreement

S in five equal annual stages commencing January 1, 1999.

ANNEX 308.2. MOST-FAVORED-NATION RATES OF DUTY ON CERTAIN COLOR CATHODE-RAY TELEVISION PICTURE TUBES

1. Any Party considering the reduction of its most-favored-nation rate of customs duty for goods provided for in item 8540.11.aa (color cathode-ray television picture tubes, including video monitor cathode-ray tubes, with a diagonal exceeding 14 inches) or 8540.11.cc (color cathode-ray television picture tubes for high definition television, with a diagonal exceeding 14 inches) during the first 10 years after the date of entry into force of this Agreement shall consult with the other Parties in advance of such reduction.

2. If any other Party objects in writing to such reduction, other than a reduction in the Uruguay Round of Multilateral Trade Negotiations, and the Party proceeds with the reduction, any objecting Party may raise its applicable rate of duty on originating goods provided for in the corresponding tariff item set out in its Schedule to Annex 302.2, up to the applicable rate of duty as if such good had been placed in staging category C for purpose of tariff elimination.

ANNEX 308.3. MOST-FAVORED-NATION DUTY-FREE TREATMENT OF LOCAL AREA NETWORK APPARATUS

To facilitate the operation of Article 308(3), the Parties shall consult regarding the tariff classification of local area network apparatus and shall endeavor to agree, no later than January 1, 1994, on the classification of such goods in each Party's tariff schedule.

ANNEX 310.1. EXISTING CUSTOMS USER FEES

Section A - Mexico

Mexico shall not increase its customs processing fee ("derechos de trímite aduanero") on originating goods, and shall eliminate such fee on originating goods by June 30, 1999.

Mexico shall not increase its customs processing fee ("derechos de trímite aduanero") on originating goods, and shall eliminate such fee on originating goods by June 30, 1999.

Section B - United States

1. The United States shall not increase its merchandise processing fee and shall eliminate such fee according to the schedule set out in Article 403 of the Canada - United States Free Trade Agreement on originating goods where those goods qualify to be marked as goods of Canada pursuant to Annex 311, without regard to whether the goods are marked.
2. The United States shall not increase its merchandise processing fee and shall eliminate such fee by June 30, 1999, on originating goods where those goods qualify to be marked as goods of Mexico pursuant to Annex 311, without regard to whether the goods are marked.

ANNEX 311. COUNTRY OF ORIGIN MARKING

1. The Parties shall establish by January 1, 1994, rules for determining whether a good is a good of a Party ("Marking Rules") for purposes of this Annex, Annex 300-B and Annex 302.2, and for such other purposes as the Parties may agree.
2. Each Party may require that a good of another Party, as determined in accordance with the Marking Rules, bear a country of origin marking, when imported into its territory, that indicates to the ultimate purchaser of that good the name of its country of origin.
3. Each Party shall permit the country of origin marking of a good of another Party to be indicated in English, French or Spanish, except that a Party may, as part of its general consumer information measures, require that an imported good be marked with its country of origin in the same manner as prescribed for goods of that Party.
4. Each Party shall, in adopting, maintaining and applying any measure relating to country of origin marking, minimize the difficulties, costs and inconveniences that the measure may cause to the commerce and industry of the other Parties.
5. Each Party shall:
   (a) accept any reasonable method of marking of a good of another Party, including the use of stickers, labels, tags or paint, that ensures that the marking is conspicuous, legible and sufficiently permanent;

(b) exempt from a country of origin marking requirement a good of another Party that

    (i)   is incapable of being marked,

    (ii) cannot be marked prior to exportation to the territory of another Party without causing injury to the goods,

    (iii) cannot be marked except at a cost that is substantial in relation to its customs value so as to discourage its exportation to the territory of the Party,

    (iv) cannot be marked without materially impairing its function or substantially detracting from its appearance,

    (v) is in a container that is marked in a manner that will reasonably indicate the good's origin to the ultimate purchaser,

    (vi) is a crude substance,

    (vii) is imported for use by the importer and is not intended for sale in the form in which it was imported,

    (viii) is to undergo production in the territory of the importing Party by the importer, or on its behalf, in a manner that would result in the good becoming a good of the importing Party under the Marking Rules, (ix) by reason of its character, or the circumstances of its importation, the ultimate purchaser would reasonably know its country of origin even though it is not marked,

    (x) was produced more than 20 years prior to its importation,

    (xi) was imported without the required marking and cannot be marked after its importation except at a cost that would be substantial in relation to its customs value, provided that the failure to mark the good before importation was not for the purpose of avoiding compliance with the requirement,

    (xii) for purposes of temporary duty-free admission, is in transit or in bond or otherwise under customs administration control,

    (xiii) is an original work of art, or

    (xiv) is provided for in subheading 6904.10, or heading 8541 or 8542.

6. Except for a good described in subparagraphs 5(b)(vi), (vii), (viii), (ix), (x), (xii), (xiii) and (xiv), a Party may provide that, wherever a good is exempted under subparagraph 5(b), its outermost usual container shall be marked so as to indicate the country of origin of the good it contains.

7. Each Party shall provide that:

    (a) a usual container imported empty, whether or not disposable, shall not be required to be marked with its own country of origin, but the container in which it is imported may be required to be marked with the country of origin of its contents; and

    (b) a usual container imported filled, whether or not disposable,

        (i)   shall not be required to be marked with its own country of origin, but

        (ii) may be required to be marked with the country of origin of its contents, unless the contents are marked with their country of origin and the container can be readily opened for inspection of the contents, or the marking of the contents is clearly visible through the container.

8. Each Party shall, wherever administratively practicable, permit an importer to mark a good of a Party subsequent to importation but prior to release of the good from

customs control or custody, unless there have been repeated violations of the country of origin marking requirements of the Party by the same importer and that importer has been previously notified in writing that such good is required to be marked prior to importation.

9. Each Party shall provide that, except with respect to importers that have been notified under paragraph 8, no special duty or penalty shall be imposed for failure to comply with country of origin marking requirements of that Party, unless the good is removed from customs custody or control without being properly marked, or a deceptive marking has been used.

10. The Parties shall cooperate and consult on matters related to this Annex, including additional exemptions from a country of origin marking requirement, in accordance with Article 513 (Customs Procedures - Working Group and Customs Subgroup).

11. For purposes of this Annex:

conspicuous means capable of being easily seen with normal handling of the good or container;

customs value means the value of a good for purposes of levying duties of customs on an imported good;

legible means capable of being easily read;

sufficiently permanent means capable of remaining in place until the good reaches the ultimate purchaser, unless deliberately removed;

the form in which it was imported means the condition of the good before it has undergone one of the changes in tariff classification described in the Marking Rules;

ultimate purchaser means the last person in the territory of an importing Party that purchases the good in the form in which it was imported; such purchaser need not be the last person that will use the good; and

usual container means the container in which a good will ordinarily reach its ultimate purchaser.

ANNEX 312.2. WINE AND DISTILLED SPIRITS

Section A - Canada and the United States

As between Canada and the United States, any measure related to the internal sale and distribution of wine and distilled spirits, other than a measure covered by Article 312(1) or 313, shall be governed under this Agreement exclusively in accordance with the relevant provisions of the Canada - United States Free Trade Agreement, which for this purpose are hereby incorporated into and made a part of this Agreement.

Section B - Canada and Mexico

As between Canada and Mexico:

1. Except as provided in paragraphs 3 through 6, in respect of any measure related to the internal sale and distribution of wine and distilled spirits, Article 301 shall not apply to:
   (a) a non-conforming provision of any existing measure;
   (b) the continuation or prompt renewal of a non-conforming provision of any existing measure; or
   (c) an amendment to a non-conforming provision of any existing measure to the extent that the amendment does not decrease its conformity with Article 301.

2. The Party asserting that paragraph 1 applies to one of its measures shall have the burden of establishing the validity of such assertion.

3.
   (a) Any measure related to the listing of wine and distilled spirits of the other Party shall:
      (i) conform with Article 301,
      (ii) be transparent, non-discriminatory and provide for prompt decision on any listing application, prompt written notification of such decision to the applicant and, in the case of a negative decision, provide for a statement of the reason for refusal,
      (iii) establish administrative appeal procedures for listing decisions that provide for prompt, fair and objective rulings,
      (iv) be based on normal commercial considerations,
      (v) not create disguised barriers to trade, and
      (vi) be published and made generally available to persons of the other Party.
   (b) Notwithstanding paragraph 3(a) and Article 301, and provided that listing measures of British Columbia otherwise conform with paragraph 3(a) and Article 301, automatic listing measures in the province of British Columbia may be maintained provided they apply only to existing estate wineries producing less than 30,000 gallons of wine annually and meeting the existing content rule.

4.
   (a) Where the distributor is a public entity, the entity may charge the actual cost-of-service differential between wine or distilled spirits of the other Party and domestic wine or distilled spirits. Any such differential shall not exceed the actual amount by which the audited cost of service for the wine or distilled spirits of the exporting Party exceeds the audited cost of service for the wine or distilled spirits of the importing Party.
   (b) Notwithstanding Article 301, Article I (Definitions) except for the definition of "distilled spirits", Article IV.3 (Wine), and Annexes A, B, and C, of the Agreement between Canada and the European Economic Community concerning Trade and Commerce in Alcoholic Beverages, dated February 28, 1989, shall apply with such changes as the circumstances may require.
   (c) All discriminatory mark-ups on distilled spirits shall be eliminated immediately on the date of entry into force of this Agreement. Cost-of-service differential mark-ups as described in subparagraph (a) shall be permitted.
   (d) Any other discriminatory pricing measure shall be eliminated on the date of entry into force of this Agreement.

5.
- (a) Any measure related to distribution of wine or distilled spirits of the other Party shall conform with Article 301.
- (b) Notwithstanding subparagraph (a), and provided that distribution measures otherwise ensure conformity with Article 301, a Party may
  - (i) maintain or introduce a measure limiting on-premise sales by a winery or distillery to those wines or distilled spirits produced on its premises, and
  - (ii) maintain a measure requiring existing private wine store outlets in the provinces of Ontario and British Columbia to discriminate in favor of wine of those provinces to a degree no greater than the discrimination required by such existing measure.
- (c) Nothing in this Agreement shall prohibit the Province of Quebec from requiring that any wine sold in grocery stores in Quebec be bottled in Quebec, provided that alternative outlets are provided in Quebec for the sale of wine of the other Party, whether or not such wine is bottled in Quebec.
6. Unless otherwise specifically provided in this Annex, the Parties retain their rights and obligations under the GATT and agreements negotiated under the GATT.
7. For purposes of this Annex:
wine includes wine and wine-containing beverages.

ANNEX 313. DISTINCTIVE PRODUCTS

1. Canada and Mexico shall recognize Bourbon Whiskey and Tennessee Whiskey, which is a straight Bourbon Whiskey authorized to be produced only in the State of Tennessee, as distinctive products of the United States. Accordingly, Canada and Mexico shall not permit the sale of any product as Bourbon Whiskey or Tennessee Whiskey, unless it has been manufactured in the United States in accordance with the laws and regulations of the United States governing the manufacture of Bourbon Whiskey and Tennessee Whiskey.
2. Mexico and the United States shall recognize Canadian Whisky as a distinctive product of Canada. Accordingly, Mexico and the United States shall not permit the sale of any product as Canadian Whisky, unless it has been manufactured in Canada in accordance with the laws and regulations of Canada governing the manufacture of Canadian Whisky for consumption in Canada.
3. Canada and the United States shall recognize Tequila and Mezcal as distinctive products of Mexico. Accordingly, Canada and the United States shall not permit the sale of any product as Tequila or Mezcal, unless it has been manufactured in Mexico in accordance with the laws and regulations of Mexico governing the manufacture of Tequila and Mezcal. This provision shall apply to Mezcal, either on the date of entry into force of this Agreement, or 90 days after the date when the official standard for this product is made obligatory by the Government of Mexico, whichever is later.

ANNEX 314. EXPORT TAXES

Mexico

1. Mexico may adopt or maintain a duty, tax or other charge on the export of those basic foodstuffs set out in paragraph 4, on their ingredients or on the goods from which such foodstuffs are derived, if such duty, tax or other charge is adopted or maintained on the export of such goods to the territory of all other Parties, and is used:

   (a) to limit to domestic consumers the benefits of a domestic food assistance program with respect to such foodstuff; or

   (b) to ensure the availability of sufficient quantities of such foodstuff to domestic consumers or of sufficient quantities of its ingredients, or of the goods from which such foodstuffs are derived, to a domestic processing industry, when the domestic price of such foodstuff is held below the world price as part of a governmental stabilization plan, provided that such duty, tax, or other charge

      (i) does not operate to increase the protection afforded to such domestic industry, and

      (ii) is maintained only for such period of time as is necessary to maintain the integrity of the stabilization plan.

2. Notwithstanding paragraph 1, Mexico may adopt or maintain a duty, tax or other charge on the export of any foodstuff to the territory of another Party if such duty, tax or other charge is temporarily applied to relieve critical shortages of that foodstuff. For purposes of this paragraph, "temporarily" means up to one year, or such longer period as the Parties may agree.

3. Mexico may maintain its existing tax on the export of goods provided for under tariff item 4001.30.02 of the Tariff Schedule of the *General Export Duty Act* ("Tarifa de la Ley del Impuesto General de Exportación") for up to 10 years after the date of entry into force of this Agreement.

4. For purposes of paragraph 1, "basic foodstuffs" means:
   - Beans
   - Beef steak or pulp
   - Beef liver
   - Beef remnants and bones ("retazo con hueso")
   - Beer
   - Bread
   - Brown sugar
   - Canned sardines
   - Canned tuna
   - Canned peppers
   - Chicken broth
   - Condensed milk
   - Cooked ham
   - Corn tortillas
   - Corn flour

- Corn dough
- Crackers
- Eggs
- Evaporated milk
- French rolls ("pan blanco")
- Gelatine
- Ground beef
- Instant coffee
- Low-priced cookies ("galletas dulces populares")
- Margarine
- Oat flakes
- Pasteurized milk
- Powdered chocolate
- Powdered milk for children
- Powdered milk
- Rice
- Roasted coffee
- Salt
- Soft drinks
- Soup paste
- Tomato puree
- Vegetable oil
- Vegetable fat
- Wheat flour
- White sugar

ANNEX 315. OTHER EXPORT MEASURES

Article 315 shall not apply as between Mexico and the other Parties

ANNEX 300-A. TRADE AND INVESTMENT IN THE AUTOMOTIVE SECTOR

1. Each Party shall accord to all existing producers of vehicles in its territory treatment no less favorable than it accords to any new producer of vehicles in its territory under the measures referred to in this Annex, except that this obligation shall not be construed to apply to any differences in treatment specifically provided for in the Appendices to this Annex.

2. The Parties shall review, no later than December 31, 2003, the status of the North American automotive sector and the effectiveness of the measures referred to in this Annex to determine actions that could be taken to strengthen the integration and global competitiveness of the sector.

3. Appendices 300-A.1, 300-A.2 and 300-A.3 apply to the Parties specified therein respecting trade and investment in the automotive sector.

4. For purposes of this Annex, unless otherwise specified in the Appendices:

    existing producer of vehicles means a producer that was producing vehicles in the territory of the relevant Party prior to model year 1992;

    new producer of vehicles means a producer that began producing vehicles in the territory of the relevant Party after model year 1991;

    used vehicle means a vehicle that:

    (a) has been sold, leased or loaned;

    (b) has been driven for more than

        (i) 1,000 kilometers if the vehicle has a gross weight of less than five metric tons, or

        (ii) 5,000 kilometers if the vehicle has a gross weight of five metric tons or more; or

    (c) was manufactured prior to the current year and at least 90 days have elapsed since the date of manufacture; and

    vehicle means an automobile, a truck, a bus or a special purpose motor vehicle, not including a motorcycle.

APPENDIX 300-A.1. CANADA

Existing Measures

1. Canada and the United States may maintain the *Agreement Concerning Automotive Products between the Government of Canada and the Government of the United States of America*, signed at Johnson City, Texas, January 16, 1965 and entered into force on September 16, 1966, in accordance with Article 1001, and Article 1002(1) and (4) (as they refer to Annex 1002.1, Part One), Article 1005(1) and (3), and Annex 1002.1, Part One (Waivers of Customs Duties) of the *Canada - United States Free Trade Agreement*, which provisions are hereby incorporated into and made a part of this Agreement for such purpose, except that for purposes of Article 1005(1) of that agreement, Chapter Four (Rules of Origin) of this Agreement shall be applied in the place of Chapter Three of *the Canada - United States Free Trade Agreement.*

2. Canada may maintain the measures referred to in Article 1002(1) and (4) (as they refer to Annex 1002.1, Parts Two and Three), Article 1002(2) and (3), Article 1003 and Parts Two (Export-Based Waivers of Customs Duties) and Three (Production-Based Waivers of Customs Duties) of Annex 1002.1 of *the Canada - United States Free Trade Agreement*. Canada shall eliminate those measures in accordance with the terms set out in that agreement.

3. For greater certainty, the differences in treatment pursuant to paragraphs 1 and 2 shall not be considered to be inconsistent with Article 1103 (Investment - Most-Favored- Nation Treatment).

Used Vehicles

4. Canada may adopt or maintain prohibitions or restrictions on imports of used vehicles from the territory of Mexico, except as follows:
   (a) beginning January 1, 2009, Canada may not adopt or maintain a prohibition or restriction on imports from the territory of Mexico of originating used vehicles that are at least 10 years old;
   (b) beginning January 1, 2011, Canada may not adopt or maintain a prohibition or restriction on imports from the territory of Mexico of originating used vehicles that are at least eight years old;
   (c) beginning January 1, 2013, Canada may not adopt or maintain a prohibition or restriction on imports from the territory of Mexico of originating used vehicles that are at least six years old;
   (d) beginning January 1, 2015, Canada may not adopt or maintain a prohibition or restriction on imports from the territory of Mexico of originating used vehicles that are at least four years old;
   (e) beginning January 1, 2017, Canada may not adopt or maintain a prohibition or restriction on imports from the territory of Mexico of originating used vehicles that are at least two years old; and
   (f) beginning January 1, 2019, Canada may not adopt or maintain a prohibition or restriction on imports from the territory of Mexico of originating used vehicles.
5. Paragraph 4 shall not be construed to allow Canada to derogate from its obligations in respect of land transportation services under Chapter Twelve (Cross-Border Trade in Services), including its Schedule to Annex I.

APPENDIX 300-A.2. MEXICO

Auto Decree and Auto Decree Implementing Regulations

1. Until January 1, 2004, Mexico may maintain the provisions of *the Decree for Development and Modernization of the Automotive Industry* ("Decreto para el Fomento y Modernización de la Industria Automotriz"), December 11, 1989, (the "Auto Decree") and the *Resolution that Establishes Rules for the Implementation of the Auto Decree* ("Acuerdo que Determina Reglas para la Aplicaci n para el Fomento y Modernización de la Industria Automotriz"), November 30, 1990, (the "Auto Decree Implementing Regulations") that would otherwise be inconsistent with this Agreement, subject to the conditions set out in paragraphs 2 through 18. No later than January 1, 2004, Mexico shall bring any inconsistent provision of the Auto Decree and the Auto Decree Implementing Regulations into conformity with the other provisions of this Agreement.

Autoparts Industry, National Suppliers and Independent Maquiladoras

2. Mexico may not require that an enterprise attain a level of national value added in excess of 20 percent of its total sales as one of the conditions to qualify as a national supplier or enterprise of the autoparts industry.

3. Mexico may require that a national supplier or an enterprise of the autoparts industry, in calculating its national value added solely for purposes of paragraph 2, include customs duties in the value of imports incorporated into the autoparts produced by such supplier or enterprise.

4. Mexico shall grant national supplier status to an independent maquiladora that requests such status and meets the requirements for that status set out in the existing Auto Decree, as modified by paragraphs 2 and 3. Mexico shall continue to grant to all independent maquiladoras that request national supplier status all existing rights and privileges accorded to independent maquiladoras under the existing *Decree for the Promotion and Operation of the Maquiladora Export Industry* ("Decreto para el Fomento y Operación de la Industria Maquiladora de Exportación"), December 22, 1989 (the "Maquiladora Decree").

National Value Added

5. Mexico shall provide that a manufacturer ("empresa de la industria terminal") calculate its required national value added from suppliers (VANp) as a percentage of:
    (a) the manufacturer's reference value as set out in paragraph 8; or
    (b) the manufacturer's total national value added (VANt),
    whichever is greater, except that Mexico shall provide that a manufacturer beginning production of motor vehicles in Mexico after model year 1991 calculate its required national value added from suppliers (VANp) as a percentage of its total national value added (VANt).

6. Mexico may not require that the percentage referred to in paragraph 5 be greater than:
    (a) 34 percent for each of the first five years beginning January 1, 1994;
    (b) 33 percent for 1999;
    (c) 32 percent for 2000;
    (d) 31 percent for 2001;
    (e) 30 percent for 2002; and
    (f) 29 percent for 2003.

7. Notwithstanding paragraph 6, Mexico shall allow a manufacturer that produced motor vehicles in Mexico before model year 1992 to use as its percentage referred to in paragraph 5 the ratio of actual national value added from suppliers (VANp) to total national value added (VANt) that the manufacturer attained in model year 1992, for so long as that ratio is lower than the applicable percentage specified under paragraph 6. In determining such ratio for model year 1992, purchases that the manufacturer made from independent maquiladoras that would have been eligible to receive national supplier status had paragraphs 2, 3 and 4 of this Appendix been in

effect at that time, shall be included in the calculation of the manufacturer's national value added from suppliers (VANp), in the same manner as autoparts from any other national supplier or enterprise of the autoparts industry.

8. The annual reference value for a manufacturer ("reference value") shall be:

    (a) for each of the years 1994 through 1997, the base value for the manufacturer, plus no more than 65 percent of the difference between the manufacturer's total sales in Mexico in that year and its base value;

    (b) for each of the years 1998 through 2000, the base value for the manufacturer, plus no more than 60 percent of the difference between the manufacturer's total sales in Mexico in that year and its base value; and

    (c) for each of the years 2001 through 2003, the base value for the manufacturer, plus no more than 50 percent of the difference between the manufacturer's total sales in Mexico in that year and its base value.

9. Mexico shall provide that where a manufacturer's total sales in Mexico in a year are lower than its base value, the reference value for the manufacturer for that year shall be equal to the manufacturer's total sales in Mexico for the year.

10. In the event an abnormal production disruption affects a manufacturer's production capability, Mexico shall allow the manufacturer to seek a reduction in its reference value before the Intersecretariat Automotive Industry Commission, established under Chapter V of the Auto Decree. If the Commission finds that the production capability of the manufacturer has been impaired by such an abnormal production disruption, the Commission shall reduce the manufacturer's reference value in an amount commensurate to the event.

11. If, on the request of a manufacturer, the Intersecretariat Automotive Industry Commission finds that the production capability of the manufacturer has been significantly disrupted as a result of a major retooling or plant conversion in the facilities of the manufacturer, the Commission shall reduce the manufacturer's reference value for that year in an amount commensurate with the disruption, provided that any reduction in that manufacturer's required national value added from suppliers (VANp) that may result from the Commission's determination to reduce the manufacturer's reference value shall be fully made up by the manufacturer over the 24 months after the date on which the retooling or plant conversion is completed.

Trade Balance

12. Mexico may not require a manufacturer to include in the calculation of its trade balance (S) a percentage of the value of direct and indirect imports of autoparts that the manufacturer incorporated into that manufacturer's production in Mexico for sale in Mexico (VTVd) in the corresponding year, greater than the following:

    (a) 80 percent for 1994;

    (b) 77.2 percent for 1995;

    (c) 74.4 percent for 1996;

    (d) 71.6 percent for 1997;

    (e) 68.9 percent for 1998;

(f) 66.1 percent for 1999;

(g) 63.3 percent for 2000;

(h) 60.5 percent for 2001;

(i) 57.7 percent for 2002; and

(j) 55.0 percent for 2003.

13. Mexico shall provide that, for purposes of determining a manufacturer's total national value added (VANt), paragraph 12 shall not apply to the calculation of the manufacturer's trade balance (S).

14. Mexico shall allow a manufacturer with a surplus in its extended trade balance to divide its extended trade balance by the applicable percentages in paragraph 12 to determine the total value of new motor vehicles that it may import.

15. Mexico shall provide that a manufacturer's adjustment factor (Y), included in the calculation of such manufacturer's extended trade balance, shall be equal to:

(a) for a manufacturer that produced motor vehicles prior to model year 1992

(i) the greater of the manufacturer's reference value or the manufacturer's total national value added (VANt), minus

(ii) the manufacturer's actual national value added from suppliers (VANp) divided by the appropriate percentage specified under paragraph 6 or 7 as appropriate;

(b) for all other manufacturers

(i) the manufacturer's total national value added (VANt), minus

(ii) the manufacturer's actual national value added from suppliers (VANp) divided by the appropriate percentage specified under paragraph 6, except that the adjustment factor (Y) shall be zero if the amount resulting from subtracting (ii) from (i), under (a) or (b), is negative.

16. In determining the annual amount that a manufacturer may apply to its extended trade balance from unused surpluses earned prior to model year 1991, Mexico shall in any year allow the manufacturer to elect:

(a) to use the procedures of the existing Auto Decree Implementing Regulations; or

(b) to apply up to the Mexican peso equivalent of US$150 million, adjusted annually for cumulative inflation, from the date of entry into force of this Agreement, based on the implicit price deflator for U.S. Gross Domestic Product (GDP) or any successor index published by the Council of Economic Advisers in its "Economic Indicators" (hereinafter "U.S. GDP price deflator"). To adjust the US$150 million ceiling for cumulative inflation up to a certain month of a year following 1994, the $150 million shall be multiplied by the ratio of

(i) the U.S. GDP price deflator current as of the month of that year, to

(ii) the U.S. GDP price deflator current as of the date of entry into force of this Agreement,

provided that the price deflators under subparagraphs (i) and (ii) have the same base year.

The resulting adjusted amount shall be rounded to the nearest million dollars.

Other Restrictions in the Auto Decree

17. Mexico shall eliminate any restriction that limits the number of motor vehicles that a manufacturer may import into Mexico in relation to the total number of motor vehicles that such manufacturer sells in Mexico.
18. For greater certainty, the differences in treatment required under paragraphs 5, 7 and 15 shall not be considered to be inconsistent with Article 1103 (Investment - Most - Favored - Nation Treatment).

Other Restrictions

19. For the first 10 years after the date of entry into force of this Agreement, Mexico may maintain prohibitions or restrictions on the importation of new automotive products provided for in existing items 8407.34.02 (gasoline engines larger than 1000 cm³ but smaller than or equal to 2000cm³. except for motorcycles), and 8407.34.99 (gasoline engines larger than 2000cm³, except for motorcycles) and 8703.10.99 (other special vehicles) in the Tariff Schedule of the *General Import Duty Act* ("Tarifa de la Ley del Impuesto General de Importación"), except that Mexico may not prohibit or restrict the importation of automotive products provided for in item 8407.34.02 (gasoline engines larger than 1000 cm³ but smaller than or equal to 2000cm³. except for motorcycles), 8407.34.99 (gasoline engines larger than 2000 cm³, except for motorcycles), or 8703.10.99 (other special vehicles) by manufacturers that comply with the Auto Decree and the Auto Decree Implementing Regulations, as modified by this Appendix.

Autotransportation Decree and Autotransportation Implementing Regulations

20. Mexico shall eliminate the Mexican *Decree for Development and Modernization of the Autotransportation Vehicle Manufacturing Industry* , ("Decreto para el Fomento y Modernización de la Industria Manufacturera de Vehículos de Autotransporte"), December 1989, and the *Resolution that Establishes Rules for the Implementation of the Autotransportation Decree* ("Acuerdo que Establece Reglas de Aplicación del Decreto para el Fomento y Modernización de la Industria Manufacturera de Vehículos de Autotransporte"), November 1990. Mexico may adopt or maintain any measure respecting autotransportation vehicles, autotransportation parts or manufacturers of autotransportation vehicles provided that the measure is not inconsistent with this Agreement.

Importation of Autotransportation Vehicles

21. Mexico may adopt or maintain a prohibition or restriction on the importation of autotransportation vehicles of another Party until January 1, 1999, except with respect to the importation of autotransportation vehicles pursuant to paragraphs 22 and 23.
22. For each of the years 1994 through 1998, Mexico shall allow any manufacturer of autotransportation vehicles to import, for each type of autotransportation vehicle, a quantity of originating autotransportation vehicles equal to at least 50 percent of the number of vehicles of such type that the manufacturer produced in Mexico in that year.
23. For each of the years 1994 through 1998, Mexico shall allow persons other than manufacturers of autotransportation vehicles to import, in a quantity to be allocated among such persons, originating autotransportation vehicles of each type as follows:
    (a) for each of the years 1994 and 1995, no less than 15 percent of the total number of vehicles of each type of autotransportation vehicle produced in Mexico;
    (b) for 1996, no less than 20 percent of the total number of vehicles of each type of autotransportation vehicle produced in Mexico; and
    (c) for each of the years 1997 and 1998, no less than 30 percent of the total number of vehicles of each type of autotransportation vehicle produced in Mexico.

    Mexico shall allocate such quantity through a non-discriminatory auction.

Used Vehicles

24. Mexico may adopt or maintain prohibitions or restrictions on imports of used vehicles from the territory of another Party, except as follows:
    (a) beginning January 1, 2009, Mexico may not adopt or maintain a prohibition or restriction on imports from the territories of Canada or the United States of originating used vehicles that are at least 10 years old;
    (b) beginning January 1, 2011, Mexico may not adopt or maintain a prohibition or restriction on imports from the territories of Canada or the United States of originating used vehicles that are at least eight years old;
    (c) beginning January 1, 2013, Mexico may not adopt or maintain a prohibition or restriction on imports from the territories of Canada or the United States of originating used vehicles that are at least six years old;
    (d) beginning January 1, 2015, Mexico may not adopt or maintain a prohibition or restriction on imports from the territories of Canada or the United States of originating used vehicles that are at least four years old;
    (e) beginning January 1, 2017, Mexico may not adopt or maintain a prohibition or restriction on imports from the territories of Canada or the United States of originating used vehicles that are at least two years old; and

(f) beginning January 1, 2019, Mexico may not adopt or maintain a prohibition or restriction on imports from the territories of Canada or the United States of originating used vehicles.

25.

(a) Paragraph 24 shall not apply to the importation on a temporary basis of a used vehicle provided for in item 8705.20.01 (mobile drilling derricks), 8705.20.99 (other mobile drilling derricks) or 8705.90.01 (street sweepers) of the Tariff Schedule of the *General Import Duty Act* . Such importation shall be subject to the conditions set out in Section 4(b) of Annex 301.3 for such time as Mexico may adopt or maintain a prohibition or restriction on the importation of the vehicle under paragraph 24.

(b) Paragraph 24 shall not be construed to allow Mexico to derogate from its obligations in respect of land transportation services under Chapter Twelve (Cross- Border Trade in Services), including its Schedule to Annex I.

Import Licensing Measures

26. Mexico may adopt or maintain import licensing measures to the extent necessary to administer restrictions pursuant to:

(a) the Auto Decree and the Auto Decree Implementing Regulations, as modified by this Appendix, on the importation of motor vehicles;

(b) paragraph 19 of this Appendix on the importation of new automotive products provided for in item 8407.34.02 (gasoline engines larger than 1000cm3, but smaller than or equal to 2000 cm³, except for motorcycles) or 8703.10.99 (other special vehicles) in the Tariff Schedule of the *General Import Duty Act* ;

(c) paragraphs 22 and 23 of this Appendix on the importation of autotransportation vehicles; and

(d) paragraph 24 (a) through (f) of this Appendix on the importation of used vehicles that are motor vehicles or autotransportation vehicles or of other used vehicles provided for in existing items 8702.90.01 (trolley buses), 8705.10.01 (mobile cranes), 8705.20.99 (other mobile drilling derricks), 8705.90.01 (street sweepers) or 8705.90.99 (other special purpose vehicles, nes) in the Tariff Schedule of the *General Import Duty Act* ;

provided that such measures shall not have trade restrictive effects on the importation of such goods additional to those due to restrictions imposed in accordance with this Appendix, and that a license shall be granted to any person that fulfills Mexico's legal requirements for the importation of the goods.

Definitions

27. For purposes of this Appendix:

abnormal production disruption means a disruption in a manufacturer's production capability resulting from a natural disaster, fire, explosion or other unforeseen event beyond the manufacturer's control;

automotive products (referred to as "productos automotrices" in rule 1, paragraph III of the Auto Decree Implementing Regulations) means motor vehicles and autoparts;

autoparts (referred to as "partes y componentes automotrices" in article 2, paragraph X of the Auto Decree) means parts and components intended for use in a motor vehicle;

autotransportation parts means parts and components intended for use in an autotransportation vehicle;

autotransportation vehicle means a vehicle of one of the following types:

(a) a vehicle without a chassis and with an integrated body, intended for the transport of more than 10 persons, with a gross vehicle weight of more than 8,864 kilograms, provided for in items 8702.10.02, 8702.10.03, 8702.90.03, 8702.90.04, 8705.20.01 or 8705.40.01 of the Tariff Schedule of *the General Import Duty Act ;*

(b) a vehicle with a chassis, intended for the transport of goods or more than 10 persons, with a gross vehicle weight of more than 8,864 kilograms, provided for in items 8702.10.01, 8702.10.03, 8702.90.02, 8702.90.04, 8704.22.99, 8704.23.99, 8704.32.99, 8705.20.01, 8705.40.01 or 8706.00.99 of the Tariff Schedule of the *General Import Duty Act ; or*

(c) a vehicle with two or three axles, either with integrated equipment or intended for the transport of goods by hauling a trailer, or semi-trailer, provided for in items 8701.20.01, 8705.20.01, 8705.40.01 or 8706.00.99 of the Tariff Schedule of the *General Import Duty Act ;*

base value means the average for model years 1991 and 1992 of a manufacturer's production in Mexico for sale in Mexico (VTVd), adjusted annually for cumulative inflation, based on the *Mexican National Producer Price Index of Vehicles, Autoparts, and other Transportation Goods* ("Indice Nacional de Precios al Productor de vehículos, refacciones y otros materiales de transporte"), or any successor index, published by the Bank of Mexico ("Banco de Mexico") in its "Economic Indicators" ("Indicadores Económicos") (hereinafter "Mexican NPPI"). To adjust the base value for cumulative inflation up to 1994 or a subsequent year, the average for model years 1991 and 1992 of the manufacturer's VTVd shall be multiplied by the ratio of:

(a) the Mexican NPPI for that year, to

(b) the Mexican NPPI for 1992,

provided that the price indices set out in subparagraphs (a) and (b) have the same base year;

enterprise of the autoparts industry (referred to as "empresa de la industria de autopartes" in article 2, paragraph V, and articles 6 and 7 of the Auto Decree) means an enterprise constituted or organized under the law of, and operating in, Mexico that produces autoparts and:

(a) whose annual invoice value of sales of autoparts to manufacturers, for use as original equipment by the manufacturer in its production of automotive products for sale in Mexico, constitutes more than 60 percent of the enterprise's annual total invoice value of sales, calculating its annual invoice value of sales of autoparts to manufacturers in accordance with rule 20 of the Auto Decree Implementing Regulations as of August 12, 1992, or any other measure adopted by Mexico that is no more restrictive than such rule;

(b) complies with the national value added requirements pursuant to paragraphs 2 and 3 of this Appendix;

(c) complies with the capital structure required under the *Law to Promote Mexican Investment and Regulate Foreign Investment* ("Ley para Promover la Inversión Mexicana y Regular la Inversión Extranjera"), March 9, 1973, and the *Regulations of the Law to Promote Mexican Investment and to Regulate Foreign Investment* ("Reglamento de la Ley para Promover la Inversión Mexicana y Regular la Inversión Extranjera"), May 16, 1989, as applied consistently with Mexico's commitments set out in its Schedule to Annex I of Part Five (Investment, Services and Related Matters); and

(d) that, on the fulfillment of the requirements under (a), (b) and (c), is registered with the Ministry of Trade and Industrial Development ("Secretaría de Comercio y Fomento Industrial") ("SECOFI") as an enterprise of the autoparts industry, except that SECOFI may grant registration to an enterprise that complies with subparagraphs (b) and (c) but does not comply with subparagraph (a);

extended trade balance for a manufacturer is equal to $S + T + W + 0.3I + SFt - Y$, where:

(a) S denotes the manufacturer's trade balance;

(b) T denotes the transfer of

(i) trade balance surpluses between the manufacturer and other manufacturers, and

(ii) foreign exchange to the manufacturer that an enterprise of the autoparts industry has earned from exports of autoparts, excluding the value of import content in such exports, and excluding foreign exchange that the enterprise has earned from exports of autoparts that were promoted by the manufacturer,

applied in accordance with rule 8 of the Auto Decree Implementing Regulations as of August 12, 1992, or any other measure adopted by Mexico that is no more restrictive than such rule;

(c) W denotes the transfer to the manufacturer of foreign exchange that a maquiladora has earned from the export of automotive products, excluding the value of the import content in such exports, provided that the maquiladora is not a national supplier, and one or more of the following conditions is met

(i) the manufacturer is, directly or indirectly, a majority shareholder of the maquiladora,

(ii) the manufacturer and the maquiladora have a majority shareholder in common, or

(iii) the manufacturer is a promoter of the automotive goods exported by such maquiladora, calculated in accordance with article 9 of the Auto Decree and rule 8 of the Auto Decree Implementing Regulations as of August 12, 1992, or any other measure adopted by Mexico that is no more restrictive than that article or rule;

(d) I denotes the value of the manufacturer's investments in fixed assets of Mexican origin destined for permanent use in Mexico, excluding machinery and equipment purchased in Mexico but not produced in Mexico, that the manufacturer may transfer to its extended trade balance, applied in accordance with article 11 of the Auto Decree and rule 8 of the Auto Decree Implementing Regulations as of August 12, 1992, or any other measure adopted by Mexico that is no more restrictive than the article or rule;

(e) SFt denotes the manufacturer's trade balance surpluses unused in prior years and transferred to the current year, calculated in accordance with rules 17 and 19 of the Auto Decree Implementing Regulations as of August 12, 1992, as modified by paragraph 16 of this Appendix, or any other measure adopted by Mexico that is no more restrictive than such rules; and

(f) Y denotes the adjustment factor calculated in accordance with paragraph 15;

independent maquiladora means an enterprise registered as an export maquiladora enterprise under the existing MaquiladoraDecree, that has no majority shareholder in common with any manufacturer, and in which no manufacturer is directly or indirectly a majority shareholder;

manufacturer (referred to as "empresa de la industria terminal"in article 2, paragraph IV, and articles 3, 4 and 5 of the Auto Decree) means an enterprise constituted or organized under the law of, and operating in, Mexico, that is:

(a) registered with SECOFI; and

(b) engaged in Mexico in the manufacture or final assembly of motor vehicles;

manufacturer of autotransportation vehicles means an enterprise constituted or organized under the law of, and operating in, Mexico:

(a) that is registered with SECOFI;

(b) that manufactures autotransportation vehicles in Mexico; and

(c) where the enterprise's

(i) total invoice value of sales of autotransportation vehicles and autotransportation parts that it produces in Mexico, minus

(ii) total invoice value of autotransportation parts that the enterprise imports directly, plus the value of the import content of autotransportation parts that it purchases in Mexico, is equal to at least 40 percent of its total invoice value of sales of autotransportation vehicles and autotransportation parts that the enterprise produces in Mexico;

manufacturer's production in Mexico for sale in Mexico (VTVd) means the total invoice value of a manufacturer's sales in Mexico of motor vehicles and autoparts it produced in Mexico, excluding the manufacturer's sales of imported motor vehicles;

manufacturer's total sales in Mexico means the manufacturer's total invoice value of sales of motor vehicles it produced in Mexico for sale in Mexico plus the total invoice value of its sales of imported motor vehicles;

model year (referred to as "año-modelo" in article 2, paragraph IX of the Auto Decree) means a 12-month period beginning November 1;

motor vehicle (referred to as "vehículos automotores" in article 2, paragraph IV of the Auto Decree) means an automobile, a compact automobile of popular use, a commercial truck, a light duty truck or a medium duty truck, where:

(a) **automobile** means a vehicle intended for the transport of up to 10 persons, provided for in items 8703.21 through 8703.33, 8703.90.99, 8706.00.01, 8706.00.02 or 8706.00.99 of the Tariff Schedule of the *General Import Duty Act*;

(b) **compact automobile of popular use** means a vehicle that complies with the characteristics set out in the existing *Decree that Establishes Exemptions for Compact Automobiles of Popular Use* ("Decreto que Otorga Exenciones a los Automóviles Compactos de Consumo Popular"), August 2, 1989, provided for in items 8703.21 through 8703.33, 8703.90.99, 8706.00.01, 8706.00.02 or 8706.00.99 of the Tariff Schedule of the *General Import Duty Act* ;

(c) **commercial truck** means a vehicle with or without a chassis, intended for the transport of goods or more than 10 persons, with a gross vehicle weight of up to 2,727 kilograms provided for in items 8702.10, 8702.90.02, 8702.90.03, 8702.90.04, 8703.21 through 8703.33, 8703.90.99, 8704.21.99, 8704.31.99, 8705.20.01, 8705.40.01, 8706.00.01, 8706.00.02 or 8706.00.99 of the Tariff Schedule of the *General Import Duty Act* ;

(d) **light duty truck** means a vehicle with or without a chassis, intended for the transport of goods or more than 10 persons, with a gross vehicle weight of more than 2,727 but no more than 7,272 kilograms provided for in items 8702.10, 8702.90.02, 8702.90.03, 8704.90.04, 8704.21.99, 8704.22.99, 8704.31.99, 8704.32.99, 8705.20.01, 8705.40.01, 8706.00.01, 8706.00.02 or 8706.00.99 of the Tariff Schedule of the *General Import Duty Act* ; and

(e) **medium duty truck** means a vehicle with or without a chassis, intended for the transport of goods or more than 10 persons, with a gross vehicle weight of more than 7,272 but no more than 8,864 kilograms provided for in items 8702.10, 8702.90.02, 8702.90.03, 8702.90.04, 8704.22.99, 8704.32.99, 8705.20.01, 8705.40.01, 8706.00.01, 8706.00.02 or 8706.00.99 of the Tariff Schedule of the *General Import Duty Act* ;

national supplier (referred to as "proveedor nacional" in article 2, paragraph VII of the Auto Decree) means an enterprise constituted or organized under the law of, and operating in, Mexico:

(a) that supplies to manufacturers autoparts classified in categories 26, 40, 41, 42, 43 and 57 of the input-output matrix of the National Institute of Statistics, Geography and Informatics ("Instituto Nacional de Estadística, Geografía e Informática"), published in 1980;

(b) that is registered with SECOFI;

(c) in which no manufacturer, directly or indirectly, is a majority shareholder;

(d) that has no majority shareholders that are also majority shareholders of any manufacturer; and

(e) that complies with the national value added requirements pursuant to paragraphs 2 and 3;

national value added from suppliers (VANp) (referred to as "VANp" in rule 18 of the Auto Decree Implementing Regulations) means, for a manufacturer, the sum of:

(a) the national value added contained in the autoparts that the manufacturer purchases from national suppliers and from enterprises of the autoparts industry, excluding purchases of autoparts from such suppliers and enterprises destined for the aftermarket, and

(b) the foreign exchange attributable to the value of exports of autoparts, excluding the value of import content in the exports, produced by national suppliers and enterprises of the autoparts industry, where the export of the autoparts was promoted by the manufacturer,

calculated in accordance with formula 7 of rule 18 in the Auto Decree Implementing Regulations as of August 12, 1992, or any other measure adopted by Mexico that is no more restrictive than such formula;

national value added means, for an enterprise of the autoparts industry or a national supplier, the total value of sales of such enterprise or supplier minus the value of its total imports, direct and indirect, excluding those imports incorporated in autoparts destined for the aftermarket, as modified by paragraphs 2 and 3;

total national value added (VANt) (referred to as "valor agregado nacional de la empresa de la industria terminal" in rule 18 of the Auto Decree Implementing Regulations) means, for a manufacturer, either:

(a) the sum of the manufacturer's production in Mexico for sale in Mexico (VTVd) plus the manufacturer's trade balance (S), where the trade balance (S) is greater than zero; or

(b) the manufacturer's production in Mexico for sale in Mexico (VTVd), where the manufacturer's trade balance (S) is negative;

total sales means, for a national supplier or an enterprise of the autoparts industry, the sum of:

(a) the invoice value of sales of autoparts by that supplier or enterprise to a manufacturer that are intended for use as original equipment in the motor vehicles or autoparts that the manufacturer produces, excluding autoparts destined for the aftermarket; and

(b) the value of autoparts that the supplier or enterprise exports, either directly or through a manufacturer, less the value of the imported content of such autoparts; and

trade balance (S) (referred to as "saldo en balanza comercial" in rule 9 of the Auto Decree Implementing Regulations), for a manufacturer, is equal to $X + TP - ID - IP$, where:

(a) X denotes the value of the manufacturer's direct exports of motor vehicles and autoparts that it produces,

(b) TP denotes the foreign exchange attributable to the value of exports of autoparts, excluding the value of import content in the exports, produced by national suppliers and enterprises of the autoparts industry, where the exportation of such autoparts was promoted by the manufacturer,

(c) ID denotes the value of the manufacturer's direct imports, excluding duties and domestic taxes, and whether the imports are for domestic consumption ("definitivas") or for re-export ("temporales"), incorporated in the motor vehicles and autoparts produced by the manufacturer, excluding autoparts destined for the aftermarket, and

(d) IP denotes the value of import content in the autoparts purchased by the manufacturer from an enterprise of the autoparts industry or a national supplier that are incorporated in the motor vehicles and autoparts produced by the manufacturer, excluding the import content of autoparts destined for the aftermarket, calculated in accordance with rules 10, 12, 13, 14, and 15 of the Auto Decree Implementing Regulations as of August 12, 1992, or any other measure adopted by Mexico that is no more restrictive than such rules,

provided that, for purposes of subparagraphs (c) and (d), the value of imports for domestic consumption ("definitivas") shall be discounted in accordance with paragraph 12.

APPENDIX 300-A.3. UNITED STATES - CORPORATE AVERAGE FUEL ECONOMY

1. In accordance with the schedule set out in paragraph 2, for purposes of the *Energy Policy and Conservation Act of 1975* , 42 U.S.C. 6201 et seq . ("the CAFE Act"), the United States shall consider an automobile to be domestically manufactured in any model year if at least 75 percent of the cost to the manufacturer of such automobile is attributable to value added in Canada, Mexico or the United States, unless the assembly of the automobile is completed in Canada or Mexico and such automobile is not imported into the United States prior to the expiration of the 30 days following the end of the model year.

2. Paragraph 1 shall apply to all automobiles produced by a manufacturer and sold in the United States, wherever produced and irrespective of car line or truck line, in accordance with the following schedule:

    (a) with respect to a manufacturer that initiated the production of automobiles in Mexico before model year 1992, the enterprise subject to the fuel economy requirements for those automobiles under the CAFE Act may make a one-time election at any time between January 1, 1997 and January 1, 2004, to have paragraph 1 applied beginning with the next model year after its election;

    (b) with respect to a manufacturer initiating the production of automobiles in Mexico after model year 1991, paragraph 1 shall apply beginning with the next model year after either January 1, 1994 or the date that the manufacturer initiates the production of automobiles in Mexico, whichever is later;

    (c) with respect to any other manufacturer producing automobiles in the territory of a Party, the enterprise subject to the fuel economy requirements for those automobiles under the CAFE Act may make a one-time election at any time between January 1, 1997 and January 1, 2004, to have paragraph 1 applied beginning with the next model year after its election. If such a manufacturer initiates the production of automobiles in Mexico, it shall be subject to subparagraph (b) on the date it initiates such production;

    (d) with respect to all manufacturers of automobiles not producing automobiles in the territory of a Party, paragraph 1 shall apply beginning with the next model year after January 1, 1994; and

(e) with respect to a manufacturer of automobiles covered by subparagraph (a) or (c), paragraph 1 shall apply beginning with the next model year after January 1, 2004, where the enterprise subject to the fuel economy requirements for those automobiles under the CAFE Act, has not made an election under subparagraph (a) or (c).

3. The United States shall ensure that any measure it adopts pertaining to the definition of domestic production in the CAFE Act or its implementing regulations shall apply equally to value added in Canada or Mexico.

4. Nothing in this Appendix shall be construed to require the United States to make any changes in its fuel economy requirements for automobiles, or to prevent the United States from making any changes in its fuel economy requirements for automobiles that are otherwise consistent with this Appendix.

5. For greater certainty, the differences in treatment pursuant to paragraphs 1 through 3 shall not be considered to be inconsistent with Article 1103 (Investment - Most-Favored- Nation Treatment).

6. For purposes of this Appendix:

    automobile means "automobile" as defined in the CAFE Act and its implementing regulations;

    manufacturer means "manufacturer" as defined in the CAFE Act and its implementing regulations; and

    model year means "model year" as defined in the CAFE Act and its implementing regulations.

ANNEX 300-B. TEXTILE AND APPAREL GOODS

Section 1: Scope and Coverage

1. This Annex applies to the textile and apparel goods set out in Appendix 1.1.

2. In the event of any inconsistency between this Agreement and the *Arrangement Regarding International Trade in Textiles* (Multifiber Arrangement), as amended and extended, including any amendment or extension after January 1, 1994, or any other existing or future agreement applicable to trade in textile or apparel goods, this Agreement shall prevail to the extent of the inconsistency, unless the Parties agree otherwise.

Section 2: Tariff Elimination

1. Except as otherwise provided in this Agreement, each Party shall progressively eliminate its customs duties on originating textile and apparel goods in accordance with its Schedule to Annex 302.2 (Tariff Elimination), and as set out for ease of reference in Appendix 2.1.

2. For purposes of this Annex:

(a) a textile or apparel good shall be considered an originating good if the applicable change in tariff classification set out in Chapter Four (Rules of Origin) has been satisfied in the territory of one or more of the Parties in accordance with Article 404 (Accumulation); and

(b) for purposes of determining which rate of customs duty and staging category is applicable to an originating textile or apparel good, a good shall be considered a good of a Party

    (i) as determined by each importing Party's regulations, practices or procedures, except that

    (ii) in the event of an agreement between the Parties pursuant to

Annex 311 as determined by such agreement.

3. An importing Party and an exporting Party may identify at any time particular textile and apparel goods that they mutually agree fall within:

(a) hand-loomed fabrics of a cottage industry;

(b) hand-made cottage industry goods made of such hand-loomed fabrics; or

(c) traditional folklore handicraft goods.

The importing Party shall grant duty-free treatment to goods so identified, if certified by the competent authority of the exporting Party.

4. Appendix 2.4 applies to the Parties specified in that Appendix respecting the elimination of tariffs on certain textile and apparel goods.

Section 3: Import and Export Prohibitions, Restrictions and Consultation Levels

1. Each Party may maintain a prohibition, restriction or consultation level only in accordance with Appendix 3.1 or as otherwise provided in this Annex.

2. Each Party shall eliminate any prohibition, restriction or consultation level on a textile or apparel good that otherwise would be permitted under this Annex if that Party is required to eliminate such measure as a result of having integrated that good into the GATT as a result of commitments undertaken by that Party under any successor agreement to the Multifiber Arrangement.

Section 4: Bilateral Emergency Actions (Tariff Actions)

1. Subject to paragraphs 2 through 5 and during the transition period only, if, as a result of the reduction or elimination of a duty provided for in this Agreement, a textile or apparel good originating in the territory of a Party, or a good that has been integrated into the GATT pursuant to a commitment undertaken by a Party under any successor agreement to the Multifiber Arrangement and entered under a tariff preference level set out in Appendix 6, is being imported into the territory of another Party in such increased quantities, in absolute terms or relative to the domestic market for that good, and under such conditions as to cause serious damage, or actual threat thereof, to a domestic industry producing a like or directly competitive good, the importing

Party may, to the minimum extent necessary to remedy the damage or actual threat thereof:

    (a) suspend the further reduction of any rate of duty provided for under this Agreement on the good; or

    (b) increase the rate of duty on the good to a level not to exceed the lesser of

        (i) the most-favored-nation (MFN) applied rate of duty in effect at the time the action is taken, and

        (ii) the MFN applied rate of duty in effect on December 31, 1993.

2. In determining serious damage, or actual threat thereof, the Party:

    (a) shall examine the effect of increased imports on the particular industry, as reflected in changes in such relevant economic variables as output, productivity, utilization of capacity, inventories, market share, exports, wages, employment, domestic prices, profits and investment, none of which is necessarily decisive; and

    (b) shall not consider changes in technology or consumer preference as factors supporting a determination of serious damage or actual threat thereof.

3. A Party shall deliver without delay to any Party that may be affected by an emergency action taken under this Section written notice of its intent to take such action, and on request shall enter into consultations with that Party.

4. The following conditions and limitations apply to any emergency action taken under this Section:

    (a) no action may be maintained for a period exceeding three years or, except with the consent of the Party against whose good the action is taken, have effect beyond the expiration of the transition period;

    (b) no action may be taken by a Party against any particular good originating in the territory of another Party more than once during the transition period; and

    (c) on termination of the action, the rate of duty shall be the rate that, according to the Schedule for the staged elimination of the tariff, would have been in effect one year after the initiation of the action, and beginning January 1 of the year following the termination of the action, at the option of the Party that has taken the action

        (i) the rate of duty shall conform to the applicable rate set out in that Party's Schedule to Annex 302.2, or

        (ii) the tariff shall be eliminated in equal annual stages ending on the date set out in that Party's Schedule to Annex 302.2 for the elimination of the tariff.

5. The Party taking an action under this Section shall provide to the Party against whose good the action is taken mutually agreed trade liberalizing compensation in the form of concessions having substantially equivalent trade effects or equivalent to the value of the additional duties expected to result from the action. Such concessions shall be limited to the textile and apparel goods set out in Appendix 1.1, unless the Parties otherwise agree. If the Parties concerned are unable to agree on compensation, the exporting Party may take tariff action having trade effects substantially equivalent to the action taken under this Section against any goods imported from the Party that initiated the action under this Section. The Party taking the tariff action shall only apply the action for the minimum period necessary to achieve the substantially equivalent effects.

6. For purposes of this Section, a good originating in the territory of a Party shall be determined in accordance with Section 2.2.

7. Paragraphs 1 through 5 shall also apply to textile and apparel goods described in Appendix 2.4.

Section 5: Bilateral Emergency Actions (Quantitative Restrictions)

1. Subject to Appendix 5.1, a Party may take bilateral emergency action against non-originating textile or apparel goods of another Party in accordance with this Section and Appendix 3.1.

2. If a Party considers that a non-originating textile or apparel good, including a good entered under a tariff preference level set out in Appendix 6, is being imported into its territory from a Party in such increased quantities, in absolute terms or relative to the domestic market for that good, under such conditions as to cause serious damage, or actual threat thereof, to a domestic industry producing a like or directly competitive good in the importing Party, the importing Party may request consultations with the other Party with a view to eliminating the serious damage or actual threat thereof.

3. The Party requesting consultations shall include in its request for consultations the reasons that it considers demonstrate that such serious damage or actual threat thereof to its domestic industry is resulting from the imports of the other Party, including the latest data concerning such damage or threat.

4. In determining serious damage, or actual threat thereof, the Party shall apply Section 4(2).

5. The Parties concerned shall begin consultations within 60 days of the request for consultations and shall endeavor to agree on a mutually satisfactory level of restraint on exports of the particular good within 90 days of the request, unless the consulting Parties agree to extend this period. In reaching a mutually satisfactory level of export restraint, the consulting Parties shall:

   (a) consider the situation in the market in the importing Party;

   (b) consider the history of trade in textile and apparel goods between the consulting Parties, including previous levels of trade; and

   (c) seek to ensure that the textile and apparel goods imported from the territory of the exporting Party are accorded equitable treatment as compared with treatment accorded like textile and apparel goods from non-Party suppliers.

6. If the consulting Parties do not agree on a mutually satisfactory level of export restraint, the Party requesting consultations may impose annual quantitative restrictions on imports of the good from the territory of the other Party, subject to paragraphs 7 through 13.

7. Any quantitative restriction imposed under paragraph 6 shall be no less than the sum of:

   (a) the quantity of the good imported into the territory of the Party requesting consultations from the Party that would be affected by the restriction, as reported in general import statistics of the importing Party, during the first 12 of the most recent 14 months preceding the month in which the request for consultations was made; and

(b) 20 percent of such quantity for cotton, man-made fiber and other non-cotton vegetable fiber good categories, and six percent for wool good categories.

8. The first period of any quantitative restriction imposed under paragraph 6 shall begin on the day after the date on which the request for consultations was made and terminate at the end of the calendar year in which the quantitative restriction is imposed. Any quantitative restriction that is imposed for a first period of less than 12 months shall be prorated to correspond to the time remaining in the calendar year in which the restriction is imposed, and the prorated amount may be adjusted in accordance with the flexibility provisions set out in paragraphs 8(b) and (c) of Appendix 3.1.

9. For each successive calendar year that the quantitative restriction imposed under paragraph 6 remains in effect, the Party imposing it shall:

(a) increase it by six percent for cotton, man-made fiber and noncotton vegetable fiber textile and apparel goods, and by two percent for wool textile and apparel goods, and

(b) accelerate the growth rate for quantitative restrictions on cotton, man-made fiber and non-cotton vegetable fiber textile and apparel goods if required by any successor agreement to the Multifiber Arrangement,

and the flexibility provisions set out in paragraphs 8(b) and (c) of Appendix 3.1 apply.

10. A quantitative restriction imposed under paragraph 6 before July 1 in any calendar year may remain in effect for the remainder of that year, plus two additional calendar years. Such a restriction imposed on or after July 1 in any calendar year may remain in effect for the remainder of that year, plus three additional calendar years. No such restriction may remain in effect beyond the transition period.

11. No Party may take an emergency action under this Section with respect to any particular textile or apparel non-originating good against which a quantitative restriction is in effect.

12. No Party may adopt or maintain a quantitative restriction under this Section on a particular textile or apparel good that otherwise would be permitted under this Annex, if that Party is required to eliminate such measure as a result of having integrated that good into the GATT as a result of commitments undertaken by that Party pursuant to any successor agreement to the Multifiber Arrangement.

13. No Party may take a bilateral emergency action after the expiration of the transition period with respect to cases of serious damage, or actual threat thereof, to domestic industry arising from the operation of this Agreement except with the consent of the Party against whose good the action would be taken.

Section 6: Special Provisions

Appendix 6 sets out special provisions applicable to certain textile and apparel goods.

Section 7: Review and Revision of Rules of Origin

1.
   (a) The Parties shall monitor the effects of the application of the rule of origin set out in Annex 401 applicable to goods of subheading 6212.10 of the Harmonized System (HS). No earlier than April 1, 1995, a Party may request consultations with the other Parties to seek a mutually satisfactory solution to any difficulties that it considers result from the application of that rule of origin.

   (b) If the consulting Parties fail to reach a mutually satisfactory solution within 90 days of a request for consultations, on request of any Party the rule of origin applicable to subheading 6212.10 shall change to the rule of origin set out in Annex 401 applicable to headings 62.06 through 62.11 with respect to trade between the requesting Party and the other Parties. Any such change shall be effective 180 days after the request. The Parties shall take measures to ease any resulting administrative burden on producers.

   (c) Unless the Parties agree otherwise, at any time after the completion of consultations held under subparagraph (a) and during the transition period only, a Party that has requested such consultations may make one additional request for consultations under subparagraph (a) and take action under subparagraph (b).

2.
   (a) On request of any Party, the Parties shall consult to consider whether particular goods should be subject to different rules of origin to address issues of availability of supply of fibers, yarns or fabrics in the free trade area.

   (b) In the consultations, each Party shall consider all data presented by a Party showing substantial production in its territory of the particular good. The consulting Parties shall consider that substantial production has been shown if that Party demonstrates that its domestic producers are capable of supplying commercial quantities of the good in a timely manner.

   (c) The Parties shall endeavor to conclude consultations within 60 days of the request. An agreement between two or more Parties resulting from the consultations shall supersede any prior rule of origin for such good when approved by each such Party in accordance with Article 2202(2) (Amendments). If no agreement is reached, a Party may have recourse to paragraph B.8 of Appendix 6.

   (d) Further to subparagraph (a), on request of any Party, the Parties shall consult to consider whether the rules of origin set out in Annex 401 applicable to the following provisions should be amended in view of increasing availability of supply of relevant yarns or fabrics within the free trade area:
      (i) Canadian tariff item 5407.60.10, Mexican tariff item 5407.60.02 and U.S. tariff item 5407.60.22,
      (ii) provisions (a) through (i) of the rule of origin for subheadings 6205.20 through 6205.30,
      (iii) goods of subheadings 6107.21, 6108.21 and 6108.31, wholly of fabric of Canadian tariff item 6002.92.10, Mexican tariff item 6002.92.01, and U.S. tariff item 6002.92.10, and exclusive of collar, cuffs, waistband, elastic or lace;

        (iv) note 2 to Chapter 62 of Annex 401, and

        (v) Canadian tariff item 6303.92.10, Mexican tariff item 6303.92.01 and U.S. tariff item 6303.92.aa.

3.   The Parties shall review the rules of origin applicable to textile and apparel goods within five years of the date of entry into force of this Agreement to take into account the effect of increasing global competition on textile and apparel goods and the implications of any integration into the GATT of textile and apparel goods pursuant to any successor agreement to the Multifiber Arrangement. The Parties shall give particular consideration to operative rules in other economic association or integration agreements and developments relating to textile and apparel production and trade.

Section 8: Labelling Requirements

The Subcommittee on Labelling of Textile and Apparel Goods established under Article 913(5) shall perform the functions set out in Annex 913.5.a4.

Section 9: Trade in Worn Clothing and Other Worn Articles

1.   The Parties hereby establish a Committee on Trade in Worn Clothing, comprising representatives of each Party. The Committee shall:

        (a) include or consult with a broadly representative group drawn from the manufacturing and retailing sectors in each Party; and

        (b) act in a transparent manner and, if no member of the Committee formally objects, make recommendations to the Commission.

2.   The Committee shall assess the potential benefits and risks that may result from the elimination of existing restrictions on trade between the Parties in worn clothing and other worn articles, as defined in heading 63.09 of the HS, including the effects on business and employment opportunities, and on the market for textile and apparel goods in each Party.

3.   A Party may maintain restrictions in effect on the date of entry into force of this Agreement on the importation of worn clothing and other worn articles classified under heading 63.09 of the HS, unless the Parties agree otherwise on the basis of the recommendations presented to the Commission by the Committee on Trade in Worn Clothing.

Section 10: Definitions

For purposes of this Annex:

average yarn number, as applied to woven fabrics of cotton or man-made fibers, means the average yarn number of the yarns contained therein. In computing the average yarn number, the length of the yarn is considered to be equal to the distance covered by it in the fabric, with all clipped yarn being measured as if continuous and with the count being taken of the total single yarns in the fabric including the single yarns in any multiple (folded) or cabled yarns. The weight shall be taken after any excessive sizing is removed by boiling or other suitable process. Any one of the following formulas can be used to determine the average yarn number:

$$N = \frac{BYT}{1,000} , \frac{100T}{Z'} , \frac{BT}{Z} \quad or \quad \frac{ST}{10}$$

when:

N is the average yarn number,
B is the breadth (width) of the fabric in centimeters,
Y is the meters (linear) of the fabric per kilogram,
T is the total single yarns per square centimeter,
S is the square meters of fabric per kilogram,
Z is the grams per linear meter of fabric, and
Z' is the grams per square meter of fabric.
Fractions in the resulting "average yarn number" shall be disregarded.

category means a grouping of textile or apparel goods, and as set out in Appendix 10.1 for the Parties specified in that Appendix;

consultation level means a level of exports for a particular textile or apparel good that may be adjusted in accordance with paragraph 7 of Appendix 3.1 and includes a designated consultation level, but does not include a specific limit;

exporting Party means the Party from whose territory a textile or apparel good is exported;

flexibility provisions means the provisions set out in paragraphs 8(b) and (c) of Appendix 3.1;

importing Party means the Party into whose territory a textile or apparel good is imported;

integrated into the GATT means subject to the obligations of the *General Agreement on Tariffs and Trade* , an agreement under the GATT or any successor agreements;

specific limit means a level of exports for a particular textile or apparel good that may be adjusted in accordance with paragraph 8 of Appendix 3.1;

square meters equivalent (SME) means that unit of measurement that results from the application of the conversion factors set out in Schedule 3.1.3 to a primary unit of measure such as unit, dozen or kilogram;

tariff preference level means a mechanism that provides for the application of a customs duty at a preferential rate to imports of a particular good up to a specified quantity, and at a different rate to imports of that good that exceed that quantity;

transition period means the 10year period beginning on January 1, 1994; and

wool apparel means:

(a) apparel in chief weight of wool;
(b) woven apparel in chief weight of man-made fibers containing 36 percent or more by weight of wool; and
(c) knitted or crocheted apparel in chief weight of man-made fibers containing 23 percent or more by weight of wool.

APPENDIX 1.1. LIST OF GOODS COVERED BY ANNEX 300-B

Note: The descriptions listed in this Appendix are provided for ease of reference only. For legal purposes, coverage shall be determined according to the terms of the Harmonized System.

HS No.	Description

Chapter 30 Pharmaceutical Products

3005 90	Wadding, gauze, bandages and the like

Chapter 39 Plastics and articles thereof

Chapter 42 Articles of Leather; Saddlery and Harness; Travel Goods, Handbags and Similar Containers

ex 4202 12	**(Luggage, handbags and flatgoods with an outer surface predominantly of textile materials)**
ex 4202 22	
ex 4202 32	
ex 4202 92	

Chapter 50 Silk

5004 00	Silk yarn (other than yarn spun from silk waste) not for retail sale
5005 00	Yarn spun from silk waste, not for retail sale
5006 00	Silk yarn and yarn spun from silk waste, for retail sale; silkworm gut
5007 10	Woven fabric of noil silk
5007 20	Woven fabric of silk or silk waste, other than noil silk, 85% or more of such fibers
5007 90	Woven fabric of silk, nes

Chapter 51 Wool, fine or coarse animal hair, horsehair yarn and fabric

5105 10	Carded wool
5105 21	Combed wool in fragments
5105 29	Wool tops and other combed wool, other than combed wool in fragments
5105 30	Fine animal hair, carded or combed
5106 10	Yarn of carded wool, >=85% wool, not for retail sale
5106 20	Yarn of carded, wool, 85% wool, not for retail sale
5107 10	Yarn of combed wool, >=85% wool, not for retail sale
5107 20	Yarn of combed wool, <85% wool, not for retail sale
5108 10	Yarn of carded fine animal hair, not for retail sale
5108 20	Yarn of combed fine animal hair, not for retail sale
5109 10	Yarn of wool or of fine animal hair, >= 85% wool and fine animal hair, for retail sale
5109 90	Yarn of wool/of fine animal hair, <85% wool and fine animal hair, for retail sale
5110 00	Yarn of coarse animal hair or of horsehair
5111 11	Woven fabric of carded wool or fine animal hair, >= 85% wool and fine animal hair, 300 g/m2
5111 19	Woven fabric of carded wool or fine animal hair, >= 85% wool or fine animal hair, >300 g/m2
5111 20	Woven fabric of carded wool or fine animal hair, <85% wool or fine animal hair, with man-made fibers
5111 30	Woven fabric of carded wool or fine animal hair, <85% wool or fine animal hair, with man-made fibers
5111 90	Woven fabric of carded wool or fine animal hair,<85%wool or fine animal hair,nes
5112 11	Woven fabric of combed wool or fine animal hair, >= 85% wool or fine animal hair, 200 g/m2
5112 19	Woven fabric of combed wool or fine animal hair, >= 85% wool or fine animal hair, >200 g/m2
5112 20	Woven fabric of combed wool or fine animal hair, <85% wool or fine animal hair, with manmade filament
5112 30	Woven fabric of combed wool or fine animal hair, <85% wool or fine animal hair, with manmade fibers
5112 90	Woven fabric of combed wool or fine animal hair, <85% wool or fine animal hair, nes
5113 00	Woven fabric of coarse animal hair or of horsehair

Chapter 52 Cotton

5203 00	Cotton, carded or combed
5204 11	Cotton sewing thread 85% cotton, not for retail sale
5204 19	Cotton sewing thread, <85% cotton, not for retail sale
5204 20	Cotton sewing thread, for retail sale
5205 11	Cotton yarn, 85% cotton, single, uncombed, 714.29 decitex, not for retail sale
5205 12	Cotton yarn, 85% cotton, single, uncombed, 714.29 >decitex 232.56, not for retail sale
5205 13	Cotton yarn, 85% cotton, single, uncombed, 232.56>decitex 192.31, not for retail sale
5205 14	Cotton yarn, 85% cotton, single, uncombed, 192.31 >decitex 125, not for retail sale
5205 15	Cotton yarn, 85% cotton, single, uncombed, <125 decitex, not for retail sale
5205 21	Cotton yarn, 85% cotton, single, combed, 714.29, not for retail sale
5205 22	Cotton yarn, 85% cotton, single, combed, 714.29 >decitex 232.56, not for retail sale
5205 23	Cotton yarn, 85% cotton, single, combed, 232.56 >decitex 192.31, not for retail sale
5205 24	Cotton yarn, 85% cotton, single, combed, 192.31 >decitex 125, not for retail sale
5205 25	Cotton yarn, 85% cotton, single, combed, <125 decitex, not for retail sale
5205 31	Cotton yarn, 85% cotton, multiple, uncombed, 714.29 decitex, not for retail sale, nes
5205 32	Cotton yarn, 85% cotton, multiple, uncombed, 714.29 >decitex 232.56, not for retail sale, nes
5205 33	Cotton yarn, 85% cotton, multiple, uncombed, 232.56 >decitex 192.31, not for retail sale, nes
5205 34	Cotton yarn, 85% cotton, multiple, uncombed, 192.31 >decitex 125, not for retail sale, nes
5205 35	Cotton yarn, 85% cotton, multiple, uncombed, <125 decitex, not for retail sale, nes
5205 41	Cotton yarn, 85% cotton, multiple, combed, 714.29 decitex, not for retail sale, nes
5205 42	Cotton yarn, 85% cotton, multiple, combed, 714.29 >decitex 232.56, not for retail sale, nes
5205 43	Cotton yarn, 85% cotton, multiple, combed, 232.56 >decitex 192.31, not for retail sale, nes
5205 44	Cotton yarn, 85% cotton, multiple, combed, 192.31 >decitex 125, not for retail sale, nes
5205 45	Cotton yarn, 85% cotton, multiple, combed, <125 decitex, not for retail sale, nes
5206 11	Cotton yarn, <85% cotton, single, uncombed, 714.29, not for retail sale
5206 12	Cotton yarn, <85% cotton, single, uncombed, 714.29 >decitex 232.56, not for retail sale
5206 13	Cotton yarn, <85% cotton, single, uncombed, 232.56 >decitex 192.31, not for retail sale
5206 14	Cotton yarn, <85% cotton, single, uncombed, 192.31 >decitex 125, not for retail sale
5206 15	Cotton yarn, <85% cotton, single, uncombed, <125 decitex, not for retail sale
5206 21	Cotton yarn, <85% cotton, single, combed, 714.29 decitex, not for retail sale
5206 22	Cotton yarn, <85% cotton, single, combed, 714.29 >decitex 232.56, not for retail sale

5206 23	Cotton yarn, <85% cotton, single, combed, 232.56 >decitex 192.31, not for retail sale
5206 24	Cotton yarn, <85% cotton, single, combed, 192.31 >decitex 125, not for retail sale
5206 25	Cotton yarn, <85% cotton, single, combed, <125 decitex, not for retail sale
5206 31	Cotton yarn, <85% cotton, multiple, uncombed, 714.29, not for retail sale, nes
5206 32	Cotton yarn, <85% cotton, multiple, uncombed, 714.29 >decitex 232.56, not for retail sale, nes
5206 33	Cotton yarn, <85% cotton, multiple, uncombed, 232.56 >decitex 192.31, not for retail sale, nes
5206 34	Cotton yarn, <85% cotton, multiple, uncombed, 192.31 >decitex 125, not for retail sale, nes
5206 35	Cotton yarn, <85% cotton, multiple, uncombed, <125 decitex, not for retail sale, nes
5206 41	Cotton yarn, <85% cotton, multiple, combed, 714.29, not for retail sale, nes
5206 42	Cotton yarn, <85% cotton, multiple, combed, 714.29 >decitex 232.56, not for retail sale, nes
5206 43	Cotton yarn, <85% cotton, multiple, combed, 232.56 >decitex 192.31, not for retail sale, nes
5206 44	Cotton yarn, <85% cotton, multiple, combed, 192.31 >decitex 125, not for retail sale, nes
5206 45	Cotton yarn, <85% cotton, multiple, combed, <125 decitex, not for retail sale, nes
5207 10	Cotton yarn (other than sewing thread) 85% cotton, for retail sale
5207 90	Cotton yarn (other than sewing thread) <85% cotton, for retail sale
5208 11	Plain weave cotton fabric, 85% cotton, 100g/m2, unbleached
5208 12	Plain weave cotton fabric, 85% cotton, >100g/m2, 200g/m2, unbleached
5208 13	Twill weave cotton fabric, 85% cotton, 200g/m2, unbleached
5208 19	Woven fabric of cotton, 85% cotton, 200g/m2, unbleached, nes
5208 21	Plain weave cotton fabric, 85% cotton, 100g/m2, bleached
5208 22	Plain weave cotton fabric, 85% cotton, >100g/m2, 200g/m2, bleached
5208 23	Twill weave cotton fabric, 85% cotton, 200g/m2, bleached
5208 29	Woven fabric of cotton, 85% cotton, 200g/m2, bleached, nes
5208 31	Plain weave cotton fabric, 85% cotton, 100g/m2, dyed
5208 32	Plain weave cotton fabric, 85% cotton, >100g/m2, 200g/m2, dyed
5208 33	Twill weave cotton fabric, 85% cotton, 200g/m2, dyed
5208 39	Woven fabric of cotton, 85% cotton, 200g/m2, dyed, nes
5208 41	Plain weave cotton fabric, 85% cotton, 100g/m2, yarn dyed
5208 42	Plain weave cotton fabric, 85% cotton, >100g/m2, 200 g/m2, yarn dyed
5208 43	Twill weave cotton fabric, 85% cotton, 200g/m2, yarn dyed
5208 49	Woven fabric of cotton, 85% cotton, 200g/m2, yarn dyed, nes
5208 51	Plain weave cotton fabric, 85% cotton, 100g/m2, printed
5208 52	Plain weave cotton fabric, 85% cotton, >100g/m2, 200 g/m2, printed
5208 53	Twill weave cotton fabric, 85% cotton, 200g/m2, printed
5208 59	Woven fabric of cotton, 85% cotton, 200g/m2, printed, nes
5209 11	Plain weave cotton fabric, 85% cotton, >200g/m2, unbleached

(Continued)

5209 12	Twill weave cotton fabric, 85% cotton, >200g/m2, unbleached
5209 19	Woven fabric of cotton, 85% cotton, >200g/m2, unbleached, nes
5209 21	Plain weave cotton fabric, 85% cotton, >200g/m2, bleached
5209 22	Twill weave cotton fabric, 85% cotton, >200g/m2, bleached
5209 29	Woven fabric of cotton, 85% cotton, >200g/m2, bleached, nes
5209 31	Plain weave cotton fabric, 85% cotton, >200g/m2, dyed
5209 32	Twill weave cotton fabric, 85% cotton, >200g/m2, dyed
5209 39	Woven fabric of cotton, 85% cotton, >200g/m2, dyed, nes
5209 41	Plain weave cotton fabric, 85% cotton, >200g/m2, yarn dyed
5209 42	Blue denim fabric of cotton, 85% cotton, >200g/m2
5209 43	Twill weave cotton fabric, other than denim, 85% cotton, >200g/m2, yarn dyed
5209 49	Woven fabric of cotton, 85% cotton, >200g/m2, yarn dyed, nes
5209 51	Plain weave cotton fabric, 85% cotton, >200g/m2, printed
5209 52	Twill weave cotton fabric, 85% cotton, >200g/m2, printed
5209 59	Woven fabric of cotton, 85% cotton, >200g/m2, printed, nes
5210 11	Plain weave cotton fabric, <85% cotton, with manmade fiber, 200g/m2, unbleached
5210 12	Twill weave cotton fabric, <85% cotton, with manmade fiber, 200g/m2, unbleached
5210 19	Woven fabric of cotton, <85% cotton, with manmade fiber, 200g/m2, unbleached, nes
5210 21	Plain weave cotton fabric, <85% cotton, with manmade fiber, 200g/m2, bleached
5210 22	Twill weave cotton fabric, <85% cotton, with manmade fiber, 200g/m2, bleached
5210 29	Woven fabric of cotton, <85% cotton, with manmade fiber, 200g/m2, bleached, nes
5210 31	Plain weave cotton fabric, <85% cotton, with manmade fiber, 200g/m2, dyed
5210 32	Twill weave cotton fabric, <85% cotton, with manmade fiber, 200g/m2, dyed
5210 39	Woven fabric of cotton, <85% cotton, with manmade fiber, 200g/m2, dyed, nes
5210 41	Plain weave cotton fabric, <85% cotton, with manmade fiber, 200g/m2, yarn dyed
5210 42	Twill weave cotton fabric, <85% cotton, with manmade fiber, 200g/m2, yarn dyed
5210 49	Woven fabric of cotton, <85% cotton, with manmade fiber, 200g/m2, yarn dyed, nes
5210 51	Plain weave cotton fabric, <85% cotton, with manmade fiber, 200g/m2, printed
5210 52	Twill weave cotton fabric, <85% cotton, with manmade fiber, 200g/m2, printed
5210 59	Woven fabric of cotton, <85% cotton, with manmade fiber, 200g/m2, printed, nes
5211 11	Plain weave cotton fabric, <85% cotton, with manmade fiber, >200g/m2, unbleached
5211 12	Twill weave cotton fabric, <85% cotton, with manmade fiber, >200g/m2, unbleached
5211 19	Woven fabric of cotton, <85% cotton, with manmade fiber, >200g/m2, unbleached, nes
5211 21	Plain weave cotton fabric, <85% cotton, with manmade fiber, >200g/m2, bleached
5211 22	Twill weave cotton fabric, <85% cotton, with manmade fiber, >200g/m2, bleached
5211 29	Woven fabric of cotton, <85% cotton, with manmade fiber, >200g/m2, bleached, nes
5211 31	Plain weave cotton fabric, <85% cotton, with manmade fiber, >200g/m2, dyed
5211 32	Twill weave cotton fabric, <85% cotton, with manmade fiber, >200g/m2, dyed

5211 39	Woven fabric of cotton, <85% cotton, with manmade fiber, >200g/m2, dyed, nes
5211 41	Plain weave cotton fabric, <85% cotton, with manmade fiber, >200g/m2, yarn dyed
5211 42	Blue denim fabric of cotton, <85% cotton, with manmade fiber, >200g/m2
5211 43	Twill weave cotton fabric, other than denim, <85% cotton, with manmade fiber, >200g/m2, yarn dyed
5211 49	Woven fabric of cotton, <85% cotton, with manmade fiber, >200g/m2, yarn dyed, nes
5211 51	Plain weave cotton fabric, <85% cotton, with manmade fiber, >200g/m2, printed
5211 52	Twill weave cotton fabric, <85% cotton, with manmade fiber, >200g/m2, printed
5211 59	Woven fabric of cotton, <85% cotton, with manmade fiber, >200g/m2, printed, nes
5212 11	Woven fabric of cotton, weighing 200g/m2, unbleached, nes
5212 12	Woven fabric of cotton, weighing 200g/m2, bleached, nes
5212 13	Woven fabric of cotton, weighing 200g/m2, dyed, nes
5212 14	Woven fabric of cotton, 200g/m2, of yarns of different colors, nes
5212 15	Woven fabric of cotton, weighing 200g/m2, printed, nes
5212 21	Woven fabric of cotton, weighing >200g/m2, unbleached, nes
5212 22	Woven fabric of cotton, weighing >200g/m2, bleached, nes
5212 23	Woven fabric of cotton, weighing >200g/m2, dyed, nes
5212 24	Woven fabric of cotton, >200g/m2, of yarns of different colors, nes
5212 25	Woven fabric of cotton, weighing >200g/m2, printed, nes

Chapter 53 Other vegetable textile fibers; paper yarn and woven fabric of paper yarn

5306 10	Flax yarn, single
5306 20	Flax yarn, multiple
5307 10	Yarn of jute or of other textile bast fibers, single
5307 20	Yarn of jute or other textile bast fibers, multiple
5308 20	True hemp yarn
5308 90	Yarn of other vegetable textile fibers
5309 11	Woven fabric, 85% flax, unbleached or bleached
5309 19	Woven fabric, 85% flax, other than unbleached or bleached
5309 21	Woven fabric of flax, <85% flax, unbleached or bleached
5309 29	Woven fabric of flax, <85% flax, other than unbleached or bleached
5310 10	Woven fabric of jute or of other textile bast fibers, unbleached
5310 90	Woven fabric of jute or of other textile bast fibers, other than unbleached
5311 00	Woven fabric of other vegetable textile fibers; woven fabric of paper yarn

Chapter 54 Manmade filaments

5401 10	Sewing thread of synthetic filaments
5401 20	Sewing thread of artificial filaments
5402 10	High tenacity yarn (other than sewing thread), nylon or other polyamide fiber, not for retail sale
5402 20	High tenacity yarn (other than sewing thread), of polyester filaments, not for retail sale
5402 31	Textured yarn nes, of nylon or other polyamide fiber, 50 tex/single yarn, not for retail sale
5402 32	Textured yarn nes, of nylon or other polyamide fiber,>50 tex/single yarn, not for retail sale
5402 33	Textured yarn nes, of polyester filaments, not for retail sale
5402 39	Textured yarn of synthetic filaments, nes, not for retail sale
5402 41	Yarn of nylon or other polyamide fiber, single, untwisted, nes, not for retail sale
5402 42	Yarn of polyester filaments, partially oriented, single, nes, not for retail sale
5402 43	Yarn of polyester filaments, single, untwisted, nes, not for retail sale
5402 49	Yarn of synthetic filaments, single, untwisted, nes, not for retail sale
5402 51	Yarn of nylon or other polyamide fiber, single >50 turns per meter, not for retail sale
5402 52	Yarn of polyester filaments, single, >50 turns per meter, not for retail sale
5402 59	Yarn of synthetic filaments, single, >50 turns per meter, nes, not for retail sale
5402 61	Yarn of nylon or other polyamide fiber, multiple, nes, not for retail sale
5402 62	Yarn of polyester filaments, multiple, nes, not for retail sale
5402 69	Yarn of synthetic filaments, multiple, nes, not for retail sale
5403 10	High tenacity yarn (other than sewing thread), of viscose rayon filaments, not for retail sale
5403 20	Textured yarn nes, of artificial filaments, not for retail sale
5403 31	Yarn of viscose rayon filaments, single, untwisted, nes, not for retail sale
5403 32	Yarn of viscose rayon filaments, single, >120 turns per meter, nes, not for retailsale
5403 33	Yarn of cellulose acetate filaments, single, nes, not for retail sale
5403 39	Yarn of artificial filaments, single, nes, not for retail sale
5403 41	Yarn of viscose rayon filaments, multiple, nes, not for retail sale
5403 42	Yarn of cellulose acetate filaments, multiple, nes, not for retail sale
5403 49	Yarn of artificial filaments, multiple, nes, not for retail sale
5404 10	Synthetic monofilament, 67 decitex, no cross sectional dimension >1 mm
5404 90	Strip and the like of synthetic textile material of an apparent width 5mm
5405 00	Artificial monofil, 67 decitex, cross sectional dimension >1mm; strip of art. tex. mat. width 5mm
5406 10	Yarn of synthetic filaments (other than sewing thread), for retail sale
5406 20	Yarn of artificial filaments (other than sewing thread), for retail sale
5407 10	Woven fabric of high tenacity filament yarn of nylon or other polyamides, or polyester
5407 20	Woven fabric obtained from strip or the like of synthetic textile materials
5407 30	Fabric specified in Note 9 Section XI (layers of parallel synthetic textile yarn)

5407 41	Woven fabric, 85%nylon or other polyamide filaments, unbleached or bleached,nes
5407 42	Woven fabric, 85% nylon or other polyamide filaments, dyed, nes
5407 43	Woven fabric, 85% nylon or other polyamide filaments, yarn dyed, nes
5407 44	Woven fabric, 85% nylon or other polyamide filaments, printed, nes
5407 51	Woven fabric, 85% textured polyester filaments, unbleached or bleached, nes
5407 52	Woven fabric, 85% textured polyester filaments, dyed, nes
5407 53	Woven fabric, 85% textured polyester filaments, yarn dyed, nes
5407 54	Woven fabric, 85% textured polyester filaments, printed, nes
5407 60	Woven fabric, 85% nontextured polyester filaments, nes
5407 71	Woven fabric, 85% synthetic filaments, unbleached or bleached, nes
5407 72	Woven fabric, 85% synthetic filaments, dyed, nes
5407 73	Woven fabric, 85% synthetic filaments, yarn dyed, nes
5407 74	Woven fabric, 85% synthetic filaments, printed, nes
5407 81	Woven fabric of synthetic filaments, <85% syn. filaments, with cotton, unbl or bl, nes
5407 82	Woven fabric of synthetic filaments, <85% with cotton, dyed, nes
5407 83	Woven fabric of synthetic filaments, <85% with cotton, yarn dyed, nes
5407 84	Woven fabric of synthetic filaments, <85% with cotton, printed, nes
5407 91	Woven fabric of synthetic filaments, unbleached or bleached, nes
5407 92	Woven fabric of synthetic filaments, dyed, nes
5407 93	Woven fabric of synthetic filaments, yarn dyed, nes
5407 94	Woven fabric of synthetic filaments, printed, nes
5408 10	Woven fabric of high tenacity filament yarn of viscose rayon
5408 21	Woven fabric, 85% artificial filament or strip, unbleached or bleached, nes
5408 22	Woven fabric, 85% artificial filament or strip, dyed, nes
5408 23	Woven fabric, 85% artificial filament or strip, yarn dyed, nes
5408 24	Woven fabric, 85% artificial filament or strip, printed, nes
5408 31	Woven fabric of artificial filaments, unbleached or bleached, nes
5408 32	Woven fabric of artificial filaments, dyed, nes
5408 33	Woven fabric of artificial filaments, yarn dyed, nes
5408 34	Woven fabric of artificial filaments, printed, nes

Chapter 55 Manmade staple fibers

5501 10	Filament tow of nylon or other polyamides
5501 20	Filament tow of polyesters
5501 30	Filament tow of acrylic or modacrylic
5501 90	Synthetic filament tow, nes
5502 00	Artificial filament tow
5503 10	Staple fibers of nylon or other polyamides, not carded or combed
5503 20	Staple fibers of polyesters, not carded or combed
5503 30	Staple fibers of acrylic or modacrylic, not carded or combed

(Continued)

5503 40	Staple fibers of polypropylene, not carded or combed
5503 90	Synthetic staple fibers, not carded or combed, nes
5504 10	Staple fibers of viscose, not carded or combed
5504 90	Artificial staple fibers, other than viscose, not carded or combed
5505 10	Waste of synthetic fibers
5505 20	Waste of artificial fibers
5506 10	Staple fibers of nylon or other polyamides, carded or combed
5506 20	Staple fibers of polyesters, carded or combed
5506 30	Staple fibers of acrylic or modacrylic, carded or combed
5506 90	Synthetic staple fibers, carded or combed, nes
5507 00	Artificial staple fibers, carded or combed
5508 10	Sewing thread of synthetic staple fibers
5508 20	Sewing thread of artificial staple fibers
5509 11	Yarn, 85% nylon or other polyamide staple fibers, single, not for retail sale
5509 12	Yarn, 85% nylon or other polyamide staple fibers, multiple, not for retail sale, nes
5509 21	Yarn, 85% of polyester staple fibers, single, not for retail sale
5509 22	Yarn, 85% of polyester staple fibers, multiple, not for retail sale, nes
5509 31	Yarn, 85% of acrylic or modacrylic staple fibers, single, not for retail sale
5509 32	Yarn, 85% acrylic/modacrylic staple fibers, multiple, not for retail sale, nes
5509 41	Yarn, 85% of other synthetic staple fibers, single, not for retail sale
5509 42	Yarn, 85% of other synthetic staple fibers, multiple, not for retail sale, nes
5509 51	Yarn of polyester staple fibers mixed with artificial staple fiber, not for retail sale, nes
5509 52	Yarn of polyester staple fiber mixed with wool or fine animal hair, not for retail sale, nes
5509 53	Yarn of polyester staple fibers mixed with cotton, not for retail sale, nes
5509 59	Yarn of polyester staple fibers, not for retail sale, nes
5509 61	Yarn of acrylic staple fiber mixed with wool or fine animal hair, not for retail sale, nes
5509 62	Yarn of acrylic staple fibers mixed with cotton, not for retail sale, nes
5509 69	Yarn of acrylic staple fibers, not for retail sale, nes
5509 91	Yarn of other synthetic staple fibers mixed with wool or fine animal hair, not for retail sale, nes
5509 92	Yarn of other synthetic staple fibers mixed with cotton, not for retail sale, nes
5509 99	Yarn of other synthetic staple fibers, not for retail sale, nes
5510 11	Yarn, 85% of artificial staple fibers, single, not for retail sale
5510 12	Yarn, 85% of artificial staple fibers, multiple, not for retail sale, nes
5510 20	Yarn of artificial staple fiber mixed with wool/fine animal hair, not for retail sale, nes
5510 30	Yarn of artificial staple fibers mixed with cotton, not for retail sale, nes
5510 90	Yarn of artificial staple fibers, not for retail sale, nes
5511 10	Yarn, 85% of synthetic staple fibers, other than sewing thread, for retail sale
5511 20	Yarn, <85% of synthetic staple fibers, for retail sale, nes

5511 30	Yarn of artificial fibers (other than sewing thread), for retail sale
5512 11	Woven fabric, 85% of polyester staple fibers, unbleached or bleached
5512 19	Woven fabric, 85% of polyester staple fibers, other than unbleached or bleached
5512 21	Woven fabric, 85% of acrylic staple fibers, unbleached or bleached
5512 29	Woven fabric, 85% of acrylic staple fibers, other than unbleached or bleached
5512 91	Woven fabric, 85% of other synthetic staple fibers, unbleached or bleached
5512 99	Woven fabric, 85% of other synthetic staple fibers, other than unbleached or bleached
5513 11	Plain weave polyester fabric, <85% syn stple fiber, with cot, 170g/m2, unbl or bl
5513 12	Twill weave polyester staple fiber fabric, <85% syn. staple fiber, with cotton, 170g/m2, unbl or bl
5513 13	Woven polyester fabric, <85% synthetic stple fiber, with cotton, 170g/m2, unbl or bl, nes
5513 19	Woven fabric of other synthetic staple fiber, <85% syn. stpl fib, with cotton, 170g/m2, unbl or bl
5513 21	Plain weave polyester staple fiber fabric,<85% synthetic staple fiber, with cotton, 170g/m2, dyed
5513 22	Twill weave polyester staple fiber fabric,<85% synthetic staple fiber, with cotton, 170g/m2, dyed
5513 23	Woven fabric of polyester staple fiber, <85% syn. staple fiber, with cotton, 170g/m2, dyed, nes
5513 29	Woven fabric of other synthetic staple fiber, <85% syn. staple fiber, with cotton, 170g/m2, dyed
5513 31	Plain weave polyester staple fiber fabric, <85% syn. staple fiber, with cotton, 170g/m2, yarn dyed
5513 32	Twill weave polyester staple fiber fabric, <85% syn. staple fiber, with cotton, 170g/m2, yarn dyed
5513 33	Woven fabric of polyester staple fiber, <85% syn. staple fiber, with cotton, 170g/m2, dyed nes
5513 39	Woven fabric of other synthetic staple fiber, <85% syn. staple fiber, with cotton, 170g/m2, yarn dyed
5513 41	Plain weave polyester staple fiber fabric, <85% syn. stpl fiber, with cotton, 170g/m2, printed
5513 42	Twill weave polyester staple fiber fabric, <85% syn. staple fiber, with cotton, <=/170g/m2, printed
5513 43	Woven fabric of polyester staple fiber, <85% syn staple fiber, with cotton, 170g/m2, printed, nes
5513 49	Woven fabric of other synthetic staple fiber, <85% syn. staple fiber, with cotton, 170g/m2, printed
5514 11	Plain weave polyester staple fiber fabric, <85% syn. staple fiber, with cotton, >170g/m2, unbl or bl
5514 12	Twill weave polyester staple fiber fabric, <85% syn. staple fiber, with cotton, >170g/m2, unbl or bl
5514 13	Woven fabric of polyester staple fiber, <85% syn. stpl fiber, with cotton, >170g/m2, unbl or bl, nes
5514 19	Woven fabric of other synthetic staple fiber, <85% syn stpl. fib, with cotton, >170g/m2, unbl or bl

(Continued)

5514 21	Plain weave polyester staple fiber fabric, <85% syn staple fiber, with cotton, >170g/m2, dyed
5514 22	Twill weave polyester staple fiber fabric, <85% synthetic staple fiber, with cotton, >170g/m2, dyed
5514 23	Woven fabric of polyester staple fiber, <85% synthetic staple fiber, with cotton, >170g/m2, dyed
5514 29	Woven fabric of other synthetic staple fiber, <85% synthetic staple fiber, with cotton, >170g/m2, dyed
5514 31	Plain weave polyester staple fiber fabric, <85% syn. staple fiber, with cotton, >170g/m2, yarn dyed
5514 32	Twill weave polyester staple fiber fabric, <85% mixed with cotton, >170g/m2, yarn dyed
5514 33	Woven fabric of polyester staple fiber, <85% syn. staple fiber, with cotton, >170g/m2, yarn dyed nes
5514 39	Woven fabric of other synthetic staple fiber, <85% syn. stpl fiber, with cotton, >170g/m2, yarn dyed
5514 41	Plain weave polyester staple fiber fabric, <85% synthetic staple fiber, with cotton, >170g/m2, printed
5514 42	Twill weave polyester staple fiber fabric, <85% synthetic staple fiber, with cotton, >170g/m2, printed
5514 43	Woven fabric of polyester staple fibers <85% syn. staple fiber, with cotton, >170g/m2, printed, nes
5514 49	Woven fabric of other synthetic staple fiber, <85% syn. staple fiber, with cotton, >170g/m2, printed
5515 11	Woven fabric of polyester staple fiber, with viscose rayon staple fiber, nes
5515 12	Woven fabric of polyester staple fiber, with manmade filaments, nes
5515 13	Woven fabric of polyester staple fiber, with wool or fine animal hair, nes
5515 19	Woven fabric of polyester staple fiber, nes
5515 21	Woven fabric of acrylic staple fiber, with manmade filaments, nes
5515 22	Woven fabric of acrylic staple fiber, with wool or fine animal hair, nes
5515 29	Woven fabric of acrylic or modacrylic staple fibers, nes
5515 91	Woven fabric of other synthetic staple fiber, with manmade filaments, nes
5515 92	Woven fabric of other synthetic staple fiber, with wool or fine animal hair, nes
5515 99	Woven fabric of synthetic staple fibers, nes
5516 11	Woven fabric, 85% artificial staple fiber, unbleached or bleached
5516 12	Woven fabric, 85% artificial staple fiber, dyed
5516 13	Woven fabric, 85% artificial staple fiber, yarn dyed
5516 14	Woven fabric, 85% artificial staple fiber, printed
5516 21	Woven fabric of artificial staple fiber, <85% artificial staple fiber, with manmade fib, unbl or bl
5516 22	Woven fabric of artificial staple fiber, <85% artificial staple fiber, with manmade fib, dyed
5516 23	Woven fabric of artificial staple fiber, <85% artificial staple fiber, with manmade fib, yarn dyed

5516 24	Woven fabric of artificial staple fiber, <85% artificial staple fiber, with manmade fib, printed
5516 31	Woven fabric of artificial staple fiber, <85% art stpl fiber, with wool/fine animal hair, unbl or bl
5516 32	Woven fabric of artificial staple fiber, <85% art staple fiber, with wool/fine animal hair, dyed
5516 33	Woven fabric of artificial staple fiber, <85% art staple fiber, with wool/fine animal hair, yarn dyed
5516 34	Woven fabric of artificial staple fiber, <85% art staple fiber, with wool/fine animal hair, printed
5516 41	Woven fabric of artificial staple fiber, <85% artificial staple fiber, with cotton, unbl or bl
5516 42	Woven fabric of artificial staple fiber, <85%artificial staple fiber, with cotton,dyed
5516 43	Woven fabric of artificial staple fiber, <85% artificial staple fiber, with cotton, yarn dyed
5516 44	Woven fabric of artificial staple fiber, <85% artificial staple fiber, with cotton, printed
5516 91	Woven fabric of artificial staple fiber, unbleached or bleached, nes
5516 92	Woven fabric of artificial staple fiber, dyed, nes
5516 93	Woven fabric of artificial staple fiber, yarn dyed, nes
5516 94	Woven fabric of artificial staple fiber, printed, nes

Chapter 56: Wadding, felt and nonwovens; special yarns, twine, cordage, ropes and cables and articles thereof

5601 10	Sanitary articles of wadding of textile materials, including sanitary towels, tampons, and diapers
5601 21	Wadding of cotton and articles thereof, other than sanitary articles
5601 22	Wadding of manmade fibers and articles thereof, other than sanitary articles
5601 29	Wedge of other textile materials and articles thereof, other than sanitary articles
5601 30	Textile flock and dust and mill neps
5602 10	Needleloom felt and stitchbonded fiber fabric
5602 21	Felt other than needleloom, of wool or fine animal hair, not impregnated, coated, covered or laminated
5602 29	Felt other than needleloom, of other textile materials, not impregnated, coated, covered or laminated
5602 90	Felt of textile materials, nes
5603 00	Nonwovens, whether or not impregnated, coated, covered or laminated
5604 10	Rubber thread and cord, textile covered
5604 20	High tenacity yarn of polyester, nylon other polyamide, viscose rayon, impregnated or coated
5604 90	Textile yarn, strip, impregnated, coated, covered or sheathed with rubber or plastics nes
5605 00	Metalized yarn, being textile yarn combined with metal thread, strip, or powder

(Continued)

5606 00	Gimped yarn nes; chenille yarn; loop waleyarn
5607 10	Twine, cordage, ropes and cables, of jute or other textile bast fibers
5607 21	Binder or baler twine, of sisal or other textile fibers of the genus Agave
5607 29	Twine nes, cordage, ropes and cables, of sisal textile fibers
5607 30	Twine, cordage, ropes and cables, of abaca or other hard (leaf) fibers
5607 41	Binder or baler twine, of polyethylene or polypropylene
5607 49	Twine nes, cordage, ropes and cables, of polyethylene or polypropylene
5607 50	Twine, cordage, ropes and cables, of other synthetic fibers
5607 90	Twine, cordage, ropes and cables, of other materials
5608 11	Made up fishing nets, of manmade textile materials
5608 19	Knotted netting of twine, cordage, or rope, and other made up nets of manmade textile materials
5608 90	Knotted netting of twine, cordage, or rope, nes, and made up nets of other textile materials
5609 00	Articles of yarn, strip, twine, cordage, rope and cables, nes

Chapter 57 Carpets and other textile floor coverings

5701 10	Carpets of wool or fine animal hair, knotted
5701 90	Carpets of other textile materials, knotted
5702 10	Kelem, Schumacks, Karamanie and similar textile handwoven rugs
5702 20	Floor coverings of coconut fibers (coir)
5702 31	Carpets of wool or fine animal hair, of woven pile construction, not made up, nes
5702 32	Carpets of manmade textile materials, of woven pile construction, not made up, nes
5702 39	Carpets of other textile materials, of woven pile construction, not made up, nes
5702 41	Carpets of wool or fine animal hair, of woven pile construction, made up, nes
5702 42	Carpets of manmade textile materials, of woven pile construction, made up, nes
5702 49	Carpets of other textile materials, of woven pile construction, made up, nes
5702 51	Carpets of wool or fine animal hair, woven, not made up, nes
5702 52	Carpets of manmade textile materials, woven, not made up, nes
5702 59	Carpets of other textile materials, woven, not made up, nes
5702 91	Carpets of wool or fine animal hair, woven, made up, nes
5702 92	Carpets of manmade textile materials, woven, made up, nes
5702 99	Carpets of other textile materials, woven, made up, nes
5703 10	Carpets of wool or fine animal hair, tufted
5703 20	Carpets of nylon or other polyamide, tufted
5703 30	Carpets of other manmade textile materials, tufted
5703 90	Carpets of other textile materials, tufted
5704 10	Tiles of felt of textile materials, having a maximum surface area of 0.3 m2
5704 90	Carpets of felt of textile materials, nes
5705 00	Carpets and other textile floor coverings, nes

Chapter 58 Special woven fabrics; tufted textile fabrics; lace; tapestries; trimmings; embroidery

5801 10	Woven pile fabric of wool or fine animal hair, other than terry and narrow fabric
5801 21	Woven uncut weft pile fabric of cotton, other than terry and narrow fabric
5801 22	Cut corduroy fabric of cotton, other than narrow fabric
5801 23	Woven weft pile fabric of cotton, nes
5801 24	Woven warp pile fabric of cotton, epingle (uncut), other than terry and narrow fabric
5801 25	Woven warp pile fabric of cotton, cut, other than terry and narrow fabric
5801 26	Chenille fabric of cotton, other than narrow fabric
5801 31	Woven uncut weft pile fabric of manmade fibers, other than terry and narrow fabric
5801 32	Cut corduroy fabric of manmade fibers, other than narrow fabric
5801 33	Woven weft pile fabric of manmade fibers, nes
5801 34	Woven warp pile fabric of manmade fiber, epingle (uncut), other than terry and narrow fabric
5801 35	Woven warp pile fabric of manmade fiber, cut, other than terry and narrow fabric
5801 36	Chenille fabric of manmade fibers, other than narrow fabric
5801 90	Woven pile fabric and chenille fabric of other textile materials, other than terry and narrow fabric
5802 11	Terry toweling and similar woven terry fabric of cotton, other than narrow fabric, unbleached
5802 19	Terry toweling and similar woven terry fabric of cotton, other than unbleached or narrow fabric
5802 20	Terry toweling and similar woven terry fabric of other textile materials, other than narrow fabric
5802 30	Tufted textile fabric, other than products of heading No 57.03
5803 10	Gauze of cotton, other than narrow fabric
5803 90	Gauze of other textile material, other than narrow fabric
5804 10	Tulles and other net fabric, not including woven, knitted or crocheted fabric
5804 21	Mechanically made lace of manmade fiber, in the piece, in strips or motifs
5804 29	Mechanically made lace of other textile materials, in the piece, in strips or in motifs
5804 30	Handmade lace, in the piece, in strips or in motifs
5805 00	Handwoven tapestries and needleworked tapestries, whether or not made up
5806 10	Narrow woven pile fabric and narrow chenille fabric
5806 20	Narrow woven fabric, containing 5% elastomeric yarn or rubber thread, nes
5806 31	Narrow woven fabric of cotton, nes
5806 32	Narrow woven fabric of manmade fibers, nes
5806 39	Narrow woven fabric of other textile materials, nes
5806 40	Fabric consisting of warp without weft, assembled by means of an adhesive
5807 10	Labels, badges and similar woven articles of textile materials
5807 90	Labels, badges and similar articles, not woven, of textile materials, nes
5808 10	Braids in the piece
5808 90	Ornamental trimmings in the piece, other than knit; tassels, pompons and similar articles
5809 00	Woven fabric of metal thread or metalized yarn, for apparel, and homefurnishings, nes
5810 10	Embroidery without visible ground, in the piece, in strips or in motifs
5810 91	Embroidery of cotton, in the piece, in strips or in motifs, nes
5810 92	Embroidery of manmade fibers, in the piece, in strips or in motifs, nes
5810 99	Embroidery of other textile materials, in the piece, in strips or motifs, nes
5811 00	Quilted textile products in the piece

Chapter 59: Impregnated, coated, covered, laminated textile fabric; textile articles suitable for industrial use

5901 10	Textile fabric coated with gum, of a kind used for outer covers of books or the like
5901 90	Tracing cloth; prepared painting canvas; stiffened textile fabric for hats, nes
5902 10	Tire cord fabric of high tenacity nylon or other polyamide yarn
5902 20	Tire cord fabric of high tenacity polyester yarn
5902 90	Tire cord fabric made of high tenacity viscose rayon yarn
5903 10	Textile fabric impregnated, coated, covered, or laminated with polyvinyl chloride, nes
5903 20	Textile fabric impregnated, coated, covered, or laminated with polyurethane, nes
5903 90	Textile fabric impregnated, coated, covered, or laminated with plastics, nes
5904 10	Linoleum, whether or not cut to shape
5904 91	Floor coverings, other than linoleum, with a base of needleloom felt or nonwovens
5904 92	Floor coverings, other than linoleum, with other textile base
5905 00	Textile wall coverings
5906 10	Rubberized textile adhesive tape of a width not exceeding 20 cm
5906 91	Rubberized textile knitted or crocheted fabric, nes
5906 99	Rubberized textile fabric, nes
5907 00	Textile fabric impregnated, coated, covered, nes; painted canvas for theater use, backdrops, etc.
5908 00	Textile wicks for lamps, stoves, candles or the like; gas mantles and knitted gas mantle fabric
5909 00	Textile hosepiping and similar textile tubing
5910 00	Transmission or conveyor belts or belting of textile material whether or not reinforced
5911 10	Felt and feltlined woven fabric combined with rubber, leather, or other material, for technical uses
5911 20	Textile bolting cloth, whether or not made up
5911 31	Textile fabric, endless or linked, for papermaking or similar machines, weighing <650 g/m2
5911 32	Textile fabric, endless or linked, for papermaking or similar machines, weighing 650 g/m2
5911 40	Textile straining cloth used in oil presses or the like, including of human hair
5911 90	Textile products and articles for technical uses, nes

Chapter 60 Knitted or crocheted fabrics

6001 10	Long pile knitted or crocheted textile fabric
6001 21	Looped pile knitted or crocheted fabric, of cotton
6001 22	Looped pile knitted or crocheted fabric, of manmade fibers
6001 29	Looped pile knitted or crocheted fabric, of other textile materials
6001 91	Pile knitted or crocheted fabric, of cotton, nes
6001 92	Pile knitted or crocheted fabric, of manmade fiber, nes

6001 99	Pile knitted or crocheted fabric, of other textile materials, nes
6002 10	Knitted or crocheted textile fabric, w 30 cm, 5% of elastomeric yarn or rubber thread, nes
6002 20	Knitted or crocheted textile fabric, width not exceeding 30 cm, nes
6002 30	Knitted or crocheted textile fabric, width > 30 cm, 5% of elastomeric yarn or rubber thread, nes
6002 41	Warp knitted fabric, of wool or fine animal hair, nes
6002 42	Warp knitted fabric, of cotton, nes
6002 43	Warp knitted fabric, of manmade fibers, nes
6002 49	Warp knitted fabric, of other materials, nes
6002 91	Knitted or crocheted fabric, of wool or of fine animal hair, nes
6002 92	Knitted or crocheted fabric, of cotton, nes
6002 93	Knitted or crocheted fabric, of manmade fibers, nes
6002 99	Knitted or crocheted fabric, of other materials, nes

Chapter 61 Articles of Apparel and Clothing Accessories, Knitted or Crocheted

6101 10	Men's or boys' overcoats, anoraks, and sim articles, of wool or fine animal hair, knitted or crocheted
6101 20	Men's or boys' overcoats, anoraks, and similar articles, of cotton, knitted or crocheted
6101 30	Men's or boys' overcoats, anoraks, and similar articles, of manmade fibers, knitted or crocheted
6101 90	Men's or boys' overcoats, anoraks, and sim articles, of other textile materials, knitted or crocheted
6102 10	Women's or girls' overcoats, anoraks and sim art, of wool or fine animal hair, knitted or crocheted
6102 20	Women's or girls' overcoats, anoraks and similar articles, of cotton, knitted or crocheted
6102 30	Women's or girls' overcoats, anoraks and similar articles, of manmade fibers, knitted or crocheted
6102 90	Women's or girls' overcoats, anoraks and sim art, of other textile materials, knitted or crocheted
6103 11	Men's or boys' suits, of wool or fine animal hair, knitted or crocheted
6103 12	Men's or boys' suits, of synthetic fibers, knitted or crocheted
6103 19	Men's or boys' suits, of other textile materials, knitted or crocheted
6103 21	Men's or boys' ensembles, of wool or fine animal hair, knitted or crocheted
6103 22	Men's or boys' ensembles, of cotton, knitted or crocheted
6103 23	Men's or boys' ensembles, of synthetic fibers, knitted or crocheted
6103 29	Men's or boys' ensembles, of other textile materials, knitted or crocheted
6103 31	Men's or boys' jackets and blazers, of wool or fine animal hair, knitted or crocheted

(Continued)

6103 32	Men's or boys' jackets and blazers, of cotton, knitted or crocheted
6103 33	Men's or boys' jackets and blazers, of synthetic fibers, knitted or crocheted
6103 39	Men's or boys' jackets and blazers, of other textile materials, knitted or crocheted
6103 41	Men's or boys' trousers and shorts, of wool or fine animal hair, knitted or crocheted
6103 42	Men's or boys' trousers and shorts, of cotton, knitted or crocheted
6103 43	Men's or boys' trousers and shorts, of synthetic fibers, knitted or crocheted
6103 49	Men's or boys' trousers and shorts, of other textile materials, knitted or crocheted
6104 11	Women's or girls' suits, of wool or fine animal hair, knitted or crocheted
6104 12	Women's or girls' suits, of cotton, knitted or crocheted
6104 13	Women's or girls' suits, of synthetic fibers, knitted or crocheted
6104 19	Women's or girls' suits, of other textile materials, knitted or crocheted
6104 21	Women's or girls' ensembles, of wool or fine animal hair, knitted or crocheted
6104 22	Women's or girls' ensembles, of cotton, knitted or crocheted
6104 23	Women's or girls' ensembles, of synthetic fibers, knitted or crocheted
6104 29	Women's or girls' ensembles, of other textile materials, knitted or crocheted
6104 31	Women's or girls' jackets, of wool or fine animal hair, knitted or crocheted
6104 32	Women's or girls' jackets, of cotton, knitted or crocheted
6104 33	Women's or girls' jackets, of synthetic fibers, knitted or crocheted
6104 39	Women's or girls' jackets, of other textile materials, knitted or crocheted
6104 41	Women's or girls' dresses, of wool or fine animal hair, knitted or crocheted
6104 42	Women's or girls' dresses, of cotton, knitted or crocheted
6104 43	Women's or girls' dresses, of synthetic fibers, knitted or crocheted
6104 44	Women's or girls' dresses, of artificial fibers, knitted or crocheted
6104 49	Women's or girls' dresses, of other textile materials, knitted or crocheted
6104 51	Women's or girls' skirts, of wool or fine animal hair, knitted or crocheted
6104 52	Women's or girls' skirts, of cotton, knitted or crocheted
6104 53	Women's or girls' skirts, of synthetic fibers, knitted or crocheted
6104 59	Women's or girls' skirts, of other textile materials, knitted or crocheted
6104 61	Women's or girls' trousers and shorts, of wool or fine animal hair, knitted or crocheted
6104 62	Women's or girls' trousers and shorts, of cotton, knitted or crocheted
6104 63	Women's or girls' trousers and shorts, of synthetic fibers, knitted or crocheted
6104 69	Women's or girls' trousers and shorts, of other textile materials, knitted or crocheted
6105 10	Men's or boys' shirts, of cotton, knitted or crocheted
6105 20	Men's or boys' shirts, of manmade fibers, knitted or crocheted
6105 90	Men's or boys' shirts, of other textile materials, knitted or crocheted
6106 10	Women's or girls' blouses and shirts, of cotton, knitted or crocheted
6106 20	Women's or girls' blouses and shirts, of manmade fibers, knitted or crocheted
6106 90	Women's or girls' blouses and shirts, of other materials, knitted or crocheted
6107 11	Men's or boys' underpants and briefs, of cotton, knitted or crocheted
6107 12	Men's or boys' underpants and briefs, of manmade fibers, knitted or crocheted
6107 19	Men's or boys' underpants and briefs, of other textile materials, knitted or crocheted

6107 21	Men's or boys' nightshirts and pajamas, of cotton, knitted or crocheted
6107 22	Men's or boys' nightshirts and pajamas, of manmade fibers, knitted or crocheted
6107 29	Men's or boys' nightshirts and pajamas, of other textile materials, knitted or crocheted
6107 91	Men's or boys' underpants, briefs, robes, and similar articles of cotton, knitted or crocheted
6107 92	Men's or boys' underpants, briefs, robes, and sim articles of manmade fibers, knitted or crocheted
6107 99	Men's or boys' underwear, briefs, robes, and sim art of other textile materials, knitted or crocheted
6108 11	Women's or girls' slips and petticoats, of manmade fibers, knitted or crocheted
6108 19	Women's or girls' slips and petticoats, of other textile materials, knitted or crocheted
6108 21	Women's or girls' briefs and panties, of cotton, knitted or crocheted
6108 22	Women's or girls' briefs and panties, of manmade fibers, knitted or crocheted
6108 29	Women's or girls' briefs and panties, of other textile materials, knitted or crocheted
6108 31	Women's or girls' nightdresses and pajamas, of cotton, knitted or crocheted
6108 32	Women's or girls' nightdresses and pajamas, of manmade fibers, knitted or crocheted
6108 39	Women's or girls' nightdresses and pajamas, of other textile materials, knitted or crocheted
6108 91	Women's or girls' robes, dressing gowns, and similar articles of cotton, nes, knitted or crocheted
6108 92	Women's or girls' robes, dressing gowns, and sim art of manmade fibers, nes, knitted or crocheted
6108 99	Women's or girls' robes, dressing gowns, and sim art of other tex materials, nes, knitted or crocheted
6109 10	Tshirts, singlets, tank tops, and similar garments, of cotton, knitted or crocheted
6109 90	Tshirts, singlets, tank tops, and similar garments, of other textile materials, knitted or crocheted
6110 10	Sweaters, pullovers, sweatshirts, and sim articles of wool or fine animal hair, knitted or crocheted
6110 20	Sweaters, pullovers, sweatshirts, and similar articles of cotton, knitted or crocheted
6110 30	Sweaters, pullovers, sweatshirts, and similar articles of manmade fibers, knitted or crocheted
6110 90	Sweaters, pullovers, sweatshirts, and sim articles of other textile materials, knitted or crocheted
6111 10	Babies' garments and clothing accessories of wool or fine animal hair, knitted or crocheted
6111 20	Babies' garments and clothing accessories of cotton, knitted or crocheted
6111 30	Babies' garments and clothing accessories of synthetic fibers, knitted or crocheted
6111 90	Babies' garments and clothing accessories of other textile materials, knitted or crocheted
6112 11	Track suits, of cotton, knitted or crocheted
6112 12	Track suits, of synthetic fibers, knitted or crocheted

(Continued)

6112 19	Track suits, of other textile materials, knitted or crocheted
6112 20	Ski suits, of textile materials, knitted or crocheted
6112 31	Men's or boys' swimwear, of synthetic fibers, knitted or crocheted
6112 39	Men's or boys' swimwear, of other textile materials, knitted or crocheted
6112 41	Women's or girls' swimwear, of synthetic fibers, knitted or crocheted
6112 49	Women's or girls' swimwear, of other textile materials, knitted or crocheted
6113 00	Garments made up of impregnated, coated, covered or laminated textile knitted or crocheted fabric
6114 10	Garments of wool or fine animal hair, knitted or crocheted, nes
6114 20	Garments of cotton, knitted or crocheted, nes
6114 30	Garments of manmade fibers, knitted or crocheted, nes
6114 90	Garments of other textile materials, knitted or crocheted, nes
6115 11	Panty hose and tights, of synthetic fiber yarn, <67decitex/single yarn, knitted or crocheted
6115 12	Panty hose and tights, of synthetic fiber yarn, 67 decitex/single yarn, knitted or crocheted
6115 19	Panty hose and tights, of other textile materials, knitted or crocheted
6115 20	Women full or knee length hosiery, of textile yarn, <67 decitex/single yarn, knitted or crocheted
6115 91	Hosiery nes, of wool or fine animal hair, knitted or crocheted
6115 92	Hosiery nes, of cotton, knitted or crocheted
6115 93	Hosiery nes, of synthetic fibers, knitted or crocheted
6115 99	Hosiery nes, of other textile materials, knitted or crocheted
6116 10	Gloves or mittens, impregnated, coated or covered with plastics or rubber, knitted or crocheted
6116 91	Gloves or mittens, nes, of wool or fine animal hair, knitted or crocheted
6116 92	Gloves or mittens, nes, of cotton, knitted or crocheted
6116 93	Gloves or mittens, nes, of synthetic fibers, knitted or crocheted
6116 99	Gloves or mittens, nes, of other textile materials, knitted or crocheted
6117 10	Shawls, scarves, veils and the like, of textile materials, knitted or crocheted
6117 20	Ties, bow ties and cravats, of textile materials, knitted or crocheted
6117 80	Clothing accessories nes, of textile materials, knitted or crocheted
6117 90	Parts of garments or clothing accessories, of textile materials, knitted or crocheted

Chapter 62: Articles of Apparel and Clothing Accessories, Not Knitted or Crocheted

6201 11	Men's or boys' overcoats, and similar articles of wool or fine animal hair, not knit
6201 12	Men's or boys' overcoats, and similar articles of cotton, not knitted or crocheted
6201 13	Men's or boys' overcoats, and similar articles of manmade fibers, not knitted or crocheted
6201 19	Men's or boys' overcoats, and similar articles of other textile materials, not knitted or crocheted

6201 91	Men's or boys' anoraks and similar articles, of wool or fine animal hair, not knitted or crocheted
6201 92	Men's or boys' anoraks and similar articles, of cotton, not knitted or crocheted
6201 93	Men's or boys' anoraks and similar articles, of manmade fibers, not knitted or crocheted
6201 99	Men's or boys' anoraks and similar articles, of other textile materials, not knitted or crocheted
6202 11	Women's or girls' overcoats and similar articles of wool or fine animal hair not knit
6202 12	Women's or girls' overcoats and similar articles of cotton, not knitted or crocheted
6202 13	Women's or girls' overcoats and similar articles of manmade fibers, not knitted or crocheted
6202 19	Women's or girls' overcoats and similar articles of other textile mat, not knit
6202 91	Women's or girls' anoraks and similar article of wool or fine animal hair, not knit
6202 92	Women's or girls' anoraks and similar article of cotton, not knitted or crocheted
6202 93	Women's or girls' anoraks and similar article of manmade fibers, not knitted or crocheted
6202 99	Women's or girls' anoraks and similar article of other textile materials, not knit
6203 11	Men's or boys' suits, of wool or fine animal hair, not knitted or crocheted
6203 12	Men's or boys' suits, of synthetic fibers, not knitted or crocheted
6203 19	Men's or boys' suits, of other textile materials, not knitted or crocheted
6203 21	Men's or boys' ensembles, of wool or fine animal hair, not knitted or crocheted
6203 22	Men's or boys' ensembles, of cotton, not knitted or crocheted
6203 23	Men's or boys' ensembles, of synthetic fibers, not knitted or crocheted
6203 29	Men's or boys' ensembles, of other textile materials, not knitted or crocheted
6203 31	Men's or boys' jackets and blazers, of wool or fine animal hair, not knitted or crocheted
6203 32	Men's or boys' jackets and blazers, of cotton, not knitted or crocheted
6203 33	Men's or boys' jackets and blazers, of synthetic fibers, not knitted or crocheted
6203 39	Men's or boys' jackets and blazers, of other textile materials, not knitted or crocheted
6203 41	Men's or boys' trousers and shorts, of wool or fine animal hair, not knitted or crocheted
6203 42	Men's or boys' trousers and shorts, of cotton, not knitted or crocheted
6203 43	Men's or boys' trousers and shorts, of synthetic fibers, not knitted or crocheted
6203 49	Men's or boys' trousers and shorts, of other textile materials, not knitted or crocheted
6204 11	Women's or girls' suits, of wool or fine animal hair, not knitted or crocheted
6204 12	Women's or girls' suits, of cotton, not knitted or crocheted
6204 13	Women's or girls' suits, of synthetic fibers, not knitted or crocheted
6204 19	Women's or girls' suits, of other textile materials, not knitted or crocheted
6204 21	Women's or girls' ensembles, of wool or fine animal hair, not knitted or crocheted
6204 22	Women's or girls' ensembles, of cotton, not knitted or crocheted
6204 23	Women's or girls' ensembles, of synthetic fibers, not knitted or crocheted
6204 29	Women's or girls' ensembles, of other textile materials, not knitted or crocheted

(Continued)

6204 31	Women's or girls' jackets, of wool or fine animal hair, not knitted or crocheted
6204 32	Women's or girls' jackets, of cotton, not knitted or crocheted
6204 33	Women's or girls' jackets, of synthetic fibers, not knitted or crocheted
6204 39	Women's or girls' jackets, of other textile materials, not knitted or crocheted
6204 41	Women's or girls' dresses, of wool or fine animal hair, not knitted or crocheted
6204 42	Women's or girls' dresses, of cotton, not knitted or crocheted
6204 43	Women's or girls' dresses, of synthetic fibers, not knitted or crocheted
6204 44	Women's or girls' dresses, of artificial fibers, not knitted or crocheted
6204 49	Women's or girls' dresses, of other textile materials, not knitted or crocheted
6204 51	Women's or girls' skirts, of wool or fine animal hair, not knitted or crocheted
6204 52	Women's or girls' skirts, of cotton, not knitted or crocheted
6204 53	Women's or girls' skirts, of synthetic fibers, not knitted or crocheted
6204 59	Women's or girls' skirts, of other textile materials, not knitted or crocheted
6204 61	Women's or girls' trousers and shorts, of wool or fine animal hair, not knitted or crocheted
6204 62	Women's or girls' trousers and shorts, of cotton, not knitted or crocheted
6204 63	Women's or girls' trousers and shorts, of synthetic fibers, not knitted or crocheted
6204 69	Women's or girls' trousers and shorts, of other textile materials, not knitted or crocheted
6205 10	Men's or boys' shirts, of wool or fine animal hair, not knitted or crocheted
6205 20	Men's or boys' shirts, of cotton, not knitted or crocheted
6205 30	Men's or boys' shirts, of manmade fibers, not knitted or crocheted
6205 90	Men's or boys' shirts, of other textile materials, not knitted or crocheted
6206 10	Women's or girls' blouses and shirts, of silk or silk waste, not knitted or crocheted
6206 20	Women's or girls' blouses and shirts, of wool or fine animal hair, not knitted or crocheted
6206 30	Women's or girls' blouses and shirts, of cotton, not knitted or crocheted
6206 40	Women's or girls' blouses and shirts, of manmade fibers, not knitted or crocheted
6206 90	Women's or girls' blouses and shirts, of other textile materials, not knitted or crocheted
6207 11	Men's or boys' underpants and briefs, of cotton, not knitted or crocheted
6207 19	Men's or boys' underpants and briefs, of other textile materials, not knitted or crocheted
6207 21	Men's or boys' nightshirts and pajamas, of cotton, not knitted or crocheted
6207 22	Men's or boys' nightshirts and pajamas, of manmade fibers, not knitted or crocheted
6207 29	Men's or boys' nightshirts and pajamas, of other textile materials, not knitted or crocheted
6207 91	Men's or boys' robes, dressing gowns, and similar articles of cotton, not knitted or crocheted
6207 92	Men's or boys' robes, dressing gowns, and sim art of manmade fibers, not knitted or crocheted
6207 99	Men's or boys' robes, dressing gowns, and similar articles of other textile materials, not knit
6208 11	Women's or girls' slips and petticoats, of manmade fibers, not knitted or crocheted

6208 19	Women's or girls' slips and petticoats, of other textile materials, not knitted or crocheted
6208 21	Women's or girls' nightdresses and pajamas, of cotton, not knitted or crocheted
6208 22	Women's or girls' nightdresses and pajamas, of manmade fibers, not knitted or crocheted
6208 29	Women's or girls' nightdresses and pajamas, of other textile materials, not knitted or crocheted
6208 91	Women's or girls' panties, robes, and similar articles of cotton, not knitted or crocheted
6208 92	Women's or girls' panties, robes, and similar articles of manmade fibers, not knitted or crocheted
6208 99	Women's or girls' panties, robes, and sim art of other textile materials, not knitted or crocheted
6209 10	Babies' garments and clothing accessories of wool or fine animal hair, not knitted or crocheted
6209 20	Babies' garments and clothing accessories of cotton, not knitted or crocheted
6209 30	Babies' garments and clothing accessories of synthetic fibers, not knitted or crocheted
6209 90	Babies' garments and clothing accessories of other textile materials, not knitted or crocheted
6210 10	Garments made up of textile felts and of nonwoven textile fabric
6210 20	Men's or boys' overcoats and similar articles of impreg, coated, covered etc, textile fabric
6210 30	Women's or girls' overcoats and sim art, of impregnated, coated, covered, or laminated woven fabric
6210 40	Men's or boys' garments nes, made up of impregnated, coated, covered, or laminated woven fabric
6210 50	Women's or girls' garments nes, of impregnated, coated, covered, or laminated woven fabric
6211 11	Men's or boys' swimwear, of textile materials not knitted or crocheted
6211 12	Women's or girls' swimwear, of textile materials, not knitted or crocheted
6211 20	Ski suits, of textile materials, not knitted or crocheted
6211 31	Men's or boys' garments nes, of wool or fine animal hair, not knitted or crocheted
6211 32	Men's or boys' garments nes, of cotton, not knitted or crocheted
6211 33	Men's or boys' garments nes, of manmade fibers, not knitted or crocheted
6211 39	Men's or boys' garments nes, of other textile materials, not knitted or crocheted
6211 41	Women's or girls' garments nes, of wool or fine animal hair, not knitted or crocheted
6211 42	Women's or girls' garments nes, of cotton, not knitted or crocheted
6211 43	Women's or girls' garments nes, of manmade fibers, not knitted or crocheted
6211 49	Women's or girls' garments nes, of other textile materials, not knitted or crocheted
6212 10	Brassieres and parts thereof, of textile materials, whether or not knitted or crocheted
6212 20	Girdles, panty girdles and parts thereof, of textile materials, whether or not crocheted

(Continued)

6212 30	Corselettes and parts thereof, of textile materials, whether or not knitted or crocheted
6212 90	Corsets, braces and sim articles and parts, of textile materials, whether or not knitted or crocheted
6213 10	Handkerchiefs, of silk or silk waste, not knitted or crocheted
6213 20	Handkerchiefs, of cotton, not knitted or crocheted
6213 90	Handkerchiefs, of other textile materials, not knitted or crocheted
6214 10	Shawls, scarves, veils and the like, of silk or silk waste, not knitted or crocheted
6214 20	Shawls, scarves, veils and the like, of wool or fine animal hair, not knitted or crocheted
6214 30	Shawls, scarves, veils and the like, of synthetic fibers, not knitted or crocheted
6214 40	Shawls, scarves, veils and the like, of artificial fibers, not knitted or crocheted
6214 90	Shawls, scarves, veils and the like, of other textile materials, not knitted or crocheted
6215 10	Ties, bow ties and cravats, of silk or silk waste, not knitted or crocheted
6215 20	Ties, bow ties and cravats, of manmade fibers, not knitted or crocheted
6215 90	Ties, bow ties and cravats, of other textile materials, not knitted or crocheted
6216 00	Gloves, mittens and mitts, of textile materials, not knitted or crocheted
6217 10	Clothing accessories of textile materials, not knitted or crocheted, nes
6217 90	Parts of garments or of clothing accessories of textile materials, not knitted or crocheted, nes

Chapter 63: Other Made Up Textile Articles; Needlecraft Sets; Worn Clothing and Worn Textile Articles; Rags

6301 10	Electric blankets, of textile materials
6301 20	Blankets (other than electric) and traveling rugs, of wool or fine animal hair
6301 30	Blankets (other than electric) and traveling rugs, of cotton
6301 40	Blankets (other than electric) and traveling rugs, of synthetic fibers
6301 90	Blankets (other than electric) and traveling rugs, of other textile materials
6302 10	Bed linen, of textile knitted or crocheted or crocheted materials
6302 21	Bed linen, of cotton, printed, not knitted or crocheted
6302 22	Bed linen, of manmade fibers, printed, not knitted or crocheted
6302 29	Bed linen, of other textile materials, printed, not knitted or crocheted
6302 31	Bed linen, of cotton, nes
6302 32	Bed linen, of manmade fibers, nes
6302 39	Bed linen, of other textile materials, nes
6302 40	Table linen, of textile knitted or crocheted materials
6302 51	Table linen, of cotton, not knitted or crocheted
6302 52	Table linen, of flax, not knitted or crocheted
6302 53	Table linen, of manmade fibers, not knitted or crocheted
6302 59	Table linen, of other textile materials, not knitted or crocheted

6302 60	Toilet and kitchen linen, of terry toweling or similar terry fabric, of cotton
6302 91	Toilet and kitchen linen, of cotton, nes
6302 92	Toilet and kitchen linen, of flax
6302 93	Toilet and kitchen linen, of manmade fibers
6302 99	Toilet and kitchen linen, of other textile materials
6303 11	Curtains, interior blinds and curtain or bed valances, of cotton, knitted or crocheted
6303 12	Curtains, interior blinds and curtain or bed valances, of synthetic fiber, knitted or crocheted
6303 19	Curtains, interior blinds and curtain or bed valances, other textile materials, knitted or crocheted
6303 91	Curtains, interior blinds and curtain or bed valances, of cotton, not knitted or crocheted
6303 92	Curtains, interior blinds and curtain or bed valances, of synthetic fiber, not knitted or crocheted
6303 99	Curtains, interior blinds and curtain or bed valances, of other tex mat, not knitted or crocheted
6304 11	Bedspreads of textile materials, nes, knitted or crocheted
6304 19	Bedspreads of textile materials, nes, not knitted or crocheted
6304 91	Furnishing articles nes, of textile materials, knitted or crocheted
6304 92	Furnishing articles nes, of cotton, not knitted or crocheted
6304 93	Furnishing articles nes, of synthetic fibers, not knitted or crocheted
6304 99	Furnishing articles nes, of other textile materials, not knitted or crocheted
6305 10	Sacks and bags of jute or of other textile bast fibers
6305 20	Sacks and bags of cotton
6305 31	Sacks and bags polyethylene or polypropylene strips
6305 39	Sacks and bags of other manmade textile materials
6305 90	Sacks and bags of other textile materials
6306 11	Tarpaulins, awnings and sunblinds, of cotton
6306 12	Tarpaulins, awnings and sunblinds, of synthetic fibers
6306 19	Tarpaulins, awnings and sunblinds, of other textile materials
6306 21	Tents, of cotton
6306 22	Tents, of synthetic fibers
6306 29	Tents, of other textile materials
6306 31	Sails, of synthetic fibers
6306 39	Sails, of other textile materials
6306 41	Pneumatic mattresses, of cotton
6306 49	Pneumatic mattresses, of other textile materials
6306 91	Camping goods nes, of cotton
6306 99	Camping goods nes, of other textile materials
6307 10	Floorcloths, dishcloths, dusters and similar cleaning cloths, of textile materials
6307 20	Life jackets and life belts, of textile materials
6307 90	Made up articles, of textile materials, nes, including dress patterns
6308 00	Sets of woven fabric and yarn, for rugs, tapestries, and similar textile articles, for retail sale
6309 00	Worn clothing and other worn articles

Chapter 64: Footwear, Gaiters, and the Like; Parts of Such Articles

ex 6405 20	Footwear with soles and uppers of wool felt
ex 6406 10	Footwear uppers of which the external surface is 50% textile material
ex 6406 99	Leg warmers and gaiters of textile materials

Chapter 65: Headgear and Parts Thereof

6501 00	Hatforms, hat bodies and hoods of felt; plateaux and manchons of felt
6502 00	Hatshapes, plaited or made by assembling strips of any material
6503 00	Felt hats and other felt headgear
6504 00	Hats and other headgear, plaited or made by assembling strips of any material
6505 90	Hats and other headgear, knitted or made up from lace, or other textile materials

Chapter 66: Umbrellas, Sun Umbrellas, Walking Sticks, Seatsticks, Whips, Ridingcrops and Parts Thereof

6601 10	Umbrellas and sun umbrellas, garden type
6601 91	Other umbrella types, telescopic shaft
6601 99	Other umbrellas

Chapter 70: Glass and Glassware

ex 7019 10	Yarn of fiber glass
7019 20	Woven fabric of fiber glass

Chapter 87: Vehicles other Than Railway or Tramway Rolling Stock, and Parts and Accessories Thereof

8708 21	Safety seat belts for motor vehicles

Chapter 88: Aircraft, Spacecraft, and Parts Thereof

8804 00	Parachutes; their parts and accessories

Chapter 91 Clocks and Watches and Parts Thereof

9113 90	Watch straps, bands and bracelets of textile materials

Chapter 94: Furniture; Bedding, Mattresses, Mattress Supports, Cushions and Similar Stuffed Furnishings

Chapter 95: Toys, games and Sports Requisites; Parts and Accessories Thereof

9502 91	Garments for dolls

Chapter 96: Miscellaneous Manufactured Articles

ex 9612 10	Woven ribbons, of manmade fibers, other than those <30 mm wide and permanently in cartridges

APPENDIX 2.1. TARIFF ELIMINATION

For purposes of this Appendix, each Party shall apply Section 2(2) to determine whether a textile or apparel good is an originating good of a particular Party.

A. Trade between Canada and the United States

As required by Article 302, Canada and the United States each shall progressively eliminate its respective customs duties on originating textile and apparel goods of the other Party in accordance with Annex 401.2, as amended, of the Canada United States Free Trade Agreement, as incorporated into Annex 302.2 and as set out in each Party's Schedule to that Annex.

B. Trade between Mexico and the United States

Except as provided in Schedule 2.1.B, and as required by Article 302, Mexico and the United States each shall progressively eliminate its respective customs duties on originating textile and apparel goods of the other Party, in accordance with its respective Schedule to Annex 302.2, as follows:

(a) duties on textile and apparel goods provided for in the items in staging category A in a Party's Schedule shall be eliminated entirely and such goods shall be dutyfree, effective January 1, 1994;

(b) duties on textile and apparel goods provided for in the items in staging category B6 in a Party's Schedule shall be reduced on January 1, 1994, by an amount equal, in percentage terms, to the base rates. Thereafter, duties shall be removed in five equal annual stages beginning on January 1, 1995, and such goods shall be dutyfree, effective January 1, 1999;

(c) duties on textile and apparel goods provided for in the items in staging category C in a Party's Schedule shall be removed in 10 equal annual stages beginning on January 1, 1994, and such goods shall be dutyfree, effective January 1, 2003; and

(d) if the application of a formula provided in subparagraph (b) or (c) for staging category B6 or C results in a duty that exceeds 20 percent ad valorem during any annual stage, the rate of duty during that stage shall be 20 percent ad valorem instead of the rate that otherwise would have applied.

C. Trade between Canada and Mexico

As required by Article 302, Canada and Mexico each shall progressively eliminate its respective customs duties on originating textile and apparel goods of the other Party, in accordance with its respective Schedule to Annex 302.2, as follows:

(a) duties on textile and apparel goods provided for in the items in staging category A in a Party's Schedule shall be eliminated entirely and such goods shall be dutyfree, effective January 1, 1994;

(b) duties on textile and apparel goods provided for in the items in staging category Bl in a Party's Schedule shall be removed in six equal annual stages beginning on January 1, 1994, and such goods shall be dutyfree, effective January 1, 1999;

(c) duties on textile and apparel goods provided for in the items in staging category B+ in a Party's Schedule shall be reduced by the following percentages of the base rates, beginning on January 1, 1994, and such goods shall be dutyfree, effective January 1, 2001

(i)   January 1, 1994, 20 percent
(ii)   January 1, 1995, 0 percent
(iii) January 1, 1996, 10 percent
(iv)   January 1, 1997, 10 percent
(v)   January 1, 1998, 10 percent
(vi)   January 1, 1999, 10 percent
(vii) January 1, 2000, 10 percent
(viii) January 1, 2001, 30 percent and

(d) duties on textile and apparel goods provided for in the items in staging category C in a Party's Schedule shall be removed in 10 equal annual stages beginning on January 1, 1994, and such goods shall be dutyfree, effective January 1, 2003.

D. Trade between All Parties

Originating textile and apparel goods provided for in the items in staging category D in a Party's Schedule to Annex 302.2 shall continue to receive dutyfree treatment.

SCHEDULE 2.1.B. EXCEPTIONS TO TARIFF PHASEOUT FORMULA SPECIFIED IN APPENDIX 2.1

1. The United States shall apply the following rates of duty on tariff items 5111.11.70, 5111.19.60, 5112.11.20 and 5112.19.90 during the transition period:

1994	25.0%
1995	24.1%
1996	18.0%
1997	12.0%
1998	6.0%
1999 and thereafter	0.0%

2. Mexico shall apply the following rates of duty on tariff items 5111.11.01, 5111.19.99, 5112.11.01 and 5112.19.99, as modified to correspond to the U.S. tariff items identified in paragraph 1, during the transition period:

1994	15.0%
1995	14.5%
1996	10.8%
1997	7.2%
1998	3.6%
1999 and thereafter	0.0%

3. The United States shall apply the following rates of duty on tariff items 5111.20.90, 5111.30.90, 5112.20.30, 5112.30.30, 5407.91.05, 5407.92.05, 5407.93.05, 5407.94.05, 5408.31.05, 5408.32.05, 5408.33.05, 5408.34.05, 5515.13.05, 5515.22.05, 5515.92.05, 5516.31.05, 5516.32.05, 5516.33.05 and 5516.34.05 during the transition period:

1994	25.0%
1995	25.0%
1996	20.0%
1997	13.3%
1998	6.7%
1999 and thereafter	0.0%

4. Mexico shall apply the following rates of duty on tariff items 5111.20.99, 5111.30.99, 5112.20.01, 5112.30.01, 5407.91.99, 5407.92.99, 5407.93.99, 5407.94.99, 5408.31.99, 5408.32.99, 5408.33.99, 5408.34.99, 5515.13.01, 5515.22.01, 5515.92.01, 5516.31.01, 5516.32.01, 5516.33.01 and 5516.34.01, as modified to correspond to the U.S. tariff items identified in paragraph 3, during the transition period:

1994	15.0%
1995	15.0%
1996	12.0%
1997	8.0%
1998	4.0%
1999 and thereafter	0.0%

5. Mexico shall apply the following rates of duty on goods of subheadings 5703.20 and 5703.30 measuring not more than 5.25 square meters in area, other than nylon handhooked, during the transition period:

1994	20.0%
1995	20.0%
1996	10.0%
1997	6.6%
1998	3.3%
1999 and thereafter	0.0%

APPENDIX 2.4. TARIFF ELIMINATION ON CERTAIN TEXTILE AND APPAREL GOODS

On January 1, 1994, the United States shall eliminate customs duties on textile and apparel goods that are assembled in Mexico from fabrics wholly formed and cut in the United States and exported from and reimported into the United States under:

(a) U.S. tariff item 9802.00.80.10; or
(b) Chapter 61, 62 or 63 if, after such assembly, those goods that would have qualified for treatment under 9802.00.80.10 have been subject to bleaching, garment dyeing, stonewashing, acidwashing or permapressing.

Thereafter, the United States shall not adopt or maintain any customs duty on textile and apparel goods of Mexico that satisfy the requirements of subparagraph (a) or (b) or the requirements of any successor provision to U.S. tariff item 9802.00.80.10.

APPENDIX 3.1. ADMINISTRATION OF IMPORT AND EXPORT PROHIBITIONS, RESTRICTIONS AND CONSULTATION LEVELS

A. Trade between Canada and Mexico and between Mexico and the United States

1. This Appendix applies to prohibitions, restrictions and consultation levels on

nonoriginating textile and apparel goods.

2. An exporting Party whose textile or apparel good is subject to a prohibition, restriction or consultation level shall limit its annual exports to the specified limits or levels, and the importing Party may assist the exporting Party in implementing the prohibition, restriction or consultation level by controlling its imports.

3. Each Party shall count exports of textile and apparel goods subject to a restriction or consultation level against the limit or level:
   (a) applicable to the calendar year in which the good was exported; or
   (b) authorized for the following year if such exports exceed the authorized limit or level for the calendar year in which the good was exported, if allowed entry into the territory of the importing Party.

4. Each exporting Party whose goods are subject to a restriction or consultation level shall endeavor to space exports of such goods to the territory of the importing Party evenly throughout each calendar year, taking into consideration normal seasonal factors.

5. On written request of an exporting Party whose goods are subject to a prohibition, restriction or consultation level, that Party and the importing Party shall consult within 30 days of receipt of the request on any matter arising from the implementation of this Appendix.

6. On written request of an exporting Party that considers the application of a prohibition, restriction or consultation level under this Annex has placed it in an inequitable position in relation to another Party or a nonParty, the exporting Party and importing Party shall consult within 60 days of receipt of the request to seek a mutually beneficial solution.

7. An importing Party and an exporting Party, at any time by mutual agreement, may adjust annual Designated Consultation Levels (DCLs) as follows:
   (a) if the exporting Party whose goods are subject to a DCL wishes to export goods in any category in excess of the applicable DCL in any calendar year, that Party may present to the importing Party a formal written request for an increase in the DCL; and
   (b) the importing Party shall respond, in writing, within 30 days of the receipt of the request. If the response is negative, the Parties concerned shall consult no later than 15 days after the receipt of the response or as soon thereafter as mutually convenient, and shall endeavor to reach a mutually satisfactory solution. The Parties concerned shall confirm any agreement reached on a new DCL by an exchange of letters.

8. Adjustments to annual specific limits (SLs), including those set out in Schedule 3.1.2, may be made as follows:
   (a) an exporting Party wishing to adjust an SL shall deliver a notice to the importing Party of its intent to make an adjustment;
   (b) the exporting Party may increase the SL for a calendar year by no more than six percent ("swing"); and
   (c) in addition to any increase of its SL under subparagraph (b), the exporting Party may increase its unadjusted SL for that year by no more than 11 percent by allocating to such SL for that calendar year (the "receiving year") an unused portion ("shortfall") of the corresponding SL for the previous calendar year

("carryover") or a portion of the corresponding SL for the following calendar year ("carryforward"), as follows:

(i) subject to subparagraph (iii), the exporting Party may utilize carryover, as available, up to 11 percent of the unadjusted SL for the receiving year,

(ii) the exporting Party may utilize carryforward charged against the corresponding SL for the following calendar year, up to six percent of the unadjusted SL for the receiving year,

(iii) the combination of the exporting Party's carryover and carryforward shall not exceed 11 percent of the unadjusted SL in the receiving year, and

(iv) carryover may be utilized only following confirmation by the importing Party that sufficient shortfall exists. If the importing Party does not consider that sufficient shortfall exists, it shall promptly provide data to the exporting Party to support that view. Where substantial statistical differences exist between the import and export data on which the shortfall is computed, the Parties concerned shall seek to resolve these differences promptly.

B. Trade between Mexico and the United States

9. During the transition period, nonoriginating textile and apparel goods of Mexico exported to the United States shall be subject to the restrictions and consultation levels specified in Schedule 3.1.2, in accordance with this Appendix and its Schedules. Such restrictions and consultation levels shall be progressively eliminated as follows:

(a) restrictions or consultation levels on items contained in the categories of textile and apparel goods in staging category 1 in Schedule 3.1.1 shall be eliminated on January 1, 1994;

(b) restrictions or consultation levels on items contained in the categories of textile and apparel goods in staging category 2 in Schedule 3.1.1 shall be eliminated on January 1, 2001; and

(c) restrictions or consultation levels on items contained in the categories of textile and apparel goods in staging category 3 in Schedule 3.1.1 shall be eliminated on January 1, 2004.

10. In addition, on January 1, 1994, the United States shall eliminate restrictions or consultation levels on textile and apparel goods that are assembled in Mexico from fabrics wholly formed and cut in the United States and exported from and reimported into the United States under:

(a) U.S. tariff item 9802.00.80.10; or

(b) Chapter 61, 62 or 63 if, after such assembly, those goods that would have qualified for treatment under 9802.00.80.10 have been subject to bleaching, garment dyeing, stonewashing, acidwashing or permapressing.

Thereafter, notwithstanding Section 5, the United States shall not adopt or maintain prohibitions, restrictions or consultation levels on textile and apparel goods of Mexico that satisfy the requirements of subparagraph (a) or (b) or the requirements of any successor provision to U.S. tariff item 9802.00.80.10.

11. Mexico and the United States may identify at any time particular textile and apparel goods that they mutually agree fall within:

    (a) handloomed fabrics of a cottage industry;

    (b) handmade cottage industry goods made of such handloomed fabrics; or

    (c) traditional folklore handicraft goods.

    The importing Party shall exempt from restrictions and consultation levels goods so identified, if certified by the competent authority of the exporting Party.

12. The Bilateral Textile Agreement Between the United States of America and the United Mexican States, signed at Mazatlán, February 13, 1988, as amended and extended (the Bilateral Agreement), shall terminate on the date of entry into force of this Agreement.

13. On request of either Party, the Parties shall consult to consider accelerating the elimination of restrictions or consultation levels set out in Schedule 3.1.2 on specific textile and apparel goods. An agreement between the Parties to accelerate the elimination of a restriction or consultation level shall supersede Schedule 3.1.1 when approved by each such Party in accordance with Article 2202(2) (Amendments).

14. During 1994, Mexico may carry over any unused portion of the 1993 limit specified in the Bilateral Agreement, or apply against the 1994 limit specified in this Appendix any exports made during 1993 in excess of the applicable limit under the Bilateral Agreement, in accordance with the flexibility provisions set forth in paragraph 8.

15. All exports of textile and apparel goods from the territory of Mexico to the territory of the United States covered by restrictions or consultation levels under this Appendix shall be accompanied by an export visa issued by the competent authority of Mexico, pursuant to any bilateral visa arrangement in effect between the Parties.

16. On written request of either Party, both Parties shall consult within 30 days of receipt of the request on any matter arising from the implementation of this Appendix. In addition, on written request of either Party, both Parties shall conduct a review of this Appendix by January 1, 1999.

17. For purposes of applying prohibitions, restrictions or consultation levels, each Party shall consider a good as being of:

    (a) man-made fibers if the good is in chief weight of manmade fibers, unless

        (i) the good is knitted or crocheted apparel in which wool equals or exceeds 23 percent by weight of all fibers, in which case it shall be of wool,

        (ii) the good is apparel, not knitted or crocheted, in which wool equals or exceeds 36 percent by weight of all fibers, in which case it shall be of wool, or

        (iii) the good is a woven fabric in which wool equals or exceeds 36 percent by weight of all fibers, in which case it shall be of wool;

    (b) cotton, if not covered by subparagraph (a) and if the good is in chief weight of cotton, unless the good is a woven fabric in which wool equals or exceeds 36 percent by weight of all fibers, in which case it shall be of wool;

    (c) wool, if not covered by subparagraph (a) or (b), and the good is in chief weight of wool; and

    (d) non-cotton vegetable fiber, if not covered by subparagraph (a), (b) or (c), and the good is in chief weight of non-cotton vegetable fiber, unless

(i) cotton with wool and/or man-made fibers in the aggregate equal or exceed 50 percent by weight of the component fibers thereof and the cotton component equals or exceeds the weight of each of the total wool and/or man-made fiber components, in which case it shall be of cotton,

(ii) if not covered by subparagraph (i) and wool exceeds 17 percent by weight of all component fibers, in which case it shall be of wool, or

(iii) if not covered by subparagraph (i) or (ii) and manmade fibers in combination with cotton and/or wool in the aggregate equal or exceed 50 percent by weight of the component fibers thereof and the man-made fiber component exceeds the weight of the total wool and/or total cotton component, in which case it shall be of man-made fibers.

For purposes of this paragraph, only the textile fibers in the component of the good that determines the tariff classification of the good are to be considered.

C. Schedules

To determine which HS provisions are contained in a U.S. category listed in the Schedules to this Appendix, the Parties shall refer to the Correlation: Textile and Apparel Categories with the Harmonized Tariff Schedule of the United States, 1992 (or successor document), U.S. Department of Commerce, International Trade Administration, Office of Textiles and Apparel, Trade and Data Division, Washington, D.C. The descriptions listed in these Schedules are provided for ease of reference only. For legal purposes, coverage of a category shall be determined according to the Correlation.

Schedule 3.1.1. SCHEDULE FOR THE ELIMINATION OF RESTRICTIONS AND CONSULTATION LEVELS ON EXPORTS FROM MEXICO TO THE UNITED STATES

A. Special Regime (SR) Goods

Category	Description	Staging Category
335 SR	C W&G Coats, Special Regime	1
336/636 SR	C/MMF Dresses, Special Regime	1
338/339/638/639 SR	C/MMF Knit Shirts, Special Regime	1
340/640 SR	C/MMF Woven Shirts, Special Regime	1
341/641 SR	C/MMF Blouses, Special Regime	1
342/642 SR	C/MMF Skirts, Special Regime	1
347/348/647/648 SR	C/MMF Trousers, Special Regime	1
351/651 SR	C/MMF Pyjamas, etc. Special Regime	1
352/652 SR	C/MMF Underwear, Special Regime	1
359C/659C SR	C/MMF Coveralls, Special Regime	1
633 SR	MMF Suit Coats, Special Regime	1
635 SR	MMF Coats, Special Regime	1

B. Non-originating Goods

Category	Description	Staging Category
Broadwoven Fabric Group	C/MMF	1
218	C/MMF Fabrics/Yarns of Different Colors	1
219	C/MMF Duck Fabric	2
220	C/MMF Fabric of Special Weave	1
225	C/MMF Denim Fabric	1
226	C/MMF Cheesecloth, Batistes	1
227	C/MMF Oxford Cloth	1
300/301/607-Y	C Combed/Carded Yarn; etc.	1
313	C Sheeting Fabric	2
314	C Poplin and Broadcloth Fabric	2
315	C Printcloth Fabric	2
317	C Twill Fabric	2
326	C Sateen Fabric	1
334/634	C/MMF Men's and Boys' Coats	1
335 NR	C Coats, Women's and Girls'	1
336/636 NR	C/MMF Dresses	1
338/339/638/639 NR	C/MMF Knit Shirts and Blouses	2
340/640 NR	C/MMF Woven Shirts	2
341/641 NR	C/MMF Woven Blouses	1
342/642	C/MMF Skirts	1
347/348/647/648 NR	C/MMF Trousers and Pants	2
351/651	C/MMF Pyjamas and Nightwear	1
352/652 NR	C/MMF Underwear	1
359C/659-C NR	C/MMF Coveralls	1
363	C Terry and Pile towels	1
410	Woven Wool Fabric	3
433	W Men's and Boys' Suittype Coats	3
435	W Women's and Girls' Coats	1
443	W Men's and Boys' Suits	3
604-A	Acrylic Spun Yarn	1
604O/607O	Staple Fiber Yarn	1
611	Artificial Staple Fiber Woven Fabric	3
613	MMF Sheeting Fabric	1
614	MMF Poplin & Broadcloth Fabric	1
615	MMF Printcloth Fabric	1
617	MMF Twill & Sateen Fabric	1
625	MMF Poplin/Broadcloth Staple/Filament	1
626	MMF Printcloth Staple/Filament	1
627	MMF Sheeting Staple/Filament	1
628	MMF Twill/Sateen Staple/Filament	1
633 NR	MMF SuitType Coats, M&B	2
635	Women's and Girls' MMF Coats	1
643	MMF Suits for Men and Boys	2
669-B	Polypropylene Bags	1
670	MMF Luggage, Flat Goods Etc.	1

For purposes of this Schedule:

C means cotton;
M&B means men's and boys';
MMF means manmade fiber;
NR means normal regime;
W means wool; and
W&G means women's and girls'.

SCHEDULE 3.1.2. RESTRICTIONS AND CONSULTATION LEVELS ON EXPORTS FROM MEXICO TO THE UNITED STATES

Category	Form	Unit of Measure	1994	1995	1996
219	DCL	SM	9,438,000	9,438,000	9,438,000
313	DCL	SM	16,854,000	16,854,000	16,854,000
314	DCL	SM	6,966,904	6,966,904	6,966,904
315	DCL	SM	6,966,904	6,966,904	6,966,904
317	DCL	SM	8,427,000	8,427,000	8,427,000
611	DCL	SM	1,267,710	1,267,710	1,267,710
410	DCL	SM	397,160	397,160	397,160
338/339/ 638/639	DCL	DZ	650,000	650,000	650,000
340/640	SL	DZ	120,439	128,822	137,788
347/348/ 647/648	DCL	DZ	650,000	650,000	650,000
433	DCL	DZ	11,000	11,000	11,000
443	SL	NO	150,000	156,000	162,240
633	DCL	DZ	10,000	10,000	10,000
643	DCL	NO	155,556	155,556	155,556

Category	1997	1998	1999	2000
219	9,438,000	9,438,000	9,438,000	9,438,000
313	16,854,000	16,854,000	16,854,000	16,854,000
314	6,966,904	6,966,904	6,966,904	6,966,904
315	6,966,904	6,966,904	6,966,904	6,966,904
317	8,427,000	8,427,000	8,427,000	8,427,000
611	1,267,710	1,267,710	1,267,710	1,267,710
410	397,160	397,160	397,160	397,160
338/339/ 638/639	650,000	650,000	650,000	650,000
340/640	147,378	160,200	174,137	189,287
347/348/ 647/648	650,000	650,000	650,000	650,000
433	11,000	11,000	11,000	11,000
443	168,730	175,479	182,498	189,798
633	10,000	10,000	10,000	10,000
643	155,556	155,556	155,556	155,556

Category	2001	2002	2003
611	1,267,710	1,267,710	1,267,710
410	397,160	397,160	397,160
433	11,000	11,000	11,000
443	197,390	205,286	213,496

SCHEDULE 3.1.3. CONVERSION FACTORS

1. This Schedule applies to restrictions and consultation levels applied pursuant to Section 5 and paragraph 9 of Appendix 3.1, and to tariff preference levels applied pursuant to Section 6 and Appendix 6.
2. Unless otherwise provided in this Annex, or as may be mutually agreed between any two Parties with respect to trade between them, the rates of conversion into SME set out in paragraphs 3 through 6 shall apply.
3. The following conversion factors shall apply to the goods covered by the following U.S. categories:

U.S. Category	Conversion Factor	Description	Primary Unit of Measure
200	6.60	YARN FOR RETAIL SALE, SEWING THREAD	KG
201	6.50	SPECIALTY YARNS	KG
218	1.00	FABRIC OF YARNS OF DIFFERENT COLORS	KG
219	1.00	DUCK FABRIC	KG
220	1.00	FABRIC OF SPECIAL WEAVE	KG
222	6.00	KNIT FABRIC	KG
223	14.00	NONWOVEN FABRIC	KG
224	1.00	PILE & TUFTED FABRIC	KG
225	1.00	BLUE DENIM FABRIC	KG
226	1.00	CHEESECLOTH, BATISTE, LAWN & VOILE	KG
227	1.00	OXFORD CLOTH	KG
229	13.60	SPECIAL PURPOSE FABRIC	KG
237	19.20	PLAYSUITS, SUNSUITS, ETC	KG
239	6.30	BABIES' GARMENTS & CLOTHING ACCESS.	KG
300	8.50	CARDED COTTON YARN	KG
301	8.50	COMBED COTTON YARN	KG
313	1.00	COTTON SHEETING FABRIC	KG
314	1.00	COTTON POPLIN & BROADCLOTH FABRIC	KG
315	1.00	COTTON PRINTCLOTH FABRIC	KG
317	1.00	COTTON TWILL FABRIC	KG
326	1.00	COTTON SATEEN FABRIC	KG
330	1.40	COTTON HANDKERCHIEFS	KG
331	2.90	COTTON GLOVES AND MITTENS	KG

(Continued)

U.S. Category	Conversion Factor	Description	Primary Unit of Measure
332	3.80	COTTON HOSIERY	KG
333	30.30	M&B SUITTYPE COATS, COTTON	KG
334	34.50	OTHER M&B COATS, COTTON	KG
335	34.50	W&G COTTON COATS	KG
336	37.90	COTTON DRESSES	KG
338	6.00	M&B COTTON KNIT SHIRTS	KG
339	6.00	W&G COTTON KNIT SHIRTS/BLOUSES	KG
340	20.10	M&B COTTON SHIRTS, NOT KNIT	KG
341	12.10	W&G COTTON SHIRTS/BLOUSES,NOT KNIT	KG
342	14.90	COTTON SKIRTS	KG
345	30.80	COTTON SWEATERS	KG
347	14.90	M&B COTTON TROUSERS/BREECHES/SHORTS	KG
348	14.90	W&G COTTON TROUSERS/BREECHES/SHORTS	KG
349	4.00	BRASSIERES, OTHER BODY SUPPORT GARMENTS	KG
350	42.60	COTTON DRESSING GOWNS, ROBES ETC.	KG
351	43.50	COTTON NIGHTWEAR/PAJAMAS	KG
352	9.20	COTTON UNDERWEAR	KG
353	34.50	M&B COTTON DOWNFILLED COATS	KG
354	34.50	W&G COTTON DOWNFILLED COATS	KG
359	8.50	OTHER COTTON APPAREL	KG
360	0.90	COTTON PILLOWCASES	KG
361	5.20	COTTON SHEETS	KG
362	5.80	OTHER COTTON BEDDING	KG
363	0.40	COTTON TERRY & OTHER PILE TOWELS	KG
369	8.50	OTHER COTTON MANUFACTURES	KG
400	3.70	WOOL YARN	KG
410	1.00	WOOL WOVEN FABRIC	KG
414	2.80	OTHER WOOL FABRIC	KG
431	1.80	WOOL GLOVES/MITTENS	KG
432	2.30	WOOL HOSIERY	KG
433	30.10	M&B WOOL SUITTYPE COATS	KG
434	45.10	OTHER M&B WOOL COATS	KG
435	45.10	W&G WOOL COATS	KG
436	41.10	WOOL DRESSES	KG
438	12.50	WOOL KNIT SHIRTS/BLOUSES	KG
439	6.30	BABIES' WOOL GARM/CLOTHING ACCESS.	KG
440	20.10	WOOL SHIRTS/BLOUSES, NOTKNIT	KG
442	15.00	WOOL SKIRTS	KG
443	3.76	M&B WOOL SUITS	KG
444	3.76	W&G WOOL SUITS	KG

U.S. Category	Conversion Factor	Description	Primary Unit of Measure
445	12.40	M&B WOOL SWEATERS	KG
446	12.40	W&G WOOL SWEATERS	KG
447	15.00	M&B WOOL TROUSERS/BREECHES/SHORTS	KG
448	15.00	W&G WOOL TROUSERS/BREECHES/SHORTS	KG
459	3.70	OTHER WOOL APPAREL	KG
464	2.40	WOOL BLANKETS	KG
465	1.00	WOOL FLOOR COVERINGS	KG
469	3.70	OTHER WOOL MANUFACTURES	KG
600	6.50	TEXTURED FILAMENT YARN	KG
603	6.30	YARN 85% ARTIFICIAL STAPLE FIBER	KG
604	7.60	YARN 85% SYNTHETIC STAPLE FIBER	KG
606	20.10	NONTEXTURED FILAMENT YARN	KG
607	6.50	OTHER STAPLE FIBER YARN	KG
611	1.00	WOVEN FABRIC 85% ARTIFICIAL STAPLE	KG
613	1.00	MMF SHEETING FABRIC	KG
614	1.00	MMF POPLIN & BROADCLOTH FABRIC	KG
615	1.00	MMF PRINTCLOTH FABRIC	KG
617	1.00	MMF TWILL AND SATEEN FABRIC	KG
618	1.00	WOVEN ARTIFICIAL FILAMENT FABRIC	KG
619	1.00	POLYESTER FILAMENT FABRIC	KG
620	1.00	OTHER SYNTHETIC FILAMENT FABRIC	KG
621	14.40	IMPRESSION FABRIC	KG
622	1.00	GLASS FIBER FABRIC	KG
624	1.00	WOVEN MMF FABRIC, 15% TO 36% WOOL	KG
625	1.00	MMF STAPLE/FILAMENT POPLIN & BROADCLOTH FABRIC	KG
626	1.00	MMF STAPLE/FILAMENT PRINTCLOTH FABRIC	KG
627	1.00	MMF STAPLE/FILAMENT SHEETING FABRIC	KG
628	1.00	MMF STAPLE/FILAMENT TWILL/SATEEN FABRIC	KG
629	1.00	OTHER MMF STAPLE/FILAMENT FABRIC	KG
630	1.40	MMF HANDKERCHIEFS	KG
631	2.90	MMF GLOVES AND MITTENS	KG
632	3.80	MMF HOSIERY	KG
633	30.30	M&B MMF SUITTYPE COATS	KG
634	34.50	OTHER M&B MMF COATS	KG
635	34.50	W&G MMF COATS	KG
636	37.90	MMF DRESSES	KG
638	15.00	M&B MMF KNIT SHIRTS	KG

(Continued)

U.S. Category	Conversion Factor	Description	Primary Unit of Measure
639	12.50	W&G MMF KNIT SHIRTS & BLOUSES	KG
640	20.10	M&B NOTKNIT MMF SHIRTS	KG
641	12.10	W&G NOTKNIT MMF SHIRTS & BLOUSES	KG
642	14.90	MMF SKIRTS	KG
644	3.76	W&G MMF SUITS	KG
645	30.80	M&B MMF SWEATERS	KG
646	30.80	W&G MMF SWEATERS	KG
647	14.90	M&B MMF TROUSERS/BREECHES/SHORTS	KG
648	14.90	W&G MMF TROUSERS/BREECHES/SHORTS	KG
649	4.00	MMF BRAS & OTHER BODY SUPPORT GARMENTS	KG
650	42.60	MMF ROBES, DRESSING GOWNS, ETC.	KG
651	43.50	MMF NIGHTWEAR & PAJAMAS	KG
652	13.40	MMF UNDERWEAR	KG
653	34.50	M&B MMF DOWNFILLED COATS	KG
654	34.50	W&G MMF DOWNFILLED COATS	KG
659	14.40	OTHER MMF APPAREL	KG
665	1.00	MMF FLOOR COVERINGS	SM
666	14.40	OTHER MMF FURNISHINGS	KG
669	14.40	OTHER MMF MANUFACTURES	KG
670	3.70	MMF FLAT GOODS, HANDBAGS, LUGGAGE	KG
800	8.50	YARN, SILK BLENDS/VEGETABLE FIBER	KG
810	1.00	WOVEN FABRIC, SILK BLENDS/VEGETABLE FIBER	KG
831	2.90	GLOVES & MITTENS, SILK BLENDS/VEGETABLE FIBER	KG
832	3.80	HOSIERY, SILK BLENDS/VEGETABLE FIBER	KG
833	30.30	M&B SUITTYPE COATS, SILK BLENDS/VEGETABLE FIBER	KG
834	34.50	OTHER M&B COATS, SILK BLENDS/VEGETABLE FIBER	KG
835	34.50	W&G COATS, SILK BLENDS/VEGETABLE FIBER	KG
836	37.90	DRESSES, SILK BLENDS/VEGETABLE FIBER	KG
838	11.70	KNIT SHIRTS & BLOUSES, SILK BLENDS/VEGETABLE FIBER	KG
839	6.30	BABIES' GARM & CLOTHING ACCESSORIES, SILK/VEG FIBER	KG
840	16.70	NOTKNIT SHIRTS & BLOUSES, SILK BLENDS/VEGETABLE FIBER	KG
842	14.90	SKIRTS, SILK BLENDS/VEGETABLE FIBERS	KG

U.S. Category	Conversion Factor	Description	Primary Unit of Measure
843	3.76	M&B SUITS, SILK BLENDS/VEGETABLE FIBER	KG
844	3.76	W&G SUITS, SILK BLENDS/VEGETABLE FIBER	KG
845	30.80	SWEATERS, NONCOTTON VEGETABLE FIBERS	KG
846	30.80	SWEATERS, SILK BLENDS	KG
847	14.90	TROUSERS/BREECHES/SHORTS, SILK BLENDS/ VEGETABLE FIBER	DZ
850	42.60	ROBES, DRESSING GOWNS, ETC, SILK BLENDS/VEGETABLE FIBER	KG
851	43.50	NIGHTWEAR & PYJAMAS, SILK BLENDS/ VEGETABLE FIBER	KG
852	11.30	UNDERWEAR, SILK BLENDS/VEGETABLE FIBER	KG
858	6.60	NECKWEAR, SILK BLENDS/VEGETABLE FIBER	KG
859	12.50	OTHER SILK BLEND/VEGETABLE FIBER APPAREL	KG
863	0.40	TOWELS, SILK BLENDS/VEGETABLE FIBERS	KG
870	3.70	LUGGAGE, SILK BLENDS/VEGETABLE FIBERS	KG
871	3.70	HANDBAGS & FLATGOODS, SILK BLENDS/VEGETABLE FIBER	KG
899	11.10	OTHER SILK BLENDS/VEGETABLE FIBER MANUFACTURES	KG

4. The following conversion factors shall apply to the following goods not covered by a U.S. category:

U.S. Harmonized System Statistical Provision	Conversion Factor	Primary Unit of Measure	Description
5208.31.2000	1.00	MC	Tejidos, 85%> algodón, <100 gr/m2, certificados como hechos con telares manuales, teñidos
5208.31.2000	1.00	SM	WOVEN FABRIC, 85%> COTTON, <100G/M2 CERTIFIED HANDLOOM FABRIC, DYED
5208.32.1000	1.00	SM	WOVEN FABRIC, 85%> COTTON, 100200G/M2 CERTIFIED HANDLOOM FABRIC, DYED
5208.41.2000	1.00	SM	WOVEN FABRIC, 85% COTTON 100G/M2 CERTIFIED HANDLOOM, YARNS OF DIFFERENT COLORS
5208.42.1000	1.00	SM	WOVEN FABRIC, 85% COTTON 100200G/M2 CERTIFIED HANDLOOM, YARNS OF DIFFERENT COLORS
5208.51.2000	1.00	SM	WOVEN FABRIC, 85%> COTTON 100G/M2 PLAIN WEAVE, CERTIFIED HANDLOOM, PRINTED

(Continued)

U.S. Harmonized System Statistical Provision	Conversion Factor	Primary Unit of Measure	Description
5208.52.1000	1.00	SM	WOVEN FABRIC, 85% COTTON 100200G/M2 PLAIN WEAVE, CERTIFIED HANDLOOM, PRINTED
5209.31.3000	1.00	SM	WOVEN FABRIC, 85%> COTTON >200G/M2 PLAIN WEAVE, CERTIFIED HANDLOOM, DYED
5209.41.3000	1.00	SM	WOVEN FABRIC, 85%> COTTON >200G/M2, PLAIN WEAVE, YARNS OF DIFFERENT COLOR
5209.51.3000	1.00	SM	WOVEN FABRIC, >85% COTTON >200G/M2, PLAIN WEAVE, CERTIFIED HANDLOOM, PRINTED
5307.10.0000	8.50	KG	YARN, JUTE OR OTHER TEXTILE BAST FIBER (EXCLUDING FLAX/HEMP/RAMIE), SINGLE
5307.20.0000	8.50	KG	YARN, JUTE OR OTHER TEXTILE BAST FIBER (EX. FLAX/HEMP/RAMIE), MULTIPLE/CABLE
5308.10.0000	8.50	KG	YARN, COIR
5308.30.0000	8.50	KG	YARN, PAPER
5310.10.0020	1.00	SM	WOVEN FABRIC, JUTE OR OTHER TEXTILE BAST FIBER (EX FLAX/HEMP/RAMIE), 130CM WIDE, UNBLEACHED
5310.10.0040	1.00	SM	WOVEN FABRIC, JUTE OR OTHER TEXTILE BAST FIBER (EX FLAX/HEMP/RAMIE) >130 TO 250 CM WIDE, UNBLEACHED
5310.10.0060	1.00	SM	WOVEN FABRIC, JUTE OR OTHER TEXTILE BAST FIBER (EX FLAX/HEMP/RAMIE), >250 CM WIDE, UNBLEACHED
5310.90.0000	1.00	SM	WOVEN FABRIC, JUTE OR OTHER TEXTILE BAST FIBER (EXCLUDING FLAX/HEMP/RAMIE), NES
5311.00.6000	1.00	SM	WOVEN FABRIC OF PAPER YARN
5402.10.3020	20.10	KG	NYLON HIGH TENACITY YARN, <5 TURNS PER METER, NOT FOR RETAIL SALE
5402.20.3020	20.10	KG	POLYESTER HIGH TENACITY YARN, <5 TURNS PER METER, NOT FOR RETAIL SALE
5402.41.0010	20.10	KG	NYLON MULTIFILAMENT YARN, PARTIALLY ORIENTED, UNTWIST/TWIST <5 TURNS/METER, NOT FOR RETAIL SALE
5402.41.0020	20.10	KG	NYLON MONO/MULTIFILAMENT YARN, UNTWIST/TWIST <5 TURNS/METER, NOT FOR RETAIL SALE, NES
5402.41.0030	20.10	KG	NYLON MONO/MULTIFILAMENT YARN, UNTWIST/ TWIST <5 TURNS/METER, NOT FOR RETAIL SALE
5402.42.0000	20.10	KG	POLYESTER YARN, PARTIALLY ORIENTED, UNTWIST/TWIST 50 TURNS/METER, NOT FOR RETAIL SALE

U.S. Harmonized System Statistical Provision	Conversion Factor	Primary Unit of Measure	Description
5402.43.0020	20.10	KG	POLYESTER YARN, MONOFILAMENT, UNTWIST/ TWIST 5 TURNS/METER, NOT FOR RETAIL SALE
5402.49.0010	20.10	KG	POLYETHYLENE/POLYPROPYL ENE FILAMENT YARN, UNTWIST/TWIST <5 TURNS/METER, NOT FOR RETAIL SALE
5402.49.0050	20.10	KG	SYNTHETIC FILAMENT YARN, UNTWIST/TWIST <5 TURNS/METER, NOT FOR RETAIL SALE, NES
5403.10.3020	20.10	KG	VISCOSE RAYON HIGH TENACITY FILAMENT YARN, UNTWIST/TWIST <5 TURNS/METER, NOT FOR RETAIL SALE
5403.31.0020	20.10	KG	VISCOSE RAYON FILAMENT YARN, SINGLE, UNTWIST/TWIST <5 TURNS/METER, NOT FOR RETAIL SALE
5403.33.0020	20.10	KG	CELLULOSE ACETATE FILAMENT YARN, SINGLE, UNTWIST/TWIST <5 TURNS/METER, NOT FOR RETAIL SALE
5403.39.0020	20.10	KG	ARTIFICIAL FILAMENT YARN, UNTWIST/TWIST <5 TURNS/METER, NOT FOR RETAIL SALE, NES
5404.10.1000	20.10	KG	SYNTHETIC MONOFILAMENT RACKET STRINGS, 67 DECITEX, CROSSSECT. DIMEMSION >1MM
5404.10.2020	20.10	KG	NYLON MONFILAMENT, 67 DECITEX, CROSSSECTIONAL DIMENSION >1MM,
5404.10.2040	20.10	KG	POLYESTER MONFILAMENT, >67 DECITEX, CROSSSECTIONAL DIMENSION >1MM
5404.10.2090	20.10	KG	SYNTHETIC MONFILAMENT 67 DECITEX, CROSSSECTIONAL DIMENSION >1MM, NES
5404.90.0000	20.10	KG	SYNTHETIC STRIP WIDTH 5MM
5405.00.3000	20.10	KG	ARTIFICIAL MONOFILAMENT, 67 DECITEX, CROSSSECTIONAL DIMENSION 1MM
5405.00.6000	20.10	KG	ARTIFICIAL STRIP AND THE LIKE, WIDTH 5MM
5407.30.1000	1.00	SM	WOVEN SYNTHETIC FILAMENT FABRIC WITH YARN AT ACUTE/RIGHT ANGLES, >60% PLASTIC
5501.10.0000	7.60	KG	NYLON/OTHER POLYAMIDE FILAMENT TOW
5501.20.0000	7.60	KG	POLYESTER FILAMENT TOW
5501.30.0000	7.60	KG	ACRYLIC OR MODACRYLIC FILAMENT TOW
5501.90.0000	7.60	KG	SYNTHETIC FILAMENT TOW, NES
5502.00.0000	6.30	KG	ARTIFICIAL FILAMENT TOW
5503.10.0000	7.60	KG	NYLON/OTHER POLAMIDE STAPLE FIBERS NOT CARDED/COMBED OR OTHERWISE PROCESSED
5503.20.0000	7.60	KG	POLYESTER STAPLE FIBERS NOT CARDED/COMBED, OR OTHERWISE PROCESSED

(Continued)

U.S. Harmonized System Statistical Provision	Conversion Factor	Primary Unit of Measure	Description
5503.30.0000	7.60	KG	ACRYLIC/MODOACRYLIC STAPLE FIBERS, NOT CARDED/COMBED OR OTHERWISE PROCESSED
5503.40.0000	7.60	KG	POLYPROPYLENE STAPLE FIBERS NOT CARDED/COMBED OR OTHERWISE PROCESSED
5503.90.0000	7.60	KG	SYNTHETIC STAPLE FIBER NOT CARDED/COMBED, OR OTHERWIDE PROCESSED, NES
5504.10.0000	6.30	KG	VISCOSE RAYON STAPLE FIBERS NOT CARDED/COMBED OR OTHERWISE PROCESSED
5504.90.0000	6.30	KG	ARTIFICIAL STAPLE FIBERS NOT CARDED/COMBED OR OTHERWISE PROCESSED, NES
5505.10.0020	7.60	KG	WASTE, NYLON AND OTHER POLYAMIDES
5505.10.0040	7.60	KG	WASTE, POLYESTER
5505.10.0060	7.60	KG	WASTE, MMF SYNTHETIC FIBERS, NES
5505.20.0000	6.30	KG	WASTE, MMF ARTIFICIAL FIBERS
5506.10.0000	7.60	KG	NYLON/OTHER POLYAMIDES FIBERS, CARDED/COMBED OR OTHERWISE PROCESSED
5506.20.0000	7.60	KG	POLYESTER STAPLE FIBER, CARDED/COMBED, OR OTHERWISE PROCESSED
5506.30.0000	7.60	KG	ACRYLIC/MODOACRYLIC STAPLE FIBER, CARDED/COMBED OR OTHERWISE PROCESSED
5506.90.0000	7.60	KG	SYNTHETIC STAPLE FIBER CARDED/COMBED OR OTHERWISE PROCESSED, NES
5507.00.0000	6.30	KG	ARTIFICIAL STAPLE FIBERS, CARDED/COMBED, OR OTHERWISE PROCESSED
5801.90.2010	1.00	SM	WOVEN PILE FABRIC, >85% SILK OR SILK WASTE
5802.20.0010	1.00	SM	TERRY TOWELING FABRIC, >85% SILK OR SILK WASTE
5802.30.0010	1.00	SM	TUFTED TEXTILE FABRIC, >85% SILK OR SILK WASTE
5803.90.4010	1.00	SM	GAUZE, >85% SILK OR SILK WASTE
5804.10.0010	11.10	KG	TULLES & OTHER NETTING FABRIC, KNIT OR CROCHETED, >85% SILK OR SILK WASTE
5804.29.0010	11.10	KG	LACE IN THE PIECE/STRIP/MOTIF, >85% SILK OR SILK WASTE
5804.30.0010	11.10	KG	HANDMADE LACE IN PIECE/STRIP/MOTIF, >85% SILK OR SILK WASTE
5805.00.1000	1.00	SM	HANDWOVEN TAPESTRIES FOR WALLHANGINGS, VALUED AT >$215\SM
5805.00.2000	1.00	SM	HANDWOVEN TAPESTRIES, NES, WOOL, CERTIFIED HANDLOOMED

U.S. Harmonized System Statistical Provision	Conversion Factor	Primary Unit of Measure	Description
5805.00.4090	1.00	SM	HANDWOVEN TAPESTRIES, NES
5806.10.3010	11.10	KG	NARROW WOVEN PILE & CHENILLE FABRIC, >85% SILK OR SILK WASTE
5806.39.3010	11.10	KG	NARROW WOVEN FABRIC, NOT PILE, >85% SILK OR SILK WASTE
5806.40.0000	13.60	KG	NARROW FABRIC, WARP WITHOUT WEFT WITH AN ADHESIVE (BOLDUCS)
5807.10.1090	11.10	KG	WOVEN LABELS, TEXTILE MATERIALS, NOT EMBROIDERED, NOT COTTON OR MMF
5807.10.2010	8.50	KG	WOVEN BADGES AND SIMILAR ARTICLES, COTTON, NOT EMBROIDERED
5807.10.2020	14.40	KG	WOVEN BADGES/SIMILAR ARTICLES, MMF, NOT EMBROIDERED
5807.10.2090	11.10	KG	WOVEN BADGES/SIMILAR ARTCLES, TEXTILE MATERIALS, NOT EMBROIDERED, NOT COTTON/MMF
5807.90.1090	11.10	KG	NOTWOVEN LABELS OF TEXTILE MATERIALS, NOT EMBROIDERED, NOT COTTON/MMF
5807.90.2010	8.50	KG	NOTWOVEN BADGES/SIMILAR ARTICLES, COTTON, NOT EMBROIDERED
5807.90.2020	14.40	KG	NOTWOVEN BADGES/SIMILAR ARTICLES, MMF, NOT EMBROIDERED
5807.90.2090	11.10	KG	NOTWOVEN BADGES/SIMILAR ARTICLES, TEX MATERIALS, NOT EMBROIDERED, NOT COTTON/MMF
5808.10.2090	11.10	KG	BRAIDS IN PIECE FOR HEADWEAR, OTHER TEXTILE MATERIALS, NES NOT KNIT OR EMBROIDERED
5808.10.3090	11.10	KG	BRAID IN PIECE, NES, NES
5808.90.0090	11.10	KG	ORNAMENTAL TRIMMING IN PIECE, TEXTILE MATERIALS, NOT KNIT OR EMBROIDERED, NOT COTTON/MMF
5810.92.0040	14.40	KG	EMBROIDERED BADGES/EMBLEMS/MOTIFS WITH VISIBLE GROUND, MMF
5810.99.0090	11.10	KG	EMBROIDERY PIECES/STRIPS/MOTIFS WITH VISIBLE GROUND, TEXTILE MATERIALS, NES
5811.00.4000	1.00	SM	QUILTED PIECES, 1 LAYER TEXTILE MATERIALS, TEXTILE MATERIALS, NES
6001.99.0010	1.00	SM	KNIT OR CROCHETED PILE FABRIC 85% SILK OR SILK WASTE
6002.99.0010	11.10	KG	KNIT OR CROCHETED FABRIC, NES 85% SILK OR SILK WASTE

(Continued)

U.S. Harmonized System Statistical Provision	Conversion Factor	Primary Unit of Measure	Description
6301.90.0020	11.10	NO	BLANKET/TRAVELING RUGS, >85% SILK OR SILK WASTE
6302.29.0010	11.10	NO	BED LINEN, PRINTED >85% SILK OR SILK WASTE
6302.39.0020	11.10	NO	BED LINEN, NES, >85% SILK OR SILK WASTE
6302.99.1000	11.10	NO	LINEN, NES, >85% SILK OR SILK WASTE
6303.99.0030	11.10	NO	CURTAINS, INTERIOR BLINDS, NOT KNIT OR CROCHETED, >85% SILK OR SILK WASTE
6304.19.3030	11.10	NO	BEDSPREADS, NOT KNIT OR CROCHETED, >85% SILK OR SILK WASTE
6304.91.0060	11.10	NO	FURNISHING ARTICLES, NES, KNIT OR CROCHETED >85% SILK OR SILK WASTE
6304.99.1000	1.00	SM	WALL HANGINGS, WOOL OR FINE ANIMAL HAIR, CERTIFIED HANDLOOMED/FOLKLORE, NOT KNIT
6304.99.2500	11.10	KG	WALL HANGINGS, JUTE, NOT KNIT
6304.99.4000	3.70	KG	PILLOW COVERS, WOOL OR FINE ANIMAL HAIR, CERTIFIED HANDLOOMED/FOLKLORE
6304.99.6030	11.10	KG	OTHER FURNISHING ARTICLES, NOT KNIT, NES >85% SILK OR SILK WASTE
6305.10.0000	11.10	KG	SACKS & BAGS, JUTE/BAST FIBERS
6306.21.0000	8.50	KG	TENTS OF COTTON
6306.22.1000	14.40	NO	BACKPACK TENTS, SYNTHETIC FIBERS
6306.22.9010	14.40	KG	SCREEN HOUSES, SYNTHETIC FIBERS
6306.29.0000	14.40	KG	TENTS, TEXTILE MATERIALS NES
6306.31.0000	14.40	KG	SAILS, SYNTHETIC FIBERS
6306.39.0000	8.50	KG	SAILS, TEXTILE MATERIALS NES
6306.41.0000	8.50	KG	PNEUMATIC MATTRESSES, COTTON
6306.49.0000	14.40	KG	PNEUMATIC MATTRESSES, TEXTILE MATERIALS NES
6306.91.0000	8.50	KG	CAMPING GOODS NES, COTTON
6306.99.0000	14.40	KG	CAMPING GOODS, TEXTILE MATERIALS NES
6307.10.2030	8.50	KG	CLEANING CLOTHS NES
6307.20.0000	11.40	KG	LIFEJACKETS AND LIFEBELTS
6307.90.6010	8.50	KG	PERINEAL TOWELS, FABRIC WITH PAPER BASE
6307.90.6090	8.50	KG	OTHER SURGICAL DRAPES, FABRIC WITH PAPER BASE
6307.90.7010	14.40	KG	SURGICAL DRAPES, DISPOSAL & NONWOVEN MMF
6307.90.7020	8.50	KG	SURGICAL DRAPES NES
6307.90.7500	8.50	NO	TOYS FOR PETS, TEXTILE MATERIALS
6307.90.8500	8.50	KG	WALL BANNERS, MANMADE FIBERS

U.S. Harmonized System Statistical Provision	Conversion Factor	Primary Unit of Measure	Description
6307.90.9425	14.50	NO	NATIONAL FLAGS OF THE UNITED STATES
6307.90.9435	14.50	NO	NATIONAL FLAGS OF NATIONS OTHER THAN THE UNITED STATES
6307.90.9490	14.50	KG	OTHER MADEUP ARTICLES NES
6309.00.0010	8.50	KG	WORN CLOTHING & OTHER WORN ARTICLES
6309.00.0020	8.50	KG	WORN CLOTHING & OTHER WORN ARTICLES, NES
6310.10.1000	3.70	KG	RAGS/SCRAP/TWINE/CORDAGE/ROPE/CABLES, SORTED, WOOL OR FINE ANIMAL HAIR
6310.10.2010	8.50	KG	RAGS/SCRAP/TWINE/CORDAGE/ROPE/CABLES, SORTED, COTTON
6310.10.2020	14.40	KG	RAGS/SCRAP/TWINE/CORDAGE/ROPE/CABLES, SORTED, MMF
6310.10.2030	11.10	KG	RAGS/SCRAP/TWINE/CORDAGE/ROPE/CABLES, SORTED, NOT COTTON/MMF
6310.90.1000	3.70	KG	RAGS/SCRAP/TWINE/CORDAGE/ROPE/CABLES, NOT SORTED, WOOL OR FINE ANIMAL HAIR
6310.90.2000	8.50	KG	RAGS/SCRAP/TWINE/CORDAGE/ROPE/CABLES, NOT SORTED, NOT WOOL
6501.00.30	4.4	DZ	HAT FORMS/BODIES, NOT BLOCKED, NO BRIMS, FUR, MEN'S AND BOYS'
6501.00.60	4.4	DZ	HAT FORMS/BODIES, NOT BLOCKED, NO BRIMS, FUR, WOMEN'S AND GIRLS'
6502.00.20	18.7	DZ	HAT SHAPES, ASSEMBLED FROM STRIPS, VEGETABLE FIBER, SEWED
6502.00.40	18.7	DZ	HAT SHAPES, PLAITED OR ASSEMBLED FROM STRIPS, VEGETABLE FIBER, NOTSEWED, NOT BLEACHED/COLORED
6502.00.60	18.7	DZ	HAT SHAPES, PLAITED OR ASSEMBLED FROM STRIPS, VEGETABLE FIBER, NOTSEWED, BLEACHED/COLORED
6503.00.30	5.8	DZ	FELT HATS AND OTHER HEADGEAR, MEN'S AND BOYS'
6503.00.60	5.8	DZ	FELT HATS AND OTHER HEADGEAR, NES
6504.00.30	7.5	DZ	HATS AND OTHER HEADGEAR, ASSEMBLED FROM STRIPS, VEGETABLE FIBER, SEWED
6504.00.60	7.5	DZ	HATS AND OTHER HEADGEAR, ASSEMBLED FROM STRIPS
6601.10.00	17.9	DZ	GARDEN OR SIMILAR UMBRELLAS
6601.91.00	17.8	DZ	OTHER UMBRELLAS, TELESCOPIC SHAFT
6601.99.00	11.2	DZ	OTHER UMBRELLAS, NES
8708.21.00	2.72	KG	SAFETY SEAT BELTS

5.

(a) The primary unit of measure for the following tariff items in U.S. category 666 shall be NO and shall be converted into SME by a factor of 5.5:

6301.10.0000	ELECTRIC BLANKETS
6301.40.0010	BLANKETS (NOT ELECTRIC) & TRAVEL RUGS OF SYNTHETIC FIBER, WOVEN
6301.40.0020	BLANKETS (NOT ELECTRIC) & TRAVEL RUGS OF SYNTHETIC FIBER, NES
6301.90.0010	BLANKETS AND TRAVELING RUGS OF ARTIFICIAL FIBER
6302.10.0020	BED LINEN, KNITTED OR CROCHETED FABRIC, EXCLUDING COTTON
6302.22.1030	SHEETS WITH TRIM, NAPPED, PRINTED, MANMADE FIBER
6302.22.1040	SHEETS WITH TRIM, NOT NAPPED, PRINTED, MANMADE FIBER
6302.22.1050	BOLSTER CASES WITH TRIM, PRINTED, MANMADE FIBER
6302.22.1060	BED LINEN WITH TRIM, PRINTED, MANMADE FIBER, NES
6302.22.2020	SHEETS, NOT TRIMMED, PRINTED, MANMADE FIBER
6302.22.2030	BED LINEN, NOT TRIMMED, PRINTED, MANMADE FIBER, NES
6302.32.1030	SHEETS WITH TRIM, NAPPED, MANMADE FIBER
6302.32.1040	SHEETS WITH TRIM, NOT NAPPED, MANMADE FIBER
6302.32.1050	BOLSTER CASES WITH TRIM, MANMADE FIBER
6302.32.1060	BED LINEN WITH TRIM, MANMADE FIBER, NES
6302.32.2030	SHEETS, NOT TRIMMED, NAPPED, MANMADE FIBER
6302.32.2040	SHEETS NOT TRIMMED, NOT NAPPED, MANMADE FIBER
6302.32.2050	BOLSTER CASES, NOT TRIMMED, MANMADE FIBER
6302.32.2060	BED LINEN NES, MANMADE FIBER
6304.11.2000	BEDSPREADS, KNIT/CROCHETED, MANMADE FIBER
6304.19.1500	BEDSPREADS WITH TRIM, MANMADE FIBER, NES
6304.19.2000	BEDSPREADS, MANMADE FIBER, NES

(b) The primary unit of measure for the following tariff items in U.S. category 666 shall be NO and shall be converted into SME by a factor of 0.9:

6302.22.1010	PILLOWCASES WITH TRIM, PRINTED, NAPPED, MANMADE FIBER
6302.22.1020	Fundas para almohadas de fibras sintéticas y artificiales, con adornos, estampadas, no afelpadas
6302.22.1020	PILLOWCASES WITH TRIM, PRINTED, NOT NAPPED, MANMADE FIBER
6302.22.2010	PILLOWCASES, NOT TRIMMED, PRINTED, MANMADE FIBER
6302.32.1010	PILLOWCASES WITH TRIM, NAPPED, MANMADE FIBER
6302.32.1020	PILLOWCASES WITH TRIM, NOT NAPPED, MANMADE FIBER
6302.32.2010	PILLOWCASES, NOT TRIMMED, NAPPED, MANMADE FIBER
6302.32.2020	PILLOWCASES NOT TRIMMED, NOT NAPPED, MANMADE FIBER

6. The primary unit of measure for garment parts of subheadings 6117.90 and 6217.90 shall be KG and shall be converted into SME by applying the following factors:

Cotton apparel	8.50
Wool apparel	3.70
Manmade fiber apparel	14.40
Other noncotton vegetable fiber apparel	12.50

7. For the purposes of this Schedule:
   DPR means dozen pair;
   DZ means dozen;
   KG means kilogram;
   NO means number; and
   SM means square meter.

APPENDIX 5.1. BILATERAL EMERGENCY ACTIONS (QUANTITATIVE RESTRICTIONS)

As between Canada and the United States, actions otherwise permitted under Section 5 shall be governed by Article 407 of the Canada United States Free Trade Agreement, which is hereby incorporated into and made a part of this Agreement solely for that purpose.

APPENDIX 6. SPECIAL PROVISIONS

A. Rules Applicable to Certain Carpets and Sweaters

For purposes of trade between Mexico and the United States, a good of either Party of HS Chapter 57, subheading 6110.30, 6103.23 or 6104.23 shall be treated as if it were an originating good only if any of the following changes in tariff classification is satisfied within the territory of one or more of the Parties:

(a) a change to subheading 5703.20 or 5703.30 or heading 57.04 from any heading outside Chapter 57 other than headings 51.06 through 51.13, 52.04 through 52.12, 53.08, 53.11 or any headings of Chapter 54 or 55; or a change to any other heading or subheading of Chapter 57 from any heading outside that chapter other than headings 51.06 through 51.13, 52.04 through 52.12, 53.08, 53.11, any heading of Chapter 54 or 55.08 through 55.16; and

(b) a change to U.S. tariff item 6110.30.10.10, 6110.30.10.20, 6110.30.15.10, 6110.30.15.20, 6110.30.20.10, 6110.30.20.20, 6110.30.30.10, 6110.30.30.15, 6110.30.30.20, or 6110.30.30.25 or Mexican tariff item 6110.30.01, or a good of those tariff items that is classified as part of an ensemble in subheading 6103.23 or 6104.23, from any heading outside Chapter 61 other than headings 51.06 through 51.13, 52.04 through 52.12, 53.07 through 53.08, 53.10 through 53.11, any heading of Chapter 54 or 55, 60.01 or 60.02, provided that the good is both cut (or knit to shape) and sewn or otherwise assembled in the territory of one or more of the Parties;

or a change to any other tariff item of subheading 6110.30 from any heading outside Chapter 61 other than headings 51.06 through 51.13, 52.04 through 52.12, 53.07 through 53.08, 53.10 through 53.11, any heading of Chapter 54, 55.08 through 55.16, 60.01 or 60.02, provided, that the good is both cut (or knit to shape) and sewn or otherwise assembled in the territory of one or more of the Parties.

B. Preferential Tariff Treatment for NonOriginating Goods of another Party

Apparel and MadeUp Goods

1.
 (a) Each Party shall apply the rate of duty applicable to originating goods set out in its Schedule to Annex 302.2, and in accordance with Appendix 2.1, up to the annual quantities specified in Schedule 6.B.1, in SME, to apparel goods provided for in Chapters 61 and 62 that are both cut (or knit to shape) and sewn or otherwise assembled in the territory of a Party from fabric or yarn produced or obtained outside the free trade area, and that meet other applicable conditions for preferred tariff treatment under this Agreement. The SME shall be determined in accordance with the conversion factors set out in Schedule 3.1.3.
 (b) The annual tariff preference levels (TPLs) of imports from Canada into the United States shall be adjusted annually for five consecutive years commencing on January 1, 1995, by the following growth factors:
    (i)   for cotton or manmade fiber apparel, 2 percent,
    (ii) for cotton or manmade fiber apparel made from fabrics woven or knit in a nonParty, 1 percent, and
    (iii) for wool apparel, 1 percent.
2. The United States shall apply the rate of duty applicable to originating goods set out in its Schedule to Annex 302.2, and in accordance with Appendix 2.1, up to the annual quantity specified in Schedule 6.B.1, to textile or apparel goods provided for in Chapters 61, 62 and 63 that are sewn or otherwise assembled in Mexico as provided for in U.S. tariff item 9802.00.80.60 from fabric which is knit or woven outside the territory of the United States or Mexico, when exported to the United States. This paragraph shall not apply after quantitative restrictions established pursuant to the Multifiber Arrangement or any successor agreement are terminated.

Exceptions

3. As between Mexico and the United States:
 (a) apparel goods provided for in Chapters 61 and 62 of the HS, in which the fabric that determines the tariff classification of the good is classified in one of the following tariff provisions, are ineligible for preferential tariff treatment provided for under the levels established in Schedule 6.B.1

(i) blue denim: subheadings 5209.42 and 5211.42, U.S. tariff items 5212.24.60.20, and 5514.32.00.10 or Mexican tariff items 5212.24.xx and 5514.32.xx; and

(ii) fabric woven as plain weave where two or more warp ends are woven as one (oxford cloth) of average yarn number less than 135 metric number: 5208.19, 5208.29, 5208.39, 5208.49, 5208.59, 5210.19, 5210.29, 5210.39, 5210.49, 5210.59, 5512.11, 5512.19, 5513.13, 5513.23, 5513.33, and 5513.43;

(b) apparel goods provided for in U.S. tariff items 6107.11.00, 6107.12.00, 6109.10.00 and 6109.90.00 or Mexican tariff items 6107.11.01, 6107.12.01, 6109.10.01 and 6109.90.01 are ineligible for preferential tariff treatment provided for under the levels established in Schedule 6.B.1 if they are composed chiefly of circular knit fabric of yarn number equal to or less than 100 metric number. Apparel goods provided for in subheadings 6108.21 and 6108.22 are ineligible for preferential tariff treatment provided for under the levels established in parts 2(a), 2(b), 3(a) and 3(b) in Schedule 6.B.1 if they are composed chiefly of circular knit fabric of yarn number equal to or less than 100 metric number; and

(c) apparel goods provided for in U.S. tariff items 6110.30.10.10, 6110.30.10.20, 6110.30.15.10, 6110.30.15.20, 6110.30.20.10, 6110.30.20.20, 6110.30.30.10, 6110.30.30.15, 6110.30.30.20, 6110.30.30.25 and items of those tariff items that are classified as parts of ensembles in U.S. tariff items 6103.23.00.30, 6103.23.00.70, 6104.23.00.22 and 6104.23.00.40 or Mexican tariff item 6110.30.01or goods of that tariff item that are classified as parts of ensembles in subheading 6103.23 or 6104.23 are ineligible for preferential tariff treatment provided for under the levels established in Schedule 6.B.1.

Fabric and Made Up Goods

4.

(a) Each Party shall apply the rate of duty applicable to originating goods set out in its Schedule to Annex 302.2, and in accordance with Appendix 2.1, up to the annual quantities specified in Schedule 6.B.2, in SME, to cotton or manmade fiber fabric and cotton or manmade fiber madeup textile goods provided for in Chapters 52 through 55, 58, 60, and 63 that are woven or knit in a Party from yarn produced or obtained outside the free trade area, or knit in a Party from yarn spun in a Party from fiber produced or obtained outside the free trade area, and to goods of subheading 9404.90 that are finished and cut and sewn or otherwise assembled from fabrics of subheadings 5208.11 through 5208.29, 5209.11 through 5209.29, 5210.11 through 5210.29, 5211.11 through 5211.29, 5212.11, 5212.12, 5212.21, 5212.22, 5407.41, 5407.51, 5407.71, 5407.81, 5407.91, 5408.21, 5408.31, 5512.11, 5512.21, 5512.91, 5513.11 through 5513.19, 5514.11 through 5514.19, 5516.11, 5516.21, 5516.31, 5516.41, 5516.91 produced or obtained outside the free trade area, and that meet other applicable conditions for preferred tariff treatment under this Agreement. The SME shall be determined in accordance with the conversion factors set out in Schedule 3.1.3.

(b) The annual TPL and sublevels on imports from Canada into the United States shall be adjusted by an annual growth factor of two percent for five consecutive years commencing on January 1, 1995.

5. For purposes of paragraph 4, the number of SME that will be counted against the TPLs applied as between Canada and the United States shall be:

(a) for textile goods that are not originating because certain nonoriginating textile materials do not undergo the applicable change in tariff classification set out in Annex 401 for that good, but where such materials are 50 percent or less by weight of the materials of that good, only 50 percent of the SME for that good, determined in accordance with the conversion factors set out in Schedule 3.1.3; and

(b) for textile goods that are not originating because certain nonoriginating textile materials do not undergo the applicable change in tariff classification set out in Annex 401 for that good, but where such materials are more than 50 percent by weight of the materials of that good, 100 percent of the SME for that good, determined in accordance with the conversion factors set out in Schedule 3.1.3.

Spun Yarn

6.

(a) Each Party shall apply the rate of duty applicable to originating goods set out in its Schedule to Annex 302.2, and in accordance with Appendix 2.1, up to the annual quantities specified in Schedule 6.B.3, in kilograms (kg), to cotton or manmade fiber yarns provided for in headings 52.05 through 52.07 or 55.09 through 55.11 that are spun in a Party from fiber of headings 52.01 through 52.03 or 55.01 through 55.07, produced or obtained outside the free trade area and that meet other applicable conditions for preferred tariff treatment under this Agreement.

(b) The annual TPL on imports from Canada into the United States shall be adjusted by an annual growth factor of two percent for five consecutive years commencing on January 1, 1995.

7. Textile or apparel goods that enter the territory of a Party under paragraph 1, 2, 4 or 6 shall not be considered to be originating goods.

Review and Consultations

8.

(a) Trade in the goods referred to in paragraphs 1, 2, 4 and 6 shall be monitored by the Parties. On request of any Party wishing to adjust any annual TPL for imports into Canada from Mexico or the United States, imports into Mexico from Canada or the United States, or imports into the United States from Mexico, based on the ability to obtain supplies of particular fibers, yarns and fabrics, as appropriate, that can be used to produce originating goods, the Parties shall consult with a view to adjusting such level. Any adjustment in the TPL requires the mutual consent of the Parties concerned.

(b) Canada and the United States shall decide, in the review referred to in Section 7(3), whether to continue to apply annual growth factors to the specified TPLs after the five consecutive years. If a growth factor for a TPL is not continued as a result of the review, subparagraph (a) shall also apply to imports from Canada into the United States of goods covered by the TPL.

SCHEDULE 6.B.1. PREFERENTIAL TARIFF TREATMENT FOR NON-ORIGINATING APPAREL AND MADE-UP GOODS

1. Imports into Canada : (a) Cotton or Manmade fiber apparel (b) Wool apparel	**from Mexico** 6,000,000 SME 250,000 SME	**from United States** 9,000,000 SME 919,740 SME
2. Imports into Mexico : (a) Cotton or Manmade fiber apparel (b) Wool apparel	**from Canada** 6,000,000 SME 250,000 SME	**from United States** 12,000,000 SME 1,000,000 SME
3. Imports into United States : (a) Cotton or Manmade fiber apparel (b) Wool apparel (c) Goods imported under U.S. tariff item 9802.00.80.60	**from Canada** 80,000,000 SME [1] 5,066,948 SME [2] n/a	**from Mexico** 45,000,000 SME 1,500,000 SME 25,000,000 SME
1. Imports into Canada :	**from Mexico** 7,000,000 SME	**from United States** 2,000,000 SME [1]
2. Imports into Mexico:	**from Canada** 7,000,000 SME	**from United States** 2,000,000 SME
3. Imports into United States :	**from Canada** 65,000,000 SME [2]	**from Mexico** 24,000,000 SME [3]

[1] Of the 80,000,000 SME annual quantity of cotton or manmade fiber apparel imports from Canada into the United States, no more than 60,000,000 SME shall be made from fabrics which are knit or woven in a nonParty.

[2] Of the 5,066,948 SME annual quantity of wool apparel imports from Canada into the United States, no more than 5,016,780 SME shall be men's or boys' wool suits of U.S. category 443.

SCHEDULE 6.B.2. PREFERENTIAL TARIFF TREATMENT FOR NON-ORIGINATING COTTON OR MAN-MADE FIBER FABRICS AND MADE-UP GOODS

1. The 2,000,000 SME annual quantity of imports from the United States into Canada shall be limited to goods of chapter 60 of the HS.

2. Of the 65,000,000 SME annual quantity of imports from Canada into the United States, no more than 35,000,000 SME may be in goods of chapters 52 through 55, 58 and 63 (other than subheading 6302.10, 6302.40, 6303.11, 6303.12, 6303.19, 6304.11or 6304.91) of the HS; and no more than 35,000,000 SME may be in goods of chapter 60 and subheading 6302.10, 6302.40, 6303.11, 6303.12, 6303.19, 6304.11 or 6304.91 of the HS.

3. Of the 24,000,000 SME annual quantity of imports from Mexico into the United States, no more than 18,000,000 SME may be in goods of chapter 60 and subheading 6302.10, 6302.40, 6303.11, 6303.12, 6303.19, 6304.11 or 6304.91 of the HS; and no more than 6,000,000 SME may be in goods of chapters 52 through 55, 58 and 63 (other than subheading 6302.10, 6302.40, 6303.11, 6303.12, 6303.19, 6304.11 or 6304.91) of the HS.

SCHEDULE 6.B.3. PREFERENTIAL TARIFF TREATMENT FOR NON-ORIGINATING COTTON OR MAN-MADE FIBER SPUN YARN

1. Imports into Canada :	from Mexico 1,000,000 kg	from United States 1,000,000 kg
2. Imports into Mexico :	from Canada 1,000,000 kg	from United States 1,000,000 kg
3. Imports into United States:	from Canada 10,700,000 kg	from Mexico 1,000,000 kg

APPENDIX 10.1. COUNTRY-SPECIFIC DEFINITIONS

Definitions Specific to Canada

general import statistics means statistics issued by Statistics Canada or, where available, import permit data provided by the Export and Import Permits Bureau of the Department of External Affairs and International Trade, or their successors.

Definitions Specific to Mexico

general import statistics means the statistics of the "Sistema de Informacion Comercial" (Trade Information System) or its successor.

Definitions Specific to the United States

category means a grouping of textile or apparel goods defined in the Correlation: Textile and Apparel Categories with the Harmonized Tariff Schedule of the United States, 1992 (or successor publication), published by the United States Department of Commerce, International Trade Administration, Office of Textiles and Apparel, Trade and Data Division, Washington, D.C.; and general import statistics means statistics of the U.S. Bureau of the Census or its successor.

4. RULES OF ORIGIN

Article 401: Originating Goods

Except as otherwise provided in this Chapter, a good shall originate in the territory of a Party where:

a) the good is wholly obtained or produced entirely in the territory of one or more of the Parties, as defined in Article 415;

b) each of the non-originating materials used in the production of the good undergoes an applicable change in tariff classification set out in Annex 401 as a result of production occurring entirely in the territory of one or more of the Parties, or the good otherwise satisfies the applicable requirements of that Annex where no change in tariff classification is required, and the good satisfies all other applicable requirements of this Chapter;

c) the good is produced entirely in the territory of one or more of the Parties exclusively from originating materials; or

d) except for a good provided for in Chapters 61 through 63 of the Harmonized System, the good is produced entirely in the territory of one or more of the Parties but one or more of the non-originating materials provided for as parts under the Harmonized System that are used in the production of the good does not undergo a change in tariff classification because

   (i) the good was imported into the territory of a Party in an unassembled or a disassembled form but was classified as an assembled good pursuant to General Rule of Interpretation 2(a) of the Harmonized System, or

   (ii) the heading for the good provides for and specifically describes both the good itself and its parts and is not further subdivided into subheadings, or the subheading for the good provides for and specifically describes both the good itself and its parts,

provided that the regional value content of the good, determined in accordance with Article 402, is not less than 60 percent where the transaction value method is used, or is not less than 50 percent where the net cost method is used, and that the good satisfies all other applicable requirements of this Chapter.

Article 402: Regional Value Content

1. Except as provided in paragraph 5, each Party shall provide that the regional value content of a good shall be calculated, at the choice of the exporter or producer of the good, on the basis of either the transaction value method set out in paragraph 2 or the net cost method set out in paragraph 3.

2. Each Party shall provide that an exporter or producer may calculate the regional value content of a good on the basis of the following transaction value method:

$$RVC = \frac{TV - VNM}{TV} \times 100$$

where

RVC	is the regional value content, expressed as a percentage;
TV	is the transaction value of the good adjusted to a F.O.B. basis; and
VNM	is the value of non-originating materials used by the producer in the production of the good.

3. Each Party shall provide that an exporter or producer may calculate the regional value content of a good on the basis of the following net cost method:

$$RVC = \frac{NC - VNM}{NC} \times 100$$

where

RVC	is the regional value content, expressed as a percentage;
NC	is the net cost of the good; and
VNM	is the value of non-originating materials used by the producer in the production of the good.

4. Except as provided in Article 403(1) and for a motor vehicle identified in Article 403(2) or a component identified in Annex 403.2, the value of non-originating materials used by the producer in the production of a good shall not, for purposes of calculating the regional value content of the good under paragraph 2 or 3, include the value of nonoriginating materials used to produce originating materials that are subsequently used in the production of the good.

5. Each Party shall provide that an exporter or producer shall calculate the regional value content of a good solely on the basis of the net cost method set out in paragraph 3 where:

    a) there is no transaction value for the good;

    b) the transaction value of the good is unacceptable under Article 1 of the Customs Valuation Code;

    c) the good is sold by the producer to a related person and the volume, by units of quantity, of sales of identical or similar goods to related persons during the six-month period immediately preceding the month in which the good is sold exceeds 85 percent of the producer's total sales of such goods during that period;

    d) the good is

        (i)   a motor vehicle provided for in heading 87.01 or 87.02, subheading 8703.21 through 8703.90, or heading 87.04, 87.05 or 87.06,

        (ii) identified in Annex 403.1 or 403.2 and is for use in a motor vehicle provided for in heading 87.01 or 87.02, subheading 8703.21 through 8703.90, or heading 87.04, 87.05 or 87.06,

        (iii) provided for in subheading 6401.10 through 6406.10, or

        (iv) provided for in tariff item 8469.10.aa (word processing machines);

e) the exporter or producer chooses to accumulate the regional value content of the good in accordance with Article 404; or

f) the good is designated as an intermediate material under paragraph 10 and is subject to a regional value-content requirement.

6. If an exporter or producer of a good calculates the regional value-content of the good on the basis of the transaction value method set out in paragraph 2 and a Party subsequently notifies the exporter or producer, during the course of a verification pursuant to Chapter Five (Customs Procedures), that the transaction value of the good, or the value of any material used in the production of the good, is required to be adjusted or is unacceptable under Article 1 of the Customs Valuation Code, the exporter or producer may then also calculate the regional value content of the good on the basis of the net cost method set out in paragraph 3.

7. Nothing in paragraph 6 shall be construed to prevent any review or appeal available under Article 510 (Review and Appeal) of an adjustment to or a rejection of:

a) the transaction value of a good; or

b) the value of any material used in the production of a good.

8. For purposes of calculating the net cost of a good under paragraph 3, the producer of the good may:

a) calculate the total cost incurred with respect to all goods produced by that producer, subtract any sales promotion, marketing and aftersales service costs, royalties, shipping and packing costs, and non-allowable interest costs that are included in the total cost of all such goods, and then reasonably allocate the resulting net cost of those goods to the good,

b) calculate the total cost incurred with respect to all goods produced by that producer, reasonably allocate the total cost to the good, and then subtract any sales promotion, marketing and aftersales service costs, royalties, shipping and packing costs and non allowable interest costs that are included in the portion of the total cost allocated to the good, or

c) reasonably allocate each cost that forms part of the total cost incurred with respect to the good so that the aggregate of these costs does not include any sales promotion, marketing and aftersales service costs, royalties, shipping and packing costs, and non-allowable interest costs,

provided that the allocation of all such costs is consistent with the provisions regarding the reasonable allocation of costs set out in the Uniform Regulations, established under Article 511 (Customs Procedures Uniform Regulations).

9. Except as provided in paragraph 11, the value of a material used in the production of a good shall:

a) be the transaction value of the material determined in accordance with Article 1 of the Customs Valuation Code; or

b) in the event that there is no transaction value or the transaction value of the material is unacceptable under Article 1 of the Customs Valuation Code, be determined in accordance with Articles 2 through 7 of the Customs Valuation Code; and

c) where not included under subparagraph (a) or (b), include

(i) freight, insurance, packing and all other costs incurred in transporting the material to the location of the producer,

(ii) duties, taxes and customs brokerage fees on the material paid in the territory of one or more of the Parties, and

(iii) the cost of waste and spoilage resulting from the use of the material in the production of the good, less the value of renewable scrap or byproduct.

10. Except as provided in Article 403(1), any self-produced material, other than a componenet identified in Annex 403.2, that is used in the production of a good may be designated by the producer of the good as an intermediate material for the purpose of calculating the regional value content of the good under paragraph 2 or 3, provided that where the intermediate material is subject to a regional value-content requirement used in the production of that intermediate material may itself be designated by the producer as an intermediate material.

11. The value of an intermediate material shall be:

a) the total cost incurred with respect to all goods produced by the producer of the good that can be reasonably allocated to that intermediate material; or

b) the aggregate of each cost that forms part of the total cost incurred with respect to that intermediate material that can be reasonably allocated to that intermediate material.

12. The value of an indirect material shall be based on the Generally Accepted Accounting Principles applicable in the territory of the Party in which the good is produced.

Article 403: Automotive Goods

1. For purposes of calculating the regional value content under the net cost method set out in Article 402(3) for:

a) a good that is a motor vehicle provided for in tariff item 8702.10.bb or 8702.90.bb (vehicles for the transport of 15 or fewer persons), or subheading 8703.21 through 8703.90, 8704.21 or 8704.31, or

b) a good provided for in the tariff provisions listed in Annex 403.1 where the good is subject to a regional value-content requirement and is for use as original equipment in the production of a good provided for in tariff item 8702.10.bb or 8702.90.bb (vehicles for the transport of 15 or fewer persons), or subheading 8702.xx, 8703.21 through 8703.90, 8704.21 or 8704.31,

the value of non-originating materials used by the producer in the production of the good shall be the sum of the values of non-originating materials, determined in accordance with Article 402(9) at the time the non-originating materials are received by the first person in the territory of a Party who takes title to them, that are imported from outside the territories of the Parties under the tariff provisions listed in Annex 403.1 and that are used in the production of the good or that are used in the production of any material used in the production of the good.

2. For purposes of calculating the regional value content under the net cost method set out in Article 402(3) for a good that is a motor vehicle provided for in heading 87.01, tariff item 8702.10.aa or 8702.90.aa (vehicles for the transport of 16 or more persons), subheading 8704.10, 8704.22, 8704.23, 8704.32 or 8704.90, or heading

87.05 or 87.06, or for a component identified in Annex 403.2 for use as original equipment in the production of the motor vehicle, the value of non-originating materials used by the producer in the production of the good shall be the sum of:

a) for each material used by the producer listed in Annex 403.2, whether or not produced by the producer, at the choice of the producer and determined in accordance with Article 402, either

   (i)   the value of such material that is non originating, or

   (ii) the value of non-originating materials used in the production of such material; and

b) the value of any other non-originating material used by the producer that is not listed in Annex 403.2, determined in accordance with Article 402.

3. For purposes of calculating the regional value content of a motor vehicle identified in paragraph 1 or 2, the producer may average its calculation over its fiscal year, using any one of the following categories, on the basis of either all motor vehicles in the category or only those motor vehicles in the category that are exported to the territory of one or more of the other Parties:

   a)   the same model line of motor vehicles in the same class of vehicles produced in the same plant in the territory of a Party;

   b)   the same class of motor vehicles produced in the same plant in the territory of a Party;

   c)   the same model line of motor vehicles produced in the territory of a Party; or

   d)   if applicable, the basis set out in Annex 403.3.

4. For purposes of calculating the regional value content for any or all goods provided for in a tariff provision listed in Annex 403.1, or a component or material identified in Annex 403.2, produced in the same plant, the producer of the good may:

   a)   average its calculation
      (i) over the fiscal year of the motor vehicle producer to whom the good is sold,
      (ii) over any quarter or month, or
      (iii) over its fiscal year, if the good is sold as an aftermarket part;

   b)   calculate the average referred to in subparagraph (a) separately for any or all goods sold to one or more motor vehicle producers; or

   c)   with respect to any calculation under this paragraph, calculate separately those goods that are exported to the territory of one or more of the Parties.

5. Notwithstanding Annex 401, and except as provided in paragraph 6, the regional value-content requirement shall be:

   a)   for a producer's fiscal year beginning on the day closest to January 1, 1998 and thereafter, 56 percent under the net cost method, and for a producer's fiscal year beginning on the day closest to January 1, 2002 and thereafter, 62.5 percent under the net cost method, for

      (i)   a good that is a motor vehicle provided for in tariff item 8702.10.bb or 8702.90.bb (vehicles for the transport of 15 or fewer persons), or subheading 8703.21 through 8703.90, 8704.21 or 8704.31, and

      (ii) a good provided for in heading 84.07 or 84.08, or subheading 8708.40, that is for use in a motor vehicle identified in subparagraph (a)(i); and

   b)   for a producer's fiscal year beginning on the day closest to January 1, 1998 and thereafter, 55 percent under the net cost method, and for a producer's fiscal year beginning on the day closest to January 1, 2002 and thereafter, 60 percent under the net cost method, for

(i) a good that is a motor vehicle provided for in heading 87.01, tariff item 8702.10.aa or 8702.90.aa (vehicles for the transport of 16 or more persons), 8704.10, 8704.22, 8704.23, 8704.32 or 8704.90, or heading 87.05 or 87.06,

(ii) a good provided for in heading 84.07 or 84.08 or subheading 8708.40 that is for use in a motor vehicle identified in subparagraph (b)(i), and

(iii) except for a good identified in subparagraph (a)(ii) or provided for in subheading 8482.10 through 8482.80, 8483.20 or 8483.30, a good identified in Annex 403.1 that is subject to a regional value content requirement and that is for use in a motor vehicle identified in subparagraphs (a)(i) or (b)(i).

6. The regional value-content requirement for a motor vehicle identified in Article 403(1) or 403(2) shall be:

a) 50 percent for five years after the date on which the first motor vehicle prototype is produced in a plant by a motor vehicle assembler, if

(i) it is a motor vehicle of a class, or marque, or, except for a motor vehicle identified in Article 403(2), size category and underbody, not previously produced by the motor vehicle assembler in the territory of any of the Parties,

(ii) the plant consists of a new building in which the motor vehicle is assembled, and

(iii) the plant contains substantially all new machinery that is used in the assembly of the motor vehicle; or

b) 50 percent for two years after the date on which the first motor vehicle prototype is produced at a plant following a refit, if it is a different motor vehicle of a class, or marque, or, except for a motor vehicle identified in Article 403(2), size category and underbody, than was assembled by the motor vehicle assembler in the plant before the refit.

Article 404: Accumulation

1. For purposes of determining whether a good is an originating good, the production of the good in the territory of one or more of the Parties by one or more producers shall, at the choice of the exporter or producer of the good for which preferential tariff treatment is claimed, be considered to have been performed in the territory of any of the Parties by that exporter or producer, provided that:

a) all non-originating materials used in the production of the good undergo an applicable tariff classification change set out in Annex 401, and the good satisfies any applicable regional value-content requirement, entirely in the territory of one or more of the Parties; and

b) the good satisfies all other applicable requirements of this Chapter.

2. For purposes of Article 402(10), the production of a producer that chooses to accumulate its production with that of other producers under paragraph 1 shall be considered to be the production of a single producer.

Article 405: De Minimis

1. Except as provided in paragraphs 3 through 6, a good shall be considered to be an originating good if the value of all non-originating materials used in the production of the good that do not undergo an applicable change in tariff classification set out in Annex 401 is not more than seven percent of the transaction value of the good, adjusted to a F.O.B. basis, or, if the transaction value of the good is unacceptable under Article 1 of the Customs Valuation Code, the value of all such non-originating materials is not more than seven percent of the total cost of the good, provided that:

    a)   if the good is subject to a regional value-content requirement, the value of such non-originating materials shall be taken into account in calculating the regional value content of the good; and

    b)   the good satisfies all other applicable requirements of this Chapter.

2. A good that is otherwise subject to a regional value-content requirement shall not be required to satisfy such requirement if the value of all non-originating materials used in the production of the good is not more than seven percent of the transaction value of the good, adjusted to a F.O.B. basis, or, if the transaction value of the good is unacceptable under Article 1 of the Customs Valuation Code, the value of all non-originating materials is not more than seven percent of the total cost of the good, provided that the good satisfies all other applicable requirements of this Chapter.

3. Paragraph 1 does not apply to:

    a)   a non-originating material provided for in Chapter 4 of the Harmonized System or tariff item 1901.90.aa (dairy preparations containing over 10 percent by weight of milk solids) that is used in the production of a good provided for in Chapter 4 of the Harmonized System;

    b)   a non-originating material provided for in Chapter 4 of the Harmonized System or tariff item 1901.90.aa (dairy preparations containing over 10 percent by weight of milk solids) that is used in the production of a good provided for in tariff item 1901.10.aa (infant preparations containing over 10 percent by weight of milk solids), 1901.20.aa (mixes and doughs, containing over 25 percent by weight of butterfat, not put up for retail sale), 1901.90.aa (dairy preparations containing over 10 percent by weight of milk solids), heading 21.05, or tariff item 2106.90.dd (preparations containing over 10 percent by weight of milk solids), 2202.90.cc (beverages containing milk) or 2309.90.aa (animal feeds containing over 10 percent by weight of milk solids);

    c)   a non-originating material provided for in heading 08.05 or subheading 2009.11 through 2009.30 that is used in the production of a good provided for in subheading 2009.11 through 2009.30 or tariff item 2106.90.bb (concentrated fruit or vegetable juice of any single fruit or vegetable, fortified with minerals or vitamins) or 2202.90.aa (fruit or vegetable juice of any single fruit or vegetable, fortified with minerals or vitamins);

    d)   a non-originating material provided for in Chapter 9 of the Harmonized System that is used in the production of a good provided for in tariff item 2101.10.aa (instant coffee, not flavored);

e) a non-originating material provided for in Chapter 15 of the Harmonized System that is used in the production of a good provided for in heading 15.01 through 15.08, 15.12, 15.14 or 15.15;

f) a non-originating material provided for in heading 17.01 that is used in the production of a good provided for in heading 17.01 through 17.03;

g) a non-originating material provided for in Chapter 17 of the Harmonized System or heading 18.05 that is used in the production of a good provided for in subheading 1806.10;

h) a non-originating material provided for in heading 22.03 through 22.08 that is used in the production of a good provided for in heading 22.07 through 22.08;

(i) a non-originating material used in the production of a good provided for in tariff item 7321.11.aa (gas stove or range), subheading 8415.10, 8415.81 through 8415.83, 8418.10 through 8418.21, 8418.29 through 8418.40, 8421.12, 8422.11, 8450.11 through 8450.20 or 8451.21 through 8451.29, Mexican tariff item 8479.82.aa (trash compactors) or Canadian or U.S. tariff item 8479.89.aa (trash compactors), or tariff item 8516.60.aa (electric stove or range); and

(j) a printed circuit assembly that is a non-originating material used in the production of a good where the applicable change in tariff classification for the good, as set out in Annex 401, places restrictions on the use of such non-originating material.

4. Paragraph 1 does not apply to a non-originating single juice ingredient provided for in heading 20.09 that is used in the production of a good provided for in subheading 2009.90, or tariff item 2106.90.cc (concentrated mixtures of fruit or vegetable juice, fortified with minerals or vitamins) or 2202.90.bb (mixtures of fruit or vegetable juices, fortified with minerals or vitamins).

5. Paragraph 1 does not apply to a non-originating material used in the production of a good provided for in Chapter 1 through 27 of the Harmonized System unless the non-originating material is provided for in a different subheading than the good for which origin is being determined under this Article.

6. A good provided for in Chapter 50 through 63 of the Harmonized System that does not originate because certain fibers or yarns used in the production of the component of the good that determines the tariff classification of the good do not undergo an applicable change in tariff classification set out in Annex 401, shall nonetheless be considered to originate if the total weight of all such fibers or yarns in that component is not more than seven percent of the total weight of that component.

Article 406: Fungible Goods and Materials

For purposes of determining whether a good is an originating good:

a) where originating and non-originating fungible materials are used in the production of a good, the determination of whether the materials are originating need not be made through the identification of any specific fungible material, but may be determined on the basis of any of the inventory management methods set out in the Uniform Regulations; and

b) where originating and non-originating fungible goods are commingled and exported in the same form, the determination may be made on the basis of any of the inventory management methods set out in the Uniform Regulations.

Article 407: Accessories, Spare Parts and Tools

Accessories, spare parts or tools delivered with the good that form part of the good's standard accessories, spare parts, or tools, shall be considered as originating if the good originates and shall be disregarded in determining whether all the nonoriginating materials used in the production of the good undergo the applicable change in tariff classification set out in Annex 401, provided that:

a) the accessories, spare parts or tools are not invoiced separately from the good;

b) the quantities and value of the accessories, spare parts or tools are customary for the good; and

c) if the good is subject to a regional value-content requirement, the value of the accessories, spare parts or tools shall be taken into account as originating or non-originating materials, as the case may be, in calculating the regional value content of the good.

Article 408: Indirect Materials

An indirect material shall be considered to be an originating material without regard to where it is produced.

Article 409: Packaging Materials and Containers for Retail Sale

Packaging materials and containers in which a good is packaged for retail sale shall, if classified with the good, be disregarded in determining whether all the nonoriginating materials used in the production of the good undergo the applicable change in tariff classification set out in Annex 401, and, if the good is subject to a regional valuecontent requirement, the value of such packaging materials and containers shall be taken into account as originating or non originating materials, as the case may be, in calculating the regional value content of the good.

Article 410: Packing Materials and Containers for Shipment

Packing materials and containers in which the good is packed for shipment shall be disregarded in determining whether:

a)   the nonoriginating materials used in the production of the good undergo an applicable change in tariff classification set out in Annex 401; and

b)   the good satisfies a regional valuecontent requirement.

Article 411: Trans-shipment

A good shall not be considered to be an originating good by reason of having undergone production that satisfies the requirements of Article 401 if, subsequent to that production, the good undergoes further production or any other operation outside the territories of the Parties, other than unloading, reloading or any other operation necessary to preserve it in good condition or to transport the good to the territory of a Party.

Article 412: NonQualifying Operations

A good shall not be considered to be an originating good merely by reason of:

a)   mere dilution with water or another substance that does not materially alter the characteristics of the good; or

(b)   any production or pricing practice in respect of which it may be demonstrated, on the basis of a preponderance of evidence, that the object was to circumvent this Chapter.

Article 413: Interpretation and Application

For purposes of this Chapter:

a)   the basis for tariff classification in this Chapter is the Harmonized System;

b)   where a good referred to by a tariff item number is described in parentheses following the tariff item number, the description is provided for purposes of reference only;

c)   where applying Article 401(d), the determination of whether a heading or subheading under the Harmonized System provides for and specifically describes both a good and its parts shall be made on the basis of the nomenclature of the heading or subheading, or the General Rules of Interpretation, the Chapter Notes or the Section Notes of the Harmonized System;

d)   in applying the Customs Valuation Code under this Chapter,

(i)   the principles of the Customs Valuation Code shall apply to domestic transactions, with such modifications as may be required by the circumstances, as would apply to international transactions,

(ii)   the provisions of this Chapter shall take precedence over the Customs Valuation Code to the extent of any difference, and (iii) the definitions in Article 415 shall take precedence over the definitions in the Customs Valuation Code to the extent of any difference; and

e) all costs referred to in this Chapter shall be recorded and maintained in accordance with the Generally Accepted Accounting Principles applicable in the territory of the Party in which the good is produced.

Article 414: Consultation and Modifications

1. The Parties shall consult regularly to ensure that this Chapter is administered effectively, uniformly and consistently with the spirit and objectives of this Agreement, and shall cooperate in the administration of this Chapter in accordance with Chapter Five.

2. Any Party that considers that this Chapter requires modification to take into account developments in production processes or other matters may submit a proposed modification along with supporting rationale and any studies to the other Parties for consideration and any appropriate action under Chapter Five.

Article 415: Definitions

For purposes of this Chapter:

class of motor vehicles means any one of the following categories of motor vehicles:

a) motor vehicles provided for in subheading 8701.20, tariff item 8702.10.aa or 8702.90.aa (vehicles for the transport of 16 or more persons), subheading 8704.10, 8704.22, 8704.23, 8704.32 or 8704.90, or heading 87.05 and 87.06;

b) motor vehicles provided for in subheading 8701.10 or 8701.30 through 8701.90;

c) motor vehicles provided for in tariff item 8702.10.bb or 8702.90.bb (vehicles for the transport of 15 or fewer persons), or subheading 8704.21 and 8704.31; or

d) motor vehicles provided for in subheading 8703.21 through 8703.90;

F.O.B. means free on board, regardless of the mode of transportation, at the point of direct shipment by the seller to the buyer;

fungible goods or fungible materials means goods or materials that are interchangeable for commercial purposes and whose properties are essentially identical;

goods wholly obtained or produced entirely in the territory of one or more of the Parties means:

a) mineral goods extracted in the territory of one or more of the Parties;

b) vegetable goods, as such goods are defined in the Harmonized System, harvested in the territory of one or more of the Parties;

c) live animals born and raised in the territory of one or more of the Parties;

d)   goods obtained from hunting, trapping or fishing in the territory of one or more of the Parties;

e)   goods (fish, shellfish and other marine life) taken from the sea by vessels registered or recorded with a Party and flying its flag;

f)   goods produced on board factory ships from the goods referred to in subparagraph (e) provided such factory ships are registered or recorded with that Party and fly its flag;

g)   goods taken by a Party or a person of a Party from the seabed or beneath the seabed outside territorial waters, provided that a Party has rights to exploit such seabed;

h)   goods taken from outer space, provided they are obtained by a Party or a person of a Party and not processed in a nonParty;

(i)   waste and scrap derived from
   (i)   production in the territory of one or more of the Parties, or
   (ii) used goods collected in the territory of one or more of the Parties, provided such goods are fit only for the recovery of raw materials; and

(j)   goods produced in the territory of one or more of the Parties exclusively from goods referred to in subparagraphs (a) through (i), or from their derivatives, at any stage of production;

identical or similar goods means "identical goods" and "similar goods", respectively, as defined in the Customs Valuation Code;

indirect material means a good used in the production, testing or inspection of a good but not physically incorporated into the good, or a good used in the maintenance of buildings or the operation of equipment associated with the production of a good, including:

a)   fuel and energy;
b)   tools, dies and molds;
c)   spare parts and materials used in the maintenance of equipment and buildings;
d)   lubricants, greases, compounding materials and other materials used in production or used to operate equipment and buildings;
e)   gloves, glasses, footwear, clothing, safety equipment and supplies;
f)   equipment, devices, and supplies used for testing or inspecting the goods;
g)   catalysts and solvents; and
h)   any other goods that are not incorporated into the good but whose use in the production of the good can reasonably be demonstrated to be a part of that production;

intermediate material means a material that is self-produced and used in the production of a good, and designated pursuant to Article 402(10);

marque means the trade name used by a separate marketing division of a motor vehicle assembler;

material means a good that is used in the production of another good, and includes a part or an ingredient;

model line means a group of motor vehicles having the same platform or model name;

motor vehicle assembler means a producer of motor vehicles and any related persons or joint ventures in which the producer participates;

new building means a new construction, including at least the pouring or construction of new foundation and floor, the erection of a new structure and roof, and installation of new plumbing, electrical and other utilities to house a complete vehicle assembly process;

net cost means total cost minus sales promotion, marketing and aftersales service costs, royalties, shipping and packing costs, and nonallowable interest costs that are included in the total cost;

net cost of a good means the net cost that can be reasonably allocated to a good using one of the methods set out in Article 402(8);

non-allowable interest costs means interest costs incurred by a producer that exceed 700 basis points above the applicable federal government interest rate identified in the Uniform Regulations for comparable maturities;

non-originating good or non-originating material means a good or material that does not qualify as originating under this Chapter;

producer means a person who grows, mines, harvests, fishes, traps, hunts, manufactures, processes or assembles a good;
production means growing, mining, harvesting, fishing, trapping, hunting, manufacturing, processing or assembling a good;

reasonably allocate means to apportion in a manner appropriate to the circumstances;

refit means a plant closure, for purposes of plant conversion or retooling, that lasts at least three months;

related person means a person related to another person on the basis that:

a) they are officers or directors of one another's businesses;
b) they are legally recognized partners in business;
c) they are employer and employee;
d) any person directly or indirectly owns, controls or holds 25 percent or more of the outstanding voting stock or shares of each of them;
e) one of them directly or indirectly controls the other;
f) both of them are directly or indirectly controlled by a third person; or
g) they are members of the same family (members of the same family are natural or adoptive children, brothers, sisters, parents, grandparents, or spouses);

royalties means payments of any kind, including payments under technical assistance or similar agreements, made as consideration for the use or right to use any copyright, literary, artistic, or scientific work, patent, trademark, design, model, plan, secret formula or process, excluding those payments under technical assistance or similar agreements that can be related to specific services such as:

a) personnel training, without regard to where performed; and

b) if performed in the territory of one or more of the Parties, engineering, tooling, diesetting, software design and similar computer services, or other services;

sales promotion, marketing and after-sales service costs means the following costs related to sales promotion, marketing and aftersales service:

a) sales and marketing promotion; media advertising; advertising and market research; promotional and demonstration materials, exhibits; sales conferences, trade shows and conventions; banners; marketing displays; free samples; sales, marketing and after sales service literature (product brochures, catalogs, technical literature, price lists, service manuals, sales aid information); establishment and protection of logos and trademarks; sponsorships; wholesale and retail restocking charges; entertainment;

b) sales and marketing incentives; consumer, retailer or wholesaler rebates; merchandise incentives;

c) salaries and wages, sales commissions, bonuses, benefits (for example, medical, insurance, pension), travelling and living expenses, membership and professional fees, for sales promotion, marketing and aftersales service personnel;

d) recruiting and training of sales promotion, marketing and aftersales service personnel, and aftersales training of customers' employees, where such costs are identified separately for sales promotion, marketing and aftersales service of goods on the financial statements or cost accounts of the producer;

e) product liability insurance;

f) office supplies for sales promotion, marketing and aftersales service of goods, where such costs are identified separately for sales promotion, marketing and aftersales service of goods on the financial statements or cost accounts of the producer;

g) telephone, mail and other communications, where such costs are identified separately for sales promotion, marketing and aftersales service of goods on the financial statements or cost accounts of the producer;

h) rent and depreciation of sales promotion, marketing and aftersales service offices and distribution centers;

(i) property insurance premiums, taxes, cost of utilities, and repair and maintenance of sales promotion, marketing and after-sales service offices and distribution centers, where such costs are identified separately for sales promotion, marketing and aftersales service of goods on the financial statements or cost accounts of the producer; and

(j) payments by the producer to other persons for warranty repairs;

self-produced material means a material that is produced by the producer of a good and used in the production of that good;

shipping and packing costs means the costs incurred in packing a good for shipment and shipping the good from the point of direct shipment to the buyer, excluding costs of preparing and packaging the good for retail sale;

size category means for a motor vehicle identified in Article 403(1)(a):

a)   85 or less cubic feet of passenger and luggage interior volume,
b)   between 85 and 100 cubic feet of passenger and luggage interior volume,
c)   100 to 110 cubic feet of passenger and luggage interior volume,
d)   between 110 and 120 cubic feet of passenger and luggage interior volume, and
e)   120 and more cubic feet of passenger and luggage interior volume;

total cost means all product costs, period costs and other costs incurred in the territory of one or more of the Parties;

transaction value means the price actually paid or payable for a good or material with respect to a transaction of, except for the application of Article 403(1) or 403(2)(a), the producer of the good, adjusted in accordance with the principles of paragraphs 1, 3 and 4 of Article 8 of the Customs Valuation Code, regardless of whether the good or material is sold for export;

used means used or consumed in the production of goods; and

underbody means the floor pan of a motor vehicle.

ANNEX 403.1. LIST OF TARIFF PROVISIONS FOR ARTICLE 403(1)

Note: For purposes of reference only, descriptions are provided next to the corresponding tariff provision.

40.09	tubes, pipes and hoses
4010.10	rubber belts
40.11	tires
4016.93.aa	rubber, gaskets, washers and other seals for automotive goods
4016.99.aa	vibration control goods
7007.11 and 7007.21	laminated safety glass
7009.10	rearview mirrors
8301.20	locks for the kind used on motor vehicles
8407.31	engines of a cylinder capacity not exceeding 50cc
8407.32	engines of a cylinder capacity exceeding 50cc but not exceeding 250cc

(Continued)

8407.33	engines of a cylinder capacity exceeding 250cc but not exceeding 1000cc
8407.34.aa	engines of a cylinder capacity exceeding 1000cc but not exceeding 2000cc
8407.34.bb	engines of a cylinder capacity exceeding 2000cc
8408.20	diesel engines for vehicles of Chapter 87
84.09	parts of engines
8413.30	pumps
8414.80.22	turbochargers and superchargers for motor vehicles, where not provided for under subheading 8414.59
8414.59.aa	turbochargers and superchargers for motor vehicles, where not provided for under subheading 8414.80
8415.81 through 8415.83	air conditioners
8421.39.aa	catalytic convertors
8481.20, 8481.30 and 8481.80	valves
8482.10 through 8482.80	ball bearings
8483.10 through 8483.40	transmission shafts and housed ball bearings
8483.50	flywheels
8501.10	electric motors
8501.20	electric motors
8501.31	electric motors
8501.32.aa	electric motors that provide primary source for electric powered vehicles of subheading 8703.90
8507.20.aa, 8507.30.aa, 8507.40.aa and 8507.80.aa	batteries that provide primary source for electric cars
8511.30	distributors
8511.40	starter motors
8511.50	other generators
8512.20	other lighting or visual signalling equipment
8512.40	windscreen wipers, defrosters
8519.91	cassette decks
8527.21	radios combined with cassette players
8527.29	radios
8536.50	switches
8536.90	junction boxes
8537.10.aa	motor control centers
8539.10	seal beamed headlamps
8539.21	tungsten halogen headlamps
8544.30	wire harnesses

87.06	chassis
87.07	bodies
8708.10.aa	bumpers but not parts thereof
8708.21	safety seat belts
8708.29.aa	body stampings
8708.29.bb	inflators and modules for airbags
8708.29.cc	door assemblies
8708.29.dd	airbags for use in motor vehicles, where not provided for under subheading 8708.99
8708.39	brakes and servobrakes, and parts thereof
8708.40	gear boxes, transmissions
8708.50	drive axles with differential, whether or not provided with other transmission components
8708.60	nondriving axles, and parts thereof
8708.70.aa	road wheels, but not parts or accessories thereof
8708.80	suspension shockabsorbers
8708.91	radiators
8708.92	silencers (mufflers) and exhaust pipes
8708.93.aa	clutches, but not parts thereof
8708.94	steering wheels, steering columns and steering boxes
8708.99.aa	vibration control goods containing rubber
8708.99.bb	double flanged wheel hub units
8708.99.cc	airbags for use in motor vehicles, where not provided for under subheading 8708.29
8708.99.dd	halfshafts and drive shafts
8708.99.ee	other parts for powertrains
8708.99.ff	parts for suspension systems
8708.99.gg	parts for steering systems
8708.99.hh	other parts and accessories not provided for elsewhere in subheading 8708.99
9031.80	monitoring devices
9032.89	automatic regulating instruments
9401.20	seats

ANNEX 403.2. LIST OF COMPONENTS AND MATERIALS

1. **Component: Engines provided for in heading 84.07 or 84.08**
    Materials: cast block, cast head, fuel nozzle, fuel injector pumps, glow plugs, turbochargers and superchargers, electronic engine controls, intake manifold, exhaust manifold, intake/exhaust valves, crankshaft/camshaft, alternator, starter, air cleaner assembly, pistons, connecting rods and assemblies made therefrom (or rotor assemblies for rotary engines), flywheel (for manual transmissions), flexplate (for automatic transmissions), oil pan, oil pump and pressure regulator, water pump, crankshaft and camshaft gears, and radiator assemblies or chargeair coolers.

2. **Component: Gear boxes (transmissions) provided for in subheading 8708.40**
    Materials: (a) for manual transmissions transmission case and clutch housing; clutch; internal shifting mechanism; gear sets, synchronizers and shafts; and (b) for torque convertor type transmissions transmission case and convertor housing; torque convertor assembly; gear sets and clutches; and electronic transmission controls.

ANNEX 403.3. REGIONAL VALUE-CONTENT CALCULATION FOR CAMI

1. For purposes of Article 403, in determining whether motor vehicles produced by CAMI Automotive, Inc. ("CAMI") in the territory of Canada and imported into the territory of the United States qualify as originating goods, CAMI may average its calculation of the regional value content of a class of motor vehicles or a model line of motor vehicles produced in a fiscal year in the territory of Canada by CAMI for sale in the territory of one or more of the Parties with the calculation of the regional value content of the corresponding class of motor vehicles or model line of motor vehicles produced in the territory of Canada by General Motors of Canada Limited in the fiscal year that corresponds most closely to CAMI's fiscal year, provided that:
    a) at the beginning of CAMI's fiscal year General Motors of Canada Limited owns 50 percent or more of the voting common stock of CAMI; and
    b) General Motors of Canada Limited, General Motors Corporation, General Motors de Mexico, S.A. de C.V., and any subsidiary directly or indirectly owned by any of them, or by any combination thereof, ("GM") acquires 75 percent or more by unit of quantity of the class of motor vehicles or model line of motor vehicles, as the case may be, that CAMI has produced in the territory of Canada in CAMI's fiscal year for sale in the territory of one or more of the Parties.

2. If GM acquires less than 75 percent by unit of quantity of the class of motor vehicles or model line of motor vehicles, as the case may be, that CAMI has produced in the territory of Canada in CAMI's fiscal year for sale in the territory of one or more of the Parties, CAMI may average in the manner set out in paragraph 1 only those motor vehicles that are acquired by GM for distribution under the GEO marque or other GM marque.

3. In calculating the regional value content of motor vehicles produced by CAMI in the territory of Canada, CAMI may choose to average the calculation in paragraph 1 or 2 over a period of two fiscal years in the event that any motor vehicle assembly plant operated by CAMI or any motor vehicle assembly plant operated by General Motors of Canada Limited with which CAMI is averaging its regional value content is closed for more than two consecutive months:
    a) for the purpose of retooling for a model change, or
    b) as the result of any event or circumstance (other than the imposition of antidumping and countervailing duties, or an interruption of operations resulting from a labor strike, lockout, labor dispute, picketing or boycott of or by employees of CAMI or GM), that CAMI or GM could not reasonably have been expected to avert by corrective action or by exercise of due care and diligence,

including a shortage of materials, failure of utilities, or inability to obtain or delay in obtaining raw materials, parts, fuel or utilities.

The averaging may be for CAMI's fiscal year in which a CAMI or any General Motors of Canada Limited plant with which CAMI is averaging is closed and either the previous or subsequent fiscal year. In the event that the period of closure spans two fiscal years, the averaging may be only for those two fiscal years.

4. For purposes of this Article, where as a result of an amalgamation, reorganization, division or similar transaction:

   a) a motor vehicle producer (the "successor producer") acquires all or substantially all of the assets used by GM, and

   b) the successor producer, directly or indirectly controls, or is controlled by, GM, or both the successor producer and GM are controlled by the same person, the successor producer shall be deemed to be GM.

5. CUSTOMS PROCEDURES

Section A - Certification of Origin

Article 501: Certificate of Origin

1. The Parties shall establish by January 1, 1994 a Certificate of Origin for the purpose of certifying that a good being exported from the territory of a Party into the territory of another Party qualifies as an originating good, and may thereafter revise the Certificate by agreement.

2. Each Party may require that a Certificate of Origin for a good imported into its territory be completed in a language required under its law.

3. Each Party shall:

   a) require an exporter in its territory to complete and sign a Certificate of Origin for any exportation of a good for which an importer may claim preferential tariff treatment on importation of the good into the territory of another Party; and

   b) provide that where an exporter in its territory is not the producer of the good, the exporter may complete and sign a Certificate on the basis of

      (i) its knowledge of whether the good qualifies as an originating good,

      (ii) its reasonable reliance on the producer's written representation that the good qualifies as an originating good, or

      (iii) a completed and signed Certificate for the good voluntarily provided to the exporter by the producer.

4. Nothing in paragraph 3 shall be construed to require a producer to provide a Certificate of Origin to an exporter.

5. Each Party shall provide that a Certificate of Origin that has been completed and signed by an exporter or a producer in the territory of another Party that is applicable to:

   a) a single importation of a good into the Party's territory, or

b) multiple importations of identical goods into the Party's territory that occur within a specified period, not exceeding 12 months, set out therein by the exporter or producer,

shall be accepted by its customs administration for four years after the date on which the Certificate was signed.

Article 502: Obligations Regarding Importations

1. Except as otherwise provided in this Chapter, each Party shall require an importer in its territory that claims preferential tariff treatment for a good imported into its territory from the territory of another Party to:
    a) make a written declaration, based on a valid Certificate of Origin, that the good qualifies as an originating good;
    b) have the Certificate in its possession at the time the declaration is made;
    c) provide, on the request of that Party's customs administration, a copy of the Certificate; and
    d) promptly make a corrected declaration and pay any duties owing where the importer has reason to believe that a Certificate on which a declaration was based contains information that is not correct.
2. Each Party shall provide that, where an importer in its territory claims preferential tariff treatment for a good imported into its territory from the territory of another Party:
    a) the Party may deny preferential tariff treatment to the good if the importer fails to comply with any requirement under this Chapter; and
    b) the importer shall not be subject to penalties for the making of an incorrect declaration, if it voluntarily makes a corrected declaration pursuant to paragraph 1(d).
3. Each Party shall provide that, where a good would have qualified as an originating good when it was imported into the territory of that Party but no claim for preferential tariff treatment was made at that time, the importer of the good may, no later than one year after the date on which the good was imported, apply for a refund of any excess duties paid as the result of the good not having been accorded preferential tariff treatment, on presentation of:
    a) a written declaration that the good qualified as an originating good at the time of importation;
    b) a copy of the Certificate of Origin; and
    c) such other documentation relating to the importation of the good as that Party may require.

Article 503: Exceptions

Each Party shall provide that a Certificate of Origin shall not be required for:

a) a commercial importation of a good whose value does not exceed US$1,000 or its equivalent amount in the Party's currency, or such higher amount as it may establish, except that it may require that the invoice accompanying the importation include a statement certifying that the good qualifies as an originating good,

b) a non-commercial importation of a good whose value does not exceed US$1,000 or its equivalent amount in the Party's currency, or such higher amount as it may establish, or

c) an importation of a good for which the Party into whose territory the good is imported has waived the requirement for a Certificate of Origin,

provided that the importation does not form part of a series of importations that may reasonably be considered to have been undertaken or arranged for the purpose of avoiding the certification requirements of Articles 501 and 502.

Article 504: Obligations Regarding Exportations

1. Each Party shall provide that:
   a) an exporter in its territory, or a producer in its territory that has provided a copy of a Certificate of Origin to that exporter pursuant to Article 501(3)(b)(iii), shall provide a copy of the Certificate to its customs administration on request; and
   b) an exporter or a producer in its territory that has completed and signed a Certificate of Origin, and that has reason to believe that the Certificate contains information that is not correct, shall promptly notify in writing all persons to whom the Certificate was given by the exporter or producer of any change that could affect the accuracy or validity of the Certificate.

2. Each Party:
   a) shall provide that a false certification by an exporter or a producer in its territory that a good to be exported to the territory of another Party qualifies as an originating good shall have the same legal consequences, with appropriate modifications, as would apply to an importer in its territory for a contravention of its customs laws and regulations regarding the making of a false statement or representation; and
   b) may apply such measures as the circumstances may warrant where an exporter or a producer in its territory fails to comply with any requirement of this Chapter.

3. No Party may impose penalties on an exporter or a producer in its territory that voluntarily provides written notification pursuant to paragraph (1)(b) with respect to the making of an incorrect certification.

Section B - Administration and Enforcement

Article 505: Records

Each Party shall provide that:

a) an exporter or a producer in its territory that completes and signs a Certificate of Origin shall maintain in its territory, for five years after the date on which the Certificate was signed or for such longer period as the Party may specify, all records relating to the origin of a good for which preferential tariff treatment was claimed in the territory of another Party, including records associated with

   (i)   the purchase of, cost of, value of, and payment for, the good that is exported from its territory,

   (ii) the purchase of, cost of, value of, and payment for, all materials, including indirect materials, used in the production of the good that is exported from its territory, and

   (iii) the production of the good in the form in which the good is exported from its territory; and

b) an importer claiming preferential tariff treatment for a good imported into the Party's territory shall maintain in that territory, for five years after the date of importation of the good or for such longer period as the Party may specify, such documentation, including a copy of the Certificate, as the Party may require relating to the importation of the good.

Article 506: Origin Verifications

1. For purposes of determining whether a good imported into its territory from the territory of another Party qualifies as an originating good, a Party may, through its customs administration, conduct a verification solely by means of:

   a) written questionnaires to an exporter or a producer in the territory of another Party;

   b) visits to the premises of an exporter or a producer in the territory of another Party to review the records referred to in Article 505(a) and observe the facilities used in the production of the good; or

   c) such other procedure as the Parties may agree.

2. Prior to conducting a verification visit pursuant to paragraph (1)(b), a Party shall, through its customs administration:

   a) deliver a written notification of its intention to conduct the visit to

   (i)   the exporter or producer whose premises are to be visited,

   (ii) the customs administration of the Party in whose territory the visit is to occur, and

   (iii) if requested by the Party in whose territory the visit is to occur, the embassy of that Party in the territory of the Party proposing to conduct the visit; and

   (b) obtain the written consent of the exporter or producer whose premises are to be visited.

3. The notification referred to in paragraph 2 shall include:

   a) the identity of the customs administration issuing the notification;

   b) the name of the exporter or producer whose premises are to be visited;

   c) the date and place of the proposed verification visit;

     d)   the object and scope of the proposed verification visit, including specific reference to the good that is the subject of the verification;

     e)   the names and titles of the officials performing the verification visit; and

     f)   the legal authority for the verification visit.

4.   Where an exporter or a producer has not given its written consent to a proposed verification visit within 30 days of receipt of notification pursuant to paragraph 2, the notifying Party may deny preferential tariff treatment to the good that would have been the subject of the visit.

5.   Each Party shall provide that, where its customs administration receives notification pursuant to paragraph 2, the customs administration may, within 15 days of receipt of the notification, postpone the proposed verification visit for a period not exceeding 60 days from the date of such receipt, or for such longer period as the Parties may agree.

6.   A Party shall not deny preferential tariff treatment to a good based solely on the postponement of a verification visit pursuant to paragraph 5.

7.   Each Party shall permit an exporter or a producer whose good is the subject of a verification visit by another Party to designate two observers to be present during the visit, provided that:

     a)   the observers do not participate in a manner other than as observers; and

     b)   the failure of the exporter or producer to designate observers shall not result in the postponement of the visit.

8.   Each Party shall, through its customs administration, conduct a verification of a regional value-content requirement in accordance with the Generally Accepted Accounting Principles applied in the territory of the Party from which the good was exported.

9.   The Party conducting a verification shall provide the exporter or producer whose good is the subject of the verification with a written determination of whether the good qualifies as an originating good, including findings of fact and the legal basis for the determination.

10. Where verifications by a Party indicate a pattern of conduct by an exporter or a producer of false or unsupported representations that a good imported into its territory qualifies as an originating good, the Party may withhold preferential tariff treatment to identical goods exported or produced by such person until that person establishes compliance with Chapter Four (Rules of Origin).

11. Each Party shall provide that where it determines that a certain good imported into its territory does not qualify as an originating good based on a tariff classification or a value applied by the Party to one or more materials used in the production of the good, which differs from the tariff classification or value applied to the materials by the Party from whose territory the good was exported, the Party's determination shall not become effective until it notifies in writing both the importer of the good and the person that completed and signed the Certificate of Origin for the good of its determination.

12. A Party shall not apply a determination made under paragraph 11 to an importation made before the effective date of the determination where:

     a)   the customs administration of the Party from whose territory the good was exported has issued an advance ruling under Article 509 or any other ruling on the tariff classification or on the value of such materials, or has given consistent treatment to the entry of the materials under the tariff classification or value at issue, on which a person is entitled to rely; and

    b) the advance ruling or consistent treatment was given prior to notification of the determination.

13. If a Party denies preferential tariff treatment to a good pursuant to a determination made under paragraph 11, it shall postpone the effective date of the denial for a period not exceeding 90 days where the importer of the good, or the person who completed and signed the Certificate of Origin for the good, demonstrates that it has relied in good faith to its detriment on the tariff classification or value applied to such materials by the customs administration of the Party from whose territory the good was exported.

Article 507: Confidentiality

1. Each Party shall maintain, in accordance with its law, the confidentiality of confidential business information collected pursuant to this Chapter and shall protect that information from disclosure that could prejudice the competitive position of the persons providing the information.

2. The confidential business information collected pursuant to this Chapter may only be disclosed to those authorities responsible for the administration and enforcement of determinations of origin, and of customs and revenue matters.

Article 508: Penalties

1. Each Party shall maintain measures imposing criminal, civil or administrative penalties for violations of its laws and regulations relating to this Chapter.

2. Nothing in Articles 502(2), 504(3) or 506(6) shall be construed to prevent a Party from applying such measures as the circumstances may warrant.

Section C - Advance Rulings

Article 509: Advance Rulings

1. Each Party shall, through its customs administration, provide for the expeditious issuance of written advance rulings, prior to the importation of a good into its territory, to an importer in its territory or an exporter or a producer in the territory of another Party, on the basis of the facts and circumstances presented by such importer, exporter or producer of the good, concerning:

    a) whether materials imported from a non-Party used in the production of a good undergo an applicable change in tariff classification set out in Annex 401 as a result of production occurring entirely in the territory of one or more of the Parties;

b) whether a good satisfies a regional value-content requirement under either the transaction value method or the net cost method set out in Chapter Four;

c) for the purpose of determining whether a good satisfies a regional value-content requirement under Chapter Four, the appropriate basis or method for value to be applied by an exporter or a producer in the territory of another Party, in accordance with the principles of the Customs Valuation Code, for calculating the transaction value of the good or of the materials used in the production of the good;

d) for the purpose of determining whether a good satisfies a regional value-content requirement under Chapter Four, the appropriate basis or method for reasonably allocating costs, in accordance with the allocation methods set out in the Uniform Regulations, for calculating the net cost of the good or the value of an intermediate material;

e) whether a good qualifies as an originating good under Chapter Four;

f) whether a good that re-enters its territory after the good has been exported from its territory to the territory of another Party for repair or alteration qualifies for dutyfree treatment in accordance with Article 307 (Goods Re-Entered after Repair or Alteration);

g) whether the proposed or actual marking of a good satisfies country of origin marking requirements under Article 311 (Country of Origin Marking);

h) whether an originating good qualifies as a good of a Party under Annex 300B (Textile and Apparel Goods), Annex 302.2 (Tariff Elimination) or Chapter Seven (Agriculture and Sanitary and Phytosanitary Measures);

i) whether a good is a qualifying good under Chapter Seven; or

j) such other matters as the Parties may agree.

2. Each Party shall adopt or maintain procedures for the issuance of advance rulings, including a detailed description of the information reasonably required to process an application for a ruling.

3. Each Party shall provide that its customs administration:

a) may, at any time during the course of an evaluation of an application for an advance ruling, request supplemental information from the person requesting the ruling;

b) shall, after it has obtained all necessary information from the person requesting an advance ruling, issue the ruling within the periods specified in the Uniform Regulations; and

c) shall, where the advance ruling is unfavorable to the person requesting it, provide to that person a full explanation of the reasons for the ruling.

4. Subject to paragraph 6, each Party shall apply an advance ruling to importations into its territory of the good for which the ruling was requested, beginning on the date of its issuance or such later date as may be specified in the ruling.

5. Each Party shall provide to any person requesting an advance ruling the same treatment, including the same interpretation and application of provisions of Chapter Four regarding a determination of origin, as it provided to any other person to whom

it issued an advance ruling, provided that the facts and circumstances are identical in all material respects.

6. The issuing Party may modify or revoke an advance ruling:

    a) if the ruling is based on an error

        (i) of fact,

        (ii) in the tariff classification of a good or a material that is the subject of the ruling,

        (iii) in the application of a regional value content requirement under Chapter Four,

        (iv) in the application of the rules for determining whether a good qualifies as a good of a Party under Annex 300B, 302.2 or Chapter Seven,

        (v) in the application of the rules for determining whether a good is a qualifying good under Chapter Seven, or

        (vi) in the application of the rules for determining whether a good that re-enters its territory after the good has been exported from its territory to the territory of another Party for repair or alteration qualifies for dutyfree treatment under Article 307;

    b) if the ruling is not in accordance with an interpretation agreed by the Parties regarding Chapter Three (National Treatment and Market Access for Goods) or Chapter Four;

    c) if there is a change in the material facts or circumstances on which the ruling is based;

    d) to conform with a modification of Chapter Three, Chapter Four, this Chapter, Chapter Seven, the Marking Rules or the Uniform Regulations; or

    e) to conform with a judicial decision or a change in its domestic law.

7. Each Party shall provide that any modification or revocation of an advance ruling shall be effective on the date on which the modification or revocation is issued, or on such later date as may be specified therein, and shall not be applied to importations of a good that have occurred prior to that date, unless the person to whom the advance ruling was issued has not acted in accordance with its terms and conditions.

8. Notwithstanding paragraph 7, the issuing Party shall postpone the effective date of such modification or revocation for a period not exceeding 90 days where the person to whom the advance ruling was issued demostrates that it has relied in good faith to its detriment on that ruling.

9. Each Party shall provide that where its customs administration examines the regional value content of a good for which it has issued an advance ruling pursuant to subparagraph 1(c), (d) or f), it shall evaluate whether:

    a) the exporter or producer has complied with the terms and conditions of the advance ruling;

    b) the exporter's or producer's operations are consistent with the material facts and circumstances on which the advance ruling is based; and

    c) the supporting data and computations used in applying the basis or method for calculating value or allocating cost were correct in all material respects.

10. Each Party shall provide that where its customs administration determines that any requirement in paragraph 9 has not been satisfied, it may modify or revoke the advance ruling as the circumstances may warrant.

11. Each Party shall provide that, where the person to whom an advance ruling was issued demonstrates that it used reasonable care and acted in good faith in presenting the facts and circumstances on which the ruling was based, and where the customs administration of a Party determines that the ruling was based on incorrect information, the person to whom the ruling was issued shall not be subject to penalties.

12. Each Party shall provide that where it issues an advance ruling to a person that has misrepresented or omitted material facts or circumstances on which the ruling is based or has failed to act in accordance with the terms and conditions of the ruling, the Party may apply such measures as the circumstances may warrant.

Section D - Review and Appeal of Origin Determinations and Advance Rulings

Article 510: Review and Appeal

1. Each Party shall grant substantially the same rights of review and appeal of marking determinations of origin, country of origin determinations and advance rulings by its customs administration as it provides to importers in its territory to any person:
   a) who completes and signs a Certificate of Origin for a good that has been the subject of a determination of origin;
   b) whose good has been the subject of a country of origin marking determination pursuant to Article 311 (Country of Origin Marking); or
   (c) who has received an advance ruling pursuant to Article 509(1).

2. Further to Articles 1804 (Administrative Proceedings) and 1805 (Review and Appeal), each Party shall provide that the rights of review and appeal referred to in paragraph 1 shall include access to:
   a) at least one level of administrative review independent of the official or office responsible for the determination under review; and
   b) in accordance with its domestic law, judicial or quasijudicial review of the determination or decision taken at the final level of administrative review.

Section E - Uniform Regulations

Article 511: Uniform Regulations
1. The Parties shall establish, and implement through their respective laws or regulations by January 1, 1994, Uniform Regulations regarding the interpretation, application and administration of Chapter Four, this Chapter and other matters as may be agreed by the Parties.
2. Each Party shall implement any modification of or addition to the Uniform Regulations no later than 180 days after the Parties agree on such modification or addition, or such other period as the Parties may agree.

Section F - Cooperation

Article 512: Cooperation

1. Each Party shall notify the other Parties of the following determinations, measures and rulings, including to the greatest extent practicable those that are prospective in application:
   a) a determination of origin issued as the result of a verification conducted pursuant to Article 506(1);
   b) a determination of origin that the Party is aware is contrary to
      (i) a ruling issued by the customs administration of another Party with respect to the tariff classification or value of a good, or of materials used in the production of a good, or the reasonable allocation of costs where calculating the net cost of a good, that is the subject of a determination of origin, or
      (ii) consistent treatment given by the customs administration of another Party with respect to the tariff classification or value of a good, or of materials used in the production of a good, or the reasonable allocation of costs where calculating the net cost of a good, that is the subject of a determination of origin;
   c) a measure establishing or significantly modifying an administrative policy that is likely to affect future determinations of origin, country of origin marking requirements or determinations as to whether a good qualifies as a good of a Party under the Marking Rules; and
   d) an advance ruling, or a ruling modifying or revoking an advance ruling, pursuant to Article 509.
2. The Parties shall cooperate:
   a) in the enforcement of their respective customs-related laws or regulations implementing this Agreement, and under any customs mutual assistance agreements or other customsrelated agreement to which they are party;
   b) for purposes of the detection and prevention of unlawful transshipments of textile and apparel goods of a non-Party, in the enforcement of prohibitions or quantitative restrictions, including the verification by a Party, in accordance with the procedures set out in this Chapter, of the capacity for production of goods by an exporter or a producer in the territory of another Party, provided that the customs administration of the Party proposing to conduct the verification, prior to conducting the verification
      (i) obtains the consent of the Party in whose territory the verification is to occur, and
      (ii) provides notification to the exporter or producer whose premises are to be visited, except that procedures for notifying the exporter or producer whose premises are to be visited shall be in accordance with such other procedures as the Parties may agree;
   c) to the extent practicable and for purposes of facilitating the flow of trade between them, in such customsrelated matters as the collection and exchange of statistics regarding the importation and exportation of goods, the harmonization

of documentation used in trade, the standardization of data elements, the acceptance of an international data syntax and the exchange of information; and

d) to the extent practicable, in the storage and transmission of customs-related documentation.

Article 513: Working Group and Customs Subgroup

1. The Parties hereby establish a Working Group on Rules of Origin, comprising representatives of each Party, to ensure:

   a) the effective implementation and administration of Articles 303 (Restriction on Drawback and Duty Deferral Programs), 308 (Most-Favored-Nation Rates of Duty on Certain Goods) and 311, Chapter Four, this Chapter, the Marking Rules and the Uniform Regulations; and

   b) the effective administration of the customsrelated aspects of Chapter Three.

2. The Working Group shall meet at least four times each year and on the request of any Party.

3. The Working Group shall:

   a) monitor the implementation and administration by the customs administrations of the Parties of Articles 303, 308 and 311, Chapter Four, this Chapter, the Marking Rules and the Uniform Regulations to ensure their uniform interpretation;

   b) endeavor to agree, on the request of any Party, on any proposed modification of or addition to Article 303, 308 or 311, Chapter Four, this Chapter, the Marking Rules or the Uniform Regulations;

   c) notify the Commission of any agreed modification of or addition to the Uniform Regulations;

   d) propose to the Commission any modification of or addition to Article 303, 308 or 311, Chapter Four, this Chapter, the Marking Rules, the Uniform Regulations or any other provision of this Agreement as may be required to conform with any change to the Harmonized System; and

   e) consider any other matter referred to it by a Party or by the Customs Subgroup established under paragraph 6.

4. Each Party shall, to the greatest extent practicable, take all necessary measures to implement any modification of or addition to this Agreement within 180 days of the date on which the Commission agrees on the modification or addition.

5. If the Working Group fails to resolve a matter referred to it pursuant to paragraph 3(e) within 30 days of such referral, any Party may request a meeting of the Commission under Article 2007 (Commission Good Offices, Conciliation and Mediation).

6. The Working Group shall establish, and monitor the work of, a Customs Subgroup, comprising representatives of each Party. The Subgroup shall meet at least four times each year and on the request of any Party and shall:

   a) endeavor to agree on

      (i) the uniform interpretation, application and administration of Articles 303, 308 and 311, Chapter Four, this Chapter, the Marking Rules and the Uniform Regulations,

      (ii) tariff classification and valuation matters relating to determinations of origin,

      (iii) equivalent procedures and criteria for the request, approval, modification, revocation and implementation of advance rulings,

      (iv) revisions to the Certificate of Origin,

      (v) any other matter referred to it by a Party, the Working Group or the Committee on Trade in Goods established under Article 316, and

      (vi) any other customs-related matter arising under this Agreement;

b) consider

      (i) the harmonization of customs-related automation requirements and documentation, and

      (ii) proposed customs-related administrative and operational changes that may affect the flow of trade between the Parties' territories;

c) report periodically to the Working Group and notify it of any agreement reached under this paragraph; and

d) refer to the Working Group any matter on which it has been unable to reach agreement within 60 days of referral of the matter to it pursuant to subparagraph (a)(v).

7. Nothing in this Chapter shall be construed to prevent a Party from issuing a determination of origin or an advance ruling relating to a matter under consideration by the Working Group or the Customs Subgroup or from taking such other action as it considers necessary, pending a resolution of the matter under this Agreement.

Article 514: Definitions

For purposes of this Chapter:

commercial importation means the importation of a good into the territory of any Party for the purpose of sale, or any commercial, industrial or other like use;

customs administration means the competent authority that is responsible under the law of a Party for the administration of customs laws and regulations;

determination of origin means a determination as to whether a good qualifies as an originating good in accordance with Chapter Four;

exporter in the territory of a Party means an exporter located in the territory of a Party and an exporter required under this Chapter to maintain records in the territory of that Party regarding exportations of a good;

identical goods means goods that are the same in all respects, including physical characteristics, quality and reputation, irrespective of minor differences in appearance that are not relevant to a determination of origin of those goods under Chapter Four;

importer in the territory of a Party means an importer located in the territory of a Party and an importer required under this Chapter to maintain records in the territory of that Party regarding importations of a good;

intermediate material means "intermediate material" as defined in Article 415; Marking Rules means "Marking Rules" established under Annex 311;

material means "material" as defined in Article 415;

net cost of a good means "net cost of a good" as defined in Article 415;

preferential tariff treatment means the duty rate applicable to an originating good;

producer means "producer" as defined in Article 415;

production means "production" as defined in Article 415;
transaction value means "transaction value" as defined in Article 415;

Uniform Regulations means "Uniform Regulations" established under Article 511;

used means "used" as defined in Article 415; and

value means value of a good or material for purposes of calculating customs duties or for purposes of applying Chapter Four.

6. ENERGY AND BASIC PETROCHEMICALS

Article 601: Principles

1. The Parties confirm their full respect for their Constitutions.
2. The Parties recognize that it is desirable to strengthen the important role that trade in energy and basic petrochemical goods plays in the free trade area and to enhance this role through sustained and gradual liberalization.
3. The Parties recognize the importance of having viable and internationally competitive energy and petrochemical sectors to further their individual national interests.

Article 602: Scope and Coverage

1. This Chapter applies to measures relating to energy and basic petrochemical goods originating in the territories of the Parties and to measures relating to investment and to the cross-border trade in services associated with such goods, as set forth in this Chapter.

2. For purposes of this Chapter, energy and basic petrochemical goods refer to those goods classified under the Harmonized System as:
    a) subheading 2612.10;
    b) headings 27.01 through 27.06;
    c) subheading 2707.50;
    d) subheading 2707.99 (only with respect to solvent naphtha, rubber extender oils and carbon black feedstocks);
    e) headings 27.08 and 27.09;
    f) heading 27.10 (except for normal paraffin mixtures in the range of C9 to C15);
    g) heading 27.11 (except for ethylene, propylene, butylene and butadiene in purities over 50 percent);
    h) headings 27.12 through 27.16;
    i) subheadings 2844.10 through 2844.50 (only with respect to uranium compounds classified under those subheadings);
    j) subheading 2845.10; and
    k) subheading 2901.10 (only with respect to ethane, butanes, pentanes, hexanes, and heptanes).

3. Except as specified in Annex 602.3, energy and petrochemical goods and activities shall be governed by the provisions of this Agreement.

Article 603: Import and Export Restrictions

1. Subject to the further rights and obligations of this Agreement, the Parties incorporate the provisions of the *General Agreement on Tariffs and Trade* (GATT), with respect to prohibitions or restrictions on trade in energy and basic petrochemical goods. The Parties agree that this language does not incorporate their respective protocols of provisional application to the GATT.

2. The Parties understand that the provisions of the GATT incorporated in paragraph 1 prohibit, in any circumstances in which any other form of quantitative restriction is prohibited, minimum or maximum export - price requirements and, except as permitted in enforcement of countervailing and antidumping orders and undertakings, minimum or maximum import-price requirements.

3. In circumstances where a Party adopts or maintains a restriction on importation from or exportation to a non-Party of an energy or basic petrochemical good, nothing in this Agreement shall be construed to prevent the Party from:
    a) limiting or prohibiting the importation from the territory of any Party of such energy or basic petrochemical good of the nonParty; or
    b) requiring as a condition of export of such energy or basic petrochemical good of

the Party to the territory of any other Party that the good be consumed within the territory of the other Party.

4. In the event that a Party adopts or maintains a restriction on imports of an energy or basic petrochemical good from non-Party countries, the Parties, on request of any Party, shall consult with a view to avoiding undue interference with or distortion of pricing, marketing and distribution arrangements in another Party.

5. Each Party may administer a system of import and export licensing for energy or basic petrochemical goods provided that such system is operated in a manner consistent with the provisions of this Agreement, including paragraph 1 and Article 1502 (Monopolies and State Enterprises).

6. This Article is subject to the reservations set out in Annex 603.6.

Article 604: Export Taxes

No Party may adopt or maintain any duty, tax or other charge on the export of any energy or basic petrochemical good to the territory of another Party, unless such duty, tax or charge is adopted or maintained on:

a) exports of any such good to the territory of all other Parties; and

b) any such good when destined for domestic consumption.

Article 605: Other Export Measures

Subject to Annex 605, a Party may adopt or maintain a restriction otherwise justified under Articles XI:2(a) or XX(g), (i) or (j) of the GATT with respect to the export of an energy or basic petrochemical good to the territory of another Party, only if:

a) the restriction does not reduce the proportion of the total export shipments of the specific energy or basic petrochemical good made available to that other Party relative to the total supply of that good of the Party maintaining the restriction as compared to the proportion prevailing in the most recent 36month period for which data are available prior to the imposition of the measure, or in such other representative period on which the Parties may agree;

b) the Party does not impose a higher price for exports of an energy or basic petrochemical good to that other Party than the price charged for such good when consumed domestically, by means of any measure such as licenses, fees, taxation and minimum price requirements. The foregoing provision does not apply to a higher price that may result from a measure taken pursuant to subparagraph (a) that only restricts the volume of exports; and

c) the restriction does not require the disruption of normal channels of supply to that other Party or normal proportions among specific energy or basic petrochemical goods supplied to that other Party, such as, for example, between crude oil and refined products and among different categories of crude oil and of refined products.

Article 606: Energy Regulatory Measures

1. The Parties recognize that energy regulatory measures are subject to the disciplines of:
    a) national treatment, as provided in Article 301;
    b) import and export restrictions, as provided in Article 603; and
    c) export taxes, as provided in Article 604.
2. Each Party shall seek to ensure that in the application of any energy regulatory measure, energy regulatory bodies within its territory avoid disruption of contractual relationships to the maximum extent practicable, and provide for orderly and equitable implementation appropriate to such measures.

Article 607: National Security Measures

Subject to Annex 607, no Party may adopt or maintain a measure restricting imports of an energy or basic petrochemical good from, or exports of an energy or basic petrochemical good to, another Party under Article XXI of the GATT or under Article 2102 (National Security), except to the extent necessary to:

a) supply a military establishment of a Party or enable fulfillment of a critical defense contract of a Party;
b) respond to a situation of armed conflict involving the Party taking the measure;
c) implement national policies or international agreements relating to the non-proliferation of nuclear weapons or other nuclear explosive devices; or
d) respond to direct threats of disruption in the supply of nuclear materials for defense purposes.

Article 608: Miscellaneous Provisions

1. The Parties agree to allow existing or future incentives for oil and gas exploration, development and related activities in order to maintain the reserve base for these energy resources.
2. Annex 608.2 applies only to the Parties specified in that Annex with respect to other agreements relating to trade in energy goods.

Article 609: Definitions

For purposes of this Chapter:
consumed means transformed so as to qualify under the rules of origin set out in Chapter Four (Rules of Origin), or actually consumed;

cross-border trade in services means "crossborder trade in services" as defined in Article 1213 (Cross-Border Trade in Services Definitions);

energy regulatory measure means any measure by federal or sub-federal entities that directly affects the transportation, transmission or distribution, purchase or sale, of an energy or basic petrochemical good;

enterprise means "enterprise" as defined in Article 1139 (Investment-Definitions);

enterprise of a Party means "enterprise of a Party" as defined in Article 1139;

facility for independent power production means a facility that is used for the generation of electric energy exclusively for sale to an electric utility for further resale;

first hand sale refers to the first commercial transaction affecting the good in question;

investment means investment as defined in Article 1139;

restriction means any limitation, whether made effective through quotas, licenses, permits, minimum or maximum price requirements or any other means;

total export shipments means the total shipments from total supply to users located in the territory of the other Party; and

total supply means shipments to domestic users and foreign users from:

a) domestic production;
b) domestic inventory; and
c) other imports, as appropriate.

ANNEX 602.3. RESERVATIONS AND SPECIAL PROVISIONS

Reservations

1. The Mexican State reserves to itself the following strategic activities, including investment in such activities and the provision of services in such activities:
   a) exploration and exploitation of crude oil and natural gas; refining or processing of crude oil and natural gas; and production of artificial gas, basic petrochemicals and their feedstocks and pipelines;
   b) foreign trade; transportation, storage and distribution, up to and including the first hand sales of the following goods:
      (i) crude oil,
      (ii) natural and artificial gas,
      (iii) goods covered by this Chapter obtained from the refining or processing of crude oil and natural gas, and

(iv) basic petrochemicals;

c) the supply of electricity as a public service in Mexico, including, except as provided in paragraph 5, the generation, transmission, transformation, distribution and sale of electricity; and

d) exploration, exploitation and processing of radioactive minerals, the nuclear fuel cycle, the generation of nuclear energy, the transportation and storage of nuclear waste, the use and reprocessing of nuclear fuel and the regulation of their applications for other purposes and the production of heavy water.

In the event of an inconsistency between this paragraph and another provision of this Agreement, this paragraph shall prevail to the extent of that inconsistency.

2. Pursuant to Article 1101(2), (Investment-Scope and Coverage), private investment is not permitted in the activities listed in paragraph 1. Chapter Twelve (CrossBorder Trade in Services) shall only apply to activities involving the provision of services covered in paragraph 1 when Mexico permits a contract to be granted in respect of such activities and only to the extent of that contract.

Trade in Natural Gas and Basic Petrochemicals

3. Where end-users and suppliers of natural gas or basic petrochemical goods consider that cross-border trade in such goods may be in their interests, each Party shall permit such end-users and suppliers, and any state enterprise of that Party as may be required under its domestic law, to negotiate supply contracts.

Each Party shall leave the modalities of the implementation of any such contract to the endusers, suppliers, and any state enterprise of the Party as may be required under its domestic law, which may take the form of individual contracts between the state enterprise and each of the other entities. Such contracts may be subject to regulatory approval.

Performance Clauses

4. Each Party shall allow its state enterprises to negotiate performance clauses in their service contracts.

Activities and Investment in Electricity Generation Facilities

5.

a) Production for Own Use

An enterprise of another Party may acquire, establish, and/or operate an electrical generating facility in Mexico to meet the enterprise's own supply needs. Electricity generated in excess of such needs must be sold to the Federal Electricity Commission (Comisi n Federal de Electricidad) (CFE) and CFE shall purchase such electricity under terms and conditions agreed to by CFE and the enterprise.

b) Co-generation

An enterprise of another Party may acquire, establish, and/or operate a co-generation facility in Mexico that generates electricity using heat, steam or other energy sources associated with an industrial process. Owners of the industrial facility need not be the owners of the co-generating facility. Electricity generated in excess of the industrial facility's supply requirements must be sold to CFE and CFE shall purchase such electricity under terms and conditions agreed to by CFE and the enterprise.

c) Independent Power Production

An enterprise of another Party may acquire, establish, and/or operate an electricity generating facility for independent power production (IPP) in Mexico. Electricity generated by such a facility for sale in Mexico shall be sold to CFE and CFE shall purchase such electricity under terms and conditions agreed to by CFE and the enterprise. Where an IPP located in Mexico and an electric utility of another Party consider that cross-border trade in electricity may be in their interests, each relevant Party shall permit these entities and CFE to negotiate terms and conditions of power purchase and power sale contracts. The modalities of implementing such supply contracts are left to the end users, suppliers and CFE and may take the form of individual contracts between CFE and each of the other entities. Each relevant Party shall determine whether such contracts are subject to regulatory approval.

ANNEX 603.6. EXCEPTION TO ARTICLE 603

For only those goods listed below, Mexico may restrict the granting of import and export licenses for the sole purpose of reserving foreign trade in these goods to itself.

2707.50	Other aromatic hydrocarbon mixtures of which 65 percent or more by volume (including losses) distills at 250 C by the ASTM D 86 method.
2707.99	Rubber extender oils, solvent naphtha and carbon black feedstocks only.
2709	Petroleum oils and oils obtained from bituminous minerals, crude.
2710	Aviation gasoline; gasoline and motor fuel blending stocks (except aviation gasoline) and reformates when used as motor fuel lending stocks; kerosene; gas oil and diesel oil; petroleum ether; fuel oil; paraffinic oils other than for lubricating purposes; pentanes; carbon black feedstocks; hexanes; heptanes and naphthas.
2711	Petroleum gases and other gaseous hydrocarbons other than: ethylene, propylene, butylene and butadiene, in purities over 50 percent.
2712.90	Only paraffin wax containing by weight more than 0.75 percent of oil, in bulk (Mexico classifies these goods under HS 2712.90.02) and only when imported to be used for further refining.
2713.11	Petroleum coke not calcined.
2713.20	Petroleum bitumen (except when used for road surfacing purposes under HS 2713.20.01).
2713.90	Other residues of petroleum oils or of oils obtained from bituminous minerals.
2714	Bitumen and asphalt, natural; bituminous or oil shale and tar sands, asphaltites and asphaltic rocks (except when used for road surfacing purposes under HS 2714.90.01).
2901.10	Ethane, butanes, pentanes, hexanes, and heptanes only.

ANNEX 605. EXCEPTION TO ARTICLE 605

Notwithstanding any other provision of this Chapter, the provisions of Article 605 shall not apply as between the other Parties and Mexico.

ANNEX 607. NATIONAL SECURITY

1. Article 607 shall impose no obligations and confer no rights on Mexico.
2. Article 2102 (National Security) shall apply as between Mexico and the other Parties.

ANNEX 608.2. OTHER AGREEMENTS

1. Canada and the United States shall act in accordance with the terms of Annexes 902.5 and 905.2 of the *Canada United States Free Trade Agreement* , which are hereby incorporated into and made a part of this Agreement for such purpose. This paragraph shall impose no obligations and confer no rights on Mexico.
2. Canada and the United States intend no inconsistency between this Chapter and the *Agreement on an International Energy Program (IEP*). In the event of any inconsistency between the IEP and this Chapter, the IEP shall prevail as between Canada and the United States to the extent of that inconsistency.

7. AGRICULTURE AND SANITARY AND PHYTOSANITARY MEASURES

Section A - Agriculture

Article 701: Scope and Coverage

1. This Section applies to measures adopted or maintained by a Party relating to agricultural trade.
2. In the event of any inconsistency between this Section and another provision of this Agreement, this Section shall prevail to the extent of the inconsistency.

Article 702: International Obligations

1. Annex 702.1 applies to the Parties specified in that Annex with respect to agricultural trade under certain agreements between them.
2. Prior to adopting pursuant to an intergovernmental commodity agreement, a measure that may affect trade in an agricultural good between the Parties, the Party proposing to adopt the measure shall consult with the other Parties with a view to avoiding

nullification or impairment of a concession granted by that Party in its Schedule to Annex 302.2.

3.   Annex 702.3 applies to the Parties specified in that Annex with respect to measures adopted or maintained pursuant to an intergovernmental coffee agreement.

Article 703: Market Access

1.   The Parties shall work together to improve access to their respective markets through the reduction or elimination of import barriers to trade between them in agricultural goods.

Customs Duties, Quantitative Restrictions, and Agricultural Grading and Marketing Standards

2.   Annex 703.2 applies to the Parties specified in that Annex with respect to customs duties and quantitative restrictions, trade in sugar and syrup goods, and agricultural grading and marketing standards.

Special Safeguard Provisions

3.   Each Party may, in accordance with its Schedule to Annex 302.2, adopt or maintain a special safeguard in the form of a tariff rate quota on an agricultural good listed in its Section of Annex 703.3. Notwithstanding Article 302.2, a Party may not apply an over-quota tariff rate under a special safeguard that exceeds the lesser of:
     a)   the most-favored-nation (MFN) rate as of July 1, 1991; and
     b)   the prevailing MFN rate.
4.   No Party may, with respect to the same good and the same country, at the same time:
     a)   apply an over-quota tariff rate under paragraph 3; and
     b)   take an emergency action covered by Chapter Eight (Emergency Action).

Article 704: Domestic Support

The Parties recognize that domestic support measures can be of crucial importance to their agricultural sectors but may also have trade distorting and production effects and that domestic support reduction commitments may result from agricultural multilateral trade negotiations under the *General Agreement on Tariffs and Trade (GATT)*. Accordingly, where a Party supports its agricultural producers, that Party should endeavor to work toward domestic support measures that:

a)   have minimal or no trade distorting or production effects; or
b)   are exempt from any applicable domestic support reduction commitments that may be negotiated under the GATT.

The Parties further recognize that a Party may change its domestic support measures, including those that may be subject to reduction commitments, at the Party's discretion, subject to its rights and obligations under the GATT.

Article 705: Export Subsidies

1. The Parties share the objective of the multilateral elimination of export subsidies for agricultural goods and shall cooperate in an effort to achieve an agreement under the GATT to eliminate those subsidies.

2. The Parties recognize that export subsidies for agricultural goods may prejudice the interests of importing and exporting Parties and, in particular, may disrupt the markets of importing Parties. Accordingly, in addition to the rights and obligations of the Parties specified in Annex 702.1, the Parties affirm that it is inappropriate for a Party to provide an export subsidy for an agricultural good exported to the territory of another Party where there are no other subsidized imports of that good into the territory of that other Party.

3. Except as provided in Annex 702.1, where an exporting Party considers that a non-Party is exporting an agricultural good to the territory of another Party with the benefit of export subsidies, the importing Party shall, on written request of the exporting Party, consult with the exporting Party with a view to agreeing on specific measures that the importing Party may adopt to counter the effect of any such subsidized imports. If the importing Party adopts the agreed-upon measures, the exporting Party shall refrain from applying, or immediately cease to apply, any export subsidy to exports of such good to the territory of the importing Party.

4. Except as provided in Annex 702.1, an exporting Party shall deliver written notice to the importing Party at least three days, excluding weekends, prior to adopting an export subsidy measure on an agricultural good exported to the territory of another Party. The exporting Party shall consult with the importing Party within 72 hours of receipt of the importing Party's written request, with a view to eliminating the subsidy or minimizing any adverse impact on the market of the importing Party for that good. The importing Party shall, when requesting consultations with the exporting Party, at the same time, deliver written notice to a third Party of the request. A third Party may request to participate in such consultations.

5. Each Party shall take into account the interests of the other Parties in the use of any export subsidy on an agricultural good, recognizing that such subsidies may have prejudicial effects on the interests of the other Parties.

6. The Parties hereby establish a Working Group on Agricultural Subsidies, comprising representatives of each Party, which shall meet at least semi-annually or as the Parties may otherwise agree, to work toward elimination of all export subsidies affecting agricultural trade between the Parties. The functions of the Working Group shall include:

   a) monitoring the volume and price of imports into the territory of any Party of agricultural goods that have benefitted from export subsidies;

   b) providing a forum for the Parties to develop mutually acceptable criteria and procedures for reaching agreement on the limitation or elimination of export subsidies for imports of agricultural goods into the territories of the Parties; and

c) reporting annually to the Committee on Agricultural Trade, established under Article 706, on the implementation of this Article.

7. Notwithstanding any other provision of this Article:

a) if the importing and exporting Parties agree to an export subsidy for an agricultural good exported to the territory of the importing Party, the exporting Party or Parties may adopt or maintain such subsidy; and

b) each Party retains its rights to apply countervailing duties to subsidized imports of agricultural goods from the territory of a Party or non-Party.

Article 706: Committee on Agricultural Trade

1. The Parties hereby establish a Committee on Agricultural Trade, comprising representatives of each Party.

2. The Committee's functions shall include:

a) monitoring and promoting cooperation on the implementation and administration of this Section;

b) providing a forum for the Parties to consult on issues related to this Section at least semi-annually and as the Parties may otherwise agree; and

c) reporting annually to the Commission on the implementation of this Section.

Article 707: Advisory Committee on Private Commercial Disputes regarding Agricultural Goods

The Committee shall establish an Advisory Committee on Private Commercial Disputes regarding Agricultural Goods, comprising persons with expertise or experience in the resolution of private commercial disputes in agricultural trade. The Advisory Committee shall report and provide recommendations to the Committee for the development of systems in the territory of each Party to achieve the prompt and effective resolution of such disputes, taking into account any special circumstance, including the perishability of certain agricultural goods.

Article 708: Definitions

For purposes of this Section:

agricultural good means a good provided for in any of the following:

Note: For purposes of reference only, descriptions are provided next to the corresponding tariff provision.

(a)

Harmonized System (HS) Chapters 1 through 24 (other than a fish or fish product); or
(b)

HS subheading	2905.43	manitol
HS subheading	2905.44	sorbitol
HS heading	33.01	essential oils
HS headings	35.01 to 35.05	albuminoidal substances, modified starches, glues
HS subheading	3809.10	finishing agents
HS subheading	3823.60	sorbitol n.e.p.
HS headings	41.01 to 41.03	hides and skins
HS heading	43.01	raw furskins
HS headings	50.01 to 50.03	raw silk and silk waste
HS headings	51.01 to 51.03	wool and animal hair
HS headings	52.01 to 52.03	raw cotton, cotton waste and cotton carded or combed
HS heading	53.01	raw flax
HS heading	53.02	raw hemp

customs duty means "customs duty" as defined in Article 318 (National Treatment and Market Access for Goods - Definitions);

duty-free means "duty-free" as defined in Article 318;

fish or fish product means a fish or crustacean, mollusc or other aquatic invertebrate, marine mammal, or a product thereof provided for in any of the following:

HS Chapter	03	fish and crustaceans, molluscs and other aquatic invertebrates
HS heading	05.07	tortoise-shell, whalebone and whalebone hair and those fish or crustaceans, molluscs or other aquatic invertebrates, marine mammals, and their products within this heading
HS heading	05.08	coral and similar materials
HS heading	05.09	natural sponges of animal origin
HS heading	05.11	products of fish or crustaceans, molluscs or other aquatic invertebrates; dead animals of Chapter 3
HS heading	15.04	fats and oils and their fractions, of fish or marine mammals
HS heading	16.03	"non-meat" extracts and juices
HS heading	16.04	prepared or preserved fish
HS heading	16.05	prepared preserved crustaceans, molluscs and other aquatic invertebrates;
HS subheading	2301.20	flours, meals, pellets of fish

material means "material" as defined in Article 415 (Rules of Origin - Definitions);

over-quota tariff rate means the rate of customs duty to be applied to quantities in excess of the quantity specified under a tariff rate quota;

sugar or syrup good means "sugar or syrup good" as defined in Annex 703.2;

tariff item means a "tariff item" as defined in Annex 401; and

tariff rate quota means a mechanism that provides for the application of a customs duty at a certain rate to imports of a particular good up to a specified quantity (in-quota quantity), and at a different rate to imports of that good that exceed that quantity.

ANNEX 702.1. INCORPORATION OF TRADE PROVISIONS

1. Articles 701, 702, 704, 705, 706, 707, 710 and 711 of the *Canada - United States Free Trade Agreement* apply, as between Canada and the United States, which Articles are hereby incorporated into and made a part of this Agreement.

2. The definitions of the terms specified in Article 711 of the *Canada - United States Free Trade Agreement* shall apply to the Articles incorporated by paragraph 1.

3. For purposes of this incorporation, any reference to Chapter Eighteen of the *Canada -United States Free Trade Agreement* shall be deemed to be a reference to Chapter Twenty (Institutional Arrangements and Dispute Settlement Procedures) of this Agreement.

4. The Parties understand that Article 710 of the *Canada - United States Free Trade Agreement* incorporates the GATT rights and obligations of Canada and the United States with respect to agricultural, food, beverage and certain related goods, including exemptions by virtue of paragraph (1)(b) of the Protocol of Provisional Application of the GATT and waivers granted under Article XXV of the GATT.

ANNEX 702.3. INTERGOVERNMENTAL COFFEE AGREEMENT

Notwithstanding Article 2101 (General Exceptions), neither Canada nor Mexico may adopt or maintain a measure, pursuant to an intergovernmental coffee agreement, that restricts trade in coffee between them.

ANNEX 703.2. MARKET ACCESS

Section A - Mexico and the United States

1. This Section applies only as between Mexico and the United States.

Customs Duties and Quantitative Restrictions

2. With respect to agricultural goods, Article 309(1) and (2) (Import and Export Restrictions) applies only to qualifying goods.

3. Each Party waives its rights under Article XI:2(c) of the GATT, and those rights as incorporated by Article 309, regarding any measure adopted or maintained with

respect to the importation of qualifying goods.

4. Except with respect to a good set out in Section B or C of Annex 703.3 or Appendix 703.2.A.4, where a Party applies an over-quota tariff rate to a qualifying good pursuant to a tariff rate quota set out in its Schedule to Annex 302.2, or increases a customs duty for a sugar or syrup good to a rate, in accordance with paragraph 18, that exceeds the rate of customs duty for that good set out in its GATT Schedule of Tariff Concessions as of July 1, 1991, the other Party waives its rights under the GATT with respect to the application of that rate of customs duty.

5. Notwithstanding Article 302(2) (Tariff Elimination), where an agreement resulting from agricultural multilateral trade negotiations under the GATT enters into force with respect to a Party pursuant to which it has agreed to convert a prohibition or restriction on its importation of an agricultural good into a tariff rate quota or a customs duty, that Party may not apply to such good that is a qualifying good an over-quota tariff rate that is higher than the lower of the over-quota tariff rate set out in:

   a) its Schedule to Annex 302.2, and

   b) that agreement, and paragraph 4 shall no longer apply to the other Party with respect to that good.

6. Each Party may count the in-quota quantity under a tariff rate quota applied to a qualifying good in accordance with its Schedule to Annex 302.2 toward the satisfaction of commitments regarding an in-quota quantity of a tariff rate quota or level of access under a restriction on the importation of that good:

   a) that have been agreed under the GATT, including as set out in its GATT Schedule of Tariff Concessions; or

   b) undertaken by the Party as a result of any agreement resulting from agricultural multilateral trade negotiations under the GATT.

7. Neither Party may count toward the satisfaction of a commitment regarding an in-quota quantity of a tariff rate quota in its Schedule to Annex 302.2 an agricultural good admitted or entered into a maquiladora or foreign-trade zone and re-exported, including subsequent to processing.

8. The United States shall not adopt or maintain, with respect to the importation of an agricultural qualifying good, any fee applied pursuant to section 22 of the *U.S. Agricultural Adjustment Act.*

9. Neither Party may seek a voluntary restraint agreement from the other Party with respect to the exportation of meat that is a qualifying good.

10. Notwithstanding Chapter Four (Rules of Origin), for purposes of applying a rate of customs duty to a good, the United States may consider as if it were non-originating a good provided for in:

   a) heading 12.02 that is exported from the territory of Mexico, if the good is not wholly obtained in the territory of Mexico;

   b) subheading 2008.11 that is exported from the territory of Mexico, if any material provided for in heading 12.02 used in the production of that good is not wholly obtained in the territory of Mexico; or

   c) U.S. tariff item 1806.10.42 or 2106.90.12 that is exported from the territory of Mexico, if any material provided for in HS heading 1701.99 used in the production of that good is not a qualifying good.

11. Notwithstanding Chapter Four, for purposes of applying a rate of customs duty to a good, Mexico may consider as if it were non-originating a good provided for in:
    a) HS heading 12.02 that is exported from the territory of the United States, if that good is not wholly obtained in the territory of the United States;
    b) HS subheading 2008.11 that is exported from the territory of the United States, if any material provided for in heading 12.02 used in the production of that good is not wholly obtained in the territory of the United States; or
    c) Mexican tariff item 1806.10.01 (except those with a sugar content less than 90 percent) or 2106.90.05 (except those that contain added flavoring matter) that is exported from the territory of the United States, if any material provided for in HS subheading 1701.99 used in the production of that good is not a qualifying good.

Restriction on Same-Condition Substitution Duty Drawback

12. Beginning on the date of entry into force of this Agreement, neither Mexico nor the United States may refund the amount of customs duties paid, or waive or reduce the amount of customs duties owed, on any agricultural good imported into its territory that is substituted for an identical or similar good that is subsequently exported to the territory of the other Party.

Trade in Sugar and Syrup Goods

13. The Parties shall consult by July 1 of each of the first 14 years beginning with 1994 to determine jointly, in accordance with Appendix 703.2.A.13, whether, and if so, by what quantity either Party:
    a) is projected to be a net surplus producer of sugar in the next marketing year; and
    b) has been a net surplus producer in any marketing year beginning after the date of entry into force of this Agreement, including the current marketing year.
14. For each of the first 14 marketing years beginning after the date of entry into force of this Agreement, each Party shall accord duty-free treatment to a quantity of sugar and syrup goods that are qualifying goods not less than the greatest of:
    a) 7,258 metric tons raw value;
    b) the quota allocated by the United States for a non-Party within the category designated "other specified countries and areas" under paragraph (b)(i) of additional U.S. note 3 to chapter 17 of the Harmonized Tariff Schedule of the United States; and
    c) subject to paragraph 15, the other Party's projected net production surplus for that marketing year, as determined under paragraph 13 and adjusted in accordance with Appendix 703.2.A.13.
15. Subject to paragraph 16, the duty-free quantity of sugar and syrup goods under paragraph 14(c); shall not exceed the following ceilings:
    a) for each of the first six marketing years, 25,000 metric tons raw value;
    b) for the seventh marketing year, 150,000 metric tons raw value; and

c) for each of the eighth through 14th marketing years, 110 percent of the previous marketing year's ceiling.

16. Beginning with the seventh marketing year, paragraph 15 shall not apply where, pursuant to paragraph 13, the Parties have determined the exporting Party to be a net surplus producer:

   a) for any two consecutive marketing years beginning after the date of entry into force of this Agreement;

   b) for the previous and current marketing years; or

   c) in the current marketing year and projected it to be a net surplus producer in the next marketing year, unless subsequently the Parties determine that, contrary to the projection, the exporting Party was not a net surplus producer for that year.

17. Mexico shall, beginning no later than six years after the date of entry into force of this Agreement, apply on a most- favored-nation (MFN) basis a tariff rate quota for sugar and syrup goods consisting of rates of customs duties no less than the lesser of the corresponding:

   a) MFN rates of the United States in effect on the date that Mexico commences to apply the tariff rate quota; and

   b) prevailing MFN rates of the United States.

18. When Mexico applies a tariff rate quota under paragraph 17, it shall not apply on a sugar or syrup good that is a qualifying good a rate of customs duty higher than the rate of customs duty applied by the United States on such good.

19. Each Party shall determine the quantity of a sugar or syrup good that is a qualifying good based on the actual weight of such good, converted as appropriate to raw value, without regard to the good's packaging or presentation.

20. If the United States eliminates its tariff rate quota for sugar and syrup goods imported from non-Parties, at such time the United States shall accord to such goods that are qualifying goods the better of the treatment, as determined by Mexico, of:

   a) the treatment provided for in paragraphs 14 through 16; or

   b) the MFN treatment granted by the United States to non-Parties.

21. Except as provided in paragraph 22, Mexico shall not be required to apply the applicable rate of customs duty provided in this Annex or in its Schedule to Annex 302.2 to a sugar or syrup good, or sugar-containing product, that is a qualifying good where the United States has granted or will grant benefits under any re-export program or any like program in connection with the export of the good. The United States shall notify Mexico in writing within two days, excluding weekends, of any export to Mexico of such a good for which the benefits of any re-export program or any other like program have been or will be claimed by the exporter.

22. Notwithstanding any other provision of this Section:

   a) the United States shall accord duty-free treatment to imports of

      (i) raw sugar that is a qualifying good that will be refined in the territory of the United States and re-exported to the territory of Mexico, and

      (ii) refined sugar that is a qualifying good that has been refined from raw sugar produced in, and exported from, the territory of the United States;

   b) Mexico shall accord duty-free treatment to imports of

      (i) raw sugar that is a qualifying good that will be refined in the territory of Mexico and re-exported to the territory of the United States, and

(ii) refined sugar that is a qualifying good that has been refined from raw sugar produced in, and exported from, the territory of Mexico; and

c) imports qualifying for duty-free treatment pursuant to subparagraphs (a) and (b) shall not be subject to, or counted under, any tariff rate quota.

Agricultural Grading and Marketing Standards.

23. Where a Party adopts or maintains a measure respecting the classification, grading or marketing of a domestic agricultural good, it shall accord treatment to a like qualifying good destined for processing no less favorable than it accords under the measure to the domestic good destined for processing. The importing Party may adopt or maintain measures to ensure that such imported good is processed.

24. Paragraph 23 shall be without prejudice to the rights of either Party under the GATT or under Chapter Three (National Treatment and Market Access) regarding measures respecting the classification, grading or marketing of an agricultural good, whether or not destined for processing.

25. The Parties hereby establish a Working Group, comprising representatives of Mexico and the United States, which shall meet annually or as otherwise agreed. The Working Group shall review, in coordination with the Committee on Standards-Related Measures established under Article 913 (Committee on Standards- Related Measures), the operation of agricultural grade and quality standards as they affect trade between the Parties, and shall resolve issues that may arise regarding the operation of the standards. This Working Group shall report to the Committee on Agricultural Trade established under Article 706.

Definitions

26. For purposes of this Section:

marketing year means a 12-month period beginning October 1;

net production surplus means the quantity by which a Party's domestic production of sugar exceeds its total consumption of sugar during a marketing year, determined in accordance with this Section;

net surplus producer means a Party that has a net production surplus;

plantation white sugar means crystalline sugar that has not been refined and is intended for human consumption without further processing or refining;

qualifying good means an originating good that is an agricultural good, except that in determining whether such good is an originating good, operations performed in or materials obtained from Canada shall be considered as if they were performed in or obtained from a non-Party;

raw value means the equivalent of a quantity of sugar in terms of raw sugar testing 96 degrees by the polariscope, determined as follows:

a) the raw value of plantation white sugar equals the number of kilograms thereof multiplied by 1.03;

b) the raw value of liquid sugar and invert sugar equals the number of kilograms of the total sugars thereof multiplied by 1.07; and

    c)   the raw value of other imported sugar and syrup goods equals the number of kilograms thereof multiplied by the greater of 0.93, or 1.07 less 0.0175 for each degree of polarization under 100 degrees (and fractions of a degree in proportion);

sugar means raw or refined sugar derived directly or indirectly from sugar cane or sugar beets, including liquid refined sugar; and

sugar-containing product means a good containing sugar; and

wholly obtained in the territory of means harvested in the territory of.

Section B - Canada and Mexico

1.   This Section applies only as between Canada and Mexico.

Customs Duties and Quantitative Restrictions

2.   With respect to agricultural goods, Article 309(1) and (2) (Import and Export Restrictions) applies only to qualifying goods.

3.   Except with respect to a good set out in Sections A or B of Annex 703.3., where a Party applies an over-quota tariff rate to a qualifying good pursuant to a tariff rate quota set out in its Schedule to Annex 302.2 or increases a customs duty for a sugar or syrup good to a rate that exceeds the rate of customs duty for that good set out in its GATT Schedule of Tariff Concessions as of July 1, 1991, the other Party waives its rights under the GATT with respect to the application of that rate of customs duty.

4.   Notwithstanding Article 302(2) (Tariff Elimination), where an agreement resulting from agricultural multilateral trade negotiations under the GATT enters into force with respect to a Party pursuant to which it has agreed to convert a prohibition or restriction on its importation of an agricultural good into a tariff rate quota or a customs duty, that Party may not apply to such good that is a qualifying good an over-quota tariff rate that is higher than the lower of the over-quota tariff rate in:

    a)   its Schedule to Annex 302.2, and

    b)   that agreement,

and paragraph 3 shall no longer apply to the other Party with respect to that good.

5.   Each Party may count the in-quota quantity under a tariff rate quota applied to a qualifying good in accordance with its Schedule to Annex 302.2 toward the satisfaction of commitments regarding an in-quota quantity of a tariff rate quota or level of access under a restriction on the importation of that good:

    a)   that have been agreed under the GATT, including as set out in its GATT Schedule of Tariff Concessions; or

    b)   undertaken by the Party as a result of any agreement resulting from agricultural multilateral trade negotiations under the GATT.

6.   Subject to this Section and for purposes of this Section, Canada and Mexico incorporate their respective rights and obligations with respect to agricultural goods under the GATT and agreements negotiated under the GATT, including their rights and obligations under Article XI of the GATT.

7. Notwithstanding paragraph 6 and Article 309:
   a) the rights and obligations of the Parties under Article XI:2(c)(i) of the GATT and those rights as incorporated by Article 309 shall apply with respect to trade in agricultural goods only to the dairy, poultry and egg goods set out in Appendix 703.2.B.7; and
   b) with respect to such dairy, poultry and egg goods that are qualifying goods, either Party may adopt or maintain a prohibition or restriction or a customs duty on the importation of such good consistent with its rights and obligations under the GATT.

8. Without prejudice to Chapter Eight (Emergency Action), neither Party may seek a voluntary restraint agreement from the other Party with respect to the exportation of a qualifying good.

9. Notwithstanding Chapter Four (Rules of Origin), Mexico may treat a good provided for in Mexican tariff item 1806.10.01 (except those with a sugar content less than 90 percent) or 2106.90.05 (except those that contain added flavoring matter) that is exported from the territory of Canada as non- originating for purposes of applying a rate of customs duty to that good, if any material provided for in HS subheading 1701.99 used in the production of such good is not a qualifying good.

10. Notwithstanding Chapter Four (Rules of Origin), Canada may treat a good provided for in Canadian tariff item 1806.10.10 or 2106.90.21 that is exported from the territory of Mexico as non-originating for purposes of applying a rate of customs duty to that good, if any material provided for in HS subheading 1701.99 used in the production of such good is not a qualifying good.

Trade in Sugar

11. Mexico shall apply a rate of customs duty equal to its most-favored-nation over-quota tariff rate to a sugar or syrup that is a qualifying good.

12. Canada may apply a rate of customs duty on a sugar or syrup good that is a qualifying good equal to the rate of customs duty applied by Mexico pursuant to paragraph 11.

Agricultural Grading and Marketing Standards

13. The Parties hereby establish a Working Group, comprising representatives of Canada and Mexico, which shall meet annually or as otherwise agreed. The Working Group shall review, in coordination with the Committee on Standards-Related Measures established under Article 913 (Committee on Standards-Related Measures), the operation of agricultural grade and quality standards as they affect trade between the Parties, and shall resolve issues that may arise regarding the operation of the standards. This Working Group shall report to the Committee on Agricultural Trade established under Article 706.

Definitions
14. For purposes of this Section:

qualifying good means an originating good that is an agricultural good except that, in determining whether such good is an originating good, operations performed in or material obtained from the United States shall be considered as if they were performed in or obtained from a non-Party.

Section C - Definitions

For purposes of this Annex:

sugar or syrup good means:

a) for imports into Canada, a good provided for in any of the current tariff items 1701.11.10, 1701.11.20, 1701.11.30, 1701.11.40, 1701.11.50, 1701.12.00, 1701.91.00, 1701.99.00, 1702.90.31, 1702.90.32, 1702.90.33, 1702.90.34, 1702.90.35, 1702.90.36, 1702.90.37, 1702.90.38, 1702.90.40, 1806.10.10 and 2106.90.21 of the Canadian Tariff Schedule;

b) for imports into Mexico, a good provided for in any of the current tariff items 1701.11.01, 1701.11.99, 1701.12.01, 1701.12.99, 1701.91 (except those that contain added flavoring matter), 1701.99.01, 1701.99.99, 1702.90.01, 1806.10.01 (except those with a sugar content less than 90 percent) and 2106.90.05 (except those that contain flavoring matter) of the *General Import Duty Act* ("Ley del Impuesto General de Importación"); and

c) for imports into the United States, a good provided for in any of the current tariff items 1701.11.03, 1701.12.02, 1701.91.22, 1701.99.02, 1702.90.32, 1806.10.42, and 2106.90.12 of the U.S. Harmonized Tariff Schedule, without regard to the quantity imported.

APPENDIX 703.2.A.4. GOODS NOT SUBJECT TO ANNEX 703.2.A.4

Note: For purposes of reference only, descriptions are provided next to the corresponding tariff provision.

Schedule of Mexico	
Mexican Tariff Item	**Description**
2009.11.01	Orange juice, frozen
2009.19.01	Orange juice, with a grade of concentration not greater than 1.5 (single-strength orange juice)
Schedule of the United States	
U.S. Tariff Item	**Description**
2009.11.00	Orange juice, frozen
2009.19.20	Orange juice, not frozen, not concentrated (single-strength orange juice

APPENDIX 703.2.A.13. DETERMINATION AND ADJUSTMENT OF NET PRODUCTION SURPLUS

1. For purposes of Section A(14)(c), where the Parties project a net production surplus for a Party for the next marketing year, the projected surplus shall be:

   a) increased by the amount, if any, by which the actual net production surplus exceeds the projected net production surplus in the most recent marketing year for which the Parties projected a net production surplus for that Party; or

   b) decreased by the amount, if any, by which the projected net production surplus exceeds the actual net production surplus in the most recent marketing year for which the Parties projected a net production surplus for that Party;

as further demonstrated by the following formulas:

$$ANPS = (PPy - CPy) + CF$$

where:

ANPS =	adjusted net production surplus
PP =	projected domestic production of sugar
CP =	projected total consumption of sugar
CF =	correction factor
y =	next marketing year,

and

$$CF = (PAys - CAys) - (PPys - CPys)$$

where:

PA =	actual domestic production of sugar
CA =	actual total consumption of sugar
ys =	most recent previous marketing year for which the Parties projected a net production surplus for that Party.

2. For purposes only of paragraph 1, neither the projected net production surplus (PPys -CPys) nor the actual net production surplus (PAys - CAys) in the most recent marketing year for which the Parties projected a net production surplus for that Party may be considered to:

   a) exceed the quantity, if any, in Section A(15) applicable to that year; or

   b) be lower than the greater of

      (i) 7,258 metric tons raw value, or

      (ii) the quantity in paragraph 14(b) of Section A applicable to that year.

3. In appropriate circumstances, a Party shall consider adjustments to projections of its net production surplus when:

F_c greater than (B + 10 %)

where

F	is the percentage change in stocks from the beginning to the end of a marketing year z, expressed as a positive percentage
c	is current marketing year
F	is calculated in accordance with the following formula:

$$F = \frac{Sb - Se}{Sb} \times 100$$

Sb	beginning stocks in marketing year z
Se	ending stocks in marketing year z
B	the average annual percentage change in stocks over the previous 5 marketing years, calculated in accordance with the following formula:

$$B = \frac{\left\{ 5 \Big/ \sum_{N=1} F_N \right\}}{5}$$

| N | previous marketing years, ranging from 1 (first preceding year) to 5 (fifth preceding year). |
| | |

4. For purposes of determining net production surplus or projected net production surplus:
   a) domestic production means all sugar and syrup goods derived from sugar cane or sugar beets grown in a Party's territory; and
   b) total consumption means all sugar and syrup goods consumed directly, or indirectly in the form of a good containing such goods, in the territory of a Party.
5. Each Party shall permit representatives from the other Party to observe and comment on its statistics on production, consumption, trade and stocks and on the methodology it uses to prepare such statistics.
6. Statistics on production, consumption, trade and stocks shall be provided by:
   a) the Secretaría de Agricultura y Recursos Hidráulicos, the Secretaría de Comercio y Fomento Industrial, and la Secretaría de Hacienda y Crédito Público; and
   b) the U.S. Department of Agriculture (USDA).

APPENDIX 703.2.B.7. DAIRY, POULTRY AND EGG GOODS

Note: (For purposes of reference only, descriptions are provided next to the corresponding tariff provision).

Schedule of Canada

For Canada, a dairy, poultry or egg good is a good provided for in one of the following Canadian tariff items:

Canadian Tariff Items	Description
0105.11.20	Broilers of the species Gallus domesticus for domestic production, weighing not more than 185 g
0105.91.00	Live fowls of the species Gallus domesticus, weighing 185g. or more
0105.99.00	Live ducks, geese, turkeys and guinea fowls, weighing 185g. or more
0207.10.00	Meat of poultry of heading No. 01.05, not cut in pieces, fresh or chilled
0207.21.00	Meat of fowls of the species Gallus domesticus, not cut in pieces, frozen
0207.22.00	Meat of turkeys, not cut in pieces, frozen
0207.39.00	Cut meat and edible offal (including livers other than fatty livers of geese or ducks), of the poultry of heading No. 01.05, fresh or chilled
0207.41.00	Cut meat and edible offal, other than livers, of fowls of the species Gallus domesticus, frozen
0207.42.00	Cut meat and edible offal, other than livers, of turkeys, frozen
0207.50.00	Livers of poultry of heading No. 01.05, frozen
0209.00.20	Poultry fat (not rendered), fresh, chilled, frozen, salted, in brine, dried or smoked
0210.90.10	Meat of poultry, salted, in brine, dried or smoked
0401.10.00	Milk and cream, not concentrated nor containing added sugar or other sweetening matter of a fat content, by weight, not exceeding 1 percent
0401.20.00	Milk and cream, not concentrated nor containing added sugar or other sweetening matter of a fat content, by weight, exceeding 1 percent but not exceeding 6 percent
0401.30.00	Milk and cream, not concentrated nor containing added sugar or other sweetening matter, of a fat content, by weight, exceeding 6 percent
0402.10.00	Milk and cream, concentrated or containing added sugar or other sweetening matter, in powder, granules or other solid forms, of a fat content, by weight, not exceeding 1.5 percent
0402.21.10	Milk, concentrated, not containing added sugar or other sweetening matter, in powder, granules or other solid forms, of a fat content, by weight, exceeding 1.5 percent
0402.21.20	Cream, concentrated, not containing added sugar or other sweetening matter, in powder, granules or other solid forms, of a fat content, by weight, exceeding 1.5 percent

(Continued)

Canadian Tariff Items	Description
0402.29.10	Milk, whether or not concentrated, containing added sugar or other sweetening matter, in powder, granules or other solid forms, of a fat content, by weight, exceeding 1.5 percent
0402.29.20	Cream, whether or not concentrated, containing added sugar or other sweetening matter, in powder, granules or other solid forms, of a fat content, by weight, exceeding 1.5 percent
0402.91.00	Milk and cream, concentrated, not containing added sugar or other sweetening matter, not in powder, granules or other solid forms
0402.99.00	Milk and cream, whether or not concentrated, containing added sugar or other sweetening matter, not in powder, granules or other solid forms
0403.10.00	Yogurt
0403.90.10	Powdered buttermilk
0403.90.90	Liquid buttermilk, curdled milk and cream, kephir and other fermented or acidified milk and cream, whether or not concentrated or containing added sugar or other sweetening matter or flavored or containing added fruit, nuts or cocoa
0404.10.10	Whey powder and modified whey powder, whether or not concentrated or containing added sugar or other sweetening matter
0404.10.90	Whey and modified whey, not in powder, whether or not concentrated or containing added sugar or other sweetening matter
0404.90.00	Products consisting of natural milk constituents, whether or not containing added sugar or other sweetening matter, not elsewhere specified or included
0405.00.10	Butter
0405.00.90	Fats and oils derived from milk, other than butter
0406.10.00	Fresh (unripened or uncured) cheese, including whey cheese, and curd
0406.20.10	Cheddar cheese and cheddar types of cheese, grated or powdered
0406.20.90	Grated or powdered cheese of all kinds, other than cheddar and cheddar types
0406.30.00	Processed cheese, not grated or powdered
0406.40.00	Blue-veined cheese
0406.90.10	Cheddar cheese and cheddar types of cheese, not grated, powdered or processed
0406.90.90	Other cheese not elsewhere specified or included
0407.00.00	Birds' eggs, in shell, fresh, preserved or cooked
0408.11.00	Dried egg yolks, whether or not containing added sugar or other sweetening matter
0408.19.00	Egg yolks, fresh, cooked by steaming or by boiling in water, moulded, frozen or otherwise preserved, whether or not containing added sugar or other sweetening matter
0408.91.00	Bird's eggs, not in shell, dried, whether or not containing added sugar or other sweetening matter
0408.99.00	Birds' eggs, not in shell, fresh, cooked by steaming or by boiling in water, moulded, frozen or otherwise preserved, whether or not containing added sugar or other sweetening matter

Canadian Tariff Items	Description
1601.00.11	Sausages and similar products of meat, meat offal or blood of poultry of heading No. 01.05 or food preparation based on these products, in airtight containers
1602.10.10	Homogenized preparations of chicken or turkey
1602.20.20	Poultry liver paste
1602.31.10	Prepared meals of prepared or preserved turkey meat, meat offal or blood, other than sausages and similar products
1602.31.91	Prepared or preserved turkey meat, meat offal or blood, other than sausages and similar products, and other than prepared meals, in air-tight containers
1602.31.99	Prepared or preserved turkey meat, meat offal of blood, other than sausages and similar products, other than prepared meals, not in air-tight containers
1602.39.10	Prepared meals of prepared or preserved meat, meat offal or blood of poultry of heading No. 01.05 other than turkey (i.e., Gallus domesticus, ducks, geese or guinea fowls), other than sausages and similar products
1602.39.91	Prepared or preserved meat, meat offal or blood of poultry of heading No. 01.05 other than turkey (i.e., Gallus domesticus, ducks, geese or guinea fowls), other than sausages and similar products, and other than prepared meals, in air-tight containers
1602.39.99	Prepared or preserved meat, meat offal or blood, of poultry of heading No. 01.05 other than turkey (i.e., Gallus domesticus, ducks, geese or guinea fowls), other than sausages and similar products, other than prepared meals, not in air-tight containers
1901.90.31	Food preparations of goods of headings Nos. 04.01 to 04.04, not containing cocoa powder or containing cocoa powder in a proportion by weight of less than 10 percent, not elsewhere specified or included, containing more than 10 percent on a dry weight basis of milk solids
2105.00.00	Ice cream and other edible ice, whether or not containing cocoa
2106.90.70	Egg preparations not elsewhere specified or included
2309.90.31	Complete feeds and feed supplements, including concentrates, containing over 50 percent by weight in the dry state of milk solids
3501.10.00	Casein
3501.90.00	Caseinates and other casein derivatives; casein glues
3502.10.10	Egg albumin, dried, evaporated, desiccated or powdered
3502.10.90	Other egg albumin

Schedule of Mexico

For Mexico, a dairy, poultry or egg good is a good provided for in one of the following tariff items:

Mexican Tariff Items	Description
0105.11.01	Day old chickens without being fed during its transportation
0105.91.01	Game cocks
0105.91.99	Other
0105.99.99	Other poultry
0207.10.01	Turkey
0207.10.99	Other
0207.21.01	Chickens
0207.22.01	Turkey
0207.39.01	Mechanically deboned of poultry or turkey (not provided for in heading 16.01 or 16.02)
0207.39.02	Turkey
0207.39.99	Other
0207.41.01	Mechanically deboned of poultry or turkey (not provided for in heading 16.01 or 16.02)
0207.41.99	Other
0207.42.01	Mechanically deboned of poultry or turkey (not provided for in heading 16.01 or 16.02)
0207.42.99	Other
0207.50.01	Poultry livers, frozen
0209.00.01	Chicken or turkey fat
0210.90.99	Other
0401.10.01	In hermetic containers milk not concentrated
0401.10.99	Other
0401.20.01	In hermetic containers
0401.20.99	Other
0401.30.01	In hermetic containers
0401.30.99	Other
0402.10.01	Milk powder
0402.10.99	Other
0402.21.01	Milk powder
0402.21.99	Other
0402.29.99	Other
0402.91.01	Evaporated milk
0402.91.99	Other
0402.99.01	Condensed milk
0402.99.99	Other
0403.10.01	Yogurt
0403.90.01	Powdered milk whey with a protein content less than or equal to 12 percent
0403.90.99	Other butter whey
0404.10.01	Whey, concentrated, sweetened
0404.90.99	Other
0405.00.01	Butter, including the immediate container, with a weight less than or equal to 1 kg

Canadian Tariff Items	Description
0405.00.02	Butter, including the immediate container, with a weight over 1 kg
0405.00.03	Butiric fat, dehydrated
0405.00.99	Other
0406.10.01	Fresh cheese, including whey cheese
0406.20.01	Cheese, grated or powdered
0406.30.01	Melted cheese, not grated or powdered
0406.30.99	Other, melted cheese
0406.40.01	Blue veined cheese
0406.90.01	Hard paste cheese called sardo
0406.90.02	Hard paste reggi cheese
0406.90.03	Soft paste cologne cheese
0406.90.04	Hard or semi-hard cheeses with a fat content by weight less than or equal to 40 percent, and with a water content by weight in non-fat matter less than or equal to 47 percent (called "grana", "parmigiana" or "reggiano,") or with a non-fat matter content by weight over 47 percent without exceeding 72 percent (called "danloo, edam, fontan, fontina, fynbo, gouda, Avarti, maribo, samsoe, esron, italico, kernhem, Saint-Nectaire, Saint-Paulin, or talegi ")
0406.90.05	Petit suisse cheese
0406.90.06	Egmont cheese
0406.90.99	Other hard and semihard cheese
0407.00.01	Fresh birds eggs, fertile
0407.00.02	Frozen eggs
0407.00.99	Other poultry eggs
0408.11.01	Dried yolks
0408.19.99	Other
0408.91.01	Frozen or powdered
0408.91.99	Other
0408.99.01	Frozen or powdered
0408.99.99	Other
1601.00.01	Sausages or similar products of poultry or turkey
1602.10.01	Homogenized preparations of poultry or turkey
1602.20.01	Prepared or preserved liver of poultry or turkey
1602.31.01	Prepared or preserved turkey meat
1602.39.99	Other
1901.90.03	Food preparations containing over 10 percent, by weight, of milk solids
2105.00.01	Ice cream and similar products
2106.90.09	Egg preparations
2309.90.11	Preparations containing over 50 percent by weight of milk solids
3501.10.01	Casein
3501.90.01	Casein glues
3501.90.02	Caseinates
3501.90.99	Other
3502.10.01	Egg albumin

ANNEX 703.3. SPECIAL SAFEGUARD GOODS

Note: (For purposes of reference only, descriptions are provided next to the corresponding tariff provision).

Section A – Canada

Canadian Tariff Items	Description
0603.10.90	Fresh cut flowers and flower buds, other than orchids, of a kind suitable for bouquets or for ornamental purposes.
0702.00.91	Tomatoes, fresh or chilled, not for processing, (dutiable period).
0703.10.31	Onions or shallots, green, fresh or chilled (dutiable period).
0707.00.91	Cucumbers or gherkins, fresh or chilled, not for processing (dutiable period).
0710.80.20	Broccoli and cauliflowers, uncooked or cooked by steaming or boiling in water, frozen.
0811.10.10	Strawberries, uncooked or cooked by steaming or boiling in water, frozen, whether or not containing added sugar or other sweetening matter, for processing.
0811.10.90	Strawberries, uncooked or cooked by steaming or boiling in water, frozen, whether or not containing added sugar or other sweetening matter, other than for processing.
2002.90.00	Tomatoes prepared or preserved otherwise than by vinegar or acetic acid, other than whole or in pieces.

Section B – Mexico

Mexican Tariff Items	Description
0103.91.99	Live swine, weighing less than 50 kilograms each, except purebred breeding animals and those with pedigree or selected breed certificate
0103.92.99	Live swine, weighing 50 kilograms or more each, except purebred breeding animals and those with pedigree or selected breed certificate
0203.11.01	Meat of swine, carcasses and half- carcasses, fresh or chilled
0203.12.01	Hams, shoulders or cuts thereof, with bone in, fresh or chilled
0203.19.99	Other swine meat, fresh or chilled
0203.21.01	Meat of swine, carcasses and half- carcasses, frozen
0203.22.01	Hams, shoulders and cuts thereof, with bone in, frozen
0203.29.99	Other swine meat, frozen
0210.11.01	Hams, shoulders and cuts thereof with bone in, salted, in brine, dried or smoked
0210.12.01	Bellies (streaky) and cuts thereof, salted, in brine, dried or smoked.
0210.19.99	Other swine meat, in brine, dried or smoked

Mexican Tariff Items	Description
0710.10.01	Potatoes, uncooked or cooked by steaming or boiling in water, frozen
0712.10.01	Dried potatoes, whole cut, sliced, broken or in powder, but not further prepared
0808.10.01	Apples, fresh
2004.10.01	Potatoes prepared or preserved otherwise than by vinegar or acetic acid, frozen
2005.20.01	Potatoes prepared or preserved otherwise than by vinegar or acetic acid, not frozen
2101.10.01	Extracts, essences or concentrates, of coffee, and preparations with a basis of these extracts, essences or concentrates or with a basis of coffee

Section C - United States

U.S. Tariff Items	Description
0702.00.06	Tomatoes (except cherry tomatoes), fresh or chilled; if entered during the period from November 15 to the last day of the following February, inclusive
0702.00.20	Tomatoes (except cherry tomatoes), fresh or chilled; if entered during the period from March 1 to July 14, inclusive
0703.10.40	Onions and shallots, fresh or chilled (not including onion sets and not including pearl onions not over 16 mm in diameter) if entered January 1 to April 30, inclusive
0709.30.20	Eggplants (aubergines), fresh or chilled, if entered during the period from April 1 to June 30, inclusive
0709.60.00	"Chili" peppers; if entered during the period from October 1 to July 31, inclusive (current 0709.60.00.20)
0709.90.20	Squash, fresh or chilled; if entered during the period from October 1 to the following June 30, inclusive
0807.10.40	Watermelons, fresh; if entered during the period from May 1 to September 30, inclusive.

Section B - Sanitary and Phytosanitary Measures

Article 709: Scope and Coverage

In order to establish a framework of rules and disciplines to guide the development, adoption and enforcement of sanitary and phytosanitary measures, this Section applies to any such measure of a Party that may, directly or indirectly, affect trade between the Parties.

Article 710: Relation to Other Chapters

Articles 301 (National Treatment) and 309 (Import and Export Restrictions), and the provisions of Article XX(b) of the GATT as incorporated into Article 2101(1) (General Exceptions), do not apply to any sanitary or phytosanitary measure.

Article 711: Reliance on Non-Governmental Entities

Each Party shall ensure that any non-governmental entity on which it relies in applying a sanitary or phytosanitary measure acts in a manner consistent with this Section.

Article 712: Basic Rights and Obligations

Right to Take Sanitary and Phytosanitary Measures

1.   Each Party may, in accordance with this Section, adopt, maintain or apply any sanitary or phytosanitary measure necessary for the protection of human, animal or plant life or health in its territory, including a measure more stringent than an international standard, guideline or recommendation.

Right to Establish Level of Protection

2.   Notwithstanding any other provision of this Section, each Party may, in protecting human, animal or plant life or health, establish its appropriate levels of protection in accordance with Article 715.

Scientific Principles

3.   Each Party shall ensure that any sanitary or phytosanitary measure that it adopts, maintains or applies is:
   a)   based on scientific principles, taking into account relevant factors including, where appropriate, different geographic conditions;
   b)   not maintained where there is no longer a scientific basis for it; and
   c)   based on a risk assessment, as appropriate to the circumstances.

Non-Discriminatory Treatment

4.   Each Party shall ensure that a sanitary or phytosanitary measure that it adopts, maintains or applies does not arbitrarily or unjustifiably discriminate between its goods and like goods of another Party, or between goods of another Party and like goods of any other country, where identical or similar conditions prevail.

Unnecessary Obstacles

5. Each Party shall ensure that any sanitary or phytosanitary measure that it adopts, maintains or applies is applied only to the extent necessary to achieve its appropriate level of protection, taking into account technical and economic feasibility.

Disguised Restrictions

6. No Party may adopt, maintain or apply any sanitary or phytosanitary measure with a view to, or with the effect of, creating a disguised restriction on trade between the Parties.

Article 713: International Standards and Standardizing Organizations

1. Without reducing the level of protection of human, animal or plant life or health, each Party shall use, as a basis for its sanitary and phytosanitary measures, relevant international standards, guidelines or recommendations with the objective, among others, of making its sanitary and phytosanitary measures equivalent or, where appropriate, identical to those of the other Parties.

2. A Party's sanitary or phytosanitary measure that conforms to a relevant international standard, guideline or recommendation shall be presumed to be consistent with Article 712. A measure that results in a level of sanitary or phytosanitary protection different from that which would be achieved by a measure based on a relevant international standard, guideline or recommendation shall not for that reason alone be presumed to be inconsistent with this Section.

3. Nothing in Paragraph 1 shall be construed to prevent a Party from adopting, maintaining or applying, in accordance with the other provisions of this Section, a sanitary or phytosanitary measure that is more stringent than the relevant international standard, guideline or recommendation.

4. Where a Party has reason to believe that a sanitary or phytosanitary measure of another Party is adversely affecting or may adversely affect its exports and the measure is not based on a relevant international standard, guideline or recommendation, it may request, and the other Party shall provide in writing, the reasons for the measure.

5. Each Party shall, to the greatest extent practicable, participate in relevant international and North American standardizing organizations, including the *Codex Alimentarius Commission, the International Office of Epizootics* , the *International Plant Protection Convention* , and the *North American Plant Protection Organization* , with a view to promoting the development and periodic review of international standards, guidelines and recommendations.

Article 714: Equivalence

1. Without reducing the level of protection of human, animal or plant life or health, the Parties shall, to the greatest extent practicable and in accordance with this Section, pursue equivalence of their respective sanitary and phytosanitary measures.

2   Each importing Party:
    a) shall treat a sanitary or phytosanitary measure adopted or maintained by an exporting Party as equivalent to its own where the exporting Party, in cooperation with the importing Party, provides to the importing Party scientific evidence or other information, in accordance with risk assessment methodologies agreed on by those Parties, to demonstrate objectively, subject to subparagraph (b), that the exporting Party's measure achieves the importing Party's appropriate level of protection;
    b) may, where it has a scientific basis, determine that the exporting Party's measure does not achieve the importing Party's appropriate level of protection; and
    c) shall provide to the exporting Party, on request, its reasons in writing for a determination under subparagraph (b).

3   For purposes of establishing equivalence, each exporting Party shall, on the request of an importing Party, take such reasonable measures as may be available to it to facilitate access in its territory for inspection, testing and other relevant procedures.

4. Each Party should, in the development of a sanitary or phytosanitary measure, consider relevant actual or proposed sanitary or phytosanitary measures of the other Parties.

Article 715: Risk Assessment and Appropriate Level of Protection

1. In conducting a risk assessment, each Party shall take into account:
    a) relevant risk assessment techniques and methodologies developed by international or North American standardizing organizations;
    b) relevant scientific evidence;
    c) relevant processes and production methods;
    d) relevant inspection, sampling and testing methods;
    e) the prevalence of relevant diseases or pests, including the existence of pest-free or disease-free areas or areas of low pest or disease prevalence;
    f) relevant ecological and other environmental conditions; and
    g) relevant treatments, such as quarantines.

2. Further to paragraph 1, each Party shall, in establishing its appropriate level of protection regarding the risk associated with the introduction, establishment or spread of an animal or plant pest or disease, and in assessing the risk, also take into account the following economic factors, where relevant:
    a) loss of production or sales that may result from the pest or disease;
    b) costs of control or eradication of the pest or disease in its territory; and
    c) the relative cost-effectiveness of alternative approaches to limiting risks.

3. Each Party, in establishing its appropriate level of protection:

a) should take into account the objective of minimizing negative trade effects; and

b) shall, with the objective of achieving consistency in such levels, avoid arbitrary or unjustifiable distinctions in such levels in different circumstances, where such distinctions result in arbitrary or unjustifiable discrimination against a good of another Party or constitute a disguised restriction on trade between the Parties.

4. Notwithstanding paragraphs (1) through (3) and Article 712(3)(c), where a Party conducting a risk assessment determines that available relevant scientific evidence or other information is insufficient to complete the assessment, it may adopt a provisional sanitary or phytosanitary measure on the basis of available relevant information, including from international or North American standardizing organizations and from sanitary or phytosanitary measures of other Parties. The Party shall, within a reasonable period after information sufficient to complete the assessment is presented to it, complete its assessment, review and, where appropriate, revise the provisional measure in the light of the assessment.

5. Where a Party is able to achieve its appropriate level of protection through the phased application of a sanitary or phytosanitary measure, it may, on the request of another Party and in accordance with this Section, allow for such a phased application, or grant specified exceptions for limited periods from the measure, taking into account the requesting Party's export interests.

Article 716: Adaptation to Regional Conditions

1. Each Party shall adapt any of its sanitary or phytosanitary measures relating to the introduction, establishment or spread of an animal or plant pest or disease, to the sanitary or phytosanitary characteristics of the area where a good subject to such a measure is produced and the area in its territory to which the good is destined, taking into account any relevant conditions, including those relating to transportation and handling, between those areas. In assessing such characteristics of an area, including whether an area is, and is likely to remain, a pest-free or disease-free area or an area of low pest or disease prevalence, each Party shall take into account, among other factors:

a) the prevalence of relevant pests or diseases in that area;

b) the existence of eradication or control programs in that area; and

c) any relevant international standard, guideline or recommendation.

2. Further to paragraph 1, each Party shall, in determining whether an area is a pest-free or disease-free area or an area of low pest or disease prevalence, base its determination on factors such as geography, ecosystems, epidemiological surveillance and the effectiveness of sanitary or phytosanitary controls in that area.

3. Each importing Party shall recognize that an area in the territory of the exporting Party is, and is likely to remain, a pest-free or disease-free area or an area of low pest or disease prevalence, where the exporting Party provides to the importing Party scientific evidence or other information sufficient to so demonstrate to the satisfaction of the importing Party. For this purpose, each exporting Party shall

provide reasonable access in its territory to the importing Party for inspection, testing and other relevant procedures.

4. Each Party may, in accordance with this Section:

   a) adopt, maintain or apply a different risk assessment procedure for a pest-free or disease-free area than for an area of low pest or disease prevalence, or

   b) make a different final determination for the disposition of a good produced in a pest-free or disease-free area than for a good produced in an area of low pest or disease prevalence, taking into account any relevant conditions, including those relating to transportation and handling.

5. Each Party shall, in adopting, maintaining or applying a sanitary or phytosanitary measure relating to the introduction, establishment or spread of an animal or plant pest or disease, accord a good produced in a pest-free or disease-free area in the territory of another Party no less favorable treatment than it accords a good produced in a pest-free or disease-free area, in another country, that poses the same level of risk. The Party shall use equivalent risk assessment techniques to evaluate relevant conditions and controls in the pest-free or disease-free area and in the area surrounding that area and take into account any relevant conditions, including those relating to transportation and handling.

6. Each importing Party shall pursue an agreement with an exporting Party, on request, on specific requirements the fulfillment of which allows a good produced in an area of low pest or disease prevalence in the territory of an exporting Party to be imported into the territory of the importing Party and achieves the importing Party's appropriate level of protection.

Article 717: Control, Inspection and Approval Procedures

1. Each Party, with respect to any control or inspection procedure that it conducts:

   (a) shall initiate and complete the procedure as expeditiously as possible and in no less favorable manner for a good of another Party than for a like good of the Party or of any other country;

   (b) shall publish the normal processing period for the procedure or communicate the anticipated processing period to the applicant on request;

   (c) shall ensure that the competent body

      (i) on receipt of an application, promptly examines the completeness of the documentation and informs the applicant in a precise and complete manner of any deficiency,

      (ii) transmits to the applicant as soon as possible the results of the procedure in a form that is precise and complete so that the applicant may take any necessary corrective action,

      (iii) where the application is deficient, proceeds as far as practicable with the procedure if the applicant so requests, and

      (iv) informs the applicant, on request, of the status of the application and the reasons for any delay;

(d) shall limit the information the applicant is required to supply to that necessary for conducting the procedure;

(e) shall accord confidential or proprietary information arising from, or supplied in connection with, the procedure conducted for a good of another Party

(i) treatment no less favorable than for a good of the Party, and

(ii) in any event, treatment that protects the applicant's legitimate commercial interests, to the extent provided under the Party's law;

(f) shall limit any requirement regarding individual specimens or samples of a good to that which is reasonable and necessary;

(g) should not impose a fee for conducting the procedure that is higher for a good of another Party than is equitable in relation to any such fee it imposes for its like goods or for like goods of any other country, taking into account communication, transportation and other related costs;

(h) should use criteria for selecting the location of facilities at which the procedure is conducted that do not cause unnecessary inconvenience to an applicant or its agent;

(i) shall provide a mechanism to review complaints concerning the operation of the procedure and to take corrective action when a complaint is justified;

(j) should use criteria for selecting samples of goods that do not cause unnecessary inconvenience to an applicant or its agent; and

(k) shall limit the procedure, for a good modified subsequent to a determination that the good fulfills the requirements of the applicable sanitary or phytosanitary measure, to that necessary to determine that the good continues to fulfill the requirements of that measure.

2. Each Party shall apply, with such modifications as may be necessary, paragraphs 1(a) through (i) to its approval procedures.

3. Where an importing Party's sanitary or phytosanitary measure requires the conduct of a control or inspection procedure at the level of production, an exporting Party shall, on the request of the importing Party, take such reasonable measures as may be available to it to facilitate access in its territory and to provide assistance necessary to facilitate the conduct of the importing Party's control or inspection procedure.

4. A Party maintaining an approval procedure may require its approval for the use of an additive, or its establishment of a tolerance for a contaminant, in a food, beverage or feedstuff, under that procedure prior to granting access to its domestic market for a food, beverage or feedstuff containing that additive or contaminant. Where such Party so requires, it shall consider using a relevant international standard, guideline or recommendation as the basis for granting access until it completes the procedure.

Article 718: Notification, Publication and Provision of Information

1. Further to Articles 1802 (Publication) and 1803 (Notification and Provision of Information), each Party proposing to adopt or modify a sanitary or phytosanitary measure of general application at the federal level shall:

(a) at least 60 days prior to the adoption or modification of the measure, other than a law, publish a notice and notify in writing the other Parties of the proposed measure and provide to the other Parties and publish the full text of the proposed measure, in such a manner as to enable interested persons to become acquainted with the proposed measure;

(b) identify in the notice and notification the good to which the measure would apply, and provide a brief description of the objective and reasons for the measure;

(c) provide a copy of the proposed measure to any Party or interested person that so requests and, wherever possible, identify any provision that deviates in substance from relevant international standards, guidelines or recommendations; and

(d) without discrimination, allow other Parties and interested persons to make comments in writing and shall, on request, discuss the comments and take the comments and the results of the discussions into account.

2. Each Party shall seek, through appropriate measures, to ensure, with respect to a sanitary or phytosanitary measure of a state or provincial government:

(a) that, at an early appropriate stage, a notice and notification of the type referred to in paragraphs 1(a) and (b) are made prior to their adoption; and

(b) observance of paragraphs 1(c) and (d).

3. Where a Party considers it necessary to address an urgent problem relating to sanitary or phytosanitary protection, it may omit any step set out in paragraph 1 or 2, provided that, on adoption of a sanitary or phytosanitary measure, it shall:

(a) immediately provide to the other Parties a notification of the type referred to in paragraph 1(b), including a brief description of the urgent problem;

(b) provide a copy of the measure to any Party or interested person that so requests; and

(c) without discrimination, allow other Parties and interested persons to make comments in writing and shall, on request, discuss the comments and take the comments and the results of the discussions into account.

4. Each Party shall, except where necessary to address an urgent problem referred to in paragraph 3, allow a reasonable period between the publication of a sanitary or phytosanitary measure of general application and the date that it becomes effective to allow time for interested persons to adapt to the measure.

5. Each Party shall designate a government authority responsible for the implementation at the federal level of the notification provisions of this Article, and shall notify the other Parties thereof. Where a Party designates two or more government authorities for this purpose, it shall provide to the other Parties complete and unambiguous information on the scope of responsibility of each such authority.

6. Where an importing Party denies entry into its territory of a good of another Party because it does not comply with a sanitary or phytosanitary measure, the importing Party shall provide a written explanation to the exporting Party, on request, that identifies the applicable measure and the reasons that the good is not in compliance.

Article 719: Inquiry Points

1. Each Party shall ensure that there is one inquiry point that is able to answer all reasonable inquiries from other Parties and interested persons, and to provide relevant documents, regarding:

   (a) any sanitary or phytosanitary measure of general application, including any control or inspection procedure or approval procedure, proposed, adopted or maintained in its territory at the federal, state or provincial government level;

   (b) the Party's risk assessment procedures and factors it considers in conducting the assessment and in establishing its appropriate levels of protection;

   (c) the membership and participation of the Party, or its relevant federal, state or provincial government authorities in international and regional sanitary and phytosanitary organizations and systems, and in bilateral and multilateral arrangements within the scope of this Section, and the provisions of those systems and arrangements; and

   (d) the location of notices published pursuant to this Section or where such information can be obtained.

2. Each Party shall ensure that where copies of documents are requested by another Party or by interested persons in accordance with this Section, they are supplied at the same price, apart from the actual cost of delivery, as the price for domestic purchase.

Article 720: Technical Cooperation

1. Each Party shall, on the request of another Party, facilitate the provision of technical advice, information and assistance, on mutually agreed terms and conditions, to enhance that Party's sanitary and phytosanitary measures and related activities, including research, processing technologies, infrastructure and the establishment of national regulatory bodies. Such assistance may include credits, donations and grants for the acquisition of technical expertise, training and equipment that will facilitate the Party's adjustment to and compliance with a Party's sanitary or phytosanitary measure.

2. Each Party shall, on the request of another Party:

   (a) provide to that Party information on its technical cooperation programs regarding sanitary or phytosanitary measures relating to specific areas of interest; and

   (b) consult with the other Party during the development of, or prior to the adoption or change in the application of, any sanitary or phytosanitary measure.

Article 721: Limitations on the Provision of Information

Nothing in this Section shall be construed to require a Party to:

(a) communicate, publish texts or provide particulars or copies of documents other than in an official language of the Party; or

(b) furnish any information the disclosure of which would impede law enforcement or otherwise be contrary to the public interest or would prejudice the legitimate commercial interests of particular enterprises.

Article 722: Committee on Sanitary and Phytosanitary Measures

1. The Parties hereby establish a Committee on Sanitary and Phytosanitary Measures, comprising representatives of each Party who have responsibility for sanitary and phytosanitary matters.

2. The Committee should facilitate:
    (a) the enhancement of food safety and improvement of sanitary and phytosanitary conditions in the territories of the Parties;
    (b) activities of the Parties pursuant to Articles 713 and 714;
    (c) technical cooperation between the Parties, including cooperation in the development, application and enforcement of sanitary or phytosanitary measures; and
    (d) consultations on specific matters relating to sanitary or phytosanitary measures.

3. The Committee:
    (a) shall, to the extent possible, in carrying out its functions, seek the assistance of relevant international and North American standardizing organizations to obtain available scientific and technical advice and minimize duplication of effort;
    (b) may draw on such experts and expert bodies as it considers appropriate;
    (c) shall report annually to the Commission on the implementation of this Section;
    (d) shall meet on the request of any Party and, unless the Parties otherwise agree, at least once each year; and
    (e) may, as it considers appropriate, establish and determine the scope and mandate of working groups.

Article 723: Technical Consultations

1. A Party may request consultations with another Party on any matter covered by this Section.

2. Each Party should use the good offices of relevant international and North American standardizing organizations, including those referred to in Article 713(5), for advice and assistance on sanitary and phytosanitary matters within their respective mandates.

3. Where a Party requests consultations regarding the application of this Section to a Party's sanitary or phytosanitary measure, and so notifies the Committee, the Committee may facilitate the consultations, if it does not consider the matter itself, by referring the matter for non-binding technical advice or recommendations to a working group, including an ad hoc working group, or to another forum.

4. The Committee should consider any matter referred to it under paragraph 3 as expeditiously as possible, particularly regarding perishable goods, and promptly forward to the Parties any technical advice or recommendations that it develops or receives concerning the matter. The Parties involved shall provide a written response to the Committee concerning the technical advice or recommendations within such time as the Committee may request.

5. Where the involved Parties have had recourse to consultations facilitated by the Committee under paragraph 3, the consultations shall, on the agreement of the Parties involved, constitute consultations under Article 2006 (Consultations).

6. The Parties confirm that a Party asserting that a sanitary or phytosanitary measure of another Party is inconsistent with this Section shall have the burden of establishing the inconsistency.

Article 724: Definitions For purposes of this Section:

animal includes fish and wild fauna;

appropriate level of protection means the level of protection of human, animal or plant life or health in the territory of a Party that the Party considers appropriate;

approval procedure means any registration, notification or other mandatory administrative procedure for:

(a) approving the use of an additive for a stated purpose or under stated conditions; or
(b) establishing a tolerance for a stated purpose or under stated conditions for a contaminant,

in a food, beverage or feedstuff prior to permitting the use of the additive or the marketing of a food, beverage or feedstuff containing the additive or contaminant;

area means a country, part of a country or all or parts of several countries;

area of low pest or disease prevalence means an area in which a specific pest or disease occurs at low levels;

contaminant includes pesticide and veterinary drug residues and extraneous matter;

control or inspection procedure means any procedure used, directly or indirectly, to determine that a sanitary or phytosanitary measure is fulfilled, including sampling, testing, inspection, evaluation, verification, monitoring, auditing, assurance of conformity, accreditation, registration, certification or other procedure involving the physical examination of a good, of the packaging of a good, or of the equipment or facilities directly related to production, marketing or use of a good, but does not mean an approval procedure;

international standard, guideline or recommendation means a standard, guideline or recommendation:

(a) regarding food safety, adopted by the *Codex Alimentarius Commission* , including one regarding decomposition elaborated by the *Codex Committee on Fish and Fishery Products* , food additives, contaminants, hygienic practice, and methods of analysis and sampling;

(b) regarding animal health and zoonoses, developed under the auspices of the *International Office of Epizootics* ;

(c) regarding plant health, developed under the auspices of the *Secretariat of the International Plant Protection Convention* in cooperation with the *North American Plant Protection Organization* ; or

(d) established by or developed under any other international organization agreed on by the Parties;

pest includes a weed;

pest-free or disease-free area means an area in which a specific pest or disease does not occur;

plant includes wild flora;

risk assessment means an evaluation of:

(a) the potential for the introduction, establishment or spread of a pest or disease and associated biological and economic consequences; or

(b) the potential for adverse effects on human or animal life or health arising from the presence of an additive, contaminant, toxin or disease-causing organism in a food, beverage or feedstuff;

sanitary or phytosanitary measure means a measure that a Party adopts, maintains or applies to:

(a) protect animal or plant life or health in its territory from risks arising from the introduction, establishment or spread of a pest or disease,

(b) protect human or animal life or health in its territory from risks arising from the presence of an additive, contaminant, toxin or disease-causing organism in a food, beverage or feedstuff,

(c) protect human life or health in its territory from risks arising from a disease-causing organism or pest carried by an animal or plant, or a product thereof, or

(d) prevent or limit other damage in its territory arising from the introduction, establishment or spread of a pest,

including end product criteria; a product-related processing or production method; a testing, inspection, certification or approval procedure; a relevant statistical method; a sampling procedure; a method of risk assessment; a packaging and labelling requirement directly related to food safety; and a quarantine treatment, such as a relevant requirement associated with the transportation of animals or plants or with material necessary for their survival during transportation; and

scientific basis means a reason based on data or information derived using scientific methods.

8. EMERGENCY ACTION

Article 801: Bilateral Actions

1. Subject to paragraphs 2 through 4 and Annex 801.1, and during the transition period only, if a good originating in the territory of a Party, as a result of the reduction or elimination of a duty provided for in this Agreement, is being imported into the territory of another Party in such increased quantities, in absolute terms, and under such conditions that the imports of the good from that Party alone constitute a substantial cause of serious injury, or threat thereof, to a domestic industry producing a like or directly competitive good, the Party into whose territory the good is being imported may, to the minimum extent necessary to remedy or prevent the injury:
    (a) suspend the further reduction of any rate of duty provided for under this Agreement on the good;
    (b) increase the rate of duty on the good to a level not to exceed the lesser of
        (i) the most-favored-nation (MFN) applied rate of duty in effect at the time the action is taken, and
        (ii) the MFN applied rate of duty in effect on the day immediately preceding the date of entry into force of this Agreement; or
    (c) in the case of a duty applied to a good on a seasonal basis, increase the rate of duty to a level not to exceed the MFN applied rate of duty that was in effect on the good for the corresponding season immediately preceding the date of entry into force of this Agreement.

2. The following conditions and limitations shall apply to a proceeding that may result in emergency action under paragraph 1:
    (a) a Party shall, without delay, deliver to any Party that may be affected written notice of, and a request for consultations regarding, the institution of a proceeding that could result in emergency action against a good originating in the territory of a Party;
    (b) any such action shall be initiated no later than one year after the date of institution of the proceeding;
    (c) no action may be maintained
        (i) for a period exceeding three years, except where the good against which the action is taken is provided for in the items in staging category C+ of the Schedule to Annex 302.2 of the Party taking the action and that Party determines that the affected industry has undertaken adjustment and requires an extension of the period of relief, in which case the period of relief may be

> extended for one year provided that the duty applied during the initial period of relief is substantially reduced at the beginning of the extension period, or
>
> (ii) beyond the expiration of the transition period, except with the consent of the Party against whose good the action is taken;

    (d) no action may be taken by a Party against any particular good originating in the territory of another Party more than once during the transition period; and

    (e) on the termination of the action, the rate of duty shall be the rate that, according to the Party's Schedule to Annex 302.2 for the staged elimination of the tariff, would have been in effect one year after the initiation of the action, and beginning January 1 of the year following the termination of the action, at the option of the Party that has taken the action

> (i) the rate of duty shall conform to the applicable rate set out in its Schedule to Annex 302.2, or
>
> (ii) the tariff shall be eliminated in equal annual stages ending on the date set out in its Schedule to Annex 302.2 for the elimination of the tariff.

3. A Party may take a bilateral emergency action after the expiration of the transition period to deal with cases of serious injury, or threat thereof, to a domestic industry arising from the operation of this Agreement only with the consent of the Party against whose good the action would be taken.

4. The Party taking an action under this Article shall provide to the Party against whose good the action is taken mutually agreed trade liberalizing compensation in the form of concessions having substantially equivalent trade effects or equivalent to the value of the additional duties expected to result from the action. If the Parties concerned are unable to agree on compensation, the Party against whose good the action is taken may take tariff action having trade effects substantially equivalent to the action taken under this Article. The Party taking the tariff action shall apply the action only for the minimum period necessary to achieve the substantially equivalent effects.

5. This Article does not apply to emergency actions respecting goods covered by Annex 300-B (Textile and Apparel Goods).

Article 802: Global Actions

1. Each Party retains its rights and obligations under Article XIX of the GATT or any safeguard agreement pursuant thereto except those regarding compensation or retaliation and exclusion from an action to the extent that such rights or obligations are inconsistent with this Article. Any Party taking an emergency action under Article XIX or any such agreement shall exclude imports of a good from each other Party from the action unless:

    (a) imports from a Party, considered individually, account for a substantial share of total imports; and

    (b) imports from a Party, considered individually, or in exceptional circumstances imports from Parties considered collectively, contribute importantly to the serious injury, or threat thereof, caused by imports.

2. In determining whether:

(a) imports from a Party, considered individually, account for a substantial share of total imports, those imports normally shall not be considered to account for a substantial share of total imports if that Party is not among the top five suppliers of the good subject to the proceeding, measured in terms of import share during the most recent three-year period; and

(b) imports from a Party or Parties contribute importantly to the serious injury, or threat thereof, the competent investigating authority shall consider such factors as the change in the import share of each Party, and the level and change in the level of imports of each Party. In this regard, imports from a Party normally shall not be deemed to contribute importantly to serious injury, or the threat thereof, if the growth rate of imports from a Party during the period in which the injurious surge in imports occurred is appreciably lower than the growth rate of total imports from all sources over the same period.

3. A Party taking such action, from which a good from another Party or Parties is initially excluded pursuant to paragraph 1, shall have the right subsequently to include that good from the other Party or Parties in the action in the event that the competent investigating authority determines that a surge in imports of such good from the other Party or Parties undermines the effectiveness of the action.

4. A Party shall, without delay, deliver written notice to the other Parties of the institution of a proceeding that may result in emergency action under paragraph 1 or 3.

5. No Party may impose restrictions on a good in an action under paragraph 1 or 3:
   (a) without delivery of prior written notice to the Commission, and without adequate opportunity for consultation with the Party or Parties against whose good the action is proposed to be taken, as far in advance of taking the action as practicable; and
   (b) that would have the effect of reducing imports of such good from a Party below the trend of imports of the good from that Party over a recent representative base period with allowance for reasonable growth.

6. The Party taking an action pursuant to this Article shall provide to the Party or Parties against whose good the action is taken mutually agreed trade liberalizing compensation in the form of concessions having substantially equivalent trade effects or equivalent to the value of the additional duties expected to result from the action. If the Parties concerned are unable to agree on compensation, the Party against whose good the action is taken may take action having trade effects substantially equivalent to the action taken under paragraph 1 or 3.

Article 803: Administration of Emergency Action Proceedings

1. Each Party shall ensure the consistent, impartial and reasonable administration of its laws, regulations, decisions and rulings governing all emergency action proceedings.

2. Each Party shall entrust determinations of serious injury, or threat thereof, in emergency action proceedings to a competent investigating authority, subject to review by judicial or administrative tribunals, to the extent provided by domestic

law. Negative injury determinations shall not be subject to modification, except by such review. The competent investigating authority empowered under domestic law to conduct such proceedings should be provided with the necessary resources to enable it to fulfill its duties.

3. Each Party shall adopt or maintain equitable, timely, transparent and effective procedures for emergency action proceedings, in accordance with the requirements set out in Annex 803.3.

4. This Article does not apply to emergency actions taken under Annex 300-B (Textile and Apparel Goods).

Article 804: Dispute Settlement in Emergency Action Matters

No Party may request the establishment of an arbitral panel under Article 2008 (Request for an Arbitral Panel) regarding any proposed emergency action.

Article 805: Definitions

For purposes of this Chapter:

competent investigating authority means the "competent investigating authority" of a Party as defined in Annex 805;

contribute importantly means an important cause, but not necessarily the most important cause;

critical circumstances means circumstances where delay would cause damage that would be difficult to repair;

domestic industry means the producers as a whole of the like or directly competitive good operating in the territory of a Party;

emergency action does not include any emergency action pursuant to a proceeding instituted prior to January 1, 1994;

good originating in the territory of a Party means an originating good, except that in determining the Party in whose territory that good originates, the relevant rules of Annex 302.2 shall apply;

serious injury means a significant overall impairment of a domestic industry;

surge means a significant increase in imports over the trend for a recent representative base period;

threat of serious injury means serious injury that, on the basis of facts and not merely on allegation, conjecture or remote possibility, is clearly imminent; and

transition period means the 10-year period beginning on January 1, 1994, except where the good against which the action is taken is provided for in the items in staging category C+ of the Schedule to Annex 302.2 of the Party taking the action, in which case the transition period shall be the period of staged tariff elimination for that good.

ANNEX 801.1. BILATERAL ACTIONS

1. Notwithstanding Article 801, bilateral emergency actions between Canada and the United States on goods originating in the territory of either Party, other than goods covered by Annex 300-B (Textile and Apparel Goods), shall be governed in accordance with the terms of Article 1101 of the *Canada - United States Free Trade Agreement* , which is hereby Incorporated into and made a part of this Agreement for such purpose.
2. For such purposes, "good originating in the territory of one Party" means "good originating in the territory of a Party" as defined in Article 805.

ANNEX 803.3. ADMINISTRATION OF EMERGENCY ACTION PROCEEDINGS

Institution of a Proceeding

1. An emergency action proceeding may be instituted by a petition or complaint by entities specified in domestic law. The entity filing the petition or complaint shall demonstrate that it is representative of the domestic industry producing a good like or directly competitive with the imported good.
2. A Party may institute a proceeding on its own motion or request the competent investigating authority to conduct a proceeding.

Contents of a Petition or Complaint

3. Where the basis for an investigation is a petition or complaint filed by an entity representative of a domestic industry, the petitioning entity shall, in its petition or complaint, provide the following information to the extent that such information is publicly available from governmental or other sources, or best estimates and the basis therefor if such information is not available:
    (a) product description - the name and description of the imported good concerned, the tariff subheading under which that good is classified, its current tariff

treatment and the name and description of the like or directly competitive domestic good concerned;

(b) representativeness -
   (i) the names and addresses of the entities filing the petition or complaint, and the locations of the establishments in which they produce the domestic good,
   (ii) the percentage of domestic production of the like or directly competitive good that such entities account for and the basis for claiming that they are representative of an industry, and
   (iii) the names and locations of all other domestic establishments in which the like or directly competitive good is produced;

(c) import data - import data for each of the five most recent full years that form the basis of the claim that the good concerned is being imported in increased quantities, either in absolute terms or relative to domestic production as appropriate;

(d) domestic production data - data on total domestic production of the like or directly competitive good for each of the five most recent full years;

(e) data showing injury - quantitative and objective data indicating the nature and extent of injury to the concerned industry, such as data showing changes in the level of sales, prices, production, productivity, capacity utilization, market share, profits and losses, and employment;

(f) cause of injury - an enumeration and description of the alleged causes of the injury, or threat thereof, and a summary of the basis for the assertion that increased imports, either actual or relative to domestic production, of the imported good are causing or threatening to cause serious injury, supported by pertinent data; and

(g) criteria for inclusion - quantitative and objective data indicating the share of imports accounted for by imports from the territory of each other Party and the petitioner's views on the extent to which such imports are contributing importantly to the serious injury, or threat thereof, caused by imports of that good.

4. Petitions or complaints, except to the extent that they contain confidential business information, shall promptly be made available for public inspection on being filed.

Notice Requirement

5. On instituting an emergency action proceeding, the competent investigating authority shall publish notice of the institution of the proceeding in the official journal of the Party. The notice shall identify the petitioner or other requester, the imported good that is the subject of the proceeding and its tariff subheading, the nature and timing of the determination to be made, the time and place of the public hearing, dates of deadlines for filing briefs, statements and other documents, the place at which the petition and any other documents filed in the course of the proceeding may be inspected, and the name, address and telephone number of the office to be contacted for more information.

6. With respect to an emergency action proceeding instituted on the basis of a petition or complaint filed by an entity asserting that it is representative of the domestic industry, the competent investigating authority shall not publish the notice required by paragraph 5 without first assessing carefully that the petition or complaint meets the requirements of paragraph 3, including representativeness.

Public Hearing

7. In the course of each proceeding, the competent investigating authority shall:
    (a) hold a public hearing, after providing reasonable notice, to allow all interested parties, and any association whose purpose is to represent the interests of consumers in the territory of the Party instituting the proceeding, to appear in person or by counsel, to present evidence and to be heard on the questions of serious injury, or threat thereof, and the appropriate remedy; and
    (b) provide an opportunity to all interested parties and any such association appearing at the hearing to cross-question interested parties making presentations at that hearing.

Confidential Information

8. The competent investigating authority shall adopt or maintain procedures for the treatment of confidential information, protected under domestic law, that is provided in the course of a proceeding, including a requirement that interested parties and consumer associations providing such information furnish non-confidential written summaries thereof, or where they indicate that the information cannot be summarized, the reasons why a summary cannot be provided.

Evidence of Injury and Causation

9. In conducting its proceeding the competent investigating authority shall gather, to the best of its ability, all relevant information appropriate to the determination it must make. It shall evaluate all relevant factors of an objective and quantifiable nature having a bearing on the situation of that industry, including the rate and amount of the increase in imports of the good concerned, in absolute and relative terms as appropriate, the share of the domestic market taken by increased imports, and changes in the level of sales, production, productivity, capacity utilization, profits and losses, and employment. In making its determination, the competent investigating authority may also consider other economic factors, such as changes in prices and inventories, and the ability of firms in the industry to generate capital.

10. The competent investigating authority shall not make an affirmative injury determination unless its investigation demonstrates, on the basis of objective evidence, the existence of a clear causal link between increased imports of the good

concerned and serious injury, or threat thereof. Where factors other than increased imports are causing injury to the domestic industry at the same time, such injury shall not be attributed to increased imports.

Deliberation and Report

11. Except in critical circumstances and in global actions involving perishable agricultural goods, the competent investigating authority, before making an affirmative determination in an emergency action proceeding, shall allow sufficient time to gather and consider the relevant information, hold a public hearing and provide an opportunity for all interested parties and consumer associations to prepare and submit their views.

12. The competent investigating authority shall publish promptly a report, including a summary thereof in the official journal of the Party, setting out its findings and reasoned conclusions on all pertinent issues of law and fact. The report shall describe the imported good and its tariff item number, the standard applied and the finding made. The statement of reasons shall set out the basis for the determination, including a description of:

    (a) the domestic industry seriously injured or threatened with serious injury;

    (b) information supporting a finding that imports are increasing, the domestic industry is seriously injured or threatened with serious injury, and increasing imports are causing or threatening serious injury; and

    (c) if provided for by domestic law, any finding or recommendation regarding the appropriate remedy and the basis therefor.

13. In its report, the competent investigating authority shall not disclose any confidential information provided pursuant to any undertaking concerning confidential information that may have been made in the course of the proceedings.

ANNEX 805. COUNTRY-SPECIFIC DEFINITIONS

For purposes of this Chapter:

competent investigating authority means:

(a) in the case of Canada, the Canadian International Trade Tribunal, or its successor;

(b) in the case of the Mexico, the designated authority within the Ministry of Trade and Industrial Development ("Secretaría de Comercio y Fomento Industrial"), or its successor; and

(c) in the case of the United States, the U.S. International Trade Commission, or its successor.

PART THREE: TECHNICAL BARRIERS TO TRADE

9. STANDARDS-RELATED MEASURES

Article 901: Scope and Coverage

1. This Chapter applies to standards-related measures of a Party, other than those covered by Section B of Chapter Seven (Sanitary and Phytosanitary Measures), that may, directly or indirectly, affect trade in goods or services between the Parties, and to measures of the Parties relating to such measures.
2. Technical specifications prepared by governmental bodies for production or consumption requirements of such bodies shall be governed exclusively by Chapter Ten (Government Procurement).

Article 902: Extent of Obligations

1. Article 105 (Extent of Obligations) does not apply to this Chapter.
2. Each Party shall seek, through appropriate measures, to ensure observance of Articles 904 through 908 by state or provincial governments and by non-governmental standardizing bodies in its territory.

Article 903: Affirmation of Agreement on Technical Barriers to Trade and Other Agreements

Further to Article 103 (Relation to Other Agreements), the Parties affirm with respect to each other their existing rights and obligations relating to standards-related measures under the *GATT Agreement on Technical Barriers to Trade* and all other international agreements, including environmental and conservation agreements, to which those Parties are party.

Article 904: Basic Rights and Obligations

Right to Take Standards-Related Measures

1. Each Party may, in accordance with this Agreement, adopt, maintain or apply any standards-related measure, including any such measure relating to safety, the protection of human, animal or plant life or health, the environment or consumers, and any measure to ensure its enforcement or implementation. Such measures include those to prohibit the importation of a good of another Party or the provision of a service by a service provider of another Party that fails to comply with the

applicable requirements of those measures or to complete the Party's approval procedures.

Right to Establish Level of Protection

2. Notwithstanding any other provision of this Chapter, each Party may, in pursuing its legitimate objectives of safety or the protection of human, animal or plant life or health, the environment or consumers, establish the levels of protection that it considers appropriate in accordance with Article 907(2).

Non-Discriminatory Treatment

3. Each Party shall, in respect of its standards-related measures, accord to goods and service providers of another Party:
    (a) national treatment in accordance with Article 301 (Market Access) or Article 1202 (Cross-Border Trade in Services); and
    (b) treatment no less favorable than that it accords to like goods, or in like circumstances to service providers, of any other country.

Unnecessary Obstacles

4. No Party may prepare, adopt, maintain or apply any standards-related measure with a view to or with the effect of creating an unnecessary obstacle to trade between the Parties. An unnecessary obstacle to trade shall not be deemed to be created where:
    (a) the demonstrable purpose of the measure is to achieve a legitimate objective; and
    (b) the measure does not operate to exclude goods of another Party that meet that legitimate objective.

Article 905. Use of International Standards

1. Each Party shall use, as a basis for its standards-related measures, relevant international standards or international standards whose completion is imminent, except where such standards would be an ineffective or inappropriate means to fulfill its legitimate objectives, for example because of fundamental climatic, geographical, technological or infrastructural factors, scientific justification or the level of protection that the Party considers appropriate.
2. A Party's standards-related measure that conforms to an international standard shall be presumed to be consistent with Article 904(3) and (4).
3. Nothing in paragraph 1 shall be construed to prevent a Party, in pursuing its legitimate objectives, from adopting, maintaining or applying any standards-related measure that results in a higher level of protection than would be achieved if the measure were based on the relevant international standard.

Article 906: Compatibility and Equivalence

1. Recognizing the crucial role of standards-related measures in achieving legitimate objectives, the Parties shall, in accordance with this Chapter, work jointly to enhance the level of safety and of protection of human, animal and plant life and health, the environment and consumers.

2. Without reducing the level of safety or of protection of human, animal or plant life or health, the environment or consumers, without prejudice to the rights of any Party under this Chapter, and taking into account international standardization activities, the Parties shall, to the greatest extent practicable, make compatible their respective standards-related measures, so as to facilitate trade in a good or service between the Parties.

3. Further to Articles 902 and 905, a Party shall, on request of another Party, seek, through appropriate measures, to promote the compatibility of a specific standard or conformity assessment procedure that is maintained in its territory with the standards or conformity assessment procedures maintained in the territory of the other Party.

4. Each importing Party shall treat a technical regulation adopted or maintained by an exporting Party as equivalent to its own where the exporting Party, in cooperation with the importing Party, demonstrates to the satisfaction of the importing Party that its technical regulation adequately fulfills the importing Party's legitimate objectives.

5. The importing Party shall provide to the exporting Party, on request, its reasons in writing for not treating a technical regulation as equivalent under paragraph 4.

6. Each Party shall, wherever possible, accept the results of a conformity assessment procedure conducted in the territory of another Party, provided that it is satisfied that the procedure offers an assurance, equivalent to that provided by a procedure it conducts or a procedure conducted in its territory the results of which it accepts, that the relevant good or service complies with the applicable technical regulation or standard adopted or maintained in the Party's territory.

7. Prior to accepting the results of a conformity assessment procedure pursuant to paragraph 6, and to enhance confidence in the continued reliability of each other's conformity assessment results, the Parties may consult on such matters as the technical competence of the conformity assessment bodies involved, including verified compliance with relevant international standards through such means as accreditation.

Article 907: Assessment of Risk

1. A Party may, in pursuing its legitimate objectives, conduct an assessment of risk. In conducting an assessment, a Party may take into account, among other factors relating to a good or service:
    (a) available scientific evidence or technical information;
    (b) intended end uses;
    (c) processes or production, operating, inspection, sampling or testing methods; or
    (d) environmental conditions.

2. Where pursuant to Article 904(2) a Party establishes a level of protection that it considers appropriate and conducts an assessment of risk, it should avoid arbitrary or unjustifiable distinctions between similar goods or services in the level of protection it considers appropriate, where the distinctions:
   (a) result in arbitrary or unjustifiable discrimination against goods or service providers of another Party;
   (b) constitute a disguised restriction on trade between the Parties; or
   (c) discriminate between similar goods or services for the same use under the same conditions that pose the same level of risk and provide similar benefits.

3. Where a Party conducting an assessment of risk determines that available scientific evidence or other information is insufficient to complete the assessment, it may adopt a provisional technical regulation on the basis of available relevant information. The Party shall, within a reasonable period after information sufficient to complete the assessment of risk is presented to it, complete its assessment, review and, where appropriate, revise the provisional technical regulation in the light of that assessment.

Article 908: Conformity Assessment

1. The Parties shall, further to Article 906 and recognizing the existence of substantial differences in the structure, organization and operation of conformity assessment procedures in their respective territories, make compatible those procedures to the greatest extent practicable.

2. Recognizing that it should be to the mutual advantage of the Parties concerned and except as set out in Annex 908.2, each Party shall accredit, approve, license or otherwise recognize conformity assessment bodies in the territory of another Party on terms no less favorable than those accorded to conformity assessment bodies in its territory.

3. Each Party shall, with respect to its conformity assessment procedures:
   (a) not adopt or maintain any such procedure that is stricter, nor apply the procedure more strictly, than necessary to give it confidence that a good or a service conforms with an applicable technical regulation or standard, taking into account the risks that non-conformity would create;
   (b) initiate and complete the procedure as expeditiously as possible;
   (c) in accordance with Article 904(3), undertake processing of applications in non-discriminatory order;
   (d) publish the normal processing period for each such procedure or communicate the anticipated processing period to an applicant on request;
   (e) ensure that the competent body
       (i) on receipt of an application, promptly examines the completeness of the documentation and informs the applicant in a precise and complete manner of any deficiency,
       (ii) transmits to the applicant as soon as possible the results of the conformity assessment procedure in a form that is precise and complete so that the applicant may take any necessary corrective action,

(iii) where the application is deficient, proceeds as far as practicable with the procedure where the applicant so requests, and

(iv) informs the applicant, on request, of the status of the application and the reasons for any delay;

(f) limit the information the applicant is required to supply to that necessary to conduct the procedure and to determine appropriate fees;

(g) accord confidential or proprietary information arising from, or supplied in connection with, the conduct of the procedure for a good of another Party or for a service provided by a person of another Party

(i) the same treatment as that for a good of the Party or a service provided by a person of the Party, and

(ii) in any event, treatment that protects an applicant's legitimate commercial interests to the extent provided under the Party's law;

(h) ensure that any fee it imposes for conducting the procedure is no higher for a good of another Party or a service provider of another Party than is equitable in relation to any such fee imposed for its like goods or service providers or for like goods or service providers of any other country, taking into account communication, transportation and other related costs;

(i) ensure that the location of facilities at which a conformity assessment procedure is conducted does not cause unnecessary inconvenience to an applicant or its agent;

(j) limit the procedure, for a good or service modified subsequent to a determination that the good or service conforms to the applicable technical regulation or standard, to that necessary to determine that the good or service continues to conform to the technical regulation or standard; and

(k) limit any requirement regarding samples of a good to that which is reasonable, and ensure that the selection of samples does not cause unnecessary inconvenience to an applicant or its agent.

4. Each Party shall apply, with such modifications as may be necessary, the relevant provisions of paragraph 3 to its approval procedures.

5. Each Party shall, on request of another Party, take such reasonable measures as may be available to it to facilitate access in its territory for conformity assessment activities.

6. Each Party shall give sympathetic consideration to a request by another Party to negotiate agreements for the mutual recognition of the results of that other Party's conformity assessment procedures.

Article 909: Notification, Publication, and Provision of Information

1. Further to Articles 1802 (Publication) and 1803 (Notification and Provision of Information), each Party proposing to adopt or modify a technical regulation shall:

(a) at least 60 days prior to the adoption or modification of the measure, other than a law, publish a notice and notify in writing the other Parties of the proposed measure in such a manner as to enable interested persons to become acquainted with the proposed measure, except that in the case of any such measure relating to perishable goods, each Party shall, to the greatest extent practicable, publish the notice and provide the notification at least 30 days prior to the adoption or modification of the measure, but no later than when notification is provided to domestic producers;

(b) identify in the notice and notification the good or service to which the measure would apply, and shall provide a brief description of the objective of, and reasons for the measure;

(c) provide a copy of the proposed measure to any Party or interested person that so requests, and shall, wherever possible, identify any provision that deviates in substance from relevant international standards; and

(d) without discrimination, allow other Parties and interested persons to make comments in writing and shall, on request, discuss the comments and take the comments and the results of the discussions into account.

2. Each Party proposing to adopt or modify a standard or any conformity assessment procedure not otherwise considered to be a technical regulation shall, where an international standard relevant to the proposed measure does not exist or such measure is not substantially the same as an international standard, and where the measure may have a significant effect on the trade of the other Parties:

(a) at an early appropriate stage, publish a notice and provide a notification of the type required in paragraph 1(a) and (b); and

(b) observe paragraph (c) and (d).

3. Each Party shall seek, through appropriate measures, to ensure, with respect to a technical regulation of a state or provincial government other than a local government:

(a) that, at an early appropriate stage, a notice and notification of the type required under paragraph 1(a) and (b) are made prior to their adoption; and

(b) observance of paragraph (c) and (d).

4. Where a Party considers it necessary to address an urgent problem relating to safety or to protection of human, animal or plant life or health, the environment or consumers, it may omit any step set out in paragraph 1 or 3, provided that on adoption of a standards-related measure it shall:

(a) immediately provide to the other Parties a notification of the type required under paragraph 1(b), including a brief description of the urgent problem;

(b) provide a copy of the measure to any Party or interested person that so requests; and

(c) without discrimination, allow other Parties and interested persons to make comments in writing, and shall, on request, discuss the comments and take the comments and the results of the discussions into account.

5. Each Party shall, except where necessary to address an urgent problem referred to in paragraph 4, allow a reasonable period between the publication of a standards-related measure and the date that it becomes effective to allow time for interested persons to adapt to the measure.

6. Where a Party allows non-governmental persons in its territory to be present during the process of development of standards-related measures, it shall also allow non-governmental persons from the territories of the other Parties to be present.

7. Each Party shall notify the other Parties of the development of, amendment to, or change in the application of its standards-related measures no later than the time at which it notifies non-governmental persons in general or the relevant sector in its territory.

8. Each Party shall seek, through appropriate measures, to ensure the observance of paragraphs 6 and 7 by a state or provincial government, and by non-governmental standardizing bodies in its territory.

9. Each Party shall designate by January 1, 1994 a government authority responsible for the implementation at the federal level of the notification provisions of this Article, and shall notify the other Parties thereof. Where a Party designates two or more government authorities for that purpose, it shall provide to the other Parties complete and unambiguous information on the scope of responsibility of each such authority.

Article 910: Inquiry Points

1. Each Party shall ensure that there is an inquiry point that is able to answer all reasonable inquiries from other Parties and interested persons, and to provide relevant documents regarding:
   (a) any standards-related measure proposed, adopted or maintained in its territory at the federal, state or provincial government level;
   (b) the membership and participation of the Party, or its relevant federal, state or provincial government authorities, in international and regional standardizing bodies and conformity assessment systems, and in bilateral and multilateral arrangements regarding standards-related measures, and the provisions of those systems and arrangements;
   (c) the location of notices published pursuant to Article 909, or where the information can be obtained;
   (d) the location of the inquiry points referred to in paragraph 3; and
   (e) the Party's procedures for assessment of risk, and factors it considers in conducting the assessment and in establishing, pursuant to Article 904(2), the levels of protection that it considers appropriate.

2. Where a Party designates more than one inquiry point, it shall:
   (a) provide to the other Parties complete and unambiguous information on the scope of responsibility of each inquiry point; and
   (b) ensure that any inquiry addressed to an incorrect inquiry point is promptly conveyed to the correct inquiry point.

3. Each Party shall take such reasonable measures as may be available to it to ensure that there is at least one inquiry point that is able to answer all reasonable inquiries from other Parties and interested persons and to provide relevant documents or information as to where they can be obtained regarding:
   (a) any standard or conformity assessment procedure proposed, adopted or maintained by non-governmental standardizing bodies in its territory; and

(b) the membership and participation of relevant non-governmental bodies in its territory in international and regional standardizing bodies and conformity assessment systems.

4. Each Party shall ensure that where copies of documents are requested by another Party or by interested persons in accordance with this Chapter, they are supplied at the same price, apart from the actual cost of delivery, as the price for domestic purchase.

Article 911: Technical Cooperation

1. Each Party shall, on request of another Party:
   (a) provide to that Party technical advice, information and assistance on mutually agreed terms and conditions to enhance that Party's standards-related measures, and related activities, processes and systems;
   (b) provide to that Party information on its technical cooperation programs regarding standards-related measures relating to specific areas of interest; and
   (c) consult with that Party during the development of, or prior to the adoption or change in the application of, any standards-related measure.
2. Each Party shall encourage standardizing bodies in its territory to cooperate with the standardizing bodies in the territories of the other Parties in their participation, as appropriate, in standardizing activities, such as through membership in international standardizing bodies.

Article 912: Limitations on the Provision of Information

Nothing in this Chapter shall be construed to require a Party to:

(a) communicate, publish texts, or provide particulars or copies of documents other than in an official language of the Party; or
(b) furnish any information the disclosure of which would impede law enforcement or otherwise be contrary to the public interest, or would prejudice the legitimate commercial interests of particular enterprises.

Article 913: Committee on Standards-Related Measures

1. The Parties hereby establish a Committee on Standards-Related Measures, comprising representatives of each Party.
2. The Committee's functions shall include:
   (a) monitoring the implementation and administration of this Chapter, including the progress of the subcommittees and working groups established under paragraph 4, and the operation of the inquiry points established under Article 910;

(b) facilitating the process by which the Parties make compatible their standards-related measures;

(c) providing a forum for the Parties to consult on issues relating to standards-related measures, including the provision of technical advice and recommendations under Article 914;

(d) enhancing cooperation on the development, application and enforcement of standards-related measures; and

(e) considering non-governmental, regional and multilateral developments regarding standards-related measures, including under the GATT.

3. The Committee shall:

(a) meet on request of any Party and, unless the Parties otherwise agree, at least once each year; and

(b) report annually to the Commission on the implementation of this Chapter.

4. The Committee may, as it considers appropriate, establish and determine the scope and mandate of subcommittees or working groups, comprising representatives of each Party. Each subcommittee or working group may:

(a) as it considers necessary or desirable, include or consult with

(i) representatives of non-governmental bodies, including standardizing bodies,

(ii) scientists, and

(iii) technical experts; and

(b) determine its work program, taking into account relevant international activities.

5. Further to paragraph 4, the Committee shall establish:

(a) the following subcommittees

(i) Land Transportation Standards Subcommittee, in accordance with Annex 913.5.a-1,

(ii) Telecommunications Standards Subcommittee, in accordance with Annex 913.5.a-2,

(iii) Automotive Standards Council, in accordance with Annex 913.5.a-3, and

(iv) Subcommittee on Labelling of Textile and Apparel Goods, in accordance with Annex 913.5.a-4; and

(b) such other subcommittees or working groups as it considers appropriate to address any topic, including:

(i) identification and nomenclature for goods subject to standards-related measures,

(ii) quality and identity standards and technical regulations,

(iii) packaging, labelling and presentation of consumer information, including languages, measurement systems, ingredients, sizes, terminology, symbols and related matters,

(iv) product approval and post-market surveillance programs,

(v) principles for the accreditation and recognition of conformity assessment bodies, procedures and systems,

(vi) development and implementation of a uniform chemical hazard classification and communication system,

(vii) enforcement programs, including training and inspections by regulatory, analytical and enforcement personnel,

(viii) promotion and implementation of good laboratory practices, (ix)promotion and implementation of good manufacturing practices,

(x) criteria for assessment of potential environmental hazards of goods,

(xi) methodologies for assessment of risk,

(xii)guidelines for testing of chemicals, including industrial and agricultural chemicals, pharmaceuticals and biologicals,

(xiii)methods by which consumer protection, including matters relating to consumer redress, can be facilitated, and

(xiv)extension of the application of this Chapter to other services.

6. Each Party shall, on request of another Party, take such reasonable measures as may be available to it to provide for the participation in the activities of the Committee, where and as appropriate, of representatives of state or provincial governments.

7. A Party requesting technical advice, information or assistance pursuant to Article 911 shall notify the Committee which shall facilitate any such request.

Article 914: Technical Consultations

1. Where a Party requests consultations regarding the application of this Chapter to a standards-related measure, and so notifies the Committee, the Committee may facilitate the consultations, if it does not consider the matter itself, by referring the matter for non-binding technical advice or recommendations to a subcommittee or working group, including an ad hoc subcommittee or working group, or to another forum.

2. The Committee should consider any matter referred to it under paragraph 1 as expeditiously as possible and promptly forward to the Parties any technical advice or recommendations that it develops or receives concerning the matter. The Parties involved shall provide a written response to the Committee concerning the technical advice or recommendations within such time as the Committee may request.

3. Where the involved Parties have had recourse to consultations facilitated by the Committee under paragraph 1, the consultations shall, on the agreement of the Parties involved, constitute consultations under Article 2006 (Consultations).

4. The Parties confirm that a Party asserting that a standards-related measure of another Party is inconsistent with this Chapter shall have the burden of establishing the inconsistency.

Article 915: Definitions

1. For purposes of this Chapter:

approval procedure means any registration, notification or other mandatory administrative procedure for granting permission for a good or service to be produced, marketed or used for a stated purpose or under stated conditions;

assessment of risk means evaluation of the potential for adverse effects;

conformity assessment procedure means any procedure used, directly or indirectly, to determine that a technical regulation or standard is fulfilled, including sampling, testing, inspection, evaluation, verification, monitoring, auditing, assurance of conformity, accreditation, registration or approval used for such a purpose, but does not mean an approval procedure;

international standard means a standards-related measure, or other guide or recommendation, adopted by an international standardizing body and made available to the public;

international standardizing body means a standardizing body whose membership is open to the relevant bodies of at least all the parties to the *GATT Agreement on Technical Barriers to Trade* , including the *International Organization for Standardization (ISO)* , the *International Electrotechnical Commission (IEC), Codex Alimentarius Commission* , the *World Health Organization (WHO)* , the *Food and Agriculture Organization (FAO)* , the *International Telecommunication Union (ITU*); or any other body that the Parties designate;

land transportation service means a transportation service provided by means of motor carrier or rail;

legitimate objective includes an objective such as:

    (a) safety,
    (b) protection of human, animal or plant life or health, the environment or consumers, including matters relating to quality and identifiability of goods or services, and
    (c) sustainable development,
        considering, among other things, where appropriate, fundamental climatic or other geographical factors, technological or infrastructural factors, or scientific justification but does not include the protection of domestic production;

make compatible means bring different standards-related measures of the same scope approved by different standardizing bodies to a level such that they are either identical, equivalent or have the effect of permitting goods or services to be used in place of one another or fulfill the same purpose;

services means land transportation services and telecommunications services;

standard means a document, approved by a recognized body, that provides, for common and repeated use, rules, guidelines or characteristics for goods or related processes and production methods, or for services or related operating methods, with which compliance is not mandatory. It may also include or deal exclusively with terminology, symbols, packaging, marking or labelling requirements as they apply to a good, process, or production or operating method;

standardizing body means a body having recognized activities in standardization;

standards-related measure means a standard, technical regulation or conformity assessment procedure;

technical regulation means a document which lays down goods characteristics or their related processes and production methods, or services characteristics or their related operating methods, including the applicable administrative provisions, with which compliance is mandatory. It may also include or deal exclusively with terminology, symbols, packaging, marking or labelling requirements as they apply to a good, process, or production or operating method; and

telecommunications service means a service provided by means of the transmission and reception of signals by any electromagnetic means, but does not mean the cable, broadcast or other electromagnetic distribution of radio or television programming to the public generally.

2. Except as they are otherwise defined in this Agreement, other terms in this Chapter shall be interpreted in accordance with their ordinary meaning in context and in the light of the objectives of this Agreement, and where appropriate by reference to the terms presented in the sixth edition of the ISO/IEC Guide 2: 1991, *General Terms and Their Definitions Concerning Standardization and Related Activities.*

ANNEX 908.2. TRANSITIONAL RULES FOR CONFORMITY ASSESSMENT PROCEDURES

1. Except in respect of governmental conformity assessment bodies, Article 908(2) shall impose no obligation and confer no right on Mexico until four years after the date of entry into force of this Agreement.
2. Where a Party charges a reasonable fee, limited in amount to the approximate cost of the service rendered, to accredit, approve, license or otherwise recognize a conformity assessment body in the territory of another Party, it need not, prior to December 31, 1998 or such earlier date as the Parties may agree, charge such a fee to a conformity assessment body in its territory.

ANNEX 913.5.A-1. LAND TRANSPORTATION STANDARDS SUBCOMMITTEE

1. The Land Transportation Standards Subcommittee, established under Article 913(5)(a)(i), shall comprise representatives of each Party.
2. The Subcommittee shall implement the following work program for making compatible the Parties' relevant standards-related measures for:
    (a) bus and truck operations

    (i) no later than one and one-half years after the date of entry into force of this Agreement, for non-medical standards-related measures respecting drivers, including measures relating to the age of and language used by drivers,

    (ii) no later than two and one-half years after the date of entry into force of this Agreement, for medical standards-related measures respecting drivers,

    (iii) no later than three years after the date of entry into force of this Agreement, for standards-related measures respecting vehicles, including measures relating to weights and dimensions, tires, brakes, parts and accessories, securement of cargo, maintenance and repair, inspections, and emissions and environmental pollution levels not covered by the Automotive Standards Council's work program established under Annex 913.5.a-3,

    (iv) no later than three years after the date of entry into force of this Agreement, for standards-related measures respecting each Party's supervision of motor carriers' safety compliance, and

    (v) no later than three years after the date of entry into force of this Agreement, for standards-related measures respecting road signs;

(b) rail operations

    (i) no later than one year after the date of entry into force of this Agreement, for standards-related measures respecting operating personnel that are relevant to cross-border operations, and

    (ii) no later than one year after the date of entry into force of this Agreement, for standards-related measures respecting locomotives and other rail equipment; and

(c) transportation of dangerous goods, no later than six years after the date of entry into force of this Agreement, using as their basis the *United Nations Recommendations on the Transport of Dangerous Goods* , or such other standards as the Parties may agree.

3. The Subcommittee may address other related standards-related measures as it considers appropriate.

ANNEX 913.5.A-2. TELECOMMUNICATIONS STANDARDS SUBCOMMITTEE

1. The Telecommunications Standards Subcommittee, established under Article 913(5)(a)(ii), shall comprise representatives of each Party.

2. The Subcommittee shall, within six months of the date of entry into force of this Agreement, develop a work program, including a timetable, for making compatible, to the greatest extent practicable, the standards-related measures of the Parties for authorized equipment as defined in Chapter Thirteen (Telecommunications).

3. The Subcommittee may address other appropriate standards-related matters respecting telecommunications equipment or services and such other matters as it considers appropriate.

4. The Subcommittee shall take into account relevant work carried out by the Parties in other forums, and that of non-governmental standardizing bodies.

ANNEX 913.5.A-3. AUTOMOTIVE STANDARDS COUNCIL

1. The Automotive Standards Council, established under Article 913.5(a)(iii), shall comprise representatives of each Party.

2. The purpose of the Council shall be, to the extent practicable, to facilitate the attainment of compatibility among, and review the implementation of, national standards-related measures of the Parties that apply to automotive goods, and to address other related matters.

3. To facilitate its objectives, the Council may establish subgroups, consultation procedures and other appropriate operational mechanisms. On the agreement of the Parties, the Council may include state and provincial government or private sector representatives in its subgroups.

4. Any recommendation of the Council shall require agreement of the Parties. Where the adoption of a law is not required for a Party, the Council's recommendations shall be implemented by the Party within a reasonable time in accordance with the legal and procedural requirements and international obligations of the Party. Where the adoption of a law is required for a Party, the Party shall use its best efforts to secure the adoption of the law and shall implement any such law within a reasonable time.

5. Recognizing the existing disparity in standards-related measures of the Parties, the Council shall develop a work program for making compatible the national standards-related measures that apply to automotive goods and other related matters based on the following criteria:
   (a) the impact on industry integration;
   (b) the extent of the barriers to trade;
   (c) the level of trade affected; and
   (d) the extent of the disparity.
   In developing its work program, the Council may address other related matters, including emissions from on-road and non-road mobile sources.

6. Each Party shall take such reasonable measures as may be available to it to promote the objectives of this Annex with respect to standards-related measures that are maintained by state and provincial government authorities and private sector organizations. The Council shall make every effort to assist these entities with such activities, especially the identification of priorities and the establishment of work schedules.

ANNEX 913.5.A-4. SUBCOMMITTEE ON LABELLING OF TEXTILE AND APPAREL GOODS

1. The Subcommittee on Labelling of Textile and Apparel Goods, established under Article 913(5)(a)(iv), shall comprise representatives of each Party.

2. The Subcommittee shall include, and consult with, technical experts as well as a broadly representative group from the manufacturing and retailing sectors in the territory of each Party.

3. The Subcommittee shall develop and pursue a work program on the harmonization of labelling requirements to facilitate trade in textile and apparel goods between the Parties through the adoption of uniform labelling provisions. The work program should include the following matters:

    (a) pictograms and symbols to replace, where possible, required written information, as well as other methods to reduce the need for labels on textile and apparel goods in multiple languages;

    (b) care instructions for textile and apparel goods;

    (c) fiber content information for textile and apparel goods;

    (d) uniform methods acceptable for the attachment of required information to textile and apparel goods; and

    (e) use in the territory of the other Parties of each Party's national registration numbers for manufacturers or importers of textile and apparel goods.

PART FOUR: GOVERNMENT PROCUREMENT

10. GOVERNMENT PROCUREMENT

Section A - Scope and Coverage and National Treatment

Article 1001: Scope and Coverage

1. This Chapter applies to measures adopted or maintained by a Party relating to procurement:

    (a) by a federal government entity set out in Annex 1001.1a-1, a government enterprise set out in Annex 1001.1a-2, or a state or provincial government entity set out in Annex 1001.1a-3 in accordance with Article 1024;

    (b) of goods in accordance with Annex 1001.1b-1, services in accordance with Annex 1001.1b-2, or construction services in accordance with Annex 1001.1b-3; and

    (c) where the value of the contract to be awarded is estimated to be equal to or greater than a threshold, calculated and adjusted according to the U.S. inflation rate as set out in Annex 1001.1c, of

        (i) for federal government entities, US$50,000 for contracts for goods, services or any combination thereof, and US$6.5 million for contracts for construction services,

        (ii) for government enterprises, US$250,000 for contracts for goods, services or any combination thereof, and US$8.0 million for contracts for construction services, and

        (iii) for state and provincial government entities, the applicable threshold, as set out in Annex 1001.1a-3 in accordance with Article 1024.

2. Paragraph 1 is subject to:

    (a) the transitional provisions set out in Annex 1001.2a;

(b) the General Notes set out in Annex 1001.2b; and

(c) Annex 1001.2c, for the Parties specified therein.

3. Subject to paragraph 4, where a contract to be awarded by an entity is not covered by this Chapter, this Chapter shall not be construed to cover any good or service component of that contract.

4. No Party may prepare, design or otherwise structure any procurement contract in order to avoid the obligations of this Chapter.

5. Procurement includes procurement by such methods as purchase, lease or rental, with or without an option to buy. Procurement does not include:

(a) non-contractual agreements or any form of government assistance, including cooperative agreements, grants, loans, equity infusions, guarantees, fiscal incentives, and government provision of goods and services to persons or state, provincial and regional governments; and

(b) the acquisition of fiscal agency or depository services, liquidation and management services for regulated financial institutions and sale and distribution services for government debt.

Article 1002: Valuation of Contracts

1. Each Party shall ensure that its entities, in determining whether a contract is covered by this Chapter, apply paragraphs 2 through 7 in calculating the value of that contract.

2. The value of a contract shall be estimated as at the time of publication of a notice in accordance with Article 1010.

3. In calculating the value of a contract, an entity shall take into account all forms of remuneration, including premiums, fees, commissions and interest.

4. Further to Article 1001(4), an entity may not select a valuation method, or divide procurement requirements into separate contracts, to avoid the obligations of this Chapter.

5. Where an individual requirement for a procurement results in the award of more than one contract, or in contracts being awarded in separate parts, the basis for valuation shall be either:

(a) the actual value of similar recurring contracts concluded over the prior fiscal year or 12 months adjusted, where possible, for anticipated changes in quantity and value over the subsequent 12 months; or

(b) the estimated value of recurring contracts in the fiscal year or 12 months subsequent to the initial contract.

6. In the case of a contract for lease or rental, with or without an option to buy, or in the case of a contract that does not specify a total price, the basis for valuation shall be:

(a) in the case of a fixed-term contract, where the term is 12 months or less, the total contract value, for its duration or, where the term exceeds 12 months, the total contract value, including the estimated residual value; or

(b) in the case of a contract for an indefinite period, the estimated monthly installment multiplied by 48.

If the entity is uncertain as to whether a contract is for a fixed or an indefinite term, the entity shall calculate the value of the contract using the method set out in subparagraph (b).

7. Where tender documentation requires option clauses, the basis for valuation shall be the total value of the maximum permissible procurement, including all possible optional purchases.

Article 1003: National Treatment and Non-Discrimination

1. With respect to measures covered by this Chapter, each Party shall accord to goods of another Party, to the suppliers of such goods and to service suppliers of another Party, treatment no less favorable than the most favorable treatment that the Party accords to:
   (a) its own goods and suppliers; and
   (b) goods and suppliers of another Party.

2. With respect to measures covered by this Chapter, no Party may:
   (a) treat a locally established supplier less favorably than another locally established supplier on the basis of degree of foreign affiliation or ownership; or
   (b) discriminate against a locally established supplier on the basis that the goods or services offered by that supplier for the particular procurement are goods or services of another Party.

3. Paragraph 1 does not apply to measures respecting customs duties or other charges of any kind imposed on or in connection with importation, the method of levying such duties or charges or other import regulations, including restrictions and formalities.

Article 1004: Rules of Origin

No Party may apply rules of origin to goods imported from another Party for purposes of government procurement covered by this Chapter that are different from or inconsistent with the rules of origin the Party applies in the normal course of trade, which may be the Marking Rules established under Annex 311 if they become the rules of origin applied by that Party in the normal course of its trade.

Article 1005: Denial of Benefits

1. Subject to prior notification and consultation in accordance with Articles 1803 (Notification and Provision of Information) and 2006 (Consultations), a Party may deny the benefits of this Chapter to a service supplier of another Party where the Party establishes that the service is being provided by an enterprise that is owned or controlled by persons of a non-Party and that has no substantial business activities in the territory of any Party.

2. A Party may deny to an enterprise of another Party the benefits of this Chapter if nationals of a non-Party own or control the enterprise and:

    (a) the circumstance set out in Article 1113(1)(a) (Denial of Benefits) is met; or

    (b) the denying Party adopts or maintains measures with respect to the non-Party that prohibit transactions with the enterprise or that would be violated or circumvented if the benefits of this Chapter were accorded to the enterprise.

Article 1006: Prohibition of Offsets

Each Party shall ensure that its entities do not, in the qualification and selection of suppliers, goods or services, in the evaluation of bids or the award of contracts, consider, seek or impose offsets. For purposes of this Article, offsets means conditions imposed or considered by an entity prior to or in the course of its procurement process that encourage local development or improve its Party's balance of payments accounts, by means of requirements of local content, licensing of technology, investment, counter-trade or similar requirements.

Article 1007: Technical Specifications

1. Each Party shall ensure that its entities do not prepare, adopt or apply any technical specification with the purpose or the effect of creating unnecessary obstacles to trade.

2. Each Party shall ensure that any technical specification prescribed by its entities is, where appropriate:

    (a) specified in terms of performance criteria rather than design or descriptive characteristics; and

    (b) based on international standards, national technical regulations, recognized national standards, or building codes.

3. Each Party shall ensure that the technical specifications prescribed by its entities do not require or refer to a particular trademark or name, patent, design or type, specific origin or producer or supplier unless there is no sufficiently precise or intelligible way of otherwise describing the procurement requirements and provided that, in such cases, words such as "or equivalent" are included in the tender documentation.

4. Each Party shall ensure that its entities do not seek or accept, in a manner that would have the effect of precluding competition, advice that may be used in the preparation or adoption of any technical specification for a specific procurement from a person that may have a commercial interest in that procurement.

Section B - Tendering Procedures

Article 1008: Tendering Procedures

1. Each Party shall ensure that the tendering procedures of its entities are:

(a) applied in a non-discriminatory manner; and

(b) consistent with this Article and Articles 1009 through 1016.

2. In this regard, each Party shall ensure that its entities:

(a) do not provide to any supplier information with regard to a specific procurement in a manner that would have the effect of precluding competition; and

(b) provide all suppliers equal access to information with respect to a procurement during the period prior to the issuance of any notice or tender documentation.

Article 1009: Qualification of Suppliers

1. Further to Article 1003, no entity of a Party may, in the process of qualifying suppliers in a tendering procedure, discriminate between suppliers of the other Parties or between domestic suppliers and suppliers of the other Parties.

2. The qualification procedures followed by an entity shall be consistent with the following:

(a) conditions for participation by suppliers in tendering procedures shall be published sufficiently in advance so as to provide the suppliers adequate time to initiate and, to the extent that it is compatible with efficient operation of the procurement process, to complete the qualification procedures;

(b) conditions for participation by suppliers in tendering procedures, including financial guarantees, technical qualifications and information necessary for establishing the financial, commercial and technical capacity of suppliers, as well as the verification of whether a supplier meets those conditions, shall be limited to those that are essential to ensure the fulfillment of the contract in question;

(c) the financial, commercial and technical capacity of a supplier shall be judged both on the basis of that supplier's global business activity, including its activity in the territory of the Party of the supplier, and its activity, if any, in the territory of the Party of the procuring entity;

(d) an entity shall not misuse the process of, including the time required for, qualification in order to exclude suppliers of another Party from a suppliers' list or from being considered for a particular procurement;

(e) an entity shall recognize as qualified suppliers those suppliers of another Party that meet the conditions for participation in a particular procurement;

(f) an entity shall consider for a particular procurement those suppliers of another Party that request to participate in the procurement and that are not yet qualified, provided there is sufficient time to complete the qualification procedure;

(g) an entity that maintains a permanent list of qualified suppliers shall ensure that suppliers may apply for qualification at any time, that all qualified suppliers so requesting are included in the list within a reasonably short period of time and that all qualified suppliers included in the list are notified of the termination of the list or of their removal from it;

(h) where, after publication of a notice in accordance with Article 1010, a supplier that is not yet qualified requests to participate in a particular procurement, the entity shall promptly start the qualification procedure;

(i) an entity shall advise any supplier that requests to become a qualified supplier of its decision as to whether that supplier has become qualified; and

(j) where an entity rejects a supplier's application to qualify or ceases to recognize a supplier as qualified, the entity shall, on request of the supplier, promptly provide pertinent information concerning the entity's reasons for doing so.

3. Each Party shall:

(a) ensure that each of its entities uses a single qualification procedure, except that an entity may use additional qualification procedures where the entity determines the need for a different procedure and is prepared, on request of another Party, to demonstrate that need; and

(b) endeavor to minimize differences in the qualification procedures of its entities.

4. Nothing in paragraphs 2 and 3 shall prevent an entity from excluding a supplier on grounds such as bankruptcy or false declarations.

Article 1010: Invitation to Participate

1. Except as otherwise provided in Article 1016, an entity shall publish an invitation to participate for all procurements in accordance with paragraphs 2, 3 and 5, in the appropriate publication referred to in Annex 1010.1.

2. The invitation to participate shall take the form of a notice of proposed procurement that shall contain the following information:

(a) a description of the nature and quantity of the goods or services to be procured, including any options for further procurement and, if possible,

(i) an estimate of when such options may be exercised, and

(ii) in the case of recurring contracts, an estimate of when the subsequent notices will be issued;

(b) a statement as to whether the procedure is open or selective and whether it will involve negotiation;

(c) any date for starting or completion of delivery of the goods or services to be procured;

(d) the address to which an application to be invited to tender or to qualify for the suppliers' lists must be submitted, the final date for receiving the application and the language or languages in which it may be submitted;

(e) the address to which tenders must be submitted, the final date for receiving tenders and the language or languages in which tenders may be submitted;

(f) the address of the entity that will award the contract and that will provide any information necessary for obtaining specifications and other documents;

(g) a statement of any economic or technical requirements and of any financial guarantees, information and documents required from suppliers;

(h) the amount and terms of payment of any sum payable for the tender documentation; and

(i) a statement as to whether the entity is inviting offers for purchase, lease or rental, with or without an option to buy.

3. Notwithstanding paragraph 2, an entity listed in Annex 1001.1a-2 or 1001.1a-3 may use as an invitation to participate a notice of planned procurement that shall contain as much of the information referred to in paragraph 2 as is available to the entity, but that shall include, at a minimum, the following information:

(a) a description of the subject matter of the procurement;

(b) the time limits set for the receipt of tenders or applications to be invited to tender;

(c) the address to which requests for documents relating to the procurement should be submitted;

(d) a statement that interested suppliers should express their interest in the procurement to the entity; and

(e) the identification of a contact point within the entity from which further information may be obtained.

4. An entity that uses a notice of planned procurement as an invitation to participate shall subsequently invite suppliers that have expressed an interest in the procurement to confirm their interest on the basis of information provided by the entity, which shall include at least the information referred to in paragraph 2.

5. Notwithstanding paragraph 2, an entity listed in Annex 1001.1a-2 or 1001.1a-3 may use as an invitation to participate a notice regarding a qualification system. An entity that uses such a notice shall, subject to the considerations referred to Article 1015(8), provide in a timely manner information that allows all suppliers that have expressed an interest in participating in the procurement to have a meaningful opportunity to assess their interest. The information shall normally include the information required for notices referred to in paragraph 2. Information provided to any interested supplier shall be provided in a non-discriminatory manner to all other interested suppliers.

6. In the case of selective tendering procedures, an entity that maintains a permanent list of qualified suppliers shall publish annually in the appropriate publication referred to in Annex 1010.1 a notice containing the following information:

(a) an enumeration of any such lists maintained, including their headings, in relation to the goods or services or categories of goods or services to be procured through the lists;

(b) the conditions to be fulfilled by suppliers in view of their inscription on the lists and the methods according to which each of those conditions will be verified by the entity concerned; and

(c) the period of validity of the lists and the formalities for their renewal.

7. Where, after publication of an invitation to participate, but before the time set for the opening or receipt of tenders as specified in the notices or the tender documentation, an entity finds that it has become necessary to amend or reissue the notice or tender documentation, the entity shall ensure that the amended or reissued notice or tender documentation is given the same circulation as the original. Any significant information given by an entity to a supplier with respect to a particular procurement shall be given simultaneously to all other interested suppliers and sufficiently in advance so as to provide all suppliers concerned adequate time to consider the information and to respond.

8. An entity shall indicate in the notices referred to in this Article that the procurement is covered by this Chapter.

Article 1011: Selective Tendering Procedures

1. To ensure optimum effective competition between the suppliers of the Parties under selective tendering procedures, an entity shall, for each procurement, invite tenders from the maximum number of domestic suppliers and suppliers of the other Parties, consistent with the efficient operation of the procurement system.

2. Subject to paragraph 3, an entity that maintains a permanent list of qualified suppliers may select suppliers to be invited to tender for a particular procurement from among those listed. In the process of making a selection, the entity shall provide for equitable opportunities for suppliers on the list.

3. Subject to Article 1009(2)(f), an entity shall allow a supplier that requests to participate in a particular procurement to submit a tender and shall consider the tender. The number of additional suppliers permitted to participate shall be limited only by the efficient operation of the procurement system.

4. Where an entity does not invite or admit a supplier to tender, the entity shall, on request of the supplier, promptly provide pertinent information concerning its reasons for not doing so.

Article 1012: Time Limits for Tendering and Delivery

1. An entity shall:
    (a) in prescribing a time limit, provide adequate time to allow suppliers of another Party to prepare and submit tenders before the closing of the tendering procedures;
    (b) in determining a time limit, consistent with its own reasonable needs, take into account such factors as the complexity of the procurement, the extent of subcontracting anticipated, and the time normally required for transmitting tenders by mail from foreign as well as domestic points; and
    (c) take due account of publication delays when setting the final date for receipt of tenders or applications to be invited to tender.

2. Subject to paragraph 3, an entity shall provide that:
    (a) in open tendering procedures, the period for the receipt of tenders is no less than 40 days from the date of publication of a notice in accordance with Article 1010;
    (b) in selective tendering procedures not involving the use of a permanent list of qualified suppliers, the period for submitting an application to be invited to tender is no less than 25 days from the date of publication of a notice in accordance with Article 1010, and the period for receipt of tenders is no less than 40 days from the date of issuance of the invitation to tender; and
    (c) in selective tendering procedures involving the use of a permanent list of qualified suppliers, the period for receipt of tenders is no less than 40 days from

the date of the initial issuance of invitations to tender, but where the date of initial issuance of invitations to tender does not coincide with the date of publication of a notice in accordance with Article 1010, there shall not be less than 40 days between those two dates.

3. An entity may reduce the periods referred to in paragraph 2 in accordance with the following:

    (a) where a notice referred to Article 1010(3) or (5) has been published for a period of no less than 40 days and no more than 12 months, the 40-day limit for receipt of tenders may be reduced to no less than 24 days;

    (b) in the case of the second or subsequent publications dealing with recurring contracts within the meaning of Article 1010(2)(a), the 40-day limit for receipt of tenders may be reduced to no less than 24 days;

    (c) where a state of urgency duly substantiated by the entity renders impracticable the periods in question, the periods may be reduced to no less than 10 days from the date of publication of a notice in accordance with Article 1010; or

    (d) where an entity listed in Annex 1001.1a-2 or 1001.1a-3 is using as an invitation to participate a notice referred to in Article 1010(5), the periods may be fixed by mutual agreement between the entity and all selected suppliers but, in the absence of agreement, the entity may fix periods that shall be sufficiently long to allow for responsive bidding and in any event shall be no less than 10 days.

4. An entity shall, in establishing a delivery date for goods or services and consistent with its own reasonable needs, take into account such factors as the complexity of the procurement, the extent of subcontracting anticipated and the time realistically required for production, destocking and transport of goods from the points of supply.

Article 1013: Tender Documentation

1. Where an entity provides tender documentation to suppliers, the documentation shall contain all information necessary to permit suppliers to submit responsive tenders, including information required to be published in the notice referred to in Article 1010(2), except for the information required under Article 1010(2)(h). The documentation shall also include:

    (a) the address of the entity to which tenders should be submitted;

    (b) the address to which requests for supplementary information should be submitted;

    (c) the language or languages in which tenders and tendering documents may be submitted;

    (d) the closing date and time for receipt of tenders and the length of time during which tenders should be open for acceptance;

    (e) the persons authorized to be present at the opening of tenders and the date, time and place of the opening;

    (f) a statement of any economic or technical requirements and of any financial guarantees, information and documents required from suppliers;

    (g) a complete description of the goods or services to be procured and any other requirements, including technical specifications, conformity certification and necessary plans, drawings and instructional materials;

    (h) the criteria for awarding the contract, including any factors other than price that are to be considered in the evaluation of tenders and the cost elements to be included in evaluating tender prices, such as transportation, insurance and inspection costs, and in the case of goods or services of another Party, customs duties and other import charges, taxes and the currency of payment;

    (i) the terms of payment; and

    (j) any other terms or conditions.

2.   An entity shall:

    (a) forward tender documentation on the request of a supplier that is participating in open tendering procedures or has requested to participate in selective tendering procedures, and reply promptly to any reasonable request for explanations relating thereto; and

    (b) reply promptly to any reasonable request for relevant information made by a supplier participating in the tendering procedure, on condition that such information does not give that supplier an advantage over its competitors in the procedure for the award of the contract.

Article 1014: Negotiation Disciplines

1.   An entity may conduct negotiations only:

    (a) in the context of procurement in which the entity has, in a notice published in accordance with Article 1010, indicated its intent to negotiate; or

    (b) where it appears to the entity from the evaluation of the tenders that no one tender is obviously the most advantageous in terms of the specific evaluation criteria set out in the notices or tender documentation.

2.   An entity shall use negotiations primarily to identify the strengths and weaknesses in the tenders.

3.   An entity shall treat all tenders in confidence. In particular, no entity may provide to any person information intended to assist any supplier to bring its tender up to the level of any other tender.

4.   No entity may, in the course of negotiations, discriminate between suppliers. In particular, an entity shall:

    (a) carry out any elimination of suppliers in accordance with the criteria set out in the notices and tender documentation;

    (b) provide in writing all modifications to the criteria or technical requirements to all suppliers remaining in the negotiations;

    (c) permit all remaining suppliers to submit new or amended tenders on the basis of the modified criteria or requirements; and

    (d) when negotiations are concluded, permit all remaining suppliers to submit final tenders in accordance with a common deadline.

Article 1015: Submission, Receipt and Opening of Tenders and Awarding of Contracts

1. An entity shall use procedures for the submission, receipt and opening of tenders and the awarding of contracts that are consistent with the following:

   (a) tenders shall normally be submitted in writing directly or by mail;

   (b) where tenders by telex, telegram, telecopy or other means of electronic transmission are permitted, the tender made thereby must include all the information necessary for the evaluation of the tender, in particular the definitive price proposed by the supplier and a statement that the supplier agrees to all the terms and conditions of the invitation to tender;

   (c) a tender made by telex, telegram, telecopy or other means of electronic transmission must be confirmed promptly by letter or by the dispatch of a signed copy of the telex, telegram, telecopy or electronic message;

   (d) the content of the telex, telegram, telecopy or electronic message shall prevail where there is a difference or conflict between that content and the content of any documentation received after the time limit for submission of tenders;

   (e) tenders presented by telephone shall not be permitted;

   (f) requests to participate in selective tendering procedures may be submitted by telex, telegram or telecopy and if permitted, may be submitted by other means of electronic transmission; and

   (g) the opportunities that may be given to suppliers to correct unintentional errors of form between the opening of tenders and the awarding of the contract shall not be administered in a manner that would result in discrimination between suppliers.

   In this paragraph, "means of electronic transmission" consists of means capable of producing for the recipient at the destination of the transmission a printed copy of the tender.

2. No entity may penalize a supplier whose tender is received in the office designated in the tender documentation after the time specified for receiving tenders if the delay is due solely to mishandling on the part of the entity. An entity may also consider, in exceptional circumstances, tenders received after the time specified for receiving tenders if the entity's procedures so provide.

3. All tenders solicited by an entity under open or selective tendering procedures shall be received and opened under procedures and conditions guaranteeing the regularity of the opening of tenders. The entity shall retain the information on the opening of tenders. The information shall remain at the disposal of the competent authorities of the Party for use, if required, under Article 1017, Article 1019 or Chapter Twenty (Institutional Arrangements and Dispute Settlement Procedures).

4. An entity shall award contracts in accordance with the following:

   (a) to be considered for award, a tender must, at the time of opening, conform to the essential requirements of the notices or tender documentation and have been submitted by a supplier that complies with the conditions for participation;

   (b) if the entity has received a tender that is abnormally lower in price than other tenders submitted, the entity may inquire of the supplier to ensure that it can comply with the conditions of participation and is or will be capable of fulfilling the terms of the contract;

(c) unless the entity decides in the public interest not to award the contract, the entity shall make the award to the supplier that has been determined to be fully capable of undertaking the contract and whose tender is either the lowest-priced tender or the tender determined to be the most advantageous in terms of the specific evaluation criteria set out in the notices or tender documentation;

(d) awards shall be made in accordance with the criteria and essential requirements specified in the tender documentation; and

(e) option clauses shall not be used in a manner that circumvents this Chapter.

5. No entity of a Party may make it a condition of the awarding of a contract that the supplier has previously been awarded one or more contracts by an entity of that Party or that the supplier has prior work experience in the territory of that Party.

6. An entity shall:

(a) on request, promptly inform suppliers participating in tendering procedures of decisions on contract awards and, if so requested, inform them in writing; and

(b) on request of a supplier whose tender was not selected for award, provide pertinent information to that supplier concerning the reasons for not selecting its tender, the relevant characteristics and advantages of the tender selected and the name of the winning supplier.

7. No later than 72 days after the award of a contract, an entity shall publish a notice in the appropriate publication referred to in Annex 1010.1 that shall contain the following information:

(a) a description of the nature and quantity of goods or services included in the contract;

(b) the name and address of the entity awarding the contract;

(c) the date of the award;

(d) the name and address of each winning supplier;

(e) the value of the contract, or the highest-priced and lowest-priced tenders considered in the process of awarding the contract; and

(f) the tendering procedure used.

8. Notwithstanding paragraphs 1 through 7, an entity may withhold certain information on the award of a contract where disclosure of the information:

(a) would impede law enforcement or otherwise be contrary to the public interest;

(b) would prejudice the legitimate commercial interest of a particular person; or

(c) might prejudice fair competition between suppliers.

Article 1016: Limited Tendering Procedures

1. An entity of a Party may, in the circumstances and subject to the conditions set out in paragraph 2, use limited tendering procedures and thus derogate from Articles 1008 through 1015, provided that such limited tendering procedures are not used with a view to avoiding maximum possible competition or in a manner that would constitute

a means of discrimination between suppliers of the other Parties or protection of domestic suppliers.

2. An entity may use limited tendering procedures in the following circumstances and subject to the following conditions, as applicable:

    (a) in the absence of tenders in response to an open or selective call for tenders, or where the tenders submitted either have resulted from collusion or do not conform to the essential requirements of the tender documentation, or where the tenders submitted come from suppliers that do not comply with the conditions for participation provided for in accordance with this Chapter, on condition that the requirements of the initial procurement are not substantially modified in the contract as awarded;

    (b) where, for works of art, or for reasons connected with the protection of patents, copyrights or other exclusive rights, or proprietary information or where there is an absence of competition for technical reasons, the goods or services can be supplied only by a particular supplier and no reasonable alternative or substitute exists;

    (c) in so far as is strictly necessary where, for reasons of extreme urgency brought about by events unforeseeable by the entity, the goods or services could not be obtained in time by means of open or selective tendering procedures;

    (d) for additional deliveries by the original supplier that are intended either as replacement parts or continuing services for existing supplies, services or installations, or as the extension of existing supplies, services or installations, where a change of supplier would compel the entity to procure equipment or services not meeting requirements of interchangeability with already existing equipment or services, including software to the extent that the initial procurement of the software was covered by this Chapter;

    (e) where an entity procures a prototype or a first good or service that is developed at its request in the course of and for a particular contract for research, experiment, study or original development. Where such contracts have been fulfilled, subsequent procurement of goods or services shall be subject to Articles 1008 through 1015. Original development of a first good may include limited production in order to incorporate the results of field testing and to demonstrate that the good is suitable for production in quantity to acceptable quality standards, but does not include quantity production to establish commercial viability or to recover research and development costs;

    (f) for goods purchased on a commodity market;

    (g) for purchases made under exceptionally advantageous conditions that only arise in the very short term, such as unusual disposals by enterprises that are not normally suppliers or disposal of assets of businesses in liquidation or receivership, but not routine purchases from regular suppliers;

    (h) for a contract to be awarded to the winner of an architectural design contest, on condition that the contest is

        (i) organized in a manner consistent with the principles of this Chapter, including regarding publication of an invitation to suitably qualified suppliers to participate in the contest,

        (ii) organized with a view to awarding the design contract to the winner, and

(iii) to be judged by an independent jury; and

(i) where an entity needs to procure consulting services regarding matters of a confidential nature, the disclosure of which could reasonably be expected to compromise government confidences, cause economic disruption or similarly be contrary to the public interest.

3. An entity shall prepare a report in writing on each contract awarded by it under paragraph 2. Each report shall contain the name of the procuring entity, indicate the value and kind of goods or services procured, the name of the country of origin, and a statement indicating the circumstances and conditions described in paragraph 2 that justified the use of limited tendering. The entity shall retain each report. They shall remain at the disposal of the competent authorities of the Party for use, if required, under Article 1017, Article 1019 or Chapter Twenty (Institutional Arrangements and Dispute Settlement Procedures).

Section C - Bid Challenge

Article 1017: Bid Challenge

1. In order to promote fair, open and impartial procurement procedures, each Party shall adopt and maintain bid challenge procedures for procurement covered by this Chapter in accordance with the following:

(a) each Party shall allow suppliers to submit bid challenges concerning any aspect of the procurement process, which for the purposes of this Article begins after an entity has decided on its procurement requirement and continues through the contract award;

(b) a Party may encourage a supplier to seek a resolution of any complaint with the entity concerned prior to initiating a bid challenge;

(c) each Party shall ensure that its entities accord fair and timely consideration to any complaint regarding procurement covered by this Chapter;

(d) whether or not a supplier has attempted to resolve its complaint with the entity, or following an unsuccessful attempt at such a resolution, no Party may prevent the supplier from initiating a bid challenge or seeking any other relief;

(e) a Party may require a supplier to notify the entity on initiation of a bid challenge;

(f) a Party may limit the period within which a supplier may initiate a bid challenge, but in no case shall the period be less than 10 working days from the time when the basis of the complaint became known or reasonably should have become known to the supplier;

(g) each Party shall establish or designate a reviewing authority with no substantial interest in the outcome of procurements to receive bid challenges and make findings and recommendations concerning them;

(h) on receipt of a bid challenge, the reviewing authority shall expeditiously investigate the challenge;

(i) a Party may require its reviewing authority to limit its considerations to the challenge itself;

(j) in investigating the challenge, the reviewing authority may delay the awarding of the proposed contract pending resolution of the challenge, except in cases of urgency or where the delay would be contrary to the public interest;

(k) the reviewing authority shall issue a recommendation to resolve the challenge, which may include directing the entity to re-evaluate offers, terminate or re-compete the contract in question;

(l) entities normally shall follow the recommendations of the reviewing authority;

(m) each Party should authorize its reviewing authority, following the conclusion of a bid challenge procedure, to make additional recommendations in writing to an entity respecting any facet of the entity's procurement process that is identified as problematic during the investigation of the challenge, including recommendations for changes in the procurement procedures of the entity to bring them into conformity with this Chapter;

(n) the reviewing authority shall provide its findings and recommendations respecting bid challenges in writing and in a timely manner, and shall make them available to the Parties and interested persons;

(o) each Party shall specify in writing and shall make generally available all its bid challenge procedures; and

(p) each Party shall ensure that each of its entities maintains complete documentation regarding each of its procurements, including a written record of all communications substantially affecting each procurement, for at least three years from the date the contract was awarded, to allow verification that the procurement process was carried out in accordance with this Chapter.

2. A Party may require that a bid challenge be initiated only after the notice of procurement has been published or, where a notice is not published, after tender documentation has been made available. Where a Party imposes such a requirement, the 10-working day period described in paragraph 1(f) shall begin no earlier than the date that the notice is published or the tender documentation is made available.

Section D - General Provisions

Article 1018: Exceptions

1. Nothing in this Chapter shall be construed to prevent a Party from taking any action or not disclosing any information which it considers necessary for the protection of its essential security interests relating to the procurement of arms, ammunition or war materials, or to procurement indispensable for national security or for national defense purposes.

2. Provided that such measures are not applied in a manner that would constitute a means of arbitrary or unjustifiable discrimination between Parties where the same conditions prevail or a disguised restriction on trade between the Parties, nothing in this Chapter shall be construed to prevent any Party from adopting or maintaining measures:

(a) necessary to protect public morals, order or safety;

(b) necessary to protect human, animal or plant life or health;

(c) necessary to protect intellectual property; or

(d) relating to goods or services of handicapped persons, of philanthropic institutions or of prison labor.

Article 1019: Provision of Information

1. Further to Article 1802(1) (Publication), each Party shall promptly publish any law, regulation, precedential judicial decision, administrative ruling of general application and any procedure, including standard contract clauses, regarding government procurement covered by this Chapter in the appropriate publications referred to in Annex 1010.1.

2. Each Party shall:

    (a) on request, explain to another Party its government procurement procedures;

    (b) ensure that its entities, on request from a supplier, promptly explain their procurement practices and procedures; and

    (c) designate by January 1, 1994 one or more contact points to

        (i) facilitate communication between the Parties, and

        (ii) answer all reasonable inquiries from other Parties to provide relevant information on matters covered by this Chapter.

3. A Party may seek such additional information on the award of the contract as may be necessary to determine whether the procurement was made fairly and impartially, in particular with respect to unsuccessful tenders. To this end, the Party of the procuring entity shall provide information on the characteristics and relative advantages of the winning tender and the contract price. Where release of this information would prejudice competition in future tenders, the information shall not be released by the requesting Party except after consultation with and agreement of the Party that provided the information.

4. On request, each Party shall provide to another Party information available to that Party and its entities concerning covered procurement of its entities and the individual contracts awarded by its entities.

5. No Party may disclose confidential information the disclosure of which would prejudice the legitimate commercial interests of a particular person or might prejudice fair competition between suppliers, without the formal authorization of the person that provided the information to that Party.

6. Nothing in this Chapter shall be construed as requiring any Party to disclose confidential information the disclosure of which would impede law enforcement or otherwise be contrary to the public interest.

7. With a view to ensuring effective monitoring of procurement covered by this Chapter, each Party shall collect statistics and provide to the other Parties an annual report in accordance with the following reporting requirements, unless the Parties otherwise agree:

    (a) statistics on the estimated value of all contracts awarded, both above and below the applicable threshold values, broken down by entities;

(b) statistics on the number and total value of contracts above the applicable threshold values, broken down by entities, by categories of goods and services established in accordance with classification systems developed under this Chapter and by the country of origin of the goods and services procured;

(c) statistics on the number and total value of contracts awarded under each use of the procedures referred to in Article 1016, broken down by entities, by categories of goods and services, and by country of origin of the goods and services procured; and

(d) statistics on the number and total value of contracts awarded under derogations to this Chapter set out in Annexes 1001.2a and 1001.2b, broken down by entities.

8. Each Party may organize by state or province any portion of a report referred to in paragraph 7 that pertains to entities listed in Annex 1001.1a-3.

Article 1020: Technical Cooperation

1. The Parties shall cooperate, on mutually agreed terms, to increase understanding of their respective government procurement systems, with a view to maximizing access to government procurement opportunities for the suppliers of all Parties.

2. Each Party shall provide to the other Parties and to the suppliers of such Parties, on a cost recovery basis, information concerning training and orientation programs regarding its government procurement system, and access on a non-discriminatory basis to any program it conducts.

3. The training and orientation programs referred to in paragraph 2 include:

(a) training of government personnel directly involved in government procurement procedures;

(b) training of suppliers interested in pursuing government procurement opportunities;

(c) an explanation and description of specific elements of each Party's government procurement system, such as its bid challenge mechanism; and

(d) information about government procurement market opportunities.

4. Each Party shall establish by January 1, 1994 at least one contact point to provide information on the training and orientation programs referred to in this Article.

Article 1021: Joint Programs for Small Business

1. The Parties shall establish, within 12 months after the date of entry into force of this Agreement, the Committee on Small Business, comprising representatives of the Parties. The Committee shall meet as mutually agreed, but not less than once each year, and shall report annually to the Commission on the efforts of the Parties to promote government procurement opportunities for their small businesses.

2. The Committee shall work to facilitate the following activities of the Parties:

(a) identification of available opportunities for the training of small business personnel in government procurement procedures;

(b) identification of small businesses interested in becoming trading partners of small businesses in the territory of another Party;

(c) development of data bases of small businesses in the territory of each Party for use by entities of another Party wishing to procure from small businesses;

(d) consultations regarding the factors that each Party uses in establishing its criteria for eligibility for any small business programs; and

(e) activities to address any related matter.

Article 1022: Rectifications or Modifications

1. A Party may modify its coverage under this Chapter only in exceptional circumstances.

2. Where a Party modifies its coverage under this Chapter, the Party shall:
   (a) notify the other Parties and its Section of the Secretariat of the modification;
   (b) reflect the change in the appropriate Annex; and
   (c) propose to the other Parties appropriate compensatory adjustments to its coverage in order to maintain a level of coverage comparable to that existing prior to the modification.

3. Notwithstanding paragraphs 1 and 2, a Party may make rectifications of a purely formal nature and minor amendments to its Schedules to Annexes 1001.1a-1 through 1001.1b-3 and Annexes 1001.2a and 1001.2b, provided that it notifies such rectifications to the other Parties and its Section of the Secretariat, and another Party does not object to such proposed rectification within 30 days. In such cases, compensation need not be proposed.

4. Notwithstanding any other provision of this Chapter, a Party may undertake reorganizations of its government procurement entities covered by this Chapter, including programs through which the procurement of such entities is decentralized or the corresponding government functions cease to be performed by any government entity, whether or not subject to this Chapter. In such cases, compensation need not be proposed. No Party may undertake such reorganizations or programs to avoid the obligations of this Chapter.

5. Where a Party considers that:
   (a) an adjustment proposed under paragraph (2)© is not adequate to maintain a comparable level of mutually agreed coverage, or
   (b) a rectification or a minor amendment under paragraph 3 or a reorganization under paragraph 4 does not meet the applicable requirements of those paragraphs and should require compensation, the Party may have recourse to dispute settlement procedures under Chapter Twenty (Institutional Arrangements and Dispute Settlement Procedures).

Article 1023: Divestiture of Entities

1. Nothing in this Chapter shall be construed to prevent a Party from divesting an entity covered by this Chapter.
2. If, on the public offering of shares of an entity listed in Annex 1001.1a-2, or through other methods, the entity is no longer subject to federal government control, the Party may delete the entity from its Schedule to that Annex, and withdraw the entity from the coverage of this Chapter, on notification to the other Parties and its Section of the Secretariat.
3. Where a Party objects to the withdrawal on the grounds that the entity remains subject to federal government control, that Party may have recourse to dispute settlement procedures under Chapter Twenty (Institutional Arrangements and Dispute Settlement Procedures).

Article 1024: Further Negotiations

1. The Parties shall commence further negotiations no later than December 31, 1998, with a view to the further liberalization of their respective government procurement markets.
2. In such negotiations, the Parties shall review all aspects of their government procurement practices for purposes of:
    (a) assessing the functioning of their government procurement systems;
    (b) seeking to expand the coverage of this Chapter, including by adding
        (i) other government enterprises, and
        (ii) procurement otherwise subject to legislated or administrative exceptions; and
    (c) reviewing thresholds.
3. Prior to such review, the Parties shall endeavor to consult with their state and provincial governments with a view to obtaining commitments, on a voluntary and reciprocal basis, to include within this Chapter procurement by state and provincial government entities and enterprises.
4. If the negotiations pursuant to Article IX:6(b) of the *GATT Agreement on Government Procurement* ("the Code") are completed prior to such review, the Parties shall:
    (a) immediately begin consultations with their state and provincial governments with a view to obtaining commitments, on a voluntary and reciprocal basis, to include within this Chapter procurement by state and provincial government entities and enterprises; and
    (b) increase the obligations and coverage of this Chapter to a level at least commensurate with that of the Code.
5. The Parties shall undertake further negotiations, to commence no later than one year after the date of entry into force of this Agreement, on the subject of electronic transmission.

Article 1025: Definitions

1.   For purposes of this Chapter:

construction services contract means a contract for the realization by any means of civil or building works listed in Appendix 1001.1b-3-A;

entity means an entity listed in Annex 1001.1a-1, 1001.1a-2 or 1001.1a-3;

goods of another Party means goods originating in the territory of another Party, determined in accordance with Article 1004;

international standard means "international standard", as defined in Article 915 (Definitions - Standards-Related Measures);

limited tendering procedures means procedures where an entity contacts suppliers individually, only in the circumstances and under the conditions specified in Article 1016;

locally established supplier includes a natural person resident in the territory of the Party, an enterprise organized or established under the Party's law, and a branch or representative office located in the Party's territory;

open tendering procedures means those procedures under which all interested suppliers may submit a tender;

selective tendering procedures means procedures under which, consistent with Article 1011(3), those suppliers invited to do so by an entity may submit a tender;

services includes construction services contracts, unless otherwise specified;

standard means "standard", as defined in Article 915;

supplier means a person that has provided or could provide goods or services in response to an entity's call for tender;

technical regulation means "technical regulation", as defined in Article 915;

technical specification means a specification which lays down goods characteristics or their related processes and production methods, or services characteristics or their related operating methods, including the applicable administrative provisions. It may also include or deal exclusively with terminology, symbols, packaging, marking or labelling requirements as they apply to a good, process, or production or operating method; and

tendering procedures means open tendering procedures, selective tendering procedures and limited tendering procedures.

ANNEX 1001.1A-1. FEDERAL GOVERNMENT ENTITIES SCHEDULE OF CANADA

1. Atlantic Canada Opportunities Agency
2. Canada Border Services Agency
3. Canada Employment Insurance Commission
4. Canada Industrial Relations Board
5. Canada Revenue Agency
6. Canada School of Public Service
7. Canadian Centre for Occupatioinal Health and Saftey Board
8. Canadian Food Inspection Agency
9. Canadian Human Rights Commission
10. Canadian Institutes of Health Research
11. Canadian Intergovernmental Conference Secretariat
12. Canadian International Development Agency (on its own account)
13. Canadian International Trade Tribunal
14. Canadian Nuclear Safety Commission
15. Canadian Radio-television and Telecommunications Commission
16. Canadian Transportation Accident Investigation and Safety Board
17. Canadian Transportation Agency
18. Copyright Board
19. Correctional Service of Canada
20. Courts Administration Service
21. Department of Agriculture and Agri-Food
22. Department of Canadian Heritage
23. Department of Citizenship and Immigration
24. Department of Finance
25. Department of Fisheries and Oceans
26. Department of Foreign Affairs and International Trade
27. Department of Health
28. Department of Human Resources and Social Development
29. Department of Indian Affairs and Northern Development
30. Department of Industry
31. Department of Justice
32. Department of National Defence
33. Department of Natural Resources
34. Department of Public Safety and Emergency Preparedness
35. Department of Public Works and Government Services (on its own account)
36. Department of the Environment
37. Department of Transport
38. Department of Veterans Affairs
39. Department of Western Economic Diversification
40. Director of Soldier Settlement
41. Director, The Veterans' Land Act
42. Economic Development Agency of Canada for the Regions of Quebec

43. Hazardous Materials Information Review Commission
44. Immigration and Refugee Board
45. Library and Archives Canada
46. Municipal Development and Loan Board
47. National Battlefields Commission
48. National Energy Board
49. National Farm Products Council
50. National Parole Board
51. National Research Council of Canada
52. Natural Sciences and Engineering Research Council of Canada
53. Northern Pipeline Agency
54. Office of the Auditor General
55. Office of the Chief Electoral Officer
56. Office of the Commissioner for Federal Judicial Affairs
57. Office of the Commissioner of Official Languages
58. Office of the Coordinator, Status of Women
59. Office of the Governor General's Secretary
60. Office of the Superintendent of Financial Institutions
61. Offices of the Information and Privacy Commissioners of Canada
62. Parks Canada Agency
63. Patented Medicine Prices Review Board
64. Privy Council Office
65. Public Health Agency of Canada
66. Public Service Commission
67. Public Service Human Resources Management Agency of Canada
68. Public Service Labour Relations Board
69. Registry of the Competition Tribunal
70. Royal Canadian Mounted Police
71. Royal Canadian Mounted Police External Review Committee
72. Royal Canadian Mounted Police Public Complaints Commission
73. Social Sciences and Humanities Research Council
74. Statistics Canada
75. Statute Revision Commission
76. Supreme Court of Canada
77. Transportation Appeal Tribunal of Canada
78. Treasury Board Secretariat

Schedule of Mexico

1. Secretaría de Gobernación
    *   Secretaría General del Consejo Nacional de Población
    *   Archivo General de la Nación
    *   Instituto Nacional de Estudios Históricos de la Revolución Mexicana
    *   Centro Nacional de Prevención de Desastres

- Instituto Nacional para el Federalismo y el Desarrollo Municipal
- Secretaría Técnica de la Comisión Calificadora de Publicaciones y Revistas Ilustradas
- Centro de Producción de Programas Informativos y Especiales
- Coordinación General de la Comisión Mexicana de Ayuda a Refugiados
- Instituto Nacional de Migración
- Secretaría Técnica de la Comisión para Asuntos de la Frontera Norte

2. Secretaría de Relaciones Exteriores
   - Sección Mexicana de la Comisión Internacional de Límites y Aguas México-EE.UU.
   - Sección Mexicana de la Comisión Internacional de Límites y Aguas México-Guatemala-Belice
   - Instituto de México

3. Secretaría de Hacienda y Crédito Público
   - Comisión Nacional Bancaria y de Valores
   - Comisión Nacional de Seguros y Fianzas
   - Instituto Nacional de Estadística, Geografía e Informática
   - Servicio de Administración Tributaria
   - Fideicomiso Programa de Mejoramiento de los Medios de Informática y de Control de las
   - Autoridades Aduaneras (FIDEMICA)
   - Servicio de Administración de Bienes Asegurados
   - Comisión Nacional del Sistema de Ahorro para el Retiro

4. Secretaría de Agricultura, Ganadería, Desarrollo Rural, Pesca y Alimentación
   - Instituto Mexicano de Tecnología del Agua
   - Instituto Nacional de Investigaciones Forestales, Agrícolas y Pecuarias
   - Apoyos y Servicios a la Comercialización Agropecuaria (ASERCA)
   - Comisión Nacional de Acuacultura y Pesca
   - Servicio Nacional de Sanidad, Inocuidad y Calidad Agroalimentaria
   - Servicio de Información y Estadística Agroalimentaria y Pesquera
   - Servicio Nacional de Inspección y Certificación de Semillas
   - Instituto Nacional de Pesca

5. Secretaría de Comunicaciones y Transportes
   - Comisión Federal de Telecomunicaciones
   - Instituto Mexicano de Transporte

6. Secretaría de Economía
   - Comisión Federal de Mejora Regulatoria
   - Comisión Federal de Competencia

7. Secretaría de Educación Pública
   - Instituto Nacional de Antropología e Historia
   - Instituto Nacional de Bellas Artes y Literatura
   - Radio Educación
   - Centro de Ingeniería y Desarrollo Industrial
   - Consejo Nacional para la Cultura y las Artes
   - Comisión Nacional del Deporte

- Instituto Nacional de Derechos de Autor
8. Secretaría de Salud
   - Administración del Patrimonio de la Beneficencia Pública
   - Centro Nacional de la Transfusión Sanguínea
   - Laboratorio de Biológicos y Reactivos de México
   - Centro Nacional de Rehabilitación
   - Centro Nacional para la Prevención y Control del VIH/SIDA
   - Centro Nacional de Vigilancia Epidemiológica
   - Centro Nacional para la Salud de la Infancia y Adolescencia
   - Comisión Federal para la Protección contra Riesgos Sanitarios
   - Servicios de Salud Mental
   - Comisión Nacional de Arbitraje Médico
   - Centro Nacional de Transplantes
9. Secretaría del Trabajo y Previsión Social
   - Procuraduría Federal de la Defensa del Trabajo
10. Secretaría de la Reforma Agraria
    - Procuraduría Agraria
    - Registro Agrario Nacional
11. Secretaría de Medio Ambiente y Recursos Naturales
12. Procuraduría General de la República
13. Secretaría de Energía
    - Comisión Nacional de Seguridad Nuclear y Salvaguardias
    - Comisión Nacional para el Ahorro de Energía
    - Comisión Reguladora de Energía
14. Secretaría de Desarrollo Social
    - Comisión Nacional de Fomento a la Vivienda
    - Coordinación Nacional del Programa de Educación, Salud y Alimentación
15. Secretaría de Turismo
16. Secretaría de la Función Pública
17. Comisión Nacional de Zonas Aridas
18. Comisión Nacional de los Libros de Texto Gratuitos
19. Comisión Nacional de Derechos Humanos
20. Consejo Nacional de Fomento Educativo
21. Secretaría de la Defensa Nacional
22. Secretaría de Marina
23. Secretaría de Seguridad Pública
    - Secretariado Ejecutivo del Sistema Nacional de Seguridad Pública
    - Policía Federal Preventiva
    - Prevención y Readaptación Social
    - Consejo de Menores

Notes:

1. This Schedule covers the numbered entities and those listed thereunder.
2. Translation provided for purposes of reference only.

Schedule of the United States

1. Department of Agriculture (Not including procurement of agricultural goods made in furtherance of agricultural support programs or human feeding programs.)
2. Department of Commerce
3. Department of Education
4. Department of Health and Human Services
5. Department of Housing and Urban Development
6. Department of the Interior, including the Bureau of Reclamation (For goods of Canada, suppliers of such goods and service suppliers of Canada, this Chapter will apply to procurements by the Bureau of Reclamation of the Department of Interior only at such time as this Chapter applies to procurements by the Canadian provincial, not including local, hydro utilities.)
7. Department of Justice
8. Department of Labor
9. Department of State
10. United States Agency for International Development
11. Department of the Treasury
12. Department of Transportation
13. Department of Energy (Not including national security procurements made in support of safeguarding nuclear materials or technology and entered into under the authority of the Atomic Energy Act, and oil purchases related to the Strategic Petroleum Reserve.)
14. General Services Administration (except Federal Supply Groups 51 and 52 and Federal Supply Class 7340)
15. National Aeronautics and Space Administration (NASA)
16. Department of Veterans Affairs
17. Environmental Protection Agency
18. Broadcasting Board of Governors
19. National Science Foundation
20. Executive Office of the President
21. Farm Credit Administration
22. National Credit Union Administration
23. Merit Systems Protection Board
24. The Corporation for National and Community Service
25. Office of Thrift Supervision
26. Federal Housing Finance Board
27. National Labor Relations Board
28. National Mediation Board
29. Railroad Retirement Board
30. American Battle Monuments Commission
31. Federal Communications Commission
32. Federal Trade Commission
33. Securities and Exchange Commission
34. Office of Personnel Management
35. United States International Trade Commission

36. Export-Import Bank of the United States
37. Federal Mediation and Conciliation Service
38. Selective Service System
39. Smithsonian Institution
40. Federal Deposit Insurance Corporation
41. Consumer Product Safety Commission
42. Equal Employment Opportunity Commission
43. Federal Maritime Commission
44. National Transportation Safety Board
45. Nuclear Regulatory Commission
46. Overseas Private Investment Corporation
47. Commission on Civil Rights
48. Commodity Futures Trading Commission
49. Peace Corps
50. National Archives and Records Administration
51. Department of Defense, including the Army Corps of Engineers
52. Rural Utilities Service (Federal buy national requirements imposed as conditions of funding by the Rural Utilities Service will not apply to goods of Mexico and Canada, suppliers of such goods, and service suppliers of Mexico and Canada.)
53. Department of Homeland Security (For purposes of Article 1018, the national security considerations applicable to the Department of Defense are equally applicable to the Coast Guard, a military unit of the United States.)

Government Enterprises Schedule of Canada

- Canada Post Corporation
- Canadian Museum of Civilization
- Canadian Museum of Nature
- Canadian Tourism Commission
- Defence Construction (1951) Ltd.
- National Capital Commission
- National Gallery of Canada
- National Museum of Science and Technology
- Royal Canadian Mint
- Via Rail Canada Inc.

Notes:

1. For greater certainty, Article 1019(5) applies to procurements by Canadian National Railway Company, St. Lawrence Seaway Authority and Via Rail Canada Inc., respecting the protection of the commercial confidentiality of information provided.
2. This Chapter does not apply to procurement by or on behalf of the Royal Canadian Mint of direct inputs for use in minting anything other than Canadian legal tender.

3. With respect to the Canadian National Railway Company, this Chapter applies to the procurement of goods, services and construction services for its railway operations, subject to any other exceptions in this Chapter.

Schedule of Mexico

Printing and Editorial

1. Talleres Gráficos de México

Communications and Transportation

2. Aeropuertos y Servicios Auxiliares (ASA)
3. Caminos y Puentes Federales de Ingresos y Servicios Conexos (CAPUFE)
4. Servicio Postal Mexicano
5. Telecomunicaciones de México (TELECOM)

Industry

6. Petróleos Mexicanos (No incluye las compras de combustibles y gas)
    - PEMEX Corporativo
    - PEMEX Exploración y Producción
    - PEMEX Refinación
    - PEMEX Gas y Petroquímica Básica
    - PEMEX Petroquímica
    - Petroquímica Camargo
    - Petroquímica Cangrejera
    - Petroquímica Cosoleacaque
    - Petroquímica Escolín
    - Petroquímica Morelos
    - Petroquímica Pajaritos
    - Petroquímica Tula
7. Comisión Federal de Electricidad
8. Consejo de Recursos Minerales

Commerce

9. Distribuidora e Impulsora Comercial Conasupo (DICONSA)
10. Leche Industrializada Conasupo (LICONSA) (No incluye las compras de bienes agrícolas adquiridos para programas de apoyo a la agricultura o bienes para la alimentación humana).
11. Procuraduría Federal del Consumidor
12. Instituto de Seguridad y Servicios Sociales de los Trabajadores del Estado (ISSSTE)
13. Instituto Mexicano del Seguro Social (IMSS)

14. Sistema Nacional para el Desarrollo Integral de la Familia (DIF) (No incluye las compras de bienes agrícolas adquiridos para programas de apoyo a la agricultura o bienes para la alimentación humana).

Social Security

15. Instituto de Seguridad Social para las Fuerzas Armadas Mexicanas
16. Instituto Nacional Indigenista (INI)
17. Instituto Nacional para la Educación de los Adultos
18. Centro de Integración Juvenil
19. Instituto Nacional de las Personas Adultas Mayores

Others

20. Comité Administrador del Programa Federal de Construcción de Escuelas (CAPFCE)
21. Comisión Nacional del Agua
22. Comisión para la Regularización de la Tenencia de la Tierra
23. Consejo Nacional de Ciencia y Tecnología (CONACYT)
24. NOTIMEX
25. Instituto Mexicano de Cinematografía
26. Lotería Nacional para la Asistencia Pública
27. Pronósticos para la Asistencia Pública
28. Instituto Nacional de las Mujeres
29. Grupo Aeroportuario de la Ciudad de México
30. Aeropuerto Internacional de la Ciudad de México
31. Servicio Aeroportuario de la Ciudad de México
32. Instituto Mexicano de la Propiedad Industrial
33. Comisión Nacional Forestal
34. Instituto Mexicano de la Juventud
35. Ferrocarril del Istmo de Tehuantepec
36. Consejo de Promoción Turística de México

Schedule of the United States

1. Tennessee Valley Authority
2. Bonneville Power Administration
3. Western Area Power Administration
4. Southeastern Power Administration
5. Southwestern Power Administration
6. St. Lawrence Seaway Development Corporation

Note: For goods of Canada, suppliers of such goods and service suppliers of Canada, this Chapter will apply to procurements by the authorities and power administrations listed as items 1 through 5 only at such time as this Chapter applies to the procurements by the Canadian provincial, not including local, hydro utilities.

ANNEX 1001.1A-3. STATE AND PROVINCIAL GOVERNMENT ENTITIES

Coverage under this Annex will be the subject of consultations with state and provincial governments in accordance with Article 1024.

ANNEX 1001.1B-1. GOODS

Section A - General Provisions

1. This Chapter applies to all goods, except to the extent set out in paragraphs 2 through 5 and Section B.
2. With respect to Canada, the goods listed in Section B purchased by the Department of National Defence and the Royal Canadian Mounted Police are included in the coverage of this Chapter, subject to Article 1018(1).
3. With respect to Mexico, the goods listed in Section B purchased by the Secretaría de la Defensa Nacional and the Secretaría de Marina are included in the coverage of this Chapter, subject to the application of Article 1018(1).
4. With respect to the United States, this Chapter will generally apply to Department of Defense purchases of the FSC categories listed in Section B subject to United States Government determinations under Article 1018(1).
5. This Chapter does not apply to the following purchases of the U.S. Department of Defense:
    (a) Federal Supply Classification (FSC) 83 - all elements other than pins, needles, sewing kits, flagstaffs, flagpoles and flagstaff trucks;
    (b) FSC 84 - all elements other than sub-class 8460 (luggage);
    (c) FSC 89 - all elements other than sub-class 8975 (tobacco products);
    (d) FSC 2310 - (buses only);
    (e) specialty metals, defined as steels melted in steel manufacturing facilities located in the United States or its possessions, where the maximum alloy content exceeds one or more of the following limits, must be used in products purchased by DOD: (1) manganese, 1.65 percent; silicon, 0.60 percent; or copper, 0.06 percent; or which contains more than 0.25 percent of any of the following elements: aluminum, chromium, cobalt, columbium, molybdenum, nickel, titanium, tungsten or vanadium; (2) metal alloys consisting of nickel, iron-nickel and cobalt base alloys containing a total of other alloying metals (except iron) in excess of 10 percent; (3) titanium and titanium alloys; or (4) zirconium base alloys;

(f) FSC 19 and 20 - that part defined as naval vessels or major components of the hull or superstructure thereof;

(g) FSC 51; and

(h) the following FSC categories are not generally covered due to application of Article 1018(1): 10, 12, 13, 14, 15, 16, 17, 19, 20, 28, 31, 58, 59 and 95.

Section B - List of Certain Goods

(Numbers refer to the Federal Supply Classification code)

22. Railway equipment
23. Motor vehicles, trailers and cycles (except buses in 2310; and, for Canada and Mexico, except military trucks and trailers in 2320 and 2330 and tracked combat, assault and tactical vehicles in 2350)
24. Tractors
25. Vehicular equipment components
26. Tires and tubes
29. Engine accessories
30. Mechanical power transmission equipment
32. Woodworking machinery and equipment
34. Metal working machinery
35. Service and trade equipment
36. Special industry machinery
37. Agricultural machinery and equipment
38. Construction, mining, excavating and highway maintenance equipment
39. Materials handling equipment
40. Rope, cable, chain and fittings
41. Refrigeration and air conditioning equipment
42. Fire fighting, rescue and safety equipment (for Canada, except 4220: Marine life-saving and diving equipment; and 4230: Decontaminating and impregnating equipment)
43. Pumps and compressors
44. Furnace, steam plant, drying equipment and nuclear reactors
45. Plumbing, heating and sanitation equipment
46. Water purification and sewage treatment equipment
47. Pipe, tubing, hose and fittings
48. Valves
49. Maintenance and repair shop equipment
52. Measuring tools
53. Hardware and abrasives
54. Prefabricated structures and scaffolding
55. Lumber, millwork, plywood and veneer
56. Construction and building materials
61. Electric wire and power and distribution equipment

62. Lighting fixtures and lamps
63. Alarm and signal systems
65. Medical, dental and veterinary equipment and supplies
66. Instruments and laboratory equipment (for Canada, except 6615: Automatic pilot mechanisms and airborne Gyro components; and 6665: Hazard-detecting instruments and apparatus)
67. Photographic equipment
68. Chemicals and chemical products
69. Training aids and devices
70. General purpose automatic data processing equipment, software, supplies and support equipment (for Canada, except 7010: ADPE configurations)
71. Furniture
72. Household and commercial furnishings and appliances
73. Food preparation and serving equipment
74. Office machines, text processing system and visible record equipment
75. Office supplies and devices
76. Books, maps and other publications (for Canada and Mexico, except 7650: drawings and specifications)
77. Musical instruments, phonographs and home-type radios
78. Recreational and athletic equipment
79. Cleaning equipment and supplies
80. Brushes, paints, sealers and adhesives
81. Containers, packaging and packing supplies
85. Toiletries
87. Agricultural supplies
88. Live animals
91. Fuels, lubricants, oils and waxes (Canada and United States only)
93. Non-metallic fabricated materials
94. Non-metallic crude materials
96. Ores, minerals and their primary products (for Mexico, except 9620: minerals, natural and synthetic)
99. Miscellaneous

ANNEX 1001.1B-2. SERVICES

Section A - General Provisions

1. This Chapter applies to all services that are procured by the entities listed in Annex 1001.1a-1 and Annex 1001.1a-2, subject to:
   (a) paragraph 3 and Section B; and
   (b) Appendix 1001.1b-2-A, for the Parties specified in that Appendix.
2. Appendix 1001.1b-2-B sets out the Common Classification System for the services procured by the entities of the Parties. The Parties shall use this System for reporting

purposes and shall update Appendix 1001.1b-2-B at such times as they mutually agree.

3.   Annex 1001.1b-3 applies to contracts for construction services.

Section B - Excluded Coverage

Schedule of Canada

Services Exclusions by Major Service Category

The following service contracts are excluded:

A.	**Research and Development**
	All Classes
B.	**Special Studies and Analysis - not R&D**
B002	Animal and fisheries studies
B003	Grazing and Range Studies
B400	Aeronautic/Space Studies
B503	Medical and health studies
B507	Legal studies (Except Advisory Services on Foreign Law)
C.	**Architecture and Engineering Services**
C112	Airfield, Communication and Missile Facilities
C216	Marine architect and engineering services
D.	**Information Processing and Related Telecommunications Services**
D304	ADP Telecommunications and Transmission Services, except those classified as "enhanced or value-added services" as defined in Article 1310 and that are expressly excluded from the reservations set out in Annex II, Schedule of Canada, II-C-3 or II-C-5. For the purposes of this provision, the procurement of "ADP elecommunications and Transmission services" does not include the ownership or furnishing of facilities for the transmission of voice or data services.
D305	ADP Teleprocessing and timesharing services
D309	Information and Data Broadcasting or Data Distribution Services
D316	Telecommunications Network Management Services
D317	Automated News Service, Data Services, or Other Information Services. Buying data, the electronic equivalent of books, periodicals, newspapers, etc.
D399	Other ADP and Telecommunications Services
F.	**Natural Resources and Conservation Services**
F004	Land Treatment Practices Services (plowing/clearing, etc).
F005	Range Seeding Services (ground equipment)
F006	Crop services inc. Seed Collection/Production Services
F007	Seedling Production/Transplanting Services
F011	Pesticides/Insecticides Support services
F010	Other Range/Forest Improvements services
F021	Veterinary/Animal Care services (inc. Livestock services)
F029	Other Animal Care /Control services
F030	Fisheries Resources Management Services
F031	Fish Hatchery Services
F059	Other natural resource and conservation services
F050	Recreation Site Maintenance services (non-construction)

G.	**Health and Social Services**
	All classes
H.	**Quality Control, Testing and Inspection and Technical Representative Services**
	Services for the Departments of Transport, Communications and Fisheries and Oceans respecting FSC 36 - (Special Industry Machinery), FSC 70 - (Automatic Data Processing Equipment, software supplies and support equipment) and FSC 74 (Office machines, text processing systems and visible record equipment).
	FSC 58 (Communications, Detection, and Coherent Radiation Equipment)
	Services with reference to transportation equipment.
J.	**Maintenance, Repair, Modification, Rebuilding and Installation of Equipment**
	Services for the Departments of Transport, Communications and Fisheries and Oceans respecting FSC 36 - (Special Industry Machinery), FSC 70 - (Automatic Data Processing Equipment, software supplies and support equipment) and FSC 74 (Office machines, text processing systems and visible record equipment).
	FSC 58 (Communications, Detection, and Coherent Radiation Equipment)
	Services with reference to transportation equipment.
J019	Maintenance, Repair, Modification, Rebuilding and Installation of Equipment related to Ships
J998	Non-nuclear Ship Repair
K.	**Custodial Operations and Related Services**
K0	Personal care services
K105	Guard Services
K109	Surveillance services
K115	Preparation and Disposal of Excess and surplus property
L.	**Financial and Related Services**
	All classes
M.	**Operation of Government Owned Facilities**

	All facilities operated by:
	  The Department of Defence The Department of Transport
	  The Department of Energy, Mines and Resources
	and for all Departments:
	  M180 and M140

R.	**Professional, Administrative and Management Support Services**
R003	Legal services (Except Advisory Services on Foreign Law)
R004	Certifications and accreditations for products and institutions other than Educational Institutions
R007	Systems Engineering Services 1/
R012	Patent and Trade Mark Services
R101	Expert Witness
R102	Weather Reporting/Observation services
R104	Transcription services
R106	Post Office services
R109	Translation and Interpreting services (inc. sign language)
R113	Data Collection services
R114	Logistics Support Services 2/
R116	Court Reporting Services
R117	Paper Shredding Services
R201	Civilian Personnel Recruitment (inc. Services of Employment Agencies)

[1] with reference to transportation systems

[2] with respect to transportation and defence

(Continued)

S.	**Utilities**	
	All classes	
T.	**Communications, Photographic, Mapping, Printing and Publications Services**	
	All classes	
U.	**Education and Training Services**	
U010	Certifications and accreditations for Educational Institutions	
V.	**Transportation, Travel and Relocation Services**	
	All classes (except V503 Travel Agent Services [not including Tour Guides.])	
W.	**Lease or Rental of Equipment**	
	Services for the Departments of Transport, Communications and Fisheries and Oceans respecting FSC 36 - (Special Industry Machinery), FSC 70 - (Automatic Data Processing Equipment, software supplies and support equipment) and FSC 74 (Office machines, text processing systems and visible record equipment).	
	FSC 58 (Communications, Detection, and Coherent Radiation Equipment)	
	Services with reference to transportation equipment.	

Notes:

1. All services, with reference to those goods purchased by the Department of National Defence, the Royal Canadian Mounted Police and the Canadian Coast Guard which are not identified as subject to coverage by this chapter (Annex 1001.1b-1), will be exempt from the disciplines of the Chapter.
2. All services purchased in support of military forces located overseas will be exempt from coverage by this chapter.
3. The Schedules of Canada as identified in Annex 1001.2b and Annex 1001.1b -3 will apply.
4. In the absence of agreed definitions for service classes under the proposed NAFTA classification system, and until such time as they are mutually agreed, Canada will continue to apply appropriate CPC definitions to identify classes which it considers exempt.

Schedule of Mexico

The following service contracts are excluded:

(Based on the United Nations Central Product Classification (CPC))

1.	All transportation services, including:		
	CPC Group	**CPC Class**	
	71		Land transportation
	72		Water transport
	73		Air transport
	74		Supporting and auxiliary transport
	75		Post and telecommunication
		8868	Repair services of other transport equipment, on a fee or contract basis
2.	Public utilities services (including telecommunications, transmission, water or energy services)		
3.	Management and operation contracts awarded to federally-funded research and development centers or related to carrying out government sponsored research programs		
4.	Financial services		
5.	Research and development services		

Schedule of the United States

Service Exclusions by Major Service Category

A.	**Research and Development**
	All classes
D.	**Information Processing and Related Telecommunications Services**
D304	ADP Telecommunications and Transmission Services, except for those services classified as "enhanced or value-added services," as defined in Article 1310 and that are expressly excluded from the reservation set out in Annex II, Schedule of the United States, II-U-3. For the purposes of this provision, the procurement of "ADP Telecommunications and Transmission services" does not include the ownership or furnishing of facilities for the transmission of voice or data services.
D305	ADP Teleprocessing and Timesharing Services
D316	Telecommunications Network Management Services
D317	Automated News Services, Data Services or Other Information Services
D399	Other ADP and Telecommunications Services
J.	**Maintenance, Repair, Modification, Rebuilding and Installation of Equipment**
J019	Maintenance, Repair, Modification, Rebuilding and Installation of Equipment Related to Ships
J998	Non-nuclear Ship Repair
M.	**Operation of Government-Owned Facilities**
	All facilities operated by the Department of Defense, Department of Energy and the National Aeronautics and Space Administration; and for all entities:
M180	Research and Development
S.	**Utilities**
	All Classes
V.	**Transportation, Travel and Relocation Services**
	All Classes except V503 Travel Agent Services

Notes:

1. All services purchased in support of military forces overseas will be excluded from coverage by this Chapter.

2. For service suppliers of Canada, this Chapter will apply to procurements by the authorities and the power administrations listed as items 1 through 6 in the U.S. Schedule in Annex 1001.1a-2 (Government Enterprises) and to procurements by the Bureau of Reclamation of the Department of Interior only at such time as this Chapter applies to the procurements by the Canadian provincial, not including local, hydro utilities.

APPENDIX 1001.1B-2-A. TEMPORARY SCHEDULE OF SERVICES FOR MEXICO

1. Until Mexico has completed its Schedule to Section B of Annex 1001.1b-2, pursuant to paragraph 2, this Chapter applies only in respect of the services set out in the Temporary Schedule.

2. Mexico shall develop and, after consultations with the other Parties, complete its list of services set out in its Schedule to Section B of Annex 1001.1b-2 no later than July 1, 1995.

3. When Mexico completes its list pursuant to paragraph 2, each Party may, after consultation with the other Parties, review and revise its Schedule to Section B to Annex 1001.1b-2.

Temporary Schedule

Note: Based on the United Nations Central Product Classification (CPC)
<> <> Integrated engineering services

CPC	Professional Services	
863	Taxation services (excluding legal services)	
	Architectural services	
	86711	Advisory and pre-design architectural services
	86712	Architectural design services
	86713	Contract administration services
	86714	Combined architectural design and contract administration services
	86719	Other architectural services
	Engineering services	
	86721	Advisory and consultative engineering services
	86722	Engineering design services for foundations and building structures
	86723	Engineering design services for mechanical and electrical installations for buildings
	86724	Engineering design services for civil engineering construction
	86725	Engineering design for industrial processes and production
	86726	Engineering design services n.e.c.
	86727	Other engineering services during the construction and installation phase
	86729	Other engineering services
	86731	Integrated engineering services for transportation, infrastructure turnkey projects
	86732	Integrated engineering and project management services for water supply and sanitation works turnkey projects
	86733	Integrated engineering services for the construction of manufacturing turnkey projects
	86739	Integrated engineering services for other turnkey projects
	8674	Urban planning and landscape architectural services
Computer and Related Services		
841	Consultancy services related to the installation of computer hardware	
842	Software implementation services, including systems and software consulting services, systems analysis, design, programming and maintenance services	
843	Data processing services, including processing, tabulation and facilities management services	
844	Data base services	
845	Maintenance and repair services of office machinery and equipment including computers	
849	Other computer services	
Real Estate Services		
821	Real estate services involving own or leased property	
822	Real estate services on a fee or contract basis	
Rental/Leasing Services without Operators		
831	Leasing or rental services concerning machinery and equipment without operator, including computers	
832	Leasing or rental services concerning personal and household goods (excluding in 83201, the rental of prerecorded records, sound cassettes, CD's and excluding 83202, rental services concerning video tapes)	
Other Business Services		
	Management consulting services	
	86501	General management consulting services

	86503	Marketing management consulting services
	86504	Human resources management consulting services
	86505	Production management consulting services
	86509	Other management consulting services, including agrology, agronomy, farm management and related consulting services
8676		Technical testing and analysis services including quality control and inspection
8814		Services incidental to forestry and logging, including forest management
883		Services incidental to mining, including, drilling and field services
		Related scientific and technical consulting services
	86751	Geological, geophysical and other scientific prospecting services, including those related to mining
	86752	Subsurface surveying services
	86753	Surface surveying services
	86754	Map making services
8861 through 8866		Repair services incidental to metal products, to machinery and equipment including computers, 8866 and communications equipment
874		Building-cleaning
876		Packaging services
Environmental Services		
940		Sewage and refuse disposal, sanitation and other environmental protection services, including sewage services, nature and landscape protection services and other environmental protection services n.e.c.
Hotels and restaurants (including catering)		
641		Hotel and other lodging services
642		Food services
643		Beverage serving services
Travel agency and tour operators services		
7471		Travel agency and tour operator services

APPENDIX 1001.1B-2-B COMMON CLASSIFICATION SYSTEM SERVICES

Notes: 1. It is understood that the Parties will continue to work on the development of definitions related to the categories and other ongoing enhancements to the Classification System. 2. The Parties will continue to review outstanding technical issues that may arise from time to time. 3. This common classification system follows the format described below:

Group = one digit Sub-group = two digit Class = four digit

A - Research and Development

Definition of research and development contracts: Procurement of research and development services include the acquisition of specialized expertise for the purposes of increasing knowledge in science; applying increased scientific knowledge or exploiting the potential of scientific discoveries and improvements in technology to advance the state of art; and systematically using increases in scientific knowledge and advances in state of art to design, develop, test, or evaluate new products or services. R&D Codes: The R&D code is composed of two alphabetic digits. The first digit is always the letter "A" to identify R&D, the second digit is alphabetic "A to Z" to identify the major sub-group.

Code Descriptions

AA	Agriculture
AB	Community Services and Development
AC	Defense Systems
AD	Defense - Other
AE	Economic Growth and Productivity
AF	Education
AG	Energy
AH	Environmental Protection
AJ	General Science and Technology
AK	Housing
AL	Income Security
AM	International Affairs and Cooperation
AN	Medical
AP	Natural Resources
AQ	Social Services
AR	Space
AS	Transportation - Modal
AT	Transportation - General
AV	Mining Activities
AZ	Other Research and Development

B - Studies and Analysis - (not R&D)

	Definition of studies and analysis:
	Procurement of special studies and analyses are organized, analytic assessments that provide insights for understanding complex issues or improving policy development or decision making. Output obtained in such acquisitions is a formal, structured document including data or other information that form the basis for conclusion or recommendations.
B0	Natural Sciences
B000	Chemical/Biological Studies and Analyses
B001	Endangered Species Studies - Plant and Animal
B002	Animal and Fisheries Studies
B003	Grazing/Range Studies
B004	Natural Resource Studies
B005	Oceanological Studies
B009	Other Natural Sciences Studies
B1	Environmental Studies
B100	Air Quality Analyses

B101	Environmental Studies Development of Environmental Impact Statements & Assessments
B102	Soil Studies
B103	Water Quality Studies
B104	Wildlife Studies
B109	Other Environmental Studies
B2	Engineering Studies
B200	Geological Studies
B201	Geophysical Studies
B202	Geotechnical Studies
B203	Scientific Data Studies
B204	Seismological Studies
B205	Building Technology Studies
B206	Energy Studies
B207	Technology Studies
B208	Housing and Community Development Studies (incl. Urban/Town Planning Studies)
B219	Other Engineering Studies
B3	Administrative Support Studies
B300	Cost Benefit Analyses
B301	Data Analyses (other than scientific)
B302	Feasibility Studies (non-construction)
B303	Mathematical/Statistical Analyses
B304	Regulatory Studies
B305	Intelligence Studies
B306	Defense Studies
B307	Security Studies (Physical and Personal)
B308	Accounting/Financial Management Studies
B309	Trade Issue Studies
B310	Foreign Policy/National Security Policy Studies
B311	Organization/Administrative/Personnel Studies
B312	Mobilization/Preparedness Studies
B313	Manpower Studies
B314	Acquisition Policy/Procedures Studies
B329	Other Administrative Support Studies
B4	Space Studies
B400	Aeronautic/Space Studies
B5	Social Studies and Humanities
B500	Archeological/Paleontological Studies
B501	Historical Studies
B502	Recreation Studies
B503	Medical and Health Studies
B504	Educational Studies and Analyses
B505	Elderly/Handicapped Studies
B506	Economic Studies
B507	Legal Studies
B509	Other Studies and Analyses

C - Architect and Engineering Services

C1	- Architect and Engineering Services - Related To Construction
C11	Building and Facility Structures
C111	Administrative and Service Buildings
C112	Airfield, Communication and Missile Facilities
C113	Educational Buildings
C114	Hospital Buildings
C115	Industrial Buildings
C116	Residential Buildings
C117	Warehouse Buildings
C118	Research and Development Facilities
C119	Other Buildings
C12	Non-Building Structures
C121	Conservation and Development
C122	Highways, Roads, Streets, Bridges and Railways
C123	Electric Power Generation (EPG)
C124	Utilities
C129	Other Non-Building Structures
C130	Restoration
C2	- Architect and Engineering Services - Not Related to Construction
C211	Architect - Engineer Services (incl. landscaping, interior layout and designing)
C212	Engineering Drafting Services
C213	A&E Inspection Services
C214	A&E Management Engineering Services
C215	A&E Production Engineering Services (incl. Design and Control and Building Programming)
C216	Marine Architect and Engineering Services
C219	Other Architect and Engineering Services

D - Information Processing and Related Telecommunications Services

D301	ADP Facility Operation and Maintenance Services
D302	ADP Systems Development Services
D303	ADP Data Entry Services
D304	ADP Telecommunications and Transmission Services
D305	ADP Teleprocessing and Timesharing Services
D306	ADP Systems Analysis Services
D307	Automated Information System Design and Integration Services
D308	Programming Services
D309	Information and Data Broadcasting or Data Distribution Services
D310	ADP Backup and Security Services
D311	ADP Data Conversion Services

D312	ADP Optical Scanning Services
D313	Computer Aided Design/Computer Aided Manufacturing (CAD/CAM) Services
D314	ADP System Acquisition Support Services (Includes preparation of statement of work, benchmarks,specifications, etc.)
D315	Digitizing Services (Includes cartographic and geographic information)
D316	Telecommunications Network Management Services
D317	Automated News Services, Data Services, or Other Information Services. Buying data (the electronic equivalent of books, periodicals, newspapers, etc.)
D399	Other ADP and Telecommunications Services (incl. data storage on tapes, Compact Disk (CD), etc.

E - Environmental Services

E101	Air Quality Support Services
E102	Industrial Investigation Surveys and Technical Support Related to Air Pollution
E103	Water Quality Support Services
E104	Industrial Investigation Surveys and Technical Support Related to Water Pollution
E106	Toxic Substances Support Services
E107	Hazardous Substance Analysis
E108	Hazardous Substance Removal, Cleanup, and Disposal Services and Operational Support
E109	Leaking Underground Storage Tank Support Services
E110	Industrial Investigations, Surveys and Technical Support for Multiple Pollutants
E111	Oil Spill Response including Cleanup, Removal, Disposal and Operational Support
E199	Other Environmental Services

F - Natural Resources Services

F0	Agriculture and Forestry Services
F001	Forest/Range Fire Suppression/Presuppression Services (incl. Water Bombing)
F002	Forest/Range Fire Rehabilitation Services (non-construction)
F003	Forest Tree Planting Services
F004	Land Treatment Practices Services (plowing/clearing, etc.)
F005	Range Seeding Services (ground equipment)
F006	Crop Services (incl. Seed Collection and Production Services)
F007	Seedling Production/Transplanting Services
F008	Tree Breeding Services (incl. ornamental shrub)
F009	Tree Thinning Services
F010	Other Range/Forest Improvements Services (non-construction)
F011	Pesticides /Insecticides Support Services
F02	Animal Care / Control Services

(Continued)

F020	Other Wildlife Management Services
F021	Veterinary/Animal Care Services (incl. Livestock Services)
F029	Other Animal Care/Control Services
F03	Fisheries and Ocean Services
F030	Fisheries Resources Management Services
F031	Fish Hatchery Services
F04	Mining
F040	Surface Mining Reclamation Services (non-construction)
F041	Well Drilling
F042	Other Services Incidental to Mining Except Those Listed in F040 and F041
F05	Other Natural Resources Services
F050	Recreation Site Maintenance Services (non-construction)
F051	Survey Line Clearing Services
F059	Other Natural Resources and Conservation Services

G - Health and Social Services

G0	Health Services
G001	Health Care
G002	Internal Medicine
G003	Surgery
G004	Pathology
G009	Other Health Services
G 1	Social Services
G100	Care of Remains and/or Funeral Services
G101	Chaplain Services
G102	Recreational Services (incl. Entertainment Services)
G103	Social Rehabilitation Services
G104	Geriatric Services
G199	Other Social Services

H - Quality Control, Testing, Inspection and Technical Representative Services

HO	Technical Representative Services
Hl	Quality Control Services
H2	Equipment and Materials Testing
H3	Inspection Services (incl. commercial testing and Laboratory Services, Except Medical/Dental)
H9	Other Quality Control, Testing, Inspection and Technical Representative Services

J - Maintenance, Repair, Modification, Rebuilding and Installation of Goods/Equipment

JO	Maintenance, Repair, Modification, Rebuilding and Installation of Goods/Equipment; includes as examples: 1. Textile Finishing, Dying and Printing 2. Welding services not related to Construction. (see CPC 5155 for Construction Welding)
J998	Non-nuclear Ship Repair (including overhauls and conversions)

K - Custodial Operations and Related Services

K0	Personal Care Services (incl. services such as Barber and Beauty Shop, Shoe Repairs and Tailoring etc.)
K1	Custodial Services
K100	Custodial - Janitorial Services
K101	Fire Protection Services
K102	Food Services
K103	Fueling and Other Petroleum Services - Excluding Storage
K104	Trash/Garbage Collection Services - Including Portable Sanitation Services
K105	Guard Services
K106	Insect and Rodent Control Services
K107	Landscaping/Groundskeeping Services
K108	Laundry and Dry Cleaning Services
K109	Surveillance Services
K110	Solid Fuel Handling Services
K111	Carpet Cleaning
K112	Interior Plantscaping
K113	Snow Removal/Salt Service (also spreading aggregate or other snow meltings material)
K114	Waste Treatment and Storage
K115	Preparation and Disposal of Excess and Surplus Property
K116	Other Salvage Services
K199	Other Custodial and Related Services

L - Financial and Related Services

L000	Government Life Insurance Programs
L001	Government Health Insurance Programs
L002	Other Government Insurance Programs
L003	Non-Government Insurance Programs
L004	Other Insurance Services
L005	Credit Reporting Services
L006	Banking Services
L007	Debt Collection Services
L008	Coin Minting
L009	Banknote Printing
L099	Other Financial Services

M - Operation of Government - Owned Facilities

M110	Administrative Facilities and Service Buildings
M120	Airfield, Communications, and Missile Facilities
M130	Educational Buildings
M140	Hospital Buildings
M150	Industrial Buildings
M160	Residential Buildings
M170	Warehouse Buildings
M180	Research and Development Facilities
M190	Other Buildings
M210	Conservation and Development Facilities
M220	Highways, Roads, Streets, Bridges and Railways
M230	Electric Power Generation (EPG) Facilities
M240	Utilities
M290	Other Non-Building Facilities

R - Professional, Administrative and Management Support Services

R0	Professional Services
R001	Specifications Development Services
R002	Technology Sharing/Utilization Services
R003	Legal Services
R004	Certifications and Accreditations for products and institutions other than Educational Institutions
R005	Technical Assistance
R006	Technical Writing Services
R007	Systems Engineering Services
R008	Engineering and Technical Services (incl. Mechanical, Electrical, Chemical, Electronic Engineering)
R009	Accounting Services
R010	Auditing Services
R011	Ongoing Audit Operations Support
R012	Patent and Trade Mark Services
R013	Real Property Appraisals Services
R014	Operations Research Studies / Quantitative Analysis Studies
R015	Simulation
R016	Personal Services Contracts
R019	Other Professional Services
R1	Administrative and Management Support Services
R100	Intelligence Services
R101	Expert Witness
R102	Weather Reporting/Observation Services

R103	Courier and Messenger Services
R104	Transcription Services
R105	Mailing and Distribution Services (Excluding Post Office Services)
R106	Post Office Services
R107	Library Services
R108	Word Processing/Typing Services
R109	Translation and Interpreting Services (Including Sign Language)
R110	Stenographic Services
R111	Personal Property Management Services
R112	Information Retrieval (non-automated)
R113	Data Collection Services
R114	Logistics Support Services
R115	Contract, Procurement, and Acquisition Support Services
R116	Court Reporting Services
R117	Paper Shredding Services
R118	Real Estate Brokerage Services
R119	Industrial Hygienics
R120	Policy Review/Development Services
R121	Program Evaluation Studies
R122	Program Management/Support Services
R123	Program Review/Development Services
R199	Other Administrative and Management Support Services
R2	Personnel Recruitment
R200	Military Personnel Recruitment
R201	Civilian Personnel Recruitment (incl. Services of Employment Agencies)

S - Utilities

S000	Gas Services
S001	Electric Services
S002	Telephone and/or Communications Services (incl. Telegraph, Telex and Cablevision Service)
S003	Water Services
S099	Other Utilities

T - Communications, Photographic, Mapping, Printing and Publication Services

T000	Communications Studies
T001	Market Research and Public Opinion Services (Formerly Telephone and Field Interview Services incl. Focus testing, Syndicated and attitude Surveys)

(Continued)

T002	Communications Services (incl. exhibit Services)
T003	Advertising Services
T004	Public Relations Services (incl. Writing Services, Event Planning and Management, Media Relations, Radio and TV Analysis, Press Services)
T005	Arts/Graphics Services
T006	Cartography Services
T007	Charting Services
T008	Film Processing Services
T009	Film/Video Tape Production Services
T010	Microfiche Services
T011	Photogrammetry Services
T012	Aerial Photographic Services
T013	General Photographic Services - Still
T014	Print/Binding Services
T015	Reproduction Services
T016	Topography Services
T017	General Photographic Services - Motion
T018	Audio/Visual Services
T019	Land Surveys, Cadastral Services (non-construction)
T099	Other Communication, Photographic, Mapping, Printing and Publication Services

U - Educational and Training Services

U001	Lectures For Training
U002	Personnel Testing
U003	Reserve Training (Military)
U004	Scientific and Management Education
U005	Tuition, Registration, and Membership Fees
U006	Vocational/Technical
U007	Faculty Salaries for Schools Overseas
U008	Training/Curriculum Development
U009	Informatics Training
U010	Certifications and Accreditations for Educational Institutions
U099	Other Education and Training Services

V - Transporation, Travel and Relocation Services

V0	Land Transport Services
V000	Motor Pool Operations
V001	Motor Freight
V002	Rail Freight

V003	Motor Charter for Things
V004	Rail Charter for Things
V005	Motor Passenger Service
V006	Rail Passenger Service
V007	Passenger Motor Charter Service
V008	Passenger Rail Charter Service
V009	Ambulance Service
V010	Taxicab Services
V011	Security Vehicle Service
V1	Water Transport Services
V100	Vessel Freight
V101	Marine Charter for Things
V102	Marine Passenger Service
V103	Passenger Marine Charter Service
V2	Air Transport Services
V200	Air Freight
V201	Air Charter for Things
V202	Air Passenger Service
V203	Passenger Air Charter Service
V204	Specialty air Services including Aerial Fertilization, Spraying and Seeding
V3	Space Transportation and Launch Services
V4	Other Transport Services
V401	Other Transportation Travel and Relocation Services
V402	Other Cargo and Freight Services
V403	Other Vehicle Charter for Transportation of Things
V5	Supporting and Auxiliary Transport Services
V500	Stevedoring
V501	Vessel Towing Service
V502	Relocation Services
V503	Travel Agent Services
V504	Packing/Crating Services
V505	Warehousing and Storage Services
V506	Salvage of Marine Vessels
V507	Salvage of Aircraft
V508	Navigational Aid and Pilotage Services

W - Lease and Rental of Equipment

WO	Lease or Rental of Equipment

ANNEX 1001.1B-3. CONSTRUCTION SERVICES

Section A - General Provisions

1. This Chapter applies to all construction services set out in Appendix 1001.1b-3-A, except those listed in Section B, that are procured by the entities listed in Annex 1001.1a-1 and 1001.1a-2.
2. The Parties shall update Appendix 1001.1b-3-A at such times as they mutually agree.

Section B - Excluded Coverage

Schedule of Canada
The following services contracts are excluded:

1. Dredging
2. Construction contracts tendered by or on behalf of Department of Transport

Schedule of the United States
The following services contracts are excluded:
Dredging

Note : In accordance with this Chapter, buy national requirements on articles, supplies and materials acquired for use in construction contracts covered by this Chapter shall not apply to goods of Canada or Mexico.

APPENDIX 1001.1B-3-A. COMMON CLASSIFICATION SYSTEM

Construction Work Codes

Note : Based on the United Nations Central Product Classification (CPC) Division 51.

Definition of Construction work:
Pre-erection work; new construction and repair, alteration, restoration and maintenance work on residential buildings, non-residential buildings or civil engineering works. This work can be carried out either by general contractors who do the complete construction work for the owner of the project, or on own account; or by subcontracting parts of the construction work to contractors specializing, e.g., in installation work, where the value of work done by subcontractors becomes part of the main contractor s work. The products classified here are services which are essential in the production process of the different types of constructions, the final output of construction activities.

Code	Descriptions
511	**Pre-erection work at construction sites**
5111	Site investigation work
5112	Demolition work
5113	Site formation and clearance work
5114	Excavating and earthmoving work
5115	Site preparation work for mining (except for mining of oil and gas which is classified under FO42)
5116	Scaffolding work
512	**Construction works for buildings**
5121	For one and two dwelling buildings
5122	For multi-dwelling buildings
5123	For warehouses and industrial buildings
5124	For commercial buildings
5125	For public entertainment buildings
5126	For hotel, restaurant and similar buildings
5127	For educational Buildings
5128	For health buildings
5129	For other buildings
513	**Construction work for civil engineering**
5131	For highways (except elevated highways), streets , roads, railways and airfield runways
5132	For bridges, elevated highways, tunnels ,subways and railroads
5133	For waterways, harbours, dams and other water works
5134	For long distance pipelines, communication and power lines (cables)
5135	For local pipelines and cables; ancillary works
5136	For constructions for mining and manufacturing
5137	For constructions for sport and recreation
5138	Dredging Services
5139	For engineering works n.e.c.
514	**Assembly and erection of prefabricated constructions**
515	**Special trade construction work**
5151	Foundation work, including pile driving
5152	Water well drilling
5153	Roofing and water proofing
5154	Concrete work
5155	Steel bending and erection, including welding
5156	Masonry work
5159	Other special trade construction work
516	**Installation work**
5161	Heating, ventilation and air conditioning work
5162	Water plumbing and drain laying work
5163	Gas fitting construction work
5164	Electrical work
5165	Insulation work (electrical wiring, water, heat, sound)

(Continued)

Code	Descriptions
5166	Fencing and railing construction work
5169	Other installation work
517	**Building completion and finishing work**
5171	Glazing work and window glass installation work
5172	Plastering work
5173	Painting work
5174	Floor and wall tiling work
5175	Other floor laying, wall covering and wall papering work
5176	Wood and metal joinery and carpentry work
5177	Interior fitting decoration work
5178	Ornamentation fitting work
5179	Other building completion and finishing work
518	**Renting services related to equipment for construction or demolition of buildings or civil engineering works, with operator .**

ANNEX 1001.1C. INDEXATION AND CONVERSION OF THRESHOLDS

1. The calculations referred to in Article 1001(1)(c) (Scope and Coverage) shall be made in accordance with the following:

    (a) the U.S. inflation rate shall be measured by the Producer Price Index for Finished Goods published by the U.S. Bureau of Labor Statistics;

    (b) the first adjustment for inflation, to take effect on January 1, 1996, shall be calculated using the period from November 1, 1993 through October 31, 1995;

    (c) all subsequent adjustments shall be calculated using two-year periods, each period beginning November 1, and shall take effect on January 1 of the year immediately following the end of the two-year period;

    (d) the United States shall notify the other Parties of the adjusted threshold values no later than November 16 of the year before the adjustment takes effect; and

    (e) the inflationary adjustment shall be estimated according to the following formula

    $$T_0 \times (1 + pi_i) = T_1$$

    T_0 = threshold value at base period

    pi_i = accumulated U.S. inflation rate for the ith two year-period

    T_1 = new threshold value.

2. Mexico and Canada shall calculate and convert the value of the thresholds set out in Article 1001(1)(c) into their national currencies using the conversion formula set out in paragraph 3 or 4, as appropriate. Mexico and Canada shall notify each other and the United States of the value, in their respective currencies, of the newly calculated thresholds no later than one month before the respective thresholds take effect.

3. Canada shall base its calculation on the official conversion rates of the Bank of Canada. From January 1, 1994 through December 31, 1995, the conversion rate shall

be the average of the weekly values of the Canadian dollar in terms of the U.S. dollar over the period October 1, 1992 through September 30, 1993. For each subsequent two-year period beginning January 1, 1996, its conversion rate shall be the average of the weekly values of the Canadian dollar in terms of the U.S. dollar over the two-year period ending September 30 of the year preceding the beginning of each two-year period.

4. Mexico shall use the conversion rate of the Bank of Mexico ("Banco de México"). Its conversion rate shall be the existing value of the Mexican peso in terms of the U.S. dollar as of December 1 and June 1 of each year, or the first working day thereafter. The conversion rate as of December 1 shall apply from January 1 to June 30 of the following year, and as of June 1 shall apply from July 1 to December 31 of that year.

Annex 1001.2a. Transitional Provisions for Mexico

Notwithstanding any other provision of this Chapter, Annexes 1001.1a-1 through 1001.1b-3 are subject to the following:

Pemex, CFE and Non-Energy Construction

1. Mexico may set aside from the obligations of this Chapter for a calendar year set out in paragraph 2 the percentage specified in that paragraph of:
   (a) the total value of procurement contracts for goods and services and any combination thereof and construction services procured by Pemex in the year that are above the thresholds set out in Article 1001(1)(c);
   (b) the total value of procurement contracts for goods and services and any combination thereof and construction services procured by CFE in the year that are above the thresholds set out in Article 1001(1)(c); and
   (c) the total value of procurement contracts for construction services procured in the year that are above the thresholds set out in Article 1001(1)(c), excluding procurement contracts for construction services procured by Pemex and CFE.

2. The calendar years to which paragraph 1 applies and the percentages for those calendar years are as follows:

1994	1995	1996	1997	1998
50%	45%	45%	40%	40%
1999	2000	2001	2002	2003 and thereafter
35%	35%	30%	30%	0%

3. The value of procurement contracts that are financed by loans from regional and multilateral financial institutions shall not be included in the calculation of the total value of procurement contracts under paragraphs 1 and 2. Procurement contracts that are financed by such loans shall also not be subject to any restrictions set out in this Chapter.

4. Mexico shall ensure that the total value of procurement contracts under any single FSC class (or other classification system agreed by Parties) that are set aside by Pemex or CFE under paragraphs 1 and 2 for any year does not exceed 10 percent of the total value of the procurement contracts that may be set aside by Pemex or CFE for that year.

5. Mexico shall ensure that, after December 31, 1998, Pemex and CFE each shall make all reasonable efforts to ensure that the total value of procurement contracts under any single FSC class (or other classification system agreed by the Parties) that are set aside by Pemex or CFE under paragraphs 1 and 2 for any year does not exceed 50 percent of the total value of all Pemex and CFE procurement contracts under that FSC class (or other classification system agreed by the Parties) for that year.

Pharmaceuticals

6. Until January 1, 2002, this Chapter shall not apply to the procurement by the Secretaría de Salud, IMSS, ISSSTE, Secretaría Defensa Nacional and the Secretaría de Marina of drugs that are not currently patented in Mexico or whose Mexican patents have expired. Nothing in this paragraph shall prejudice rights under Chapter Seventeen (Intellectual Property).

Time Limits for Tendering and Delivery

7. Mexico shall use its best efforts to comply with the 40- day time limit requirements of Article 1012, and in any event shall fully comply with that obligation no later than January 1, 1995.

Provision of Information

8. The Parties recognize that Mexico may be required to undertake extensive retraining of personnel, introduce new data maintenance and reporting systems and make major adjustments to the procurement systems of certain entities in order to comply with Article 1019. The Parties also recognize that Mexico may encounter difficulties in making the transition to procurement systems that facilitate full compliance with this Chapter.

9. The Parties shall consult on an annual basis for the first five years after the date of entry into force of this Agreement to review transitional problems and to develop mutually agreed solutions. Such solutions may include, when appropriate, temporary adjustment to the obligations of Mexico under this Chapter, such as those related to reporting requirements.

10. Canada and the United States shall cooperate with Mexico to provide technical assistance, as appropriate and mutually agreed pursuant to Article 1020, to aid Mexico's transition.

11. Nothing in paragraphs 8 through 10 shall be construed to excuse compliance with the obligations of this Chapter.

Note : The General Notes for Mexico set out in Annex 1001.2b apply to this Annex.

ANNEX 1001.2B. GENERAL NOTES

Schedule of Canada

1. This Chapter does not apply to procurements in respect of:
   (a) shipbuilding and repair;
   (b) urban rail and urban transportation equipment, systems, components and materials incorporated there in as well as all project related materials of iron or steel;
   (c) contracts respecting FSC 58 (communications, detection and coherent radiation equipment);
   (d) set-asides for small and minority businesses;
   (e) the Departments of Transport, Communications and Fisheries and Oceans respecting Federal Supply Classification (FSC) 70 (automatic data processing equipment, software supplies and support equipment), FSC 74 (office machines, text processing systems and visible record equipment) and FSC 36 (special industry machinery); and
   (f) agricultural products made in furtherance of agricultural support programs or human feeding programs.
2. This Chapter does not apply to the procurement of transportation services that form a part of, or are incidental to, a procurement contract.
3. Pursuant to Article 1018, national security exemptions include oil purchases related to any strategic reserve requirements.
4. National security exceptions include procurements made in support of safeguarding nuclear materials or technology.
5. The most-favored-nation obligation of Article 1003 does not apply to procurements covered by Annex 1001.2c.

Schedule of Mexico

1. This Chapter does not apply to procurements made:
   (a) with a view to commercial resale by government-owned retail stores;
   (b) pursuant to loans from regional or multilateral financial institutions to the extent that different procedures are imposed by such institutions (except for national content requirements); or
   (c) by one entity from another entity of Mexico.
2. This Chapter does not apply to the procurement of transportation services that form a part of, or are incidental to, a procurement contract.

3. Notwithstanding any other provision in this Chapter, Mexico may set aside procurement contracts from the obligations of this Chapter, subject to the following:
    (a) the total value of the contracts set aside that may be allocated by all entities, except Pemex and CFE, may not exceed the Mexican peso equivalent of
        (i) US$1.0 billion, in each year until December 31, 2002, and
        (ii) US$1.2 billion, in each year beginning January 1, 2003;
    (b) no contract may be set aside under this paragraph by Pemex or CFE prior to January 1, 2003;
    (c) the total value of the contracts set aside by Pemex and CFE under this paragraph may not exceed the Mexican peso equivalent of US$300 million, in each year beginning January 1, 2003;
    (d) the total value of contracts under any single FSC class (or other classification system agreed by the Parties) that may be set aside under this paragraph in any year shall not exceed 10 percent of the total value of contracts that may be set aside under this paragraph for that year; and
    (e) no entity subject to subparagraph (a) may set aside contracts in any year of a value of more than 20 percent of the total value of contracts that may be set aside for that year.

4. Beginning one year after the date of entry into force of this Agreement, the dollar values referred to in paragraph 3 shall be adjusted annually for cumulative inflation from the date of entry into force of this Agreement, based on the implicit price deflator for U.S. Gross Domestic Product (GDP) or any successor index published by the Council of Economic Advisors in "Economic Indicators".
    The dollar values adjusted for cumulative inflation up to January of each year following 1994 shall be equal to the original dollar values multiplied by the ratio of:
    (a) the implicit U.S. GDP price deflator or any successor index published by the Council of Economic Advisors in "Economic Indicators", current as of January of that year, to
    (b) the implicit U.S. GDP price deflator or any successor index published by the Council of Economic Advisors in "Economic Indicators", current as of the date of entry into force of this Agreement, provided that the price deflators under paragraphs (a) and (b) have the same base year.
    The resulting adjusted dollar values shall be rounded to the nearest million dollars.

5. National security exceptions include procurements made in support of safeguarding nuclear materials or technology.

6. Notwithstanding any other provision of this Chapter, an entity may impose a local content requirement of no more than:
    (a) 40 percent, for labor-intensive turnkey or major integrated projects; or
    (b) 25 percent, for capital-intensive turnkey or major integrated projects.
        For purposes of this paragraph, a **turnkey or major integrated project** means, in general, a construction, supply or installation project undertaken by a person pursuant to a right granted by an entity with respect to which:
    (c) the prime contractor is vested with the authority to select the general contractors or subcontractors;
    (d) neither the Government of Mexico nor its entities fund the project;

    (e) the person bears the risks associated with non- performance; and

    (f) the facility will be operated by an entity or through a procurement contract of that entity.

7.   Notwithstanding the thresholds set out in Article 1001(1)(c), Article 1003 shall apply to any procurement from locally-established suppliers of oil and gas field supplies or equipment by Pemex at any project site where it performs works.

8.   In the event that Mexico exceeds in any given year the total value of the contracts it may set aside for that year in accordance with paragraph 3 or the reserved procurement under Annex 1001.2a(1)(2) or (4), Mexico shall consult with the other Parties with a view to agreement on compensation in the form of additional procurement opportunities during the following year. The consultations shall be without prejudice to the rights of any Party under Chapter Twenty (Institutional Arrangements and Dispute Settlement Procedures).

9.   Notwithstanding Annex 1001.2a(6), Mexico may not set aside from the obligations of this Chapter procurement contracts by its entities of biologicals and drugs patented in Mexico.

10. Nothing in this Chapter shall be construed to require Pemex to enter into risk-sharing contracts.

Schedule of the United States

1.   This Chapter does not apply to set asides on behalf of small and minority businesses.

2.   This Chapter does not apply to the procurement of transportation services that form a part of, or are incidental to, a procurement contract.

3.   The most-favored-nation obligation of Article 1003 does not apply to procurements covered by Annex 1001.2c.

ANNEX 1001.2C. COUNTRY-SPECIFIC THRESHOLDS

As between Canada and United States,

(a) for any entity listed in the Schedule of Canada or of the United States in Annex 1001.1a-1, the applicable threshold for goods contracts, which may include incidental services such as delivery and transportation, shall be US$25,000 and the equivalent in Canadian dollars, as the case may be;

(b) Annex 1001.1c, except paragraphs 2 and 3 of that Annex for the purpose of calculating and converting the value of the threshold set out in subparagraph (a), does not apply to such goods contracts; and

(c) Chapter Thirteen of the *Canada - United States Free Trade Agreement* shall govern any procurement procedures that began before January 1, 1994, and that Chapter is hereby incorporated and made a part of this Agreement solely for that purpose.

ANNEX 1010.1. PUBLICATIONS

Section A - Publications for Notices of Procurement in Accordance with Article 1010 (Invitation to Participate)

Schedule of Canada

1. Government Business Opportunities (GBO)
2. Open Bidding Service, ISM Publishing

Schedule of Mexico

1. Major daily newspapers of national circulation or the Official Gazette of the Federation ("Diario Oficial de la Federación") .
2. Mexico shall endeavor to establish a specialized publication for purposes of notices of procurement. When established, the publication shall substitute for those referred to in paragraph 1.

Schedule of United States

Commerce Business Daily (CBD)

Section B - Publications for Measures in Accordance with Article 1019 (Provision of Information)

Schedule of Canada

1. Laws and regulations:
   (a) Statutes of Canada; and
   (b) Canada Gazette.
2. Precedential judicial decisions:
   (a) Dominion Law Reports;
   (b) Supreme Court Reports;
   (c) Federal Court Reports; and
   (d) National Reporter.
3. Administrative rulings and procedures:
   (a) Government Business Opportunities; and
   (b) Canada Gazette.

Schedule of Mexico

1. Official Gazette of the Federation ("Diario Oficial de la Federación")
2. Judicial Weekly of the Federation ("Semanario Judicial de la Federación") (for precedential judicial decisions only).

3.   Mexico shall endeavor to establish a specialized publication for administrative rulings of general application and any procedure, including standard contract clauses regarding procurements. When established, the publication shall substitute for those set out in paragraphs 1 and 2 for this purpose.

Schedule of United States

1.   Laws and regulations:
     (a) U.S. Statutes at Large
     (b) U.S. Code of Federal Regulations.
2.   Precedential decisions:
     (a) U.S. Reports (U.S. Supreme Court);
     (b) Federal Reporter (Circuit Court of Appeals);
     (c) Federal Supplement Reporter (District Courts);
     (d) Claims Court Reporter (Claims Court);
     (e) Boards of Contract Appeals (unofficial publication by Commerce Clearing House); and
     (f) Comptroller General of the United States (Those not officially published as decisions of the Comptroller General are published unofficially by Federal Publications, Inc.).
3.   All U.S. laws, regulations, judicial decisions, administrative rulings and procedures regarding government procurement covered by this Chapter are codified in the Defense Federal Acquisition Regulation Supplement (DFARS) and the Federal Acquisition Regulation (FAR), both of which are published as a part of the U.S. Code of Federal Regulations (CFR). The DFARS and the FAR are published in title 48 of CFR.

PART FIVE: INVESTMENT, SERVICES AND RELATED MATTERS

11. INVESTMENT

Section A - Investment

Article 1101: Scope and Coverage

1.   This Chapter applies to measures adopted or maintained by a Party relating to:
     (a) investors of another Party;
     (b) investments of investors of another Party in the territory of the Party; and
     (c) with respect to Articles 1106 and 1114, all investments in the territory of the Party.
2.   A Party has the right to perform exclusively the economic activities set out in Annex III and to refuse to permit the establishment of investment in such activities.
3.   This Chapter does not apply to measures adopted or maintained by a Party to the extent that they are covered by Chapter Fourteen (Financial Services).

4. Nothing in this Chapter shall be construed to prevent a Party from providing a service or performing a function such as law enforcement, correctional services, income security or insurance, social security or insurance, social welfare, public education, public training, health, and child care, in a manner that is not inconsistent with this Chapter.

Article 1102: National Treatment

1. Each Party shall accord to investors of another Party treatment no less favorable than that it accords, in like circumstances, to its own investors with respect to the establishment, acquisition, expansion, management, conduct, operation, and sale or other disposition of investments.
2. Each Party shall accord to investments of investors of another Party treatment no less favorable than that it accords, in like circumstances, to investments of its own investors with respect to the establishment, acquisition, expansion, management, conduct, operation, and sale or other disposition of investments.
3. The treatment accorded by a Party under paragraphs 1 and 2 means, with respect to a state or province, treatment no less favorable than the most favorable treatment accorded, in like circumstances, by that state or province to investors, and to investments of investors, of the Party of which it forms a part.
4. For greater certainty, no Party may:
    (a) impose on an investor of another Party a requirement that a minimum level of equity in an enterprise in the territory of the Party be held by its nationals, other than nominal qualifying shares for directors or incorporators of corporations; or
    (b) require an investor of another Party, by reason of its nationality, to sell or otherwise dispose of an investment in the territory of the Party.

Article 1103: Most-Favored-Nation Treatment

1. Each Party shall accord to investors of another Party treatment no less favorable than that it accords, in like circumstances, to investors of any other Party or of a non-Party with respect to the establishment, acquisition, expansion, management, conduct, operation, and sale or other disposition of investments.
2. Each Party shall accord to investments of investors of another Party treatment no less favorable than that it accords, in like circumstances, to investments of investors of any other Party or of a non-Party with respect to the establishment, acquisition, expansion, management, conduct, operation, and sale or other disposition of investments.

Article 1104: Standard of Treatment

Each Party shall accord to investors of another Party and to investments of investors of another Party the better of the treatment required by Articles 1102 and 1103.

Article 1105: Minimum Standard of Treatment

1. Each Party shall accord to investments of investors of another Party treatment in accordance with international law, including fair and equitable treatment and full protection and security.
2. Without prejudice to paragraph 1 and notwithstanding Article 1108(7)(b), each Party shall accord to investors of another Party, and to investments of investors of another Party, non-discriminatory treatment with respect to measures it adopts or maintains relating to losses suffered by investments in its territory owing to armed conflict or civil strife.
3. Paragraph 2 does not apply to existing measures relating to subsidies or grants that would be inconsistent with Article 1102 but for Article 1108(7)(b).

Article 1106: Performance Requirements

1. No Party may impose or enforce any of the following requirements, or enforce any commitment or undertaking, in connection with the establishment, acquisition, expansion, management, conduct or operation of an investment of an investor of a Party or of a non-Party in its territory:
    (a) to export a given level or percentage of goods or services;
    (b) to achieve a given level or percentage of domestic content;
    (c) to purchase, use or accord a preference to goods produced or services provided in its territory, or to purchase goods or services from persons in its territory;
    (d) to relate in any way the volume or value of imports to the volume or value of exports or to the amount of foreign exchange inflows associated with such investment;
    (e) to restrict sales of goods or services in its territory that such investment produces or provides by relating such sales in any way to the volume or value of its exports or foreign exchange earnings;
    (f) to transfer technology, a production process or other proprietary knowledge to a person in its territory, except when the requirement is imposed or the commitment or undertaking is enforced by a court, administrative tribunal or competition authority to remedy an alleged violation of competition laws or to act in a manner not inconsistent with other provisions of this Agreement; or
    (g) to act as the exclusive supplier of the goods it produces or services it provides to a specific region or world market.
2. A measure that requires an investment to use a technology to meet generally applicable health, safety or environmental requirements shall not be construed to be

inconsistent with paragraph 1(f). For greater certainty, Articles 1102 and 1103 apply to the measure.

3.   No Party may condition the receipt or continued receipt of an advantage, in connection with an investment in its territory of an investor of a Party or of a non-Party, on compliance with any of the following requirements:

   (a) to achieve a given level or percentage of domestic content;

   (b) to purchase, use or accord a preference to goods produced in its territory, or to purchase goods from producers in its territory;

   (c) to relate in any way the volume or value of imports to the volume or value of exports or to the amount of foreign exchange inflows associated with such investment; or

   (d) to restrict sales of goods or services in its territory that such investment produces or provides by relating such sales in any way to the volume or value of its exports or foreign exchange earnings.

4.   Nothing in paragraph 3 shall be construed to prevent a Party from conditioning the receipt or continued receipt of an advantage, in connection with an investment in its territory of an investor of a Party or of a non-Party, on compliance with a requirement to locate production, provide a service, train or employ workers, construct or expand particular facilities, or carry out research and development, in its territory.

5.   Paragraphs 1 and 3 do not apply to any requirement other than the requirements set out in those paragraphs.

6.   Provided that such measures are not applied in an arbitrary or unjustifiable manner, or do not constitute a disguised restriction on international trade or investment, nothing in paragraph 1(b) or (c) or 3(a) or (b) shall be construed to prevent any Party from adopting or maintaining measures, including environmental measures:

   (a) necessary to secure compliance with laws and regulations that are not inconsistent with the provisions of this Agreement;

   (b) necessary to protect human, animal or plant life or health; or

   (c) necessary for the conservation of living or non-living exhaustible natural resources.

Article 1107: Senior Management and Boards of Directors

1.   No Party may require that an enterprise of that Party that is an investment of an investor of another Party appoint to senior management positions individuals of any particular nationality.

2.   A Party may require that a majority of the board of directors, or any committee thereof, of an enterprise of that Party that is an investment of an investor of another Party, be of a particular nationality, or resident in the territory of the Party, provided that the requirement does not materially impair the ability of the investor to exercise control over its investment.

Article 1108: Reservations and Exceptions

1. Articles 1102, 1103, 1106 and 1107 do not apply to:
   (a) any existing non-conforming measure that is maintained by
      (i) a Party at the federal level, as set out in its Schedule to Annex I or III,
      (ii) a state or province, for two years after the date of entry into force of this Agreement, and thereafter as set out by a Party in its Schedule to Annex I in accordance with paragraph 2, or
      (iii) a local government;
   (b) the continuation or prompt renewal of any non-conforming measure referred to in subparagraph (a); or
   (c) an amendment to any non-conforming measure referred to in subparagraph (a) to the extent that the amendment does not decrease the conformity of the measure, as it existed immediately before the amendment, with Articles 1102, 1103, 1106 and 1107.
2. Each Party may set out in its Schedule to Annex I, within two years of the date of entry into force of this Agreement, any existing nonconforming measure maintained by a state or province, not including a local government.
3. Articles 1102, 1103, 1106 and 1107 do not apply to any measure that a Party adopts or maintains with respect to sectors, subsectors or activities, as set out in its Schedule to Annex II.
4. No Party may, under any measure adopted after the date of entry into force of this Agreement and covered by its Schedule to Annex II, require an investor of another Party, by reason of its nationality, to sell or otherwise dispose of an investment existing at the time the measure becomes effective.
5. Articles 1102 and 1103 do not apply to any measure that is an exception to, or derogation from, the obligations under Article 1703 (Intellectual Property National Treatment) as specifically provided for in that Article.
6. Article 1103 does not apply to treatment accorded by a Party pursuant to agreements, or with respect to sectors, set out in its Schedule to Annex IV.
7. Articles 1102, 1103 and 1107 do not apply to:
   (a) procurement by a Party or a state enterprise; or
   (b) subsidies or grants provided by a Party or a state enterprise, including government supported loans, guarantees and insurance.
8. The provisions of:
   (a) Article 1106(1)(a), (b) and (c), and (3)(a) and (b) do not apply to qualification requirements for goods or services with respect to export promotion and foreign aid programs;
   (b) Article 1106(1)(b), (c), (f) and (g), and (3)(a) and (b) do not apply to procurement by a Party or a state enterprise; and
   (c) Article 1106(3)(a) and (b) do not apply to requirements imposed by an importing Party relating to the content of goods necessary to qualify for preferential tariffs or preferential quotas.

Article 1109: Transfers

1. Each Party shall permit all transfers relating to an investment of an investor of another Party in the territory of the Party to be made freely and without delay. Such transfers include:
    (a) profits, dividends, interest, capital gains, royalty payments, management fees, technical assistance and other fees, returns in kind and other amounts derived from the investment;
    (b) proceeds from the sale of all or any part of the investment or from the partial or complete liquidation of the investment;
    (c) payments made under a contract entered into by the investor, or its investment, including payments made pursuant to a loan agreement;
    (d) payments made pursuant to Article 1110; and
    (e) payments arising under Section B.
2. Each Party shall permit transfers to be made in a freely usable currency at the market rate of exchange prevailing on the date of transfer with respect to spot transactions in the currency to be transferred.
3. No Party may require its investors to transfer, or penalize its investors that fail to transfer, the income, earnings, profits or other amounts derived from, or attributable to, investments in the territory of another Party.
4. Notwithstanding paragraphs 1 and 2, a Party may prevent a transfer through the equitable, non-discriminatory and good faith application of its laws relating to:
    (a) bankruptcy, insolvency or the protection of the rights of creditors;
    (b) issuing, trading or dealing in securities;
    (c) criminal or penal offenses;
    (d) reports of transfers of currency or other monetary instruments; or
    (e) ensuring the satisfaction of judgments in adjudicatory proceedings.
5. Paragraph 3 shall not be construed to prevent a Party from imposing any measure through the equitable, non-discriminatory and good faith application of its laws relating to the matters set out in subparagraphs (a) through (e) of paragraph 4.
6. Notwithstanding paragraph 1, a Party may restrict transfers of returns in kind in circumstances where it could otherwise restrict such transfers under this Agreement, including as set out in paragraph 4.

Article 1110: Expropriation and Compensation

1. No Party may directly or indirectly nationalize or expropriate an investment of an investor of another Party in its territory or take a measure tantamount to nationalization or expropriation of such an investment ("expropriation"), except:
    (a) for a public purpose;
    (b) on a non-discriminatory basis;
    (c) in accordance with due process of law and Article 1105(1); and
    (d) on payment of compensation in accordance with paragraphs 2 through 6.

2. Compensation shall be equivalent to the fair market value of the expropriated investment immediately before the expropriation took place ("date of expropriation"), and shall not reflect any change in value occurring because the intended expropriation had become known earlier. Valuation criteria shall include going concern value, asset value including declared tax value of tangible property, and other criteria, as appropriate, to determine fair market value.

3. Compensation shall be paid without delay and be fully realizable.

4. If payment is made in a G7 currency, compensation shall include interest at a commercially reasonable rate for that currency from the date of expropriation until the date of actual payment.

5. If a Party elects to pay in a currency other than a G7 currency, the amount paid on the date of payment, if converted into a G7 currency at the market rate of exchange prevailing on that date, shall be no less than if the amount of compensation owed on the date of expropriation had been converted into that G7 currency at the market rate of exchange prevailing on that date, and interest had accrued at a commercially reasonable rate for that G7 currency from the date of expropriation until the date of payment.

6. On payment, compensation shall be freely transferable as provided in Article 1109.

7. This Article does not apply to the issuance of compulsory licenses granted in relation to intellectual property rights, or to the revocation, limitation or creation of intellectual property rights, to the extent that such issuance, revocation, limitation or creation is consistent with Chapter Seventeen (Intellectual Property).

8. For purposes of this Article and for greater certainty, a non-discriminatory measure of general application shall not be considered a measure tantamount to an expropriation of a debt security or loan covered by this Chapter solely on the ground that the measure imposes costs on the debtor that cause it to default on the debt.

Article 1111: Special Formalities and Information Requirements

1. Nothing in Article 1102 shall be construed to prevent a Party from adopting or maintaining a measure that prescribes special formalities in connection with the establishment of investments by investors of another Party, such as a requirement that investors be residents of the Party or that investments be legally constituted under the laws or regulations of the Party, provided that such formalities do not materially impair the protections afforded by a Party to investors of another Party and investments of investors of another Party pursuant to this Chapter.

2. Notwithstanding Articles 1102 or 1103, a Party may require an investor of another Party, or its investment in its territory, to provide routine information concerning that investment solely for informational or statistical purposes. The Party shall protect such business information that is confidential from any disclosure that would prejudice the competitive position of the investor or the investment. Nothing in this paragraph shall be construed to prevent a Party from otherwise obtaining or disclosing information in connection with the equitable and good faith application of its law.

Article 1112: Relation to Other Chapters

1. In the event of any inconsistency between this Chapter and another Chapter, the other Chapter shall prevail to the extent of the inconsistency.
2. A requirement by a Party that a service provider of another Party post a bond or other form of financial security as a condition of providing a service into its territory does not of itself make this Chapter applicable to the provision of that crossborder service. This Chapter applies to that Party's treatment of the posted bond or financial security.

Article 1113: Denial of Benefits

1. A Party may deny the benefits of this Chapter to an investor of another Party that is an enterprise of such Party and to investments of such investor if investors of a non-Party own or control the enterprise and the denying Party:
    (a) does not maintain diplomatic relations with the non-Party; or
    (b) adopts or maintains measures with respect to the non-Party that prohibit transactions with the enterprise or that would be violated or circumvented if the benefits of this Chapter were accorded to the enterprise or to its investments.
2. Subject to prior notification and consultation in accordance with Articles 1803 (Notification and Provision of Information) and 2006 (Consultations), a Party may deny the benefits of this Chapter to an investor of another Party that is an enterprise of such Party and to investments of such investors if investors of a non-Party own or control the enterprise and the enterprise has no substantial business activities in the territory of the Party under whose law it is constituted or organized.

Article 1114: Environmental Measures

1. Nothing in this Chapter shall be construed to prevent a Party from adopting, maintaining or enforcing any measure otherwise consistent with this Chapter that it considers appropriate to ensure that investment activity in its territory is undertaken in a manner sensitive to environmental concerns.
2. The Parties recognize that it is inappropriate to encourage investment by relaxing domestic health, safety or environmental measures. Accordingly, a Party should not waive or otherwise derogate from, or offer to waive or otherwise derogate from, such measures as an encouragement for the establishment, acquisition, expansion or retention in its territory of an investment of an investor. If a Party considers that another Party has offered such an encouragement, it may request consultations with the other Party and the two Parties shall consult with a view to avoiding any such encouragement.

Section B - Settlement of Disputes between a Party and an Investor of Another Party

Article 1115: Purpose

Without prejudice to the rights and obligations of the Parties under Chapter Twenty (Institutional Arrangements and Dispute Settlement Procedures), this Section establishes a mechanism for the settlement of investment disputes that assures both equal treatment among investors of the Parties in accordance with the principle of international reciprocity and due process before an impartial tribunal.

Article 1116: Claim by an Investor of a Party on Its Own Behalf

1. An investor of a Party may submit to arbitration under this Section a claim that another Party has breached an obligation under:
   (a) Section A or Article 1503(2) (State Enterprises), or
   (b) Article 1502(3)(a) (Monopolies and State Enterprises) where the monopoly has acted in a manner inconsistent with the Party's obligations under Section A,
   and that the investor has incurred loss or damage by reason of, or arising out of, that breach.
2. An investor may not make a claim if more than three years have elapsed from the date on which the investor first acquired, or should have first acquired, knowledge of the alleged breach and knowledge that the investor has incurred loss or damage.

Article 1117: Claim by an Investor of a Party on Behalf of an Enterprise

1. An investor of a Party, on behalf of an enterprise of another Party that is a juridical person that the investor owns or controls directly or indirectly, may submit to arbitration under this Section a claim that the other Party has breached an obligation under:
   (a) Section A or Article 1503(2) (State Enterprises), or
   (b) Article 1502(3)(a) (Monopolies and State Enterprises) where the monopoly has acted in a manner inconsistent with the Party's obligations under Section A, and that the enterprise has incurred loss or damage by reason of, or arising out of, that breach.
2. An investor may not make a claim on behalf of an enterprise described in paragraph 1 if more than three years have elapsed from the date on which the enterprise first acquired, or should have first acquired, knowledge of the alleged breach and knowledge that the enterprise has incurred loss or damage.
3. Where an investor makes a claim under this Article and the investor or a non-controlling investor in the enterprise makes a claim under Article 1116 arising out of the same events that gave rise to the claim under this Article, and two or more of the claims are submitted to arbitration under Article 1120, the claims should be heard

together by a Tribunal established under Article 1126, unless the Tribunal finds that the interests of a disputing party would be prejudiced thereby.

4.   An investment may not make a claim under this Section.

Article 1118: Settlement of a Claim through Consultation and Negotiation

The disputing parties should first attempt to settle a claim through consultation or negotiation.

Article 1119: Notice of Intent to Submit a Claim to Arbitration

The disputing investor shall deliver to the disputing Party written notice of its intention to submit a claim to arbitration at least 90 days before the claim is submitted, which notice shall specify:

(a)   the name and address of the disputing investor and, where a claim is made under Article 1117, the name and address of the enterprise;
(b)   the provisions of this Agreement alleged to have been breached and any other relevant provisions;
(c)   the issues and the factual basis for the claim; and
(d)   the relief sought and the approximate amount of damages claimed.

Article 1120: Submission of a Claim to Arbitration

1.   Except as provided in Annex 1120.1, and provided that six months have elapsed since the events giving rise to a claim, a disputing investor may submit the claim to arbitration under:
     (a)   the ICSID Convention, provided that both the disputing Party and the Party of the investor are parties to the Convention;
     (b)   the Additional Facility Rules of ICSID, provided that either the disputing Party or the Party of the investor, but not both, is a party to the ICSID Convention; or
     (c)   the UNCITRAL Arbitration Rules.
2.   The applicable arbitration rules shall govern the arbitration except to the extent modified by this Section.

Article 1121: Conditions Precedent to Submission of a Claim to Arbitration

1.   A disputing investor may submit a claim under Article 1116 to arbitration only if:
     (a)   the investor consents to arbitration in accordance with the procedures set out in this Agreement; and

(b) the investor and, where the claim is for loss or damage to an interest in an enterprise of another Party that is a juridical person that the investor owns or controls directly or indirectly, the enterprise, waive their right to initiate or continue before any administrative tribunal or court under the law of any Party, or other dispute settlement procedures, any proceedings with respect to the measure of the disputing Party that is alleged to be a breach referred to in Article 1116, except for proceedings for injunctive, declaratory or other extraordinary relief, not involving the payment of damages, before an administrative tribunal or court under the law of the disputing Party.

2. A disputing investor may submit a claim under Article 1117 to arbitration only if both the investor and the enterprise:

   (a) consent to arbitration in accordance with the procedures set out in this Agreement; and

   (b) waive their right to initiate or continue before any administrative tribunal or court under the law of any Party, or other dispute settlement procedures, any proceedings with respect to the measure of the disputing Party that is alleged to be a breach referred to in Article 1117, except for proceedings for injunctive, declaratory or other extraordinary relief, not involving the payment of damages, before an administrative tribunal or court under the law of the disputing Party.

3. A consent and waiver required by this Article shall be in writing, shall be delivered to the disputing Party and shall be included in the submission of a claim to arbitration.

4. Only where a disputing Party has deprived a disputing investor of control of an enterprise:

   (a) a waiver from the enterprise under paragraph 1(b) or 2(b) shall not be required; and

   (b) Annex 1120.1(b) shall not apply.

Article 1122: Consent to Arbitration

1. Each Party consents to the submission of a claim to arbitration in accordance with the procedures set out in this Agreement.

2. The consent given by paragraph 1 and the submission by a disputing investor of a claim to arbitration shall satisfy the requirement of:

   (a) Chapter II of the ICSID Convention (Jurisdiction of the Centre) and the Additional Facility Rules for written consent of the parties;

   (b) Article II of the New York Convention for an agreement in writing; and

   (c) Article I of the InterAmerican Convention for an agreement.

Article 1123: Number of Arbitrators and Method of Appointment

Except in respect of a Tribunal established under Article 1126, and unless the disputing parties otherwise agree, the Tribunal shall comprise three arbitrators, one arbitrator appointed by each of the disputing parties and the third, who shall be the presiding arbitrator, appointed by agreement of the disputing parties.

Article 1124: Constitution of a Tribunal When a Party Fails to Appoint an Arbitrator or the Disputing Parties Are Unable to Agree on a Presiding Arbitrator

1. The Secretary-General shall serve as appointing authority for an arbitration under this Section.
2. If a Tribunal, other than a Tribunal established under Article 1126, has not been constituted within 90 days from the date that a claim is submitted to arbitration, the Secretary-General, on the request of either disputing party, shall appoint, in his discretion, the arbitrator or arbitrators not yet appointed, except that the presiding arbitrator shall be appointed in accordance with paragraph 3.
3. The Secretary-General shall appoint the presiding arbitrator from the roster of presiding arbitrators referred to in paragraph 4, provided that the presiding arbitrator shall not be a national of the disputing Party or a national of the Party of the disputing investor. In the event that no such presiding arbitrator is available to serve, the Secretary-General shall appoint, from the ICSID Panel of Arbitrators, a presiding arbitrator who is not a national of any of the Parties.
4. On the date of entry into force of this Agreement, the Parties shall establish, and thereafter maintain, a roster of 45 presiding arbitrators meeting the qualifications of the Convention and rules referred to in Article 1120 and experienced in international law and investment matters. The roster members shall be appointed by consensus and without regard to nationality.

Article 1125: Agreement to Appointment of Arbitrators

For purposes of Article 39 of the ICSID Convention and Article 7 of Schedule C to the ICSID Additional Facility Rules, and without prejudice to an objection to an arbitrator based on Article 1124(3) or on a ground other than nationality:

(a) the disputing Party agrees to the appointment of each individual member of a Tribunal established under the ICSID Convention or the ICSID Additional Facility Rules;
(b) a disputing investor referred to in Article 1116 may submit a claim to arbitration, or continue a claim, under the ICSID Convention or the ICSID Additional Facility Rules, only on condition that the disputing investor agrees in writing to the appointment of each individual member of the Tribunal; and
(c) a disputing investor referred to in Article 1117(1) may submit a claim to arbitration, or continue a claim, under the ICSID Convention or the ICSID Additional Facility Rules, only on condition that the disputing investor and the enterprise agree in writing to the appointment of each individual member of the Tribunal.

Article 1126: Consolidation

1. A Tribunal established under this Article shall be established under the UNCITRAL Arbitration Rules and shall conduct its proceedings in accordance with those Rules, except as modified by this Section.

2. Where a Tribunal established under this Article is satisfied that claims have been submitted to arbitration under Article 1120 that have a question of law or fact in common, the Tribunal may, in the interests of fair and efficient resolution of the claims, and after hearing the disputing parties, by order:

   (a) assume jurisdiction over, and hear and determine together, all or part of the claims; or

   (b) assume jurisdiction over, and hear and determine one or more of the claims, the determination of which it believes would assist in the resolution of the others.

3. A disputing party that seeks an order under paragraph 2 shall request the Secretary-General to establish a Tribunal and shall specify in the request:

   (a) the name of the disputing Party or disputing investors against which the order is sought;

   (b) the nature of the order sought; and

   (c) the grounds on which the order is sought.

4. The disputing party shall deliver to the disputing Party or disputing investors against which the order is sought a copy of the request.

5. Within 60 days of receipt of the request, the Secretary-General shall establish a Tribunal comprising three arbitrators. The Secretary-General shall appoint the presiding arbitrator from the roster referred to in Article 1124(4). In the event that no such presiding arbitrator is available to serve, the Secretary-General shall appoint, from the ICSID Panel of Arbitrators, a presiding arbitrator who is not a national of any of the Parties. The Secretary-General shall appoint the two other members from the roster referred to in Article 1124(4), and to the extent not available from that roster, from the ICSID Panel of Arbitrators, and to the extent not available from that Panel, in the discretion of the Secretary-General. One member shall be a national of the disputing Party and one member shall be a national of a Party of the disputing investors.

6. Where a Tribunal has been established under this Article, a disputing investor that has submitted a claim to arbitration under Article 1116 or 1117 and that has not been named in a request made under paragraph 3 may make a written request to the Tribunal that it be included in an order made under paragraph 2, and shall specify in the request:

   (a) the name and address of the disputing investor;

   (b) the nature of the order sought; and

   (c) the grounds on which the order is sought.

7. A disputing investor referred to in paragraph 6 shall deliver a copy of its request to the disputing parties named in a request made under paragraph 3.

8. A Tribunal established under Article 1120 shall not have jurisdiction to decide a claim, or a part of a claim, over which a Tribunal established under this Article has assumed jurisdiction.

9. On application of a disputing party, a Tribunal established under this Article, pending its decision under paragraph 2, may order that the proceedings of a Tribunal established under Article 1120 be stayed, unless the latter Tribunal has already adjourned its proceedings.

10. A disputing Party shall deliver to the Secretariat, within 15 days of receipt by the disputing Party, a copy of:

   (a) a request for arbitration made under paragraph (1) of Article 36 of the ICSID Convention;

   (b) a notice of arbitration made under Article 2 of Schedule C of the ICSID Additional Facility Rules; or

   (c) a notice of arbitration given under the UNCITRAL Arbitration Rules.

11. A disputing Party shall deliver to the Secretariat a copy of a request made under paragraph 3:

   (a) within 15 days of receipt of the request, in the case of a request made by a disputing investor;

   (b) within 15 days of making the request, in the case of a request made by the disputing Party.

12. A disputing Party shall deliver to the Secretariat a copy of a request made under paragraph 6 within 15 days of receipt of the request.

13. The Secretariat shall maintain a public register of the documents referred to in paragraphs 10, 11 and 12.

Article 1127: Notice

A disputing Party shall deliver to the other Parties:

(a) written notice of a claim that has been submitted to arbitration no later than 30 days after the date that the claim is submitted; and

(b) copies of all pleadings filed in the arbitration.

Article 1128: Participation by a Party

On written notice to the disputing parties, a Party may make submissions to a Tribunal on a question of interpretation of this Agreement.

Article 1129: Documents

1. A Party shall be entitled to receive from the disputing Party, at the cost of the requesting Party a copy of:

   (a) the evidence that has been tendered to the Tribunal; and

   (b) the written argument of the disputing parties.

2. A Party receiving information pursuant to paragraph 1 shall treat the information as if it were a disputing Party.

Article 1130: Place of Arbitration

Unless the disputing parties agree otherwise, a Tribunal shall hold an arbitration in the territory of a Party that is a party to the New York Convention, selected in accordance with:

(a) the ICSID Additional Facility Rules if the arbitration is under those Rules or the ICSID Convention; or
(b) the UNCITRAL Arbitration Rules if the arbitration is under those Rules.

Article 1131: Governing Law

1. A Tribunal established under this Section shall decide the issues in dispute in accordance with this Agreement and applicable rules of international law.
2. An interpretation by the Commission of a provision of this Agreement shall be binding on a Tribunal established under this Section.

Article 1132: Interpretation of Annexes

1. Where a disputing Party asserts as a defense that the measure alleged to be a breach is within the scope of a reservation or exception set out in Annex I, Annex II, Annex III or Annex IV, on request of the disputing Party, the Tribunal shall request the interpretation of the Commission on the issue. The Commission, within 60 days of delivery of the request, shall submit in writing its interpretation to the Tribunal.
2. Further to Article 1131(2), a Commission interpretation submitted under paragraph 1 shall be binding on the Tribunal. If the Commission fails to submit an interpretation within 60 days, the Tribunal shall decide the issue.

Article 1133: Expert Reports

Without prejudice to the appointment of other kinds of experts where authorized by the applicable arbitration rules, a Tribunal, at the request of a disputing party or, unless the disputing parties disapprove, on its own initiative, may appoint one or more experts to report to it in writing on any factual issue concerning environmental, health, safety or other scientific matters raised by a disputing party in a proceeding, subject to such terms and conditions as the disputing parties may agree.

Article 1134: Interim Measures of Protection

A Tribunal may order an interim measure of protection to preserve the rights of a disputing party, or to ensure that the Tribunal's jurisdiction is made fully effective, including an order to preserve evidence in the possession or control of a disputing party or to protect the Tribunal's jurisdiction. A Tribunal may not order attachment or enjoin the application of the measure alleged to constitute a breach referred to in Article 1116 or 1117. For purposes of this paragraph, an order includes a recommendation.

Article 1135: Final Award

1. Where a Tribunal makes a final award against a Party, the Tribunal may award, separately or in combination, only:
    (a) monetary damages and any applicable interest;
    (b) restitution of property, in which case the award shall provide that the disputing Party may pay monetary damages and any applicable interest in lieu of restitution.
    A tribunal may also award costs in accordance with the applicable arbitration rules.
2. Subject to paragraph 1, where a claim is made under Article 1117(1):
    (a) an award of restitution of property shall provide that restitution be made to the enterprise;
    (b) an award of monetary damages and any applicable interest shall provide that the sum be paid to the enterprise; and
    (c) the award shall provide that it is made without prejudice to any right that any person may have in the relief under applicable domestic law.
3. A Tribunal may not order a Party to pay punitive damages.

Article 1136: Finality and Enforcement of an Award

1. An award made by a Tribunal shall have no binding force except between the disputing parties and in respect of the particular case.
2. Subject to paragraph 3 and the applicable review procedure for an interim award, a disputing party shall abide by and comply with an award without delay.
3. A disputing party may not seek enforcement of a final award until:
    (a) in the case of a final award made under the ICSID Convention
        (i) 120 days have elapsed from the date the award was rendered and no disputing party has requested revision or annulment of the award, or
        (ii) revision or annulment proceedings have been completed; and
    (b) in the case of a final award under the ICSID Additional Facility Rules or the UNCITRAL Arbitration Rules
        (i) three months have elapsed from the date the award was rendered and no disputing party has commenced a proceeding to revise, set aside or annul the award, or

(ii) a court has dismissed or allowed an application to revise, set aside or annul the award and there is no further appeal.

4. Each Party shall provide for the enforcement of an award in its territory.

5. If a disputing Party fails to abide by or comply with a final award, the Commission, on delivery of a request by a Party whose investor was a party to the arbitration, shall establish a panel under Article 2008 (Request for an Arbitral Panel). The requesting Party may seek in such proceedings:

   (a) a determination that the failure to abide by or comply with the final award is inconsistent with the obligations of this Agreement; and

   (b) a recommendation that the Party abide by or comply with the final award.

6. A disputing investor may seek enforcement of an arbitration award under the ICSID Convention, the New York Convention or the InterAmerican Convention regardless of whether proceedings have been taken under paragraph 5.

7. A claim that is submitted to arbitration under this Section shall be considered to arise out of a commercial relationship or transaction for purposes of Article I of the New York Convention and Article I of the InterAmerican Convention.

Article 1137: General

Time when a Claim is Submitted to Arbitration

1. A claim is submitted to arbitration under this Section when:

   (a) the request for arbitration under paragraph (1) of Article 36 of the ICSID Convention has been received by the Secretary-General;

   (b) the notice of arbitration under Article 2 of Schedule C of the ICSID Additional Facility Rules has been received by the Secretary-General; or

   (c) the notice of arbitration given under the UNCITRAL Arbitration Rules is received by the disputing Party.

Service of Documents

2. Delivery of notice and other documents on a Party shall be made to the place named for that Party in Annex 1137.2.

Receipts under Insurance or Guarantee Contracts

2. In an arbitration under this Section, a Party shall not assert, as a defense, counterclaim, right of setoff or otherwise, that the disputing investor has received or will receive, pursuant to an insurance or guarantee contract, indemnification or other compensation for all or part of its alleged damages.

Publication of an Award

4. Annex 1137.4 applies to the Parties specified in that Annex with respect to publication of an award.

Article 1138: Exclusions

1. Without prejudice to the applicability or non-applicability of the dispute settlement provisions of this Section or of Chapter Twenty (Institutional Arrangements and Dispute Settlement Procedures) to other actions taken by a Party pursuant to Article 2102 (National Security), a decision by a Party to prohibit or restrict the acquisition of an investment in its territory by an investor of another Party, or its investment, pursuant to that Article shall not be subject to such provisions.
2. The dispute settlement provisions of this Section and of Chapter Twenty shall not apply to the matters referred to in Annex 1138.2.

Section C - Definitions

Article 1139: Definitions

For purposes of this Chapter:

disputing investor means an investor that makes a claim under Section B;

disputing parties means the disputing investor and the disputing Party;

disputing party means the disputing investor or the disputing Party;

disputing Party means a Party against which a claim is made under Section B;

enterprise means an "enterprise" as defined in Article 201 (Definitions of General Application), and a branch of an enterprise;

enterprise of a Party means an enterprise constituted or organized under the law of a Party, and a branch located in the territory of a Party and carrying out business activities there.

equity or debt securities includes voting and non-voting shares, bonds, convertible debentures, stock options and warrants;

G7 Currency means the currency of Canada, France, Germany, Italy, Japan, the United Kingdom of Great Britain and Northern Ireland or the United States;

ICSID means the International Centre for Settlement of Investment Disputes;

ICSID Convention means the *Convention on the Settlement of Investment Disputes between States and Nationals of other States* , done at Washington, March 18, 1965;

InterAmerican Convention means the *InterAmerican Convention on International Commercial Arbitration* , done at Panama, January 30, 1975;

investment means:

(a) an enterprise;

(b) an equity security of an enterprise;

(c) a debt security of an enterprise
(i)   where the enterprise is an affiliate of the investor, or
(ii) where the original maturity of the debt security is at least three years, but does not include a debt security, regardless of original maturity, of a state enterprise;

(d) a loan to an enterprise
(i)   where the enterprise is an affiliate of the investor, or
(ii) where the original maturity of the loan is at least three years, but does not include a loan, regardless of original maturity, to a state enterprise;

(e) an interest in an enterprise that entitles the owner to share in income or profits of the enterprise;

(f) an interest in an enterprise that entitles the owner to share in the assets of that enterprise on dissolution, other than a debt security or a loan excluded from subparagraph (c) or (d);

(g) real estate or other property, tangible or intangible, acquired in the expectation or used for the purpose of economic benefit or other business purposes; and

(h) interests arising from the commitment of capital or other resources in the territory of a Party to economic activity in such territory, such as under
(i)   contracts involving the presence of an investor's property in the territory of the Party, including turnkey or construction contracts, or concessions, or
(ii) contracts where remuneration depends substantially on the production, revenues or profits of an enterprise;
but investment does not mean,

(i) claims to money that arise solely from
(i)   commercial contracts for the sale of goods or services by a national or enterprise in the territory of a Party to an enterprise in the territory of another Party, or
(ii) the extension of credit in connection with a commercial transaction, such as trade financing, other than a loan covered by subparagraph (d); or

(j) any other claims to money,
that do not involve the kinds of interests set out in subparagraphs (a) through (h);

investment of an investor of a Party means an investment owned or controlled directly or indirectly by an investor of such Party;

investor of a Party means a Party or state enterprise thereof, or a national or an enterprise of such Party, that seeks to make, is making or has made an investment;

investor of a non-Party means an investor other than an investor of a Party, that seeks to make, is making or has made an investment;

New York Convention means the *United Nations Convention on the Recognition and Enforcement of Foreign Arbitral Awards* , done at New York, June 10, 1958;

Secretary-General means the Secretary-General of ICSID;

transfers means transfers and international payments;

Tribunal means an arbitration tribunal established under Article 1120 or 1126; and

UNCITRAL Arbitration Rules means the arbitration rules of the United Nations Commission on International Trade Law, approved by the United Nations General Assembly on December 15, 1976.

ANNEX 1120.1. SUBMISSION OF A CLAIM TO ARBITRATION

Mexico

With respect to the submission of a claim to arbitration:

(a) an investor of another Party may not allege that Mexico has breached an obligation under:
    (i)   Section A or Article 1503(2) (State Enterprises), or
    (ii) Article 1502(3)(a) (Monopolies and State Enterprises) where the monopoly has acted in a manner inconsistent with the Party's obligations under Section A,
both in an arbitration under this Section and in proceedings before a Mexican court or administrative tribunal; and

(b) where an enterprise of Mexico that is a juridical person that an investor of another Party owns or controls directly or indirectly alleges in proceedings before a Mexican court or administrative tribunal that Mexico has breached an obligation under:
    (i)   Section A or Article 1503(2) (State Enterprises), or
    (ii) Article 1502(3)(a) (Monopolies and State Enterprises) where the monopoly has acted in a manner inconsistent with the Party's obligations under Section A,
the investor may not allege the breach in an arbitration under this Section.

ANNEX 1137.2. SERVICE OF DOCUMENTS ON A PARTY UNDER SECTION B

Each Party shall set out in this Annex and publish in its official journal by January 1, 1994, the place for delivery of notice and other documents under this Section.

ANNEX 1137.4.PUBLICATION OF AN AWARD

Canada

Where Canada is the disputing Party, either Canada or a disputing investor that is a party to the arbitration may make an award public.

Mexico

Where Mexico is the disputing Party, the applicable arbitration rules apply to the publication of an award.

United States

Where the United States is the disputing Party, either the United States or a disputing investor that is a party to the arbitration may make an award public.

ANNEX 1138.2. EXCLUSIONS FROM DISPUTE SETTLEMENT

Canada

A decision by Canada following a review under the *Investment Canada Act* , with respect to whether or not to permit an acquisition that is subject to review, shall not be subject to the dispute settlement provisions of Section B or of Chapter Twenty (Institutional Arrangements and Dispute Settlement Procedures).

Mexico

A decision by the National Commission on Foreign Investment ("Comisión Nacional de Inversiones Extranjeras") following a review pursuant to Annex I, page IM4, with respect to whether or not to permit an acquisition that is subject to review, shall not be subject to the dispute settlement provisions of Section B or of Chapter Twenty (Institutional Arrangements and Dispute Settlement Procedures).

PART FIVE: INVESTMENT, SERVICES AND RELATED MATTERS

12. CROSS-BORDER TRADE IN SERVICES

Article 1201: Scope and Coverage

1. This Chapter applies to measures adopted or maintained by a Party relating to cross-border trade in services by service providers of another Party, including measures respecting:
    (a) the production, distribution, marketing, sale and delivery of a service;
    (b) the purchase or use of, or payment for, a service;
    (c) the access to and use of distribution and transportation systems in connection with the provision of a service;
    (d) the presence in its territory of a service provider of another Party; and
    (e) the provision of a bond or other form of financial security as a condition for the provision of a service.
2. This Chapter does not apply to:
    (a) financial services, as defined in Chapter Fourteen (Financial Services);
    (b) air services, including domestic and international air transportation services, whether scheduled or non-scheduled, and related services in support of air services, other than
        (i) aircraft repair and maintenance services during which an aircraft is withdrawn from service, and
        (ii) specialty air services;
    (c) procurement by a Party or a state enterprise; or
    (d) subsidies or grants provided by a Party or a state enterprise, including government-supported loans, guarantees and insurance.
3. Nothing in this Chapter shall be construed to:
    (a) impose any obligation on a Party with respect to a national of another Party seeking access to its employment market, or employed on a permanent basis in its territory, or to confer any right on that national with respect to that access or employment; or
    (b) prevent a Party from providing a service or performing a function such as law enforcement, correctional services, income security or insurance, social security or insurance, social welfare, public education, public training, health, and child care, in a manner that is not inconsistent with this Chapter.

Article 1202: National Treatment

1. Each Party shall accord to service providers of another Party treatment no less favorable than that it accords, in like circumstances, to its own service providers.
2. The treatment accorded by a Party under paragraph 1 means, with respect to a state or province, treatment no less favorable than the most favorable treatment accorded,

in like circumstances, by that state or province to service providers of the Party of which it forms a part.

Article 1203: Most-Favored-Nation Treatment

Each Party shall accord to service providers of another Party treatment no less favorable than that it accords, in like circumstances, to service providers of any other Party or of a non-Party.

Article 1204: Standard of Treatment

Each Party shall accord to service providers of any other Party the better of the treatment required by Articles 1202 and 1203.

Article 1205: Local Presence

No Party may require a service provider of another Party to establish or maintain a representative office or any form of enterprise, or to be resident, in its territory as a condition for the cross-border provision of a service.

Article 1206: Reservations

1. Articles 1202, 1203 and 1205 do not apply to:
   (a) any existing non-conforming measure that is maintained by
      (i) a Party at the federal level, as set out in its Schedule to Annex I,
      (ii) a state or province, for two years after the date of entry into force of this Agreement, and thereafter as set out by a Party in its Schedule to Annex I in accordance with paragraph 2, or
      (iii) a local government;
   (b) the continuation or prompt renewal of any non-conforming measure referred to in subparagraph (a); or
   (c) an amendment to any non-conforming measure referred to in subparagraph (a) to the extent that the amendment does not decrease the conformity of the measure, as it existed immediately before the amendment, with Articles 1202, 1203 and 1205.
2. Each Party may set out in its Schedule to Annex I, within two years of the date of entry into force of this Agreement, any existing non-conforming measure maintained by a state or province, not including a local government.
3. Articles 1202, 1203 and 1205 do not apply to any measure that a Party adopts or maintains with respect to sectors, subsectors or activities, as set out in its Schedule to Annex II.

Article 1207: Quantitative Restrictions

1. Each Party shall set out in its Schedule to Annex V any quantitative restriction that it maintains at the federal level.
2. Within one year of the date of entry into force of this Agreement, each Party shall set out in its Schedule to Annex V any quantitative restriction maintained by a state or province, not including a local government.
3. Each Party shall notify the other Parties of any quantitative restriction that it adopts, other than at the local government level, after the date of entry into force of this Agreement and shall set out the restriction in its Schedule to Annex V.
4. The Parties shall periodically, but in any event at least every two years, endeavor to negotiate the liberalization or removal of the quantitative restrictions set out in Annex V pursuant to paragraphs 1 through 3.

Article 1208: Liberalization of Non-Discriminatory Measures

Each Party shall set out in its Schedule to Annex VI its commitments to liberalize quantitative restrictions, licensing requirements, performance requirements or other non-discriminatory measures.

Article 1209: Procedures

The Commission shall establish procedures for:

(a) a Party to notify and include in its relevant Schedule
    (i)   state or provincial measures in accordance with Article 1206(2),
    (ii) quantitative restrictions in accordance with Article 1207(2) and (3),
    (iii) commitments pursuant to Article 1208, and
    (iv) amendments of measures referred to in Article 1206(1)(c); and
(b) consultations on reservations, quantitative restrictions or commitments with a view to further liberalization.

Article 1210: Licensing and Certification

1. With a view to ensuring that any measure adopted or maintained by a Party relating to the licensing or certification of nationals of another Party does not constitute an unnecessary barrier to trade, each Party shall endeavor to ensure that any such measure:
    (a) is based on objective and transparent criteria, such as competence and the ability to provide a service;
    (b) is not more burdensome than necessary to ensure the quality of a service; and

    (c) does not constitute a disguised restriction on the cross-border provision of a service.

2. Where a Party recognizes, unilaterally or by agreement, education, experience, licenses or certifications obtained in the territory of another Party or of a non-Party:

    (a) nothing in Article 1203 shall be construed to require the Party to accord such recognition to education, experience, licenses or certifications obtained in the territory of another Party; and

    (b) the Party shall afford another Party an adequate opportunity to demonstrate that education, experience, licenses or certifications obtained in that other Party's territory should also be recognized or to conclude an agreement or arrangement of comparable effect.

3. Each Party shall, within two years of the date of entry into force of this Agreement, eliminate any citizenship or permanent residency requirement set out in its Schedule to Annex I that it maintains for the licensing or certification of professional service providers of another Party. Where a Party does not comply with this obligation with respect to a particular sector, any other Party may, in the same sector and for such period as the noncomplying Party maintains its requirement, solely have recourse to maintaining an equivalent requirement set out in its Schedule to Annex I or reinstating:

    (a) any such requirement at the federal level that it eliminated pursuant to this Article; or

    (b) on notification to the non-complying Party, any such requirement at the state or provincial level existing on the date of entry into force of this Agreement.

4. The Parties shall consult periodically with a view to determining the feasibility of removing any remaining citizenship or permanent residency requirement for the licensing or certification of each other's service providers.

5. Annex 1210.5 applies to measures adopted or maintained by a Party relating to the licensing or certification of professional service providers.

Article 1211: Denial of Benefits

1. A Party may deny the benefits of this Chapter to a service provider of another Party where the Party establishes that:

    (a) the service is being provided by an enterprise owned or controlled by nationals of a non-Party, and

        (i) the denying Party does not maintain diplomatic relations with the non-Party, or

        (ii) the denying Party adopts or maintains measures with respect to the non-Party that prohibit transactions with the enterprise or that would be violated or circumvented if the benefits of this Chapter were accorded to the enterprise; or

    (b) the cross-border provision of a transportation service covered by this Chapter is provided using equipment not registered by any Party.

2. Subject to prior notification and consultation in accordance with Articles 1803 (Notification and Provision of Information) and 2006 (Consultations), a Party may deny the benefits of this Chapter to a service provider of another Party where the Party establishes that the service is being provided by an enterprise that is owned or controlled by persons of a non-Party and that has no substantial business activities in the territory of any Party.

Article 1212: Sectoral Annex

Annex 1212 applies to specific sectors.

Article 1213: Definitions

1. For purposes of this Chapter, a reference to a federal, state or provincial government includes any non-governmental body in the exercise of any regulatory, administrative or other governmental authority delegated to it by that government.
2. For purposes of this Chapter:

    cross-border provision of a service or cross-border trade in services means the provision of a service:

    (a) from the territory of a Party into the territory of another Party,

    (b) in the territory of a Party by a person of that Party to a person of another Party, or

    (c) by a national of a Party in the territory of another Party,

    but does not include the provision of a service in the territory of a Party by an investment, as defined in Article 1139 (Investment Definitions), in that territory;

enterprise means an "enterprise" as defined in Article 201 (Definitions of General Application), and a branch of an enterprise;

enterprise of a Party means an enterprise constituted or organized under the law of a Party, and a branch located in the territory of a Party and carrying out business activities there;

professional services means services, the provision of which requires specialized post-secondary education, or equivalent training or experience, and for which the right to practice is granted or restricted by a Party, but does not include services provided by tradespersons or vessel and aircraft crew members;

quantitative restriction means a non-discriminatory measure that imposes limitations on:

(a) the number of service providers, whether in the form of a quota, a monopoly or an economic needs test, or by any other quantitative means; or

(b) the operations of any service provider, whether in the form of a quota or an economic needs test, or by any other quantitative means;

service provider of a Party means a person of a Party that seeks to provide or provides a service; and

specialty air services means aerial mapping, aerial surveying, aerial photography, forest fire management, fire fighting, aerial advertising, glider towing, parachute jumping, aerial construction, helilogging, aerial sightseeing, flight training, aerial inspection and surveillance, and aerial spraying services.

ANNEX 1210.5. PROFESSIONAL SERVICES

Section A General Provisions

Processing of Applications for Licenses and Certifications

1. Each Party shall ensure that its competent authorities, within a reasonable time after the submission by a national of another Party of an application for a license or certification:
   (a) where the application is complete, make a determination on the application and inform the applicant of that determination; or
   (b) where the application is not complete, inform the applicant without undue delay of the status of the application and the additional information that is required under the Party's law.

Development of Professional Standards

2. The Parties shall encourage the relevant bodies in their respective territories to develop mutually acceptable standards and criteria for licensing and certification of professional service providers and to provide recommendations on mutual recognition to the Commission.
3. The standards and criteria referred to in paragraph 2 may be developed with regard to the following matters:
   (a) education - accreditation of schools or academic programs;
   (b) examinations - qualifying examinations for licensing, including alternative methods of assessment such as oral examinations and interviews;
   (c) experience length and nature of experience required for licensing;
   (d) conduct and ethics - standards of professional conduct and the nature of disciplinary action for non-conformity with those standards;
   (e) professional development and re-certification - continuing education and ongoing requirements to maintain professional certification;
   (f) scope of practice - extent of, or limitations on, permissible activities;
   (g) local knowledge - requirements for knowledge of such matters as local laws, regulations, language, geography or climate; and

(h) consumer protection - alternatives to residency requirements, including bonding, professional liability insurance and client restitution funds, to provide for the protection of consumers.

4. On receipt of a recommendation referred to in paragraph 2, the Commission shall review the recommendation within a reasonable time to determine whether it is consistent with this Agreement. Based on the Commission's review, each Party shall encourage its respective competent authorities, where appropriate, to implement the recommendation within a mutually agreed time.

Temporary Licensing

5. Where the Parties agree, each Party shall encourage the relevant bodies in its territory to develop procedures for the temporary licensing of professional service providers of another Party.

Review

6. The Commission shall periodically, and at least once every three years, review the implementation of this Section.

Section B - Foreign Legal Consultants

1. Each Party shall, in implementing its obligations and commitments regarding foreign legal consultants as set out in its relevant Schedules and subject to any reservations therein, ensure that a national of another Party is permitted to practice or advise on the law of any country in which that national is authorized to practice as a lawyer.

Consultations With Professional Bodies

2. Each Party shall consult with its relevant professional bodies to obtain their recommendations on:
   (a) the form of association or partnership between lawyers authorized to practice in its territory and foreign legal consultants;
   (b) the development of standards and criteria for the authorization of foreign legal consultants in conformity with Article 1210; and
   (c) other matters relating to the provision of foreign legal consultancy services.

3. Prior to initiation of consultations under paragraph 7, each Party shall encourage its relevant professional bodies to consult with the relevant professional bodies designated by each of the other Parties regarding the development of joint recommendations on the matters referred to in paragraph 2.

Future Liberalization

4. Each Party shall establish a work program to develop common procedures throughout its territory for the authorization of foreign legal consultants.

5. Each Party shall promptly review any recommendation referred to in paragraphs 2 and 3 to ensure its consistency with this Agreement. If the recommendation is consistent with this Agreement, each Party shall encourage its competent authorities to implement the recommendation within one year.

6. Each Party shall report to the Commission within one year of the date of entry into force of this Agreement, and each year thereafter, on its progress in implementing the work program referred to in paragraph 4.

7. The Parties shall meet within one year of the date of entry into force of this Agreement with a view to:
    (a) assessing the implementation of paragraphs 2 through 5;
    (b) amending or removing, where appropriate, reservations on foreign legal consultancy services; and
    (c) assessing further work that may be appropriate regarding foreign legal consultancy services.

Section C - Temporary Licensing of Engineers

1. The Parties shall meet within one year of the date of entry into force of this Agreement to establish a work program to be undertaken by each Party, in conjunction with its relevant professional bodies, to provide for the temporary licensing in its territory of nationals of another Party who are licensed as engineers in the territory of that other Party.

2. To this end, each Party shall consult with its relevant professional bodies to obtain their recommendations on:
    (a) the development of procedures for the temporary licensing of such engineers to permit them to practice their engineering specialties in each jurisdiction in its territory;
    (b) the development of model procedures for adoption by the competent authorities throughout its territory to facilitate the temporary licensing of such engineers;
    (c) the engineering specialties to which priority should be given in developing temporary licensing procedures; and
    (d) other matters relating to the temporary licensing of engineers identified by the Party in such consultations.

3. Each Party shall request its relevant professional bodies to make recommendations on the matters referred to in paragraph 2 within two years of the date of entry into force of this Agreement.

4. Each Party shall encourage its relevant professional bodies to meet at the earliest opportunity with the relevant professional bodies of the other Parties with a view to cooperating in the development of joint recommendations on the matters referred to in paragraph 2 within two years of the date of entry into force of this Agreement.

Each Party shall request an annual report from its relevant professional bodies on the progress achieved in developing those recommendations.

5. The Parties shall promptly review any recommendation referred to in paragraphs 3 or 4 to ensure its consistency with this Agreement. If the recommendation is consistent with this Agreement, each Party shall encourage its competent authorities to implement the recommendation within one year.

6. The Commission shall review the implementation of this Section within two years of the date of entry into force of this Section.

7. Appendix 1210.5C applies to the Parties specified therein.

Appendix 1210.5-C. Civil Engineers

The rights and obligations of Section C of Annex 1210.5 apply to Mexico with respect to civil engineers ("ingenieros civiles") and to such other engineering specialties that Mexico may designate.

Annex 1212. Land Transportation

Contact Points

1. Further to Article 1801 (Contact Points), each Party shall designate by January 1, 1994 contact points to provide information published by that Party relating to land transportation services regarding operating authority, safety requirements, taxation, data, studies and technology, and to provide assistance in contacting its relevant government agencies.

Review Process

2. The Commission shall, during the fifth year after the date of entry into force of this Agreement and during every second year thereafter until the liberalization for bus and truck transportation set out in the Parties' Schedules to Annex I is complete, receive and consider a report from the Parties that assesses progress respecting liberalization, including:
    (a) the effectiveness of the liberalization;
    (b) specific problems for, or unanticipated effects on, each Party's bus and truck transportation industries arising from liberalization; and
    (c) modifications to the period for liberalization.
    The Commission shall endeavor to resolve any matter arising from its consideration of a report.

3. The Parties shall consult, no later than seven years after the date of entry into force of this Agreement, to consider further liberalization commitments.

PART FIVE: INVESTMENT, SERVICES AND RELATED MATTERS

13. TELECOMMUNICATIONS

Article 1301: Scope and Coverage

1. This Chapter applies to:
   (a) measures adopted or maintained by a Party relating to access to and use of public telecommunications transport networks or services by persons of another Party, including access and use by such persons operating private networks;
   (b) measures adopted or maintained by a Party relating to the provision of enhanced or value-added services by persons of another Party in the territory, or across the borders, of a Party; and
   (c) standards-related measures relating to attachment of terminal or other equipment to public telecommunications transport networks.

2. Except to ensure that persons operating broadcast stations and cable systems have continued access to and use of public telecommunications transport networks and services, this Chapter does not apply to any measure adopted or maintained by a Party relating to cable or broadcast distribution of radio or television programming.

3. Nothing in this Chapter shall be construed to:
   (a) require a Party to authorize a person of another Party to establish, construct, acquire, lease, operate or provide telecommunications transport networks or telecommunications transport services;
   (b) require a Party, or require a Party to compel any person, to establish, construct, acquire, lease, operate or provide telecommunications transport networks or telecommunications transport services not offered to the public generally;
   (c) prevent a Party from prohibiting persons operating private networks from using their networks to provide public telecommunications transport networks or services to third persons; or
   (d) require a Party to compel any person engaged in the cable or broadcast distribution of radio or television programming to make available its cable or broadcast facilities as a public telecommunications transport network.

Article 1302: Access to and Use of Public Telecommunications Transport Networks and Services

1. Each Party shall ensure that persons of another Party have access to and use of any public telecommunications transport network or service, including private leased circuits, offered in its territory or across its borders for the conduct of their business, on reasonable and non-discriminatory terms and conditions, including as set out in paragraphs 2 through 8.

2. Subject to paragraphs 6 and 7, each Party shall ensure that such persons are permitted to:

(a) purchase or lease, and attach terminal or other equipment that interfaces with the public telecommunications transport network;

(b) interconnect private leased or owned circuits with public telecommunications transport networks in the territory, or across the borders, of that Party, including for use in providing dial-up access to and from their customers or users, or with circuits leased or owned by another person on terms and conditions mutually agreed by those persons;

(c) perform switching, signalling and processing functions; and

(d) use operating protocols of their choice.

3. Each Party shall ensure that:

(a) the pricing of public telecommunications transport services reflects economic costs directly related to providing the services; and

(b) private leased circuits are available on a flat-rate pricing basis.

Nothing in this paragraph shall be construed to prevent cross-subsidization between public telecommunications transport services.

4. Each Party shall ensure that persons of another Party may use public telecommunications transport networks or services for the movement of information in its territory or across its borders, including for intracorporate communications, and for access to information contained in data bases or otherwise stored in machine-readable form in the territory of any Party.

5. Further to Article 2101 (General Exceptions), nothing in this Chapter shall be construed to prevent a Party from adopting or enforcing any measure necessary to:

(a) ensure the security and confidentiality of messages; or

(b) protect the privacy of subscribers to public telecommunications transport networks or services.

6. Each Party shall ensure that no condition is imposed on access to and use of public telecommunications transport networks or services, other than that necessary to:

(a) safeguard the public service responsibilities of providers of public telecommunications transport networks or services, in particular their ability to make their networks or services available to the public generally; or

(b) protect the technical integrity of public telecommunications transport networks or services.

7. Provided that conditions for access to and use of public telecommunications transport networks or services satisfy the criteria set out in paragraph 6, such conditions may include:

(a) a restriction on resale or shared use of such services;

(b) a requirement to use specified technical interfaces, including interface protocols, for interconnection with such networks or services;

(c) a restriction on interconnection of private leased or owned circuits with such networks or services or with circuits leased or owned by another person, where the circuits are used in the provision of public telecommunications transport networks or services; and

(d) a licensing, permit, registration or notification procedure which, if adopted or maintained, is transparent and applications filed thereunder are processed expeditiously.

8. For purposes of this Article, "non-discriminatory" means on terms and conditions no less favorable than those accorded to any other customer or user of like public telecommunications transport networks or services in like circumstances.

Article 1303: Conditions for the Provision of Enhanced or Value-Added Services

1. Each Party shall ensure that:
    (a) any licensing, permit, registration or notification procedure that it adopts or maintains relating to the provision of enhanced or value-added services is transparent and non-discriminatory, and that applications filed thereunder are processed expeditiously; and
    (b) information required under such procedures is limited to that necessary to demonstrate that the applicant has the financial solvency to begin providing services or to assess conformity of the applicant's terminal or other equipment with the Party's applicable standards or technical regulations.
2. No Party may require a person providing enhanced or value-added services to:
    (a) provide those services to the public generally;
    (b) cost-justify its rates;
    (c) file a tariff;
    (d) interconnect its networks with any particular customer or network; or
    (e) conform with any particular standard or technical regulation for interconnection other than for interconnection to a public telecommunications transport network.
3. Notwithstanding paragraph 2(c), a Party may require the filing of a tariff by:
    (a) such provider to remedy a practice of that provider that the Party has found in a particular case to be anticompetitive under its law; or
    (b) a monopoly to which Article 1305 applies.

ARTICLE 1304: STANDARDS-RELATED MEASURES

1. Further to Article 904(4) (Unnecessary Obstacles), each Party shall ensure that its standards-related measures relating to the attachment of terminal or other equipment to the public telecommunications transport networks, including those measures relating to the use of testing and measuring equipment for conformity assessment procedures, are adopted or maintained only to the extent necessary to:
    (a) prevent technical damage to public telecommunications transport networks;
    (b) prevent technical interference with, or degradation of, public telecommunications transport services;
    (c) prevent electromagnetic interference, and ensure compatibility, with other uses of the electromagnetic spectrum;
    (d) prevent billing equipment malfunction; or
    (e) ensure users' safety and access to public telecommunications transport networks or services.

2. A Party may require approval for the attachment to the public telecommunications transport network of terminal or other equipment that is not authorized, provided that the criteria for that approval are consistent with paragraph 1.

3. Each Party shall ensure that the network termination points for its public telecommunications transport networks are defined on a reasonable and transparent basis.

4. No Party may require separate authorization for equipment that is connected on the customer's side of authorized equipment that serves as a protective device fulfilling the criteria of paragraph 1.

5. Further to Article 904(3) (Non-Discriminatory Treatment), each Party shall:
    (a) ensure that its conformity assessment procedures are transparent and non-discriminatory and that applications filed thereunder are processed expeditiously;
    (b) permit any technically qualified entity to perform the testing required under the Party's conformity assessment procedures for terminal or other equipment to be attached to the public telecommunications transport network, subject to the Party's right to review the accuracy and completeness of the test results; and
    (c) ensure that any measure that it adopts or maintains requiring persons to be authorized to act as agents for suppliers of telecommunications equipment before the Party's relevant conformity assessment bodies is non-discriminatory.

6. No later than one year after the date of entry into force of this Agreement, each Party shall adopt, as part of its conformity assessment procedures, provisions necessary to accept the test results from laboratories or testing facilities in the territory of another Party for tests performed in accordance with the accepting Party's standards-related measures and procedures.

7. The Telecommunications Standards Subcommittee established under Article 913(5) (Committee on Standards-Related Measures) shall perform the functions set out in Annex 913.5.a2.

Article 1305: Monopolies

1. Where a Party maintains or designates a monopoly to provide public telecommunications transport networks or services, and the monopoly, directly or through an affiliate, competes in the provision of enhanced or value-added services or other telecommunications-related services or telecommunications-related goods, the Party shall ensure that the monopoly does not use its monopoly position to engage in anticompetitive conduct in those markets, either directly or through its dealings with its affiliates, in such a manner as to affect adversely a person of another Party. Such conduct may include cross-subsidization, predatory conduct and the discriminatory provision of access to public telecommunications transport networks or services.

2. To prevent such anticompetitive conduct, each Party shall adopt or maintain effective measures, such as:
    (a) accounting requirements;
    (b) requirements for structural separation;

(c) rules to ensure that the monopoly accords its competitors access to and use of its public telecommunications transport networks or services on terms and conditions no less favorable than those it accords to itself or its affiliates; or

(d) rules to ensure the timely disclosure of technical changes to public telecommunications transport networks and their interfaces.

Article 1306: Transparency

Further to Article 1802 (Publication), each Party shall make publicly available its measures relating to access to and use of public telecommunications transport networks or services, including measures relating to:

(a) tariffs and other terms and conditions of service;

(b) specifications of technical interfaces with the networks or services;

(c) information on bodies responsible for the preparation and adoption of standards-related measures affecting such access and use;

(d) conditions applying to attachment of terminal or other equipment to the networks; and

(e) notification, permit, registration or licensing requirements.

Article 1307: Relation to Other Chapters

In the event of any inconsistency between this Chapter and another Chapter, this Chapter shall prevail to the extent of the inconsistency.

Article 1308: Relation to International Organizations and Agreements

The Parties recognize the importance of international standards for global compatibility and interoperability of telecommunication networks or services and undertake to promote those standards through the work of relevant international bodies, including the International Telecommunication Union and the International Organization for Standardization.

Article 1309: Technical Cooperation and Other Consultations

1. To encourage the development of interoperable telecommunications transport services infrastructure, the Parties shall cooperate in the exchange of technical information, the development of government-to-government training programs and other related activities. In implementing this obligation, the Parties shall give special emphasis to existing exchange programs.

2. The Parties shall consult with a view to determining the feasibility of further liberalizing trade in all telecommunications services, including public telecommunications transport networks and services.

Article 1310: Definitions

For purposes of this Chapter:

authorized equipment means terminal or other equipment that has been approved for attachment to the public telecommunications transport network in accordance with a Party's conformity assessment procedures;

conformity assessment procedure means "conformity assessment procedure" as defined in Article 915 (Standards-Related Measures-Definitions), and includes the procedures referred to in Annex 1310;

enhanced or value-added services means those telecommunications services employing computer processing applications that:

(a) act on the format, content, code, protocol or similar aspects of a customer's transmitted information;
(b) provide a customer with additional, different or restructured information; or
(c) involve customer interaction with stored information;

flat-rate pricing basis means pricing on the basis of a fixed charge per period of time regardless of the amount of use;

intracorporate communications means telecommunications through which an enterprise communicates:

(a) internally or with or among its subsidiaries, branches or affiliates, as defined by each Party, or
(b) on a non-commercial basis with other persons that are fundamental to the economic activity of the enterprise and that have a continuing contractual relationship with it, but does not include telecommunications services provided to persons other than those described herein;

network termination point means the final demarcation of the public telecommunications transport network at the customer's premises;

private network means a telecommunications transport network that is used exclusively for intracorporate communications;

protocol means a set of rules and formats that govern the exchange of information between two peer entities for purposes of transferring signaling or data information;

public telecommunications transport network means public telecommunications infrastructure that permits telecommunications between defined network termination points;

public telecommunications transport networks or services means public telecommunications transport networks or public telecommunications transport services;

public telecommunications transport service means any telecommunications transport service required by a Party, explicitly or in effect, to be offered to the public generally, including telegraph, telephone, telex and data transmission, that typically involves the real-time transmission of customer-supplied information between two or more points without any end-to-end change in the form or content of the customer's information;

standards-related measure means a "standards-related measure" as defined in Article 915;

telecommunications means the transmission and reception of signals by any electromagnetic means; and

terminal equipment means any digital or analog device capable of processing, receiving, switching, signaling or transmitting signals by electromagnetic means and that is connected by radio or wire to a public telecommunications transport network at a termination point.

ANNEX 1310. CONFORMITY ASSESSMENT PROCEDURES

For Canada

Department of Communications, Terminal Attachment Program Certification Procedures (CP01)

Department of Communications Act , R.S.C. 1985, c. C35

Railway Act , R.S.C. 1985, c. R3

Radiocommunication Act , R.S.C. 1985, c. R2, as amended by S.C. 1989, c. 17

Telecommunications Act (Bill C62)

For Mexico

Secretaría de Comunicaciones y Transportes
Subsecretaría de Comunicaciones y Desarrollo Technológico

Reglamento de Telecomunicaciones , Capítulo X

For the United States

Part 15 and Part 68 of the *Federal Communications Commission's Rules* , Title 47 of the *Code of Federal Regulations*

PART FIVE: INVESTMENT, SERVICES AND RELATED MATTERS

14. FINANCIAL SERVICES

Article 1401: Scope and Coverage

1. This Chapter applies to measures adopted or maintained by a Party relating to:
   (a) financial institutions of another Party;
   (b) investors of another Party, and investments of such investors, in financial institutions in the Party's territory; and
   (c) cross-border trade in financial services.
2. Articles 1109 through 1111, 1113, 1114 and 1211 are hereby incorporated into and made a part of this Chapter. Articles 1115 through 1138 are hereby incorporated into and made a part of this Chapter solely for breaches by a Party of Articles 1109 through 1111, 1113 and 1114, as incorporated into this Chapter.
3. Nothing in this Chapter shall be construed to prevent a Party, including its public entities, from exclusively conducting or providing in its territory:
   (a) activities or services forming part of a public retirement plan or statutory system of social security; or
   (b) activities or services for the account or with the guarantee or using the financial resources of the Party, including its public entities.
4. Annex 1401.4 applies to the Parties specified in that Annex.

Article 1402: Self-Regulatory Organizations

Where a Party requires a financial institution or a cross-border financial service provider of another Party to be a member of, participate in, or have access to, a selfregulatory organization to provide a financial service in or into the territory of that Party, the Party shall ensure observance of the obligations of this Chapter by such selfregulatory organization.

Article 1403: Establishment of Financial Institutions

1. The Parties recognize the principle that an investor of another Party should be permitted to establish a financial institution in the territory of a Party in the juridical form chosen by such investor.

2. The Parties also recognize the principle that an investor of another Party should be permitted to participate widely in a Party's market through the ability of such investor to:

    (a) provide in that Party's territory a range of financial services through separate financial institutions as may be required by that Party;

    (b) expand geographically in that Party's territory; and

    (c) own financial institutions in that Party's territory without being subject to ownership requirements specific to foreign financial institutions.

3. Subject to Annex 1403.3, at such time as the United States permits commercial banks of another Party located in its territory to expand through subsidiaries or direct branches into substantially all of the United States market, the Parties shall review and assess market access provided by each Party in relation to the principles in paragraphs 1 and 2 with a view to adopting arrangements permitting investors of another Party to choose the juridical form of establishment of commercial banks.

4. Each Party shall permit an investor of another Party that does not own or control a financial institution in the Party's territory to establish a financial institution in that territory. A Party may:

    (a) require an investor of another Party to incorporate under the Party's law any financial institution it establishes in the Party's territory; or

    (b) impose terms and conditions on establishment that are consistent with Article 1405.

5. For purposes of this Article, "investor of another Party" means an investor of another Party engaged in the business of providing financial services in the territory of that Party.

Article 1404: Cross-Border Trade

1. No Party may adopt any measure restricting any type of cross-border trade in financial services by cross-border financial service providers of another Party that the Party permits on the date of entry into force of this Agreement, except to the extent set out in Section B of the Party's Schedule to Annex VII.

2. Each Party shall permit persons located in its territory, and its nationals wherever located, to purchase financial services from cross-border financial service providers of another Party located in the territory of that other Party or of another Party. This obligation does not require a Party to permit such providers to do business or solicit in its territory. Subject to paragraph 1, each Party may define "doing business" and "solicitation" for purposes of this obligation.

3. Without prejudice to other means of prudential regulation of cross-border trade in financial services, a Party may require the registration of cross-border financial service providers of another Party and of financial instruments.

4. The Parties shall consult on future liberalization of cross-border trade in financial services as set out in Annex 1404.4.

Article 1405: National Treatment

1. Each Party shall accord to investors of another Party treatment no less favorable than that it accords to its own investors, in like circumstances, with respect to the establishment, acquisition, expansion, management, conduct, operation, and sale or other disposition of financial institutions and investments in financial institutions in its territory.

2. Each Party shall accord to financial institutions of another Party and to investments of investors of another Party in financial institutions treatment no less favorable than that it accords to its own financial institutions and to investments of its own investors in financial institutions, in like circumstances, with respect to the establishment, acquisition, expansion, management, conduct, operation, and sale or other disposition of financial institutions and investments.

3. Subject to Article 1404, where a Party permits the cross-border provision of a financial service it shall accord to the cross-border financial service providers of another Party treatment no less favorable than that it accords to its own financial service providers, in like circumstances, with respect to the provision of such service.

4. The treatment that a Party is required to accord under paragraphs 1, 2 and 3 means, with respect to a measure of any state or province:

    (a) in the case of an investor of another Party with an investment in a financial institution, an investment of such investor in a financial institution, or a financial institution of such investor, located in a state or province, treatment no less favorable than the treatment accorded to an investor of the Party in a financial institution, an investment of such investor in a financial institution, or a financial institution of such investor, located in that state or province, in like circumstances; and

    (b) in any other case, treatment no less favorable than the most favorable treatment accorded to an investor of the Party in a financial institution, its financial institution or its investment in a financial institution, in like circumstances.
    For greater certainty, in the case of an investor of another Party with investments in financial institutions or financial institutions of such investor, located in more than one state or province, the treatment required under subparagraph (a) means:

    (c) treatment of the investor that is no less favorable than the most favorable treatment accorded to an investor of the Party with an investment located in such states, or provinces in like circumstances; and

    (d) with respect to an investment of the investor in a financial institution or a financial institution of such investor, located in a state or province, treatment no less favorable than that accorded to an investment of an investor of the Party, or a financial institution of such investor, located in that state or province, in like circumstances.

5. A Party's treatment of financial institutions and cross-border financial service providers of another Party, whether different or identical to that accorded to its own institutions or providers in like circumstances, is consistent with paragraphs 1 through 3 if the treatment affords equal competitive opportunities.

6. A Party's treatment affords equal competitive opportunities if it does not disadvantage financial institutions and cross-border financial services providers of another Party in their ability to provide financial services as compared with the ability of the Party's own financial institutions and financial services providers to provide such services, in like circumstances.

7. Differences in market share, profitability or size do not in themselves establish a denial of equal competitive opportunities, but such differences may be used as evidence regarding whether a Party's treatment affords equal competitive opportunities.

Article 1406: Most-Favored-Nation Treatment

1. Each Party shall accord to investors of another Party, financial institutions of another Party, investments of investors in financial institutions and cross-border financial service providers of another Party treatment no less favorable than that it accords to the investors, financial institutions, investments of investors in financial institutions and cross-border financial service providers of any other Party or of a non-Party, in like circumstances.

2. A Party may recognize prudential measures of another Party or of a non-Party in the application of measures covered by this Chapter. Such recognition may be:
    (a) accorded unilaterally;
    (b) achieved through harmonization or other means; or
    (c) based upon an agreement or arrangement with the other Party or non-Party.

3. A Party according recognition of prudential measures under paragraph 2 shall provide adequate opportunity to another Party to demonstrate that circumstances exist in which there are or would be equivalent regulation, oversight, implementation of regulation, and if appropriate, procedures concerning the sharing of information between the Parties.

4. Where a Party accords recognition of prudential measures under paragraph 2(c); and the circumstances set out in paragraph 3 exist, the Party shall provide adequate opportunity to another Party to negotiate accession to the agreement or arrangement, or to negotiate a comparable agreement or arrangement.

Article 1407: New Financial Services and Data Processing

1. Each Party shall permit a financial institution of another Party to provide any new financial service of a type similar to those services that the Party permits its own

financial institutions, in like circumstances, to provide under its domestic law. A Party may determine the institutional and juridical form through which the service may be provided and may require authorization for the provision of the service. Where such authorization is required, a decision shall be made within a reasonable time and the authorization may only be refused for prudential reasons.

2. Each Party shall permit a financial institution of another Party to transfer information in electronic or other form, into and out of the Party's territory, for data processing where such processing is required in the ordinary course of business of such institution.

Article 1408: Senior Management and Boards of Directors

1. No Party may require financial institutions of another Party to engage individuals of any particular nationality as senior managerial or other essential personnel.
2. No Party may require that more than a simple majority of the board of directors of a financial institution of another Party be composed of nationals of the Party, persons residing in the territory of the Party, or a combination thereof.

Article 1409: Reservations and Specific Commitments

1. Articles 1403 through 1408 do not apply to:
   (a) any existing non-conforming measure that is maintained by
      (i) a Party at the federal level, as set out in Section A of its Schedule to Annex VII,
      (ii) a state or province, for the period ending on the date specified in Annex 1409.1 for that state or province, and thereafter as described by the Party in Section A of its Schedule to Annex VII in accordance with Annex 1409.1, or
      (iii) a local government;
   (b) the continuation or prompt renewal of any non-conforming measure referred to in subparagraph (a); or
   (c) an amendment to any non-conforming measure referred to in subparagraph (a) to the extent that the amendment does not decrease the conformity of the measure, as it existed immediately before the amendment, with Articles 1403 through 1408.
2. Articles 1403 through 1408 do not apply to any non-conforming measure that a Party adopts or maintains in accordance with Section B of its Schedule to Annex VII.
3. Section C of each Party's Schedule to Annex VII sets out certain specific commitments by that Party.
4. Where a Party has set out a reservation to Article 1102, 1103, 1202 or 1203 in its Schedule to Annex I, II, III or IV, the reservation shall be deemed to constitute a reservation to Article 1405 or 1406, as the case may be, to the extent that the measure, sector, subsector or activity set out in the reservation is covered by this Chapter.

Article 1410: Exceptions

1. Nothing in this Part shall be construed to prevent a Party from adopting or maintaining reasonable measures for prudential reasons, such as:
   (a) the protection of investors, depositors, financial market participants, policyholders, policy claimants, or persons to whom a fiduciary duty is owed by a financial institution or cross-border financial service provider;
   (b) the maintenance of the safety, soundness, integrity or financial responsibility of financial institutions or cross-border financial service providers; and
   (c) ensuring the integrity and stability of a Party's financial system.
2. Nothing in this Part applies to non-discriminatory measures of general application taken by any public entity in pursuit of monetary and related credit policies or exchange rate policies. This paragraph shall not affect a Party's obligations under Article 1106 (Investment Performance Requirements) with respect to measures covered by Chapter Eleven (Investment) or Article 1109 (Investments Transfers).
3. Article 1405 shall not apply to the granting by a Party to a financial institution of an exclusive right to provide a financial service referred to in Article 1401(3)(a).
4. Notwithstanding Article 1109(1), (2) and (3), as incorporated into this Chapter, and without limiting the applicability of Article 1109(4), as incorporated into this Chapter, a Party may prevent or limit transfers by a financial institution or cross-border financial services provider to, or for the benefit of, an affiliate of or person related to such institution or provider, through the equitable, non-discriminatory and good faith application of measures relating to maintenance of the safety, soundness, integrity or financial responsibility of financial institutions or cross-border financial service providers. This paragraph does not prejudice any other provision of this Agreement that permits a Party to restrict transfers.

Article 1411: Transparency

1. In lieu of Article 1802(2) (Publication), each Party shall, to the extent practicable, provide in advance to all interested persons any measure of general application that the Party proposes to adopt in order to allow an opportunity for such persons to comment on the measure. Such measure shall be provided:
   (a) by means of official publication;
   (b) in other written form; or
   (c) in such other form as permits an interested person to make informed comments on the proposed measure.
2. Each Party's regulatory authorities shall make available to interested persons their requirements for completing applications relating to the provision of financial services.
3. On the request of an applicant, the regulatory authority shall inform the applicant of the status of its application. If such authority requires additional information from the applicant, it shall notify the applicant without undue delay.

4. A regulatory authority shall make an administrative decision on a completed application of an investor in a financial institution, a financial institution or a cross-border financial service provider of another Party relating to the provision of a financial service within 120 days, and shall promptly notify the applicant of the decision. An application shall not be considered complete until all relevant hearings are held and all necessary information is received. Where it is not practicable for a decision to be made within 120 days, the regulatory authority shall notify the applicant without undue delay and shall endeavor to make the decision within a reasonable time thereafter.

5. Nothing in this Chapter requires a Party to furnish or allow access to:
   (a) information related to the financial affairs and accounts of individual customers of financial institutions or cross-border financial service providers; or
   (b) any confidential information, the disclosure of which would impede law enforcement or otherwise be contrary to the public interest or prejudice legitimate commercial interests of particular enterprises.

6. Each Party shall maintain or establish one or more inquiry points no later than 180 days after the date of entry into force of this Agreement, to respond in writing as soon as practicable, to all reasonable inquiries from interested persons regarding measures of general application covered by this Chapter.

Article 1412: Financial Services Committee

1. The Parties hereby establish the Financial Services Committee. The principal representative of each Party shall be an official of the Party's authority responsible for financial services set out in Annex 1412.1.

2. Subject to Article 2001(2)(d) (Free Trade Commission), the Committee shall:
   (a) supervise the implementation of this Chapter and its further elaboration;
   (b) consider issues regarding financial services that are referred to it by a Party; and
   (c) participate in the dispute settlement procedures in accordance with Article 1415.

3. The Committee shall meet annually to assess the functioning of this Agreement as it applies to financial services. The Committee shall inform the Commission of the results of each annual meeting.

Article 1413: Consultations

1. A Party may request consultations with another Party regarding any matter arising under this Agreement that affects financial services. The other Party shall give sympathetic consideration to the request. The consulting Parties shall report the results of their consultations to the Committee at its annual meeting.

2. Consultations under this Article shall include officials of the authorities specified in Annex 1412.1.

3. A Party may request that regulatory authorities of another Party participate in consultations under this Article regarding that other Party's measures of general

application which may affect the operations of financial institutions or cross-border financial service providers in the requesting Party's territory.

4. Nothing in this Article shall be construed to require regulatory authorities participating in consultations under paragraph 3 to disclose information or take any action that would interfere with individual regulatory, supervisory, administrative or enforcement matters.

5. Where a Party requires information for supervisory purposes concerning a financial institution in another Party's territory or a cross-border financial service provider in another Party's territory, the Party may approach the competent regulatory authority in the other Party's territory to seek the information.

6. Annex 1413.6 shall apply to further consultations and arrangements.

Article 1414: Dispute Settlement

1. Section B of Chapter Twenty (Institutional Arrangements and Dispute Settlement Procedures) applies as modified by this Article to the settlement of disputes arising under this Chapter.

2. The Parties shall establish by January 1, 1994 and maintain a roster of up to 15 individuals who are willing and able to serve as financial services panelists. Financial services roster members shall be appointed by consensus for terms of three years, and may be reappointed.

3. Financial services roster members shall:
   (a) have expertise or experience in financial services law or practice, which may include the regulation of financial institutions;
   (b) be chosen strictly on the basis of objectivity, reliability and sound judgment; and
   (c) meet the qualifications set out in Article 2009(2)(b) and (c) (Roster).

4. Where a Party claims that a dispute arises under this Chapter, Article 2011 (Panel Selection) shall apply, except that:
   (a) where the disputing Parties so agree, the panel shall be composed entirely of panelists meeting the qualifications in paragraph 3; and
   (b) in any other case,
      (i) each disputing Party may select panelists meeting the qualifications set out in paragraph 3 or in Article 2010(1) (Qualifications of Panelists), and
      (ii) if the Party complained against invokes Article 1410, the chair of the panel shall meet the qualifications set out in paragraph 3.

5. In any dispute where a panel finds a measure to be inconsistent with the obligations of this Agreement and the measure affects:
   (a) only the financial services sector, the complaining Party may suspend benefits only in the financial services sector;
   (b) the financial services sector and any other sector, the complaining Party may suspend benefits in the financial services sector that have an effect equivalent to the effect of the measure in the Party's financial services sector; or
   (c) only a sector other than the financial services sector, the complaining Party may not suspend benefits in the financial services sector.

Article 1415: Investment Disputes in Financial Services

1. Where an investor of another Party submits a claim under Article 1116 or 1117 to arbitration under Section B of Chapter Eleven (Investment Settlement of Disputes between a Party and an Investor of Another Party) against a Party and the disputing Party invokes Article 1410, on request of the disputing Party, the Tribunal shall refer the matter in writing to the Committee for a decision. The Tribunal may not proceed pending receipt of a decision or report under this Article.

2. In a referral pursuant to paragraph 1, the Committee shall decide the issue of whether and to what extent Article 1410 is a valid defense to the claim of the investor. The Committee shall transmit a copy of its decision to the Tribunal and to the Commission. The decision shall be binding on the Tribunal.

3. Where the Committee has not decided the issue within 60 days of the receipt of the referral under paragraph 1, the disputing Party or the Party of the disputing investor may request the establishment of an arbitral panel under Article 2008 (Request for an Arbitral Panel). The panel shall be constituted in accordance with Article 1414. Further to Article 2017 (Final Report), the panel shall transmit its final report to the Committee and to the Tribunal. The report shall be binding on the Tribunal.

4. Where no request for the establishment of a panel pursuant to paragraph 3 has been made within 10 days of the expiration of the 60day period referred to in paragraph 3, the Tribunal may proceed to decide the matter.

Article 1416: Definitions

For purposes of this Chapter:

cross-border financial service provider of a Party means a person of a Party that is engaged in the business of providing a financial service within the territory of the Party and that seeks to provide or provides financial services through the cross-border provision of such services;

cross-border provision of a financial service or **cross-border trade in financial services** means the provision of a financial service:

(a) from the territory of a Party into the territory of another Party,
(b) in the territory of a Party by a person of that Party to a person of another Party, or
(c) by a national of a Party in the territory of another Party,
but does not include the provision of a service in the territory of a Party by an investment in that territory;

financial institution means any financial intermediary or other enterprise that is authorized to do business and regulated or supervised as a financial institution under the law of the Party in whose territory it is located;

financial institution of another Party means a financial institution, including a branch, located in the territory of a Party that is controlled by persons of another Party;

financial service means a service of a financial nature, including insurance, and a service incidental or auxiliary to a service of a financial nature;

financial service provider of a Party means a person of a Party that is engaged in the business of providing a financial service within the territory of that Party;

investment means "investment" as defined in Article 1139 (Investment Definitions), except that, with respect to "loans" and "debt securities" referred to in that Article:

(a) a loan to or debt security issued by a financial institution is an investment only where it is treated as regulatory capital by the Party in whose territory the financial institution is located; and

(b) a loan granted by or debt security owned by a financial institution, other than a loan to or debt security of a financial institution referred to in subparagraph (a), is not an investment;
for greater certainty:

(c) a loan to, or debt security issued by, a Party or a state enterprise thereof is not an investment; and

(d) a loan granted by or debt security owned by a cross-border financial service provider, other than a loan to or debt security issued by a financial institution, is an investment if such loan or debt security meets the criteria for investments set out in Article 1139;

investor of a Party means a Party or state enterprise thereof, or a person of that Party, that seeks to make, makes, or has made an investment;

new financial service means a financial service not provided in the Party's territory that is provided within the territory of another Party, and includes any new form of delivery of a financial service or the sale of a financial product that is not sold in the Party's territory;

person of a Party means "person of a Party" as defined in Chapter Two (General Definitions) and, for greater certainty, does not include a branch of an enterprise of a non-Party;

public entity means a central bank or monetary authority of a Party, or any financial institution owned or controlled by a Party; and

self-regulatory organization means any non-governmental body, including any securities or futures exchange or market, clearing agency, or other organization or association, that exercises its own or delegated regulatory or supervisory authority over financial service providers or financial institutions.

ANNEX 1401.4. COUNTRY-SPECIFIC COMMITMENTS

For Canada and the United States, Article 1702(1) and (2) of the Canada United States Free Trade Agreement is hereby incorporated into and made a part of this Agreement.

ANNEX 1403.3. REVIEW OF MARKET ACCESS

The review of market access referred to in Article 1403(3) shall not include the market access limitations specified in Section B of the Schedule of Mexico to Annex VII.

ANNEX 1404.4. CONSULTATIONS ON LIBERALIZATION OF CROSS-BORDER TRADE

No later than January 1, 2000, the Parties shall consult on further liberalization of cross-border trade in financial services. In such consultations the Parties shall, with respect to insurance:

(a) consider the possibility of allowing a wider range of insurance services to be provided on a cross-border basis in or into their respective territories; and

(b) determine whether the limitations on cross-border insurance services specified in Section A of the Schedule of Mexico to Annex VII shall be maintained, modified or eliminated.

ANNEX 1409.1. PROVINCIAL AND STATE RESERVATIONS

1. Canada may set out in Section A of its Schedule to Annex VII by the date of entry into force of this Agreement any existing non-conforming measure maintained at the provincial level.

2. The United States may set out in Section A of its Schedule to Annex VII by the date of entry into force of this Agreement any existing non-conforming measures maintained by California, Florida, Illinois, New York, Ohio and Texas. Existing non-conforming state measures of all other states may be set out by January 1, 1995.

ANNEX 1412.1. AUTHORITIES RESPONSIBLE FOR FINANCIAL SERVICES

The authority of each Party responsible for financial services shall be:

(a) for Canada, the Department of Finance of Canada;

(b) for Mexico, the Secretaría de Hacienda y Crédito Público; and

(c) for the United States, the Department of the Treasury for banking and other financial services and the Department of Commerce for insurance services.

ANNEX 1413.6. FURTHER CONSULTATIONS AND ARRANGEMENTS

Section A Limited Scope Financial Institutions

Three years after the date of entry into force of this Agreement, the Parties shall consult on the aggregate limit on limited scope financial institutions described in paragraph 8 of Section B of the Schedule of Mexico to Annex VII.

Section B Payments System Protection

1. If the sum of the authorized capital of foreign commercial bank affiliates (as such term is defined in the Schedule of Mexico to Annex VII), measured as a percentage of the aggregate capital of all commercial banks in Mexico, reaches 25 percent, Mexico may request consultations with the other Parties on the potential adverse effects arising from the presence of commercial banks of the other Parties in the Mexican market and the possible need for remedial action, including further temporary limitations on market participation. The consultations shall be completed expeditiously.

2. In considering the potential adverse effects, the Parties shall take into account:
   (a) the threat that the Mexican payments system may be controlled by non-Mexican persons;
   (b) the effects foreign commercial banks established in Mexico may have on Mexico's ability to conduct monetary and exchangerate policy effectively; and
   (c) the adequacy of this Chapter in protecting the Mexican payments system.

3. If no consensus is reached on the matters referred to in paragraph 1, any Party may request the establishment of an arbitral panel under Article 1414 or Article 2008 (Request for an Arbitral Panel). The panel proceedings shall be conducted in accordance with the Model Rules of Procedure established under Article 2012 (Rules of Procedure). The Panel shall present its determination within 60 days after the last panelist is selected or such other period as the Parties to the proceeding may agree. Article 2018 (Implementation of Final Report) and 2019 (Non-Implementation-Suspension of Benefits) shall not apply in such proceedings.

15. COMPETITION POLICY, MONOPOLIES AND STATE ENTERPRISES

Article 1501: Competition Law

1. Each Party shall adopt or maintain measures to proscribe anticompetitive business conduct and take appropriate action with respect thereto, recognizing that such measures will enhance the fulfillment of the objectives of this Agreement. To this end the Parties shall consult from time to time about the effectiveness of measures undertaken by each Party.

2. Each Party recognizes the importance of cooperation and coordination among their authorities to further effective competition law enforcement in the free trade area. The Parties shall cooperate on issues of competition law enforcement policy, including mutual legal assistance, notification, consultation and exchange of information relating to the enforcement of competition laws and policies in the free trade area.

3. No Party may have recourse to dispute settlement under this Agreement for any matter arising under this Article.

Article 1502: Monopolies and State Enterprises

1. Nothing in this Agreement shall be construed to prevent a Party from designating a monopoly.

2. Where a Party intends to designate a monopoly and the designation may affect the interests of persons of another Party, the Party shall:
   (a) wherever possible, provide prior written notification to the other Party of the designation; and
   (b) endeavor to introduce at the time of the designation such conditions on the operation of the monopoly as will minimize or eliminate any nullification or impairment of benefits in the sense of Annex 2004 (Nullification and Impairment).

3. Each Party shall ensure, through regulatory control, administrative supervision or the application of other measures, that any privately owned monopoly that it designates and any government monopoly that it maintains or designates:
   (a) acts in a manner that is not inconsistent with the Party's obligations under this Agreement wherever such a monopoly exercises any regulatory, administrative or other governmental authority that the Party has delegated to it in connection with the monopoly good or service, such as the power to grant import or export licenses, approve commercial transactions or impose quotas, fees or other charges;
   (b) except to comply with any terms of its designation that are not inconsistent with subparagraph (c) or (d), acts solely in accordance with commercial considerations in its purchase or sale of the monopoly good or service in the relevant market, including with regard to price, quality, availability, marketability, transportation and other terms and conditions of purchase or sale;

(c) provides non-discriminatory treatment to investments of investors, to goods and to service providers of another Party in its purchase or sale of the monopoly good or service in the relevant market; and

(d) does not use its monopoly position to engage, either directly or indirectly, including through its dealings with its parent, its subsidiary or other enterprise with common ownership, in anticompetitive practices in a non-monopolized market in its territory that adversely affect an investment of an investor of another Party, including through the discriminatory provision of the monopoly good or service, crosssubsidization or predatory conduct.

4. Paragraph 3 does not apply to procurement by governmental agencies of goods or services for governmental purposes and not with a view to commercial resale or with a view to use in the production of goods or the provision of services for commercial sale.

5. For purposes of this Article "maintain" means designate prior to the date of entry into force of this Agreement and existing on January 1, 1994.

Article 1503: State Enterprises

1. Nothing in this Agreement shall be construed to prevent a Party from maintaining or establishing a state enterprise.

2. Each Party shall ensure, through regulatory control, administrative supervision or the application of other measures, that any state enterprise that it maintains or establishes acts in a manner that is not inconsistent with the Party's obligations under Chapters Eleven (Investment) and Fourteen (Financial Services) wherever such enterprise exercises any regulatory, administrative or other governmental authority that the Party has delegated to it, such as the power to expropriate, grant licenses, approve commercial transactions or impose quotas, fees or other charges.

3. Each Party shall ensure that any state enterprise that it maintains or establishes accords non-discriminatory treatment in the sale of its goods or services to investments in the Party's territory of investors of another Party.

Article 1504: Working Group on Trade and Competition

The Commission shall establish a Working Group on Trade and Competition, comprising representatives of each Party, to report, and to make recommendations on further work as appropriate, to the Commission within five years of the date of entry into force of this Agreement on relevant issues concerning the relationship between competition laws and policies and trade in the free trade area.

Article 1505: Definitions

For purposes of this Chapter:

designate means to establish, designate or authorize, or to expand the scope of a monopoly to cover an additional good or service, after the date of entry into force of this Agreement;

discriminatory provision includes treating:

(a) a parent, a subsidiary or other enterprise with common ownership more favorably than an unaffiliated enterprise, or

(b) one class of enterprises more favorably than another,

in like circumstances;

government monopoly means a monopoly that is owned, or controlled through ownership interests, by the federal government of a Party or by another such monopoly;

in accordance with commercial considerations means consistent with normal business practices of privately held enterprises in the relevant business or industry;

market means the geographic and commercial market for a good or service;

monopoly means an entity, including a consortium or government agency, that in any relevant market in the territory of a Party is designated as the sole provider or purchaser of a good or service, but does not include an entity that has been granted an exclusive intellectual property right solely by reason of such grant;

non-discriminatory treatment means the better of national treatment and most favored nation treatment, as set out in the relevant provisions of this Agreement; and

state enterprise means, except as set out in Annex 1505, an enterprise owned, or controlled through ownership interests, by a Party.

ANNEX 1505. COUNTRY-SPECIFIC DEFINITIONS OF STATE ENTERPRISES

For purposes of Article 1503(3), "state enterprise":

(a) with respect to Canada, means a Crown corporation within the meaning of the *Financial Administration Act* (Canada), a Crown corporation within the meaning of any comparable provincial law or equivalent entity that is incorporated under other applicable provincial law; and

(b) with respect to Mexico, does not include, the Compañía Nacional de Subsistencias Populares (National Company for Basic Commodities) and its existing affiliates, or any successor enterprise or its affiliates, for purposes of sales of maize, beans and powdered milk.

16. TEMPORARY ENTRY FOR BUSINESS PERSONS

Article 1601: General Principles

Further to Article 102 (Objectives), this Chapter reflects the preferential trading relationship between the Parties, the desirability of facilitating temporary entry on a reciprocal basis and of establishing transparent criteria and procedures for temporary entry, and the need to ensure border security and to protect the domestic labor force and permanent employment in their respective territories.

Article 1602: General Obligations

1. Each Party shall apply its measures relating to the provisions of this Chapter in accordance with Article 1601 and, in particular, shall apply expeditiously those measures so as to avoid unduly impairing or delaying trade in goods or services or conduct of investment activities under this Agreement.
2. The Parties shall endeavor to develop and adopt common criteria, definitions and interpretations for the implementation of this Chapter.

Article 1603: Grant of Temporary Entry

1. Each Party shall grant temporary entry to business persons who are otherwise qualified for entry under applicable measures relating to public health and safety and national security, in accordance with this Chapter, including the provisions of Annex 1603.
2. A Party may refuse to issue an immigration document authorizing employment to a business person where the temporary entry of that person might affect adversely:
   (a) the settlement of any labor dispute that is in progress at the place or intended place of employment; or
   (b) the employment of any person who is involved in such dispute.
3. When a Party refuses pursuant to paragraph 2 to issue an immigration document authorizing employment, it shall:
   (a) inform in writing the business person of the reasons for the refusal; and
   (b) promptly notify in writing the Party whose business person has been refused entry of the reasons for the refusal.
4. Each Party shall limit any fees for processing applications for temporary entry of business persons to the approximate cost of services rendered.

Article 1604: Provision of Information

1. Further to Article 1802 (Publication), each Party shall:

    (a) provide to the other Parties such materials as will enable them to become acquainted with its measures relating to this Chapter; and

    (b) no later than one year after the date of entry into force of this Agreement, prepare, publish and make available in its own territory, and in the territories of the other Parties, explanatory material in a consolidated document regarding the requirements for temporary entry under this Chapter in such a manner as will enable business persons of the other Parties to become acquainted with them.

2.   Subject to Annex 1604.2, each Party shall collect and maintain, and make available to the other Parties in accordance with its domestic law, data respecting the granting of temporary entry under this Chapter to business persons of the other Parties who have been issued immigration documentation, including data specific to each occupation, profession or activity.

Article 1605: Working Group

1.   The Parties hereby establish a Temporary Entry Working Group, comprising representatives of each Party, including immigration officials.

2.   The Working Group shall meet at least once each year to consider:

    (a) the implementation and administration of this Chapter;

    (b) the development of measures to further facilitate temporary entry of business persons on a reciprocal basis;

    (c) the waiving of labor certification tests or procedures of similar effect for spouses of business persons who have been granted temporary entry for more than one year under Section B, C or D of Annex 1603; and

    (d) proposed modifications of or additions to this Chapter.

Article 1606: Dispute Settlement

1.   A Party may not initiate proceedings under Article 2007 (Commission Good Offices, Conciliation and Mediation) regarding a refusal to grant temporary entry under this Chapter or a particular case arising under Article 1602(1) unless:

    (a) the matter involves a pattern of practice; and

    (b) the business person has exhausted the available administrative remedies regarding the particular matter.

2.   The remedies referred to in paragraph (1)(b) shall be deemed to be exhausted if a final determination in the matter has not been issued by the competent authority within one year of the institution of an administrative proceeding, and the failure to issue a determination is not attributable to delay caused by the business person.

Article 1607: Relation to Other Chapters

Except for this Chapter, Chapters One (Objectives), Two (General Definitions), Twenty (Institutional Arrangements and Dispute Settlement Procedures) and TwentyTwo (Final Provisions) and Articles 1801 (Contacts Points), 1802 (Publication), 1803 (Notification and Provision of Information) and 1804 (Administrative Proceedings), no provision of this Agreement shall impose any obligation on a Party regarding its immigration measures.

Article 1608: Definitions

For purposes of this Chapter:

business person means a citizen of a Party who is engaged in trade in goods, the provision of services or the conduct of investment activities;

citizen means "citizen" as defined in Annex 1608 for the Parties specified in that Annex;

existing means "existing" as defined in Annex 1608 for the Parties specified in that Annex; and

temporary entry means entry into the territory of a Party by a business person of another Party without the intent to establish permanent residence.

ANNEX 1603. TEMPORARY ENTRY FOR BUSINESS PERSONS

Section A - Business Visitors

1. Each Party shall grant temporary entry to a business person seeking to engage in a business activity set out in Appendix 1603.A.1, without requiring that person to obtain an employment authorization, provided that the business person otherwise complies with existing immigration measures applicable to temporary entry, on presentation of:
   (a) proof of citizenship of a Party;
   (b) documentation demonstrating that the business person will be so engaged and describing the purpose of entry; and
   (c) evidence demonstrating that the proposed business activity is international in scope and that the business person is not seeking to enter the local labor market.
2. Each Party shall provide that a business person may satisfy the requirements of paragraph 1(c) by demonstrating that:
   (a) the primary source of remuneration for the proposed business activity is outside the territory of the Party granting temporary entry; and
   (b) the business person's principal place of business and the actual place of accrual of profits, at least predominantly, remain outside such territory.

A Party shall normally accept an oral declaration as to the principal place of business and the actual place of accrual of profits. Where the Party requires further proof, it shall normally consider a letter from the employer attesting to these matters as sufficient proof.

3. Each Party shall grant temporary entry to a business person seeking to engage in a business activity other than those set out in Appendix 1603.A.1, without requiring that person to obtain an employment authorization, on a basis no less favorable than that provided under the existing provisions of the measures set out in Appendix 1603.A.3, provided that the business person otherwise complies with existing immigration measures applicable to temporary entry.

4. No Party may:
    (a) as a condition for temporary entry under paragraph 1 or 3, require prior approval procedures, petitions, labor certification tests or other procedures of similar effect; or
    (b) impose or maintain any numerical restriction relating to temporary entry under paragraph 1 or 3.

5. Notwithstanding paragraph 4, a Party may require a business person seeking temporary entry under this Section to obtain a visa or its equivalent prior to entry. Before imposing a visa requirement, the Party shall consult, on request, with a Party whose business persons would be affected with a view to avoiding the imposition of the requirement. With respect to an existing visa requirement, a Party shall consult, on request, with a Party whose business persons are subject to the requirement with a view to its removal.

Section B - Traders and Investors

1. Each Party shall grant temporary entry and provide confirming documentation to a business person seeking to:
    (a) carry on substantial trade in goods or services principally between the territory of the Party of which the business person is a citizen and the territory of the Party into which entry is sought, or
    (b) establish, develop, administer or provide advice or key technical services to the operation of an investment to which the business person or the business person's enterprise has committed, or is in the process of committing, a substantial amount of capital,

    in a capacity that is supervisory, executive or involves essential skills, provided that the business person otherwise complies with existing immigration measures applicable to temporary entry.

2. No Party may:
    (a) as a condition for temporary entry under paragraph 1, require labor certification tests or other procedures of similar effect; or
    (b) impose or maintain any numerical restriction relating to temporary entry under paragraph 1.

3. Notwithstanding paragraph 2, a Party may require a business person seeking temporary entry under this Section to obtain a visa or its equivalent prior to entry.

Section C - Intra-Company Transferees

1. Each Party shall grant temporary entry and provide confirming documentation to a business person employed by an enterprise who seeks to render services to that enterprise or a subsidiary or affiliate thereof, in a capacity that is managerial, executive or involves specialized knowledge, provided that the business person otherwise complies with existing immigration measures applicable to temporary entry. A Party may require the business person to have been employed continuously by the enterprise for one year within the threeyear period immediately preceding the date of the application for admission.

2. No Party may:
    (a) as a condition for temporary entry under paragraph 1, require labor certification tests or other procedures of similar effect; or
    (b) impose or maintain any numerical restriction relating to temporary entry under paragraph 1.

3. Notwithstanding paragraph 2, a Party may require a business person seeking temporary entry under this Section to obtain a visa or its equivalent prior to entry. Before imposing a visa requirement, the Party shall consult with a Party whose business persons would be affected with a view to avoiding the imposition of the requirement. With respect to an existing visa requirement, a Party shall consult, on request, with a Party whose business persons are subject to the requirement with a view to its removal.

Section D - Professionals

1. Each Party shall grant temporary entry and provide confirming documentation to a business person seeking to engage in a business activity at a professional level in a profession set out in Appendix 1603.D.1, if the business person otherwise complies with existing immigration measures applicable to temporary entry, on presentation of:
    (a) proof of citizenship of a Party; and
    (b) documentation demonstrating that the business person will be so engaged and describing the purpose of entry.

2. No Party may:
    (a) as a condition for temporary entry under paragraph 1, require prior approval procedures, petitions, labor certification tests or other procedures of similar effect; or
    (b) impose or maintain any numerical restriction relating to temporary entry under paragraph 1.

3. Notwithstanding paragraph 2, a Party may require a business person seeking temporary entry under this Section to obtain a visa or its equivalent prior to entry. Before imposing a visa requirement, the Party shall consult with a Party whose business persons would be affected with a view to avoiding the imposition of the requirement. With respect to an existing visa requirement, a Party shall consult, on request, with a Party whose business persons are subject to the requirement with a view to its removal.

4. Notwithstanding paragraphs 1 and 2, a Party may establish an annual numerical limit, which shall be set out in Appendix 1603.D.4, regarding temporary entry of business persons of another Party seeking to engage in business activities at a professional level in a profession set out in Appendix 1603.D.1, if the Parties concerned have not agreed otherwise prior to the date of entry into force of this Agreement for those Parties. In establishing such a limit, the Party shall consult with the other Party concerned.

5. A Party establishing a numerical limit pursuant to paragraph 4, unless the Parties concerned agree otherwise:

    (a) shall, for each year after the first year after the date of entry into force of this Agreement, consider increasing the numerical limit set out in Appendix 1603.D.4 by an amount to be established in consultation with the other Party concerned, taking into account the demand for temporary entry under this Section;

    (b) shall not apply its procedures established pursuant to paragraph 1 to the temporary entry of a business person subject to the numerical limit, but may require the business person to comply with its other procedures applicable to the temporary entry of professionals; and

    (c) may, in consultation with the other Party concerned, grant temporary entry under paragraph 1 to a business person who practices in a profession where accreditation, licensing, and certification requirements are mutually recognized by those Parties.

6. Nothing in paragraph 4 or 5 shall be construed to limit the ability of a business person to seek temporary entry under a Party's applicable immigration measures relating to the entry of professionals other than those adopted or maintained pursuant to paragraph 1.

7. Three years after a Party establishes a numerical limit pursuant to paragraph 4, it shall consult with the other Party concerned with a view to determining a date after which the limit shall cease to apply.

APPENDIX 1603.A.1. BUSINESS VISITORS

Research and Design

- Technical, scientific and statistical researchers conducting independent research or research for an enterprise located in the territory of another Party.

Growth, Manufacture and Production

- Harvester owner supervising a harvesting crew admitted under applicable law.
- Purchasing and production management personnel conducting commercial transactions for an enterprise located in the territory of another Party.

Marketing

- Market researchers and analysts conducting independent research or analysis or research or analysis for an enterprise located in the territory of another Party.
- Trade fair and promotional personnel attending a trade convention.

Sales

- Sales representatives and agents taking orders or negotiating contracts for goods or services for an enterprise located in the territory of another Party but not delivering goods or providing services.
- Buyers purchasing for an enterprise located in the territory of another Party.

Distribution

- Transportation operators transporting goods or passengers to the territory of a Party from the territory of another Party or loading and transporting goods or passengers from the territory of a Party, with no unloading in that territory, to the territory of another Party.
- With respect to temporary entry into the territory of the United States, Canadian customs brokers performing brokerage duties relating to the export of goods from the territory of the United States to or through the territory of Canada.
- With respect to temporary entry into the territory of Canada, United States customs brokers performing brokerage duties relating to the export of goods from the territory of Canada to or through the territory of the United States.
- Customs brokers providing consulting services regarding the facilitation of the import or export of goods.

After Sales Service

- Installers, repair and maintenance personnel, and supervisors, possessing specialized knowledge essential to a seller's contractual obligation, performing services or training workers to perform services, pursuant to a warranty or other service contract incidental to the sale of commercial or industrial equipment or machinery, including computer software, purchased from an enterprise located outside the territory of the

Party into which temporary entry is sought, during the life of the warranty or service agreement.

General Service

- Professionals engaging in a business activity at a professional level in a profession set out in Appendix 1603.D.1.
- Management and supervisory personnel engaging in a commercial transaction for an enterprise located in the territory of another Party.
- Financial services personnel (insurers, bankers or investment brokers) engaging in commercial transactions for an enterprise located in the territory of another Party.
- Public relations and advertising personnel consulting with business associates, or attending or participating in conventions.
- Tourism personnel (tour and travel agents, tour guides or tour operators) attending or participating in conventions or conducting a tour that has begun in the territory of another Party.
- Tour bus operators entering the territory of a Party:
  - (a) with a group of passengers on a bus tour that has begun in, and will return to, the territory of another Party;
  - (b) to meet a group of passengers on a bus tour that will end, and the predominant portion of which will take place, in the territory of another Party; or
  - (c) with a group of passengers on a bus tour to be unloaded in the territory of the Party into which temporary entry is sought, and returning with no passengers or reloading with the group for transportation to the territory of another Party.
- Translators or interpreters performing services as employees of an enterprise located in the territory of another Party.

Definitions

For purposes of this Appendix:

territory of another Party means the territory of a Party other than the territory of the Party into which temporary entry is sought;

tour bus operator means a natural person, including relief personnel accompanying or following to join, necessary for the operation of a tour bus for the duration of a trip; and
transportation operator means a natural person, other than a tour bus operator, including relief personnel accompanying or following to join, necessary for the operation of a vehicle for the duration of a trip.

APPENDIX 1603.A.3. EXISTING IMMIGRATION MEASURES

1. In the case of Canada, subsection 19(1) of the *Immigration Regulations, 1978* , SOR/78172, as amended, made under the *Immigration Act* , R.S.C. 1985, c. I2, as amended.
2. In the case of the United States, section 101(a)(15)(B) of the *Immigration and Nationality Act* , 1952, as amended.
3. In the case of Mexico, Chapter III of the *General Demography Law* ("Ley General de Población"), 1974, as amended.

APPENDIX 1603.D.1. PROFESSIONALS

PROFESSION[1]	MINIMUM EDUCATION REQUIREMENTS AND ALTERNATIVE CREDENTIALS
General	
Accountant	Baccalaureate or Licenciatura Degree; or C.P.A., C.A., C.G.A. or C.M.A.
Architect	Baccalaureate or Licenciatura Degree; or state/provincial license [2]
Computer Systems Analyst	Baccalaureate or Licenciatura Degree; or PostSecondary Diploma [3] or PostSecondary Certificate [4] , and three years experience
Disaster Relief Insurance Claims Adjuster (claims Adjuster employed by an insurance company located in the territory of a Party, or an independent claims adjuster)	Baccalaureate or Licenciatura Degree, and successful completion of training in the appropriate areas of insurance adjustment pertaining to disaster relief claims; or three years experience in claims adjustment and successful completion of training in the appropriate areas of insurance adjustment pertaining to disaster relief claims.
Economist	Baccalaureate or Licenciatura Degree
Engineer	Baccalaureate or Licenciatura Degree; or state/provincial license
Forester	Baccalaureate or Licenciatura Degree; or state/provincial license
Graphic Designer	Baccalaureate or Licenciatura Degree; or PostSecondary Diploma or PostSecondary Certificate, and three years experience
Hotel Manager	Baccalaureate or Licenciatura Degree in hotel/restaurant management; or PostSecondary Diploma or PostSecondary Certificate in hotel/restaurant management, and three years experience in hotel/restaurant management
Industrial Designer	Baccalaureate or Licenciatura Degree; or PostSecondary Diploma or PostSecondary Certificate, and three years experience
Interior Designer	Baccalaureate or Licenciatura Degree; or PostSecondary Diploma or PostSecondary Certificate, and three years experience
Land Surveyor	Baccalaureate or Licenciatura Degree; or state/provincial/federal license
Landscape Architect	Baccalaureate or Licenciatura Degree
Lawyer (including Notary in the Province of Quebec)	LL.B., J.D., LL.L., B.C.L. or Licenciatura Degree (five years); or membership in a state/provincial bar
Librarian	M.L.S. or B.L.S. (for which another Baccalaureate or Licenciatura Degree was a prerequisite)
Management Consultant	Baccalaureate or Licenciatura Degree; or equivalent professional experience as established by statement or professional credential attesting to five years experience as a management consultant, or five

(Continued)

PROFESSION[1]	MINIMUM EDUCATION REQUIREMENTS AND ALTERNATIVE CREDENTIALS
	years experience in a field of specialty related to the consulting agreement
Mathematician (including Statistician)	Baccalaureate or Licenciatura Degree
Range Manager/Range Conservationalist	Baccalaureate or Licenciatura Degree
Research Assistant (working in a post-secondary educational institution)	Baccalaureate or Licenciatura Degree
Scientific Technician/Technologist [5]	Possession of (a) theoretical knowledge of any of the following disciplines: agricultural sciences, astronomy, biology, chemistry, engineering, forestry, geology, geophysics, meteorology or physics; and (b) the ability to solve practical problems in any of those disciplines, or the ability to apply principles of any of those disciplines to basic or applied research
Social Worker	Baccalaureate or Licenciatura Degree
Sylviculturist (including Forestry Specialist)	Baccalaureate or Licenciatura Degree
Technical Publications Writer	Baccalaureate or Licenciatura Degree; or PostSecondary Dip-loma or PostSecondary Certificate, and three years experience
Urban Planner (including Geographer)	Baccalaureate or Licenciatura Degree
Vocational Counsellor	Baccalaureate or Licenciatura Degree
Medical/Allied Professional	
Dentist	D.D.S., D.M.D., Doctor en Odontologia or Doctor en Cirugia Dental; or state/provincial license
Dietitian	Baccalaureate or Licenciatura Degree; or state/provincial license
Medical Laboratory Technologist (Canada)/ Medical Technologist (Mexico and the United States) [6]	Baccalaureate or Licenciatura Degree; or Post-Secondary Diploma or Post-Secondary Certificate, and three years experience
Nutritionist	Baccalaureate or Licenciatura Degree
Occupational Therapist	Baccalaureate or Licenciatura Degree; or state/provincial license
Pharmacist	Baccalaureate or Licenciatura Degree; or state/provincial license
Physician (teaching or research only)	M.D. or Doctor en Medicina; or state/provincial license
Physiotherapist/Physical Therapist	Baccalaureate or Licenciatura Degree; or state/provincial license
Psychologist	State/provincial license; or Licenciatura Degree
Recreational Therapist	Baccalaureate or Licenciatura Degree
Registered Nurse	State/provincial license; or Licenciatura Degree
Veterinarian	D.V.M., D.M.V. or Doctor en Veterinaria; or state/provincial license
Scientist	
Agriculturist (including Agronomist)	Baccalaureate or Licenciatura Degree
Animal Breeder	Baccalaureate or Licenciatura Degree
Animal Scientist	Baccalaureate or Licenciatura Degree
Apiculturist	Baccalaureate or Licenciatura Degree
Astronomer	Baccalaureate or Licenciatura Degree

PROFESSION[1]	MINIMUM EDUCATION REQUIREMENTS AND ALTERNATIVE CREDENTIALS
Biochemist	Baccalaureate or Licenciatura Degree
Biologist	Baccalaureate or Licenciatura Degree
Chemist	Baccalaureate or Licenciatura Degree
Dairy Scientist	Baccalaureate or Licenciatura Degree
Entomologist	Baccalaureate or Licenciatura Degree
Epidemiologist	Baccalaureate or Licenciatura Degree
Geneticist	Baccalaureate or Licenciatura Degree
Geologist	Baccalaureate or Licenciatura Degree
Geochemist	Baccalaureate or Licenciatura Degree
Geophysicist (including Oceanographer in Mexico and the United States)	Baccalaureate or Licenciatura Degree
Horticulturist	Baccalaureate or Licenciatura Degree
Meteorologist	Baccalaureate or Licenciatura Degree
Pharmacologist	Baccalaureate or Licenciatura Degree
Physicist (including Oceanographer in Canada)	Baccalaureate or Licenciatura Degree
Plant Breeder	Baccalaureate or Licenciatura Degree
Poultry Scientist	Baccalaureate or Licenciatura Degree
Soil Scientist	Baccalaureate or Licenciatura Degree
Zoologist	Baccalaureate or Licenciatura Degree
Teacher	
College	Baccalaureate or Licenciatura Degree
Seminary	Baccalaureate or Licenciatura Degree
University	Baccalaureate or Licenciatura Degree

[1] A business person seeking temporary entry under this Appendix may also perform training functions relating to the profession, including conducting seminars.

[2] "State/provincial license" and "state/provincial/federal license" mean any document issued by a state, provincial or federal government, as the case may be, or under its authority, but not by a local government, that permits a person to engage in a regulated activity or profession.

[3] "Post-Secondary Diploma" means a credential issued, on completion of two or more years of postsecondary education, by an accredited academic institution in Canada or the United States.

[4] "Post-Secondary Certificate" means a certificate issued, on completion of two or more years of postsecondary education at an academic institution, by the federal government of Mexico or a state government in Mexico, an academic institution recognized by the federal government or a state government, or an academic institution created by federal or state law.

[5] A business person in this category must be seeking temporary entry to work in direct support of professionals in agricultural sciences, astronomy, biology, chemistry, engineering, forestry, geology, geophysics, meteorology or physics.

[6] A business person in this category must be seeking temporary entry to perform in a laboratory chemical, biological, hematological, immunologic, microscopic or bacteriological tests and analyses for diagnosis, treatment or prevention of disease.

APPENDIX 1603.D.4. UNITED STATES

1. Beginning on the date of entry into force of this Agreement as between the United States and Mexico, the United States shall annually approve as many as 5,500 initial petitions of business persons of Mexico seeking temporary entry under Section D of Annex 1603 to engage in a business activity at a professional level in a profession set out in Appendix 1603.D.1.

2. For purposes of paragraph 1, the United States shall not take into account:
   (a) the renewal of a period of temporary entry;
   (b) the entry of a spouse or children accompanying or following to join the principal business person;
   (c) an admission under section 101(a)(15)(H)(i)(b) of the *Immigration and Nationality Act, 1952* , as may be amended, including the worldwide numerical limit established by section 214(g)(1)(A) of that Act; or
   (d) an admission under any other provision of section 101(a)(15) of that Act relating to the entry of professionals.

3. Paragraphs 4 and 5 of Section D of Annex 1603 shall apply as between the United States and Mexico for no longer than:
   (a) the period that such paragraphs or similar provisions may apply as between the United States and any other Party other than Canada or any non Party; or
   (b) 10 years after the date of entry into force of this Agreement as between such Parties, whichever period is shorter.

ANNEX 1604.2. PROVISION OF INFORMATION

The obligations under Article 1604(2) shall take effect with respect to Mexico one year after the date of entry into force of this Agreement.

ANNEX 1608. COUNTRY SPECIFIC DEFINITIONS

For purposes of this Chapter:

citizen means, with respect to Mexico, a national or a citizen according to the existing provisions of Articles 30 and 34, respectively, of the Mexican Constitution; and

existing means, as between:

   (a) Canada and Mexico, and Mexico and the United States, in effect on the date of entry into force of this Agreement; and
   (b) Canada and the United States, in effect on January 1, 1989.

PART SIX: INTELLECTUAL PROPERTY

17. INTELLECTUAL PROPERTY

Article 1701: Nature and Scope of Obligations

1. Each Party shall provide in its territory to the nationals of another Party adequate and effective protection and enforcement of intellectual property rights, while ensuring that measures to enforce intellectual property rights do not themselves become barriers to legitimate trade.

2. To provide adequate and effective protection and enforcement of intellectual property rights, each Party shall, at a minimum, give effect to this Chapter and to the substantive provisions of:

    (a) the *Geneva Convention for the Protection of Producers of Phonograms Against Unauthorized Duplication of their Phonograms* , 1971 (Geneva Convention);

    (b) the *Berne Convention for the Protection of Literary and Artistic Works* , 1971 (Berne Convention);

    (c) the *Paris Convention for the Protection of Industrial Property* , 1967 (Paris Convention); and

    (d) the *International Convention for the Protection of New Varieties of Plants*, 1978 (UPOV Convention), or the *International Convention for the Protection of New Varieties of Plants*, 1991 (UPOV Convention).

    If a Party has not acceded to the specified text of any such Conventions on or before the date of entry into force of this Agreement, it shall make every effort to accede.

3. Annex 1701.3 applies to the Parties specified in that Annex.

Article 1702: More Extensive Protection

A Party may implement in its domestic law more extensive protection of intellectual property rights than is required under this Agreement, provided that such protection is not inconsistent with this Agreement.

Article 1703: National Treatment

1. Each Party shall accord to nationals of another Party treatment no less favorable than that it accords to its own nationals with regard to the protection and enforcement of all intellectual property rights. In respect of sound recordings, each Party shall provide such treatment to producers and performers of another Party, except that a Party may limit rights of performers of another Party in respect of secondary uses of sound recordings to those rights its nationals are accorded in the territory of such other Party.

2. No Party may, as a condition of according national treatment under this Article, require right holders to comply with any formalities or conditions in order to acquire rights in respect of copyright and related rights.

3. A Party may derogate from paragraph 1 in relation to its judicial and administrative procedures for the protection or enforcement of intellectual property rights, including any procedure requiring a national of another Party to designate for service of process an address in the Party's territory or to appoint an agent in the Party's territory, if the derogation is consistent with the relevant Convention listed in Article 1701(2), provided that such derogation:

   (a) is necessary to secure compliance with measures that are not inconsistent with this Chapter; and

   (b) is not applied in a manner that would constitute a disguised restriction on trade.

4. No Party shall have any obligation under this Article with respect to procedures provided in multilateral agreements concluded under the auspices of the World Intellectual Property Organization relating to the acquisition or maintenance of intellectual property rights.

Article 1704: Control of Abusive or Anticompetitive Practices or Conditions

Nothing in this Chapter shall prevent a Party from specifying in its domestic law licensing practices or conditions that may in particular cases constitute an abuse of intellectual property rights having an adverse effect on competition in the relevant market. A Party may adopt or maintain, consistent with the other provisions of this Agreement, appropriate measures to prevent or control such practices or conditions.

Article 1705: Copyright

1. Each Party shall protect the works covered by Article 2 of the Berne Convention, including any other works that embody original expression within the meaning of that Convention. In particular:

   (a) all types of computer programs are literary works within the meaning of the Berne Convention and each Party shall protect them as such; and

   (b) compilations of data or other material, whether in machine readable or other form, which by reason of the selection or arrangement of their contents constitute intellectual creations, shall be protected as such.

   The protection a Party provides under subparagraph (b) shall not extend to the data or material itself, or prejudice any copyright subsisting in that data or material.

2. Each Party shall provide to authors and their successors in interest those rights enumerated in the Berne Convention in respect of works covered by paragraph 1, including the right to authorize or prohibit:

   (a) the importation into the Party's territory of copies of the work made without the right holder's authorization;

(b) the first public distribution of the original and each copy of the work by sale, rental or otherwise;

(c) the communication of a work to the public; and

(d) the commercial rental of the original or a copy of a computer program.
Subparagraph (d) shall not apply where the copy of the computer program is not itself an essential object of the rental. Each Party shall provide that putting the original or a copy of a computer program on the market with the right holder's consent shall not exhaust the rental right.

3. Each Party shall provide that for copyright and related rights:

(a) any person acquiring or holding economic rights may freely and separately transfer such rights by contract for purposes of their exploitation and enjoyment by the transferee; and

(b) any person acquiring or holding such economic rights by virtue of a contract, including contracts of employment underlying the creation of works and sound recordings, shall be able to exercise those rights in its own name and enjoy fully the benefits derived from those rights.

4. Each Party shall provide that, where the term of protection of a work, other than a photographic work or a work of applied art, is to be calculated on a basis other than the life of a natural person, the term shall be not less than 50 years from the end of the calendar year of the first authorized publication of the work or, failing such authorized publication within 50 years from the making of the work, 50 years from the end of the calendar year of making.

5. Each Party shall confine limitations or exceptions to the rights provided for in this Article to certain special cases that do not conflict with a normal exploitation of the work and do not unreasonably prejudice the legitimate interests of the right holder.

6. No Party may grant translation and reproduction licenses permitted under the Appendix to the Berne Convention where legitimate needs in that Party's territory for copies or translations of the work could be met by the right holder's voluntary actions but for obstacles created by the Party's measures.

7. Annex 1705.7 applies to the Parties specified in that Annex.

Article 1706: Sound Recordings

1. Each Party shall provide to the producer of a sound recording the right to authorize or prohibit:

(a) the direct or indirect reproduction of the sound recording;

(b) the importation into the Party's territory of copies of the sound recording made without the producer's authorization;

(c) the first public distribution of the original and each copy of the sound recording by sale, rental or otherwise; and

(d) the commercial rental of the original or a copy of the sound recording, except where expressly otherwise provided in a contract between the producer of the sound recording and the authors of the works fixed therein.

Each Party shall provide that putting the original or a copy of a sound recording on the market with the right holder's consent shall not exhaust the rental right.

2. Each Party shall provide a term of protection for sound recordings of at least 50 years from the end of the calendar year in which the fixation was made.

3. Each Party shall confine limitations or exceptions to the rights provided for in this Article to certain special cases that do not conflict with a normal exploitation of the sound recording and do not unreasonably prejudice the legitimate interests of the right holder.

Article 1707: Protection of Encrypted ProgramCarrying Satellite Signals

Within one year from the date of entry into force of this Agreement, each Party shall make it:

(a) a criminal offense to manufacture, import, sell, lease or otherwise make available a device or system that is primarily of assistance in decoding an encrypted program carrying satellite signal without the authorization of the lawful distributor of such signal; and

(b) a civil offense to receive, in connection with commercial activities, or further distribute, an encrypted program carrying satellite signal that has been decoded without the authorization of the lawful distributor of the signal or to engage in any activity prohibited under subparagraph (a).

Each Party shall provide that any civil offense established under subparagraph (b) shall be actionable by any person that holds an interest in the content of such signal.

Article 1708: Trademarks

1. For purposes of this Agreement, a trademark consists of any sign, or any combination of signs, capable of distinguishing the goods or services of one person from those of another, including personal names, designs, letters, numerals, colors, figurative elements, or the shape of goods or of their packaging. Trademarks shall include service marks and collective marks, and may include certification marks. A Party may require, as a condition for registration, that a sign be visually perceptible.

2. Each Party shall provide to the owner of a registered trademark the right to prevent all persons not having the owner's consent from using in commerce identical or similar signs for goods or services that are identical or similar to those goods or services in respect of which the owner's trademark is registered, where such use would result in a likelihood of confusion. In the case of the use of an identical sign for identical goods or services, a likelihood of confusion shall be presumed. The rights described above shall not prejudice any prior rights, nor shall they affect the possibility of a Party making rights available on the basis of use.

3. A Party may make registrability depend on use. However, actual use of a trademark shall not be a condition for filing an application for registration. No Party may refuse an application solely on the ground that intended use has not taken place before the expiry of a period of three years from the date of application for registration.

4. Each Party shall provide a system for the registration of trademarks, which shall include:

    (a) examination of applications;
    (b) notice to be given to an applicant of the reasons for the refusal to register a trademark;
    (c) a reasonable opportunity for the applicant to respond to the notice;
    (d) publication of each trademark either before or promptly after it is registered; and
    (e) a reasonable opportunity for interested persons to petition to cancel the registration of a trademark.

    A Party may provide for a reasonable opportunity for interested persons to oppose the registration of a trademark.

5. The nature of the goods or services to which a trademark is to be applied shall in no case form an obstacle to the registration of the trademark.

6. Article 6bis of the Paris Convention shall apply, with such modifications as may be necessary, to services. In determining whether a trademark is wellknown, account shall be taken of the knowledge of the trademark in the relevant sector of the public, including knowledge in the Party's territory obtained as a result of the promotion of the trademark. No Party may require that the reputation of the trademark extend beyond the sector of the public that normally deals with the relevant goods or services.

7. Each Party shall provide that the initial registration of a trademark be for a term of at least 10 years and that the registration be indefinitely renewable for terms of not less than 10 years when conditions for renewal have been met.

8. Each Party shall require the use of a trademark to maintain a registration. The registration may be canceled for the reason of non-use only after an uninterrupted period of at least two years of non-use, unless valid reasons based on the existence of obstacles to such use are shown by the trademark owner. Each Party shall recognize, as valid reasons for non- use, circumstances arising independently of the will of the trademark owner that constitute an obstacle to the use of the trademark, such as import restrictions on, or other government requirements for, goods or services identified by the trademark.

9. Each Party shall recognize use of a trademark by a person other than the trademark owner, where such use is subject to the owner's control, as use of the trademark for purposes of maintaining the registration.

10. No Party may encumber the use of a trademark in commerce by special requirements, such as a use that reduces the trademark's function as an indication of source or a use with another trademark.

11. A Party may determine conditions on the licensing and assignment of trademarks, it being understood that the compulsory licensing of trademarks shall not be permitted and that the owner of a registered trademark shall have the right to assign its trademark with or without the transfer of the business to which the trademark belongs.

12. A Party may provide limited exceptions to the rights conferred by a trademark, such as fair use of descriptive terms, provided that such exceptions take into account the legitimate interests of the trademark owner and of other persons.

13. Each Party shall prohibit the registration as a trademark of words, at least in English, French or Spanish, that generically designate goods or services or types of goods or services to which the trademark applies.

14. Each Party shall refuse to register trademarks that consist of or comprise immoral, deceptive or scandalous matter, or matter that may disparage or falsely suggest a connection with persons, living or dead, institutions, beliefs or any Party's national symbols, or bring them into contempt or disrepute.

Article 1709: Patents

1. Subject to paragraphs 2 and 3, each Party shall make patents available for any inventions, whether products or processes, in all fields of technology, provided that such inventions are new, result from an inventive step and are capable of industrial application. For purposes of this Article, a Party may deem the terms "inventive step" and "capable of industrial application" to be synonymous with the terms "non-obvious" and "useful", respectively.

2. A Party may exclude from patentability inventions if preventing in its territory the commercial exploitation of the inventions is necessary to protect ordre public or morality, including to protect human, animal or plant life or health or to avoid serious prejudice to nature or the environment, provided that the exclusion is not based solely on the ground that the Party prohibits commercial exploitation in its territory of the subject matter of the patent.

3. A Party may also exclude from patentability:
   (a) diagnostic, therapeutic and surgical methods for the treatment of humans or animals;
   (b) plants and animals other than microorganisms; and
   (c) essentially biological processes for the production of plants or animals, other than non-biological and microbiological processes for such production.
   Notwithstanding subparagraph (b), each Party shall provide for the protection of plant varieties through patents, an effective scheme of *sui generis* protection, or both.

4. If a Party has not made available product patent protection for pharmaceutical or agricultural chemicals commensurate with paragraph 1:
   (a) as of January 1, 1992, for subject matter that relates to naturally occurring substances prepared or produced by, or significantly derived from, microbiological processes and intended for food or medicine, and
   (b) as of July 1, 1991, for any other subject matter,
   that Party shall provide to the inventor of any such product or its assignee the means to obtain product patent protection for such product for the unexpired term of the patent for such product granted in another Party, as long as the product has not been marketed in the Party providing protection under this paragraph and the person seeking such protection makes a timely request.

5. Each Party shall provide that:
   (a) where the subject matter of a patent is a product, the patent shall confer on the patent owner the right to prevent other persons from making, using or selling the subject matter of the patent, without the patent owner's consent; and
   (b) where the subject matter of a patent is a process, the patent shall confer on the patent owner the right to prevent other persons from using that process and from using, selling, or importing at least the product obtained directly by that process, without the patent owner's consent.

6. A Party may provide limited exceptions to the exclusive rights conferred by a patent, provided that such exceptions do not unreasonably conflict with a normal exploitation of the patent and do not unreasonably prejudice the legitimate interests of the patent owner, taking into account the legitimate interests of other persons.

7. Subject to paragraphs 2 and 3, patents shall be available and patent rights enjoyable without discrimination as to the field of technology, the territory of the Party where the invention was made and whether products are imported or locally produced.

8. A Party may revoke a patent only when:
   (a) grounds exist that would have justified a refusal to grant the patent; or
   (b) the grant of a compulsory license has not remedied the lack of exploitation of the patent.

9. Each Party shall permit patent owners to assign and transfer by succession their patents, and to conclude licensing contracts.

10. Where the law of a Party allows for use of the subject matter of a patent, other than that use allowed under paragraph 6, without the authorization of the right holder, including use by the government or other persons authorized by the government, the Party shall respect the following provisions:
    (a) authorization of such use shall be considered on its individual merits;
    (b) such use may only be permitted if, prior to such use, the proposed user has made efforts to obtain authorization from the right holder on reasonable commercial terms and conditions and such efforts have not been successful within a reasonable period of time. The requirement to make such efforts may be waived by a Party in the case of a national emergency or other circumstances of extreme urgency or in cases of public non-commercial use. In situations of national emergency or other circumstances of extreme urgency, the right holder shall, nevertheless, be notified as soon as reasonably practicable. In the case of public non-commercial use, where the government or contractor, without making a patent search, knows or has demonstrable grounds to know that a valid patent is or will be used by or for the government, the right holder shall be informed promptly;
    (c) the scope and duration of such use shall be limited to the purpose for which it was authorized;
    (d) such use shall be non-exclusive;
    (e) such use shall be non-assignable, except with that part of the enterprise or goodwill that enjoys such use;
    (f) any such use shall be authorized predominantly for the supply of the Party's domestic market;

(g) authorization for such use shall be liable, subject to adequate protection of the legitimate interests of the persons so authorized, to be terminated if and when the circumstances that led to it cease to exist and are unlikely to recur. The competent authority shall have the authority to review, on motivated request, the continued existence of these circumstances;

(h) the right holder shall be paid adequate remuneration in the circumstances of each case, taking into account the economic value of the authorization;

(i) the legal validity of any decision relating to the authorization shall be subject to judicial or other independent review by a distinct higher authority;

(j) any decision relating to the remuneration provided in respect of such use shall be subject to judicial or other independent review by a distinct higher authority;

(k) the Party shall not be obliged to apply the conditions set out in subparagraphs (b) and (f) where such use is permitted to remedy a practice determined after judicial or administrative process to be anticompetitive. The need to correct anticompetitive practices may be taken into account in determining the amount of remuneration in such cases. Competent authorities shall have the authority to refuse termination of authorization if and when the conditions that led to such authorization are likely to recur;

(l) the Party shall not authorize the use of the subject matter of a patent to permit the exploitation of another patent except as a remedy for an adjudicated violation of domestic laws regarding anticompetitive practices.

11. Where the subject matter of a patent is a process for obtaining a product, each Party shall, in any infringement proceeding, place on the defendant the burden of establishing that the allegedly infringing product was made by a process other than the patented process in one of the following situations:

(a) the product obtained by the patented process is new; or

(b) a substantial likelihood exists that the allegedly infringing product was made by the process and the patent owner has been unable through reasonable efforts to determine the process actually used.

In the gathering and evaluation of evidence, the legitimate interests of the defendant in protecting its trade secrets shall be taken into account.

12. Each Party shall provide a term of protection for patents of at least 20 years from the date of filing or 17 years from the date of grant. A Party may extend the term of patent protection, in appropriate cases, to compensate for delays caused by regulatory approval processes.

Article 1710: Layout Designs of Semiconductor Integrated Circuits

1. Each Party shall protect layout designs (topographies) of integrated circuits ("layout designs") in accordance with Articles 2 through 7, 12 and 16(3), other than Article 6(3), of the *Treaty on Intellectual Property in Respect of Integrated Circuits* as opened for signature on May 26, 1989.

2. Subject to paragraph 3, each Party shall make it unlawful for any person without the right holder's authorization to import, sell or otherwise distribute for commercial purposes any of the following:
   (a) a protected layout design;
   (b) an integrated circuit in which a protected layout design is incorporated; or
   (c) an article incorporating such an integrated circuit, only insofar as it continues to contain an unlawfully reproduced layout design.

3. No Party may make unlawful any of the acts referred to in paragraph 2 performed in respect of an integrated circuit that incorporates an unlawfully reproduced layout design, or any article that incorporates such an integrated circuit, where the person performing those acts or ordering those acts to be done did not know and had no reasonable ground to know, when it acquired the integrated circuit or article incorporating such an integrated circuit, that it incorporated an unlawfully reproduced layout design.

4. Each Party shall provide that, after the person referred to in paragraph 3 has received sufficient notice that the layout design was unlawfully reproduced, such person may perform any of the acts with respect to the stock on hand or ordered before such notice, but shall be liable to pay the right holder for doing so an amount equivalent to a reasonable royalty such as would be payable under a freely negotiated license in respect of such a layout design.

5. No Party may permit the compulsory licensing of layout designs of integrated circuits.

6. Any Party that requires registration as a condition for protection of a layout design shall provide that the term of protection shall not end before the expiration of a period of 10 years counted from the date of:
   (a) filing of the application for registration; or
   (b) the first commercial exploitation of the layout design, wherever in the world it occurs.

7. Where a Party does not require registration as a condition for protection of a layout design, the Party shall provide a term of protection of not less than 10 years from the date of the first commercial exploitation of the layout design, wherever in the world it occurs.

8. Notwithstanding paragraphs 6 and 7, a Party may provide that the protection shall lapse 15 years after the creation of the layout design.

9. Annex 1710.9 applies to the Parties specified in that Annex.

Article 1711: Trade Secrets

1. Each Party shall provide the legal means for any person to prevent trade secrets from being disclosed to, acquired by, or used by others without the consent of the person lawfully in control of the information in a manner contrary to honest commercial practices, in so far as:
   (a) the information is secret in the sense that it is not, as a body or in the precise configuration and assembly of its components, generally known among or

readily accessible to persons that normally deal with the kind of information in question;

(b) the information has actual or potential commercial value because it is secret; and

(c) the person lawfully in control of the information has taken reasonable steps under the circumstances to keep it secret.

2. A Party may require that to qualify for protection a trade secret must be evidenced in documents, electronic or magnetic means, optical discs, microfilms, films or other similar instruments.

3. No Party may limit the duration of protection for trade secrets, so long as the conditions in paragraph 1 exist.

4. No Party may discourage or impede the voluntary licensing of trade secrets by imposing excessive or discriminatory conditions on such licenses or conditions that dilute the value of the trade secrets.

5. If a Party requires, as a condition for approving the marketing of pharmaceutical or agricultural chemical products that utilize new chemical entities, the submission of undisclosed test or other data necessary to determine whether the use of such products is safe and effective, the Party shall protect against disclosure of the data of persons making such submissions, where the origination of such data involves considerable effort, except where the disclosure is necessary to protect the public or unless steps are taken to ensure that the data is protected against unfair commercial use.

6. Each Party shall provide that for data subject to paragraph 5 that are submitted to the Party after the date of entry into force of this Agreement, no person other than the person that submitted them may, without the latter's permission, rely on such data in support of an application for product approval during a reasonable period of time after their submission. For this purpose, a reasonable period shall normally mean not less than five years from the date on which the Party granted approval to the person that produced the data for approval to market its product, taking account of the nature of the data and the person's efforts and expenditures in producing them. Subject to this provision, there shall be no limitation on any Party to implement abbreviated approval procedures for such products on the basis of bioequivalence and bioavailability studies.

7. Where a Party relies on a marketing approval granted by another Party, the reasonable period of exclusive use of the data submitted in connection with obtaining the approval relied on shall begin with the date of the first marketing approval relied on.

Article 1712: Geographical Indications

1. Each Party shall provide, in respect of geographical indications, the legal means for interested persons to prevent:

(a) the use of any means in the designation or presentation of a good that indicates or suggests that the good in question originates in a territory, region or locality other than the true place of origin, in a manner that misleads the public as to the geographical origin of the good;

    (b) any use that constitutes an act of unfair competition within the meaning of Article 10bis of the Paris Convention.

2.   Each Party shall, on its own initiative if its domestic law so permits or at the request of an interested person, refuse to register, or invalidate the registration of, a trademark containing or consisting of a geographical indication with respect to goods that do not originate in the indicated territory, region or locality, if use of the indication in the trademark for such goods is of such a nature as to mislead the public as to the geographical origin of the good.

3.   Each Party shall also apply paragraphs 1 and 2 to a geographical indication that, although correctly indicating the territory, region or locality in which the goods originate, falsely represents to the public that the goods originate in another territory, region or locality.

4.   Nothing in this Article shall be construed to require a Party to prevent continued and similar use of a particular geographical indication of another Party in connection with goods or services by any of its nationals or domiciliaries who have used that geographical indication in a continuous manner with regard to the same or related goods or services in that Party's territory, either:

    (a) for at least 10 years, or

    (b) in good faith,

before the date of signature of this Agreement.

5.   Where a trademark has been applied for or registered in good faith, or where rights to a trademark have been acquired through use in good faith, either:

    (a) before the date of application of these provisions in that Party, or

    (b) before the geographical indication is protected in its Party of origin,

no Party may adopt any measure to implement this Article that prejudices eligibility for, or the validity of, the registration of a trademark, or the right to use a trademark, on the basis that such a trademark is identical with, or similar to, a geographical indication.

6.   No Party shall be required to apply this Article to a geographical indication if it is identical to the customary term in common language in that Party's territory for the goods or services to which the indication applies.

7.   A Party may provide that any request made under this Article in connection with the use or registration of a trademark must be presented within five years after the adverse use of the protected indication has become generally known in that Party or after the date of registration of the trademark in that Party, provided that the trademark has been published by that date, if such date is earlier than the date on which the adverse use became generally known in that Party, provided that the geographical indication is not used or registered in bad faith.

8.   No Party shall adopt any measure implementing this Article that would prejudice any person's right to use, in the course of trade, its name or the name of its predecessor in business, except where such name forms all or part of a valid trademark in existence before the geographical indication became protected and with which there is a likelihood of confusion, or such name is used in such a manner as to mislead the public.

9. Nothing in this Chapter shall be construed to require a Party to protect a geographical indication that is not protected, or has fallen into disuse, in the Party of origin.

Article 1713: Industrial Designs

1. Each Party shall provide for the protection of independently created industrial designs that are new or original. A Party may provide that:
    (a) designs are not new or original if they do not significantly differ from known designs or combinations of known design features; and
    (b) such protection shall not extend to designs dictated essentially by technical or functional considerations.
2. Each Party shall ensure that the requirements for securing protection for textile designs, in particular in regard to any cost, examination or publication, do not unreasonably impair a person's opportunity to seek and obtain such protection. A Party may comply with this obligation through industrial design law or copyright law.
3. Each Party shall provide the owner of a protected industrial design the right to prevent other persons not having the owner's consent from making or selling articles bearing or embodying a design that is a copy, or substantially a copy, of the protected design, when such acts are undertaken for commercial purposes.
4. A Party may provide limited exceptions to the protection of industrial designs, provided that such exceptions do not unreasonably conflict with the normal exploitation of protected industrial designs and do not unreasonably prejudice the legitimate interests of the owner of the protected design, taking into account the legitimate interests of other persons.
5. Each Party shall provide a term of protection for industrial designs of at least 10 years.

Article 1714: Enforcement of Intellectual Property Rights: General Provisions

1. Each Party shall ensure that enforcement procedures, as specified in this Article and Articles 1715 through 1718, are available under its domestic law so as to permit effective action to be taken against any act of infringement of intellectual property rights covered by this Chapter, including expeditious remedies to prevent infringements and remedies to deter further infringements. Such enforcement procedures shall be applied so as to avoid the creation of barriers to legitimate trade and to provide for safeguards against abuse of the procedures.
2. Each Party shall ensure that its procedures for the enforcement of intellectual property rights are fair and equitable, are not unnecessarily complicated or costly, and do not entail unreasonable timelimits or unwarranted delays.
3. Each Party shall provide that decisions on the merits of a case in judicial and administrative enforcement proceedings shall:

(a) preferably be in writing and preferably state the reasons on which the decisions are based;

(b) be made available at least to the parties in a proceeding without undue delay; and

(c) be based only on evidence in respect of which such parties were offered the opportunity to be heard.

4. Each Party shall ensure that parties in a proceeding have an opportunity to have final administrative decisions reviewed by a judicial authority of that Party and, subject to jurisdictional provisions in its domestic laws concerning the importance of a case, to have reviewed at least the legal aspects of initial judicial decisions on the merits of a case. Notwithstanding the above, no Party shall be required to provide for judicial review of acquittals in criminal cases.

5. Nothing in this Article or Articles 1715 through 1718 shall be construed to require a Party to establish a judicial system for the enforcement of intellectual property rights distinct from that Party's system for the enforcement of laws in general.

6. For the purposes of Articles 1715 through 1718, the term "right holder" includes federations and associations having legal standing to assert such rights.

Article 1715: Specific Procedural and Remedial Aspects of Civil and Administrative Procedures

1. Each Party shall make available to right holders civil judicial procedures for the enforcement of any intellectual property right provided in this Chapter. Each Party shall provide that:

(a) defendants have the right to written notice that is timely and contains sufficient detail, including the basis of the claims;

(b) parties in a proceeding are allowed to be represented by independent legal counsel;

(c) the procedures do not include imposition of overly burdensome requirements concerning mandatory personal appearances;

(d) all parties in a proceeding are duly entitled to substantiate their claims and to present relevant evidence; and

(e) the procedures include a means to identify and protect confidential information.

2. Each Party shall provide that its judicial authorities shall have the authority:

(a) where a party in a proceeding has presented reasonably available evidence sufficient to support its claims and has specified evidence relevant to the substantiation of its claims that is within the control of the opposing party, to order the opposing party to produce such evidence, subject in appropriate cases to conditions that ensure the protection of confidential information;

(b) where a party in a proceeding voluntarily and without good reason refuses access to, or otherwise does not provide relevant evidence under that party's control within a reasonable period, or significantly impedes a proceeding relating to an enforcement action, to make preliminary and final determinations, affirmative or negative, on the basis of the evidence presented, including the complaint or the allegation presented by the party adversely affected by the denial of access to evidence, subject to providing the parties an opportunity to be heard on the allegations or evidence;

(c) to order a party in a proceeding to desist from an infringement, including to prevent the entry into the channels of commerce in their jurisdiction of imported goods that involve the infringement of an intellectual property right, which order shall be enforceable at least immediately after customs clearance of such goods;

(d) to order the infringer of an intellectual property right to pay the right holder damages adequate to compensate for the injury the right holder has suffered because of the infringement where the infringer knew or had reasonable grounds to know that it was engaged in an infringing activity;

(e) to order an infringer of an intellectual property right to pay the right holder's expenses, which may include appropriate attorney's fees; and

(f) to order a party in a proceeding at whose request measures were taken and who has abused enforcement procedures to provide adequate compensation to any party wrongfully enjoined or restrained in the proceeding for the injury suffered because of such abuse and to pay that party's expenses, which may include appropriate attorney's fees.

3. With respect to the authority referred to in subparagraph 2(c), no Party shall be obliged to provide such authority in respect of protected subject matter that is acquired or ordered by a person before that person knew or had reasonable grounds to know that dealing in that subject matter would entail the infringement of an intellectual property right.

4. With respect to the authority referred to in subparagraph 2(d), a Party may, at least with respect to copyrighted works and sound recordings, authorize the judicial authorities to order recovery of profits or payment of pre-established damages, or both, even where the infringer did not know or had no reasonable grounds to know that it was engaged in an infringing activity.

5. Each Party shall provide that, in order to create an effective deterrent to infringement, its judicial authorities shall have the authority to order that:

(a) goods that they have found to be infringing be, without compensation of any sort, disposed of outside the channels of commerce in such a manner as to avoid any injury caused to the right holder or, unless this would be contrary to existing constitutional requirements, destroyed; and

(b) materials and implements the predominant use of which has been in the creation of the infringing goods be, without compensation of any sort, disposed of outside the channels of commerce in such a manner as to minimize the risks of further infringements.

In considering whether to issue such an order, judicial authorities shall take into account the need for proportionality between the seriousness of the infringement and the remedies ordered as well as the interests of other persons. In regard to counterfeit goods, the simple removal of the trademark unlawfully affixed shall not be sufficient, other than in exceptional cases, to permit release of the goods into the channels of commerce.

6. In respect of the administration of any law pertaining to the protection or enforcement of intellectual property rights, each Party shall only exempt both public authorities and officials from liability to appropriate remedial measures where

actions are taken or intended in good faith in the course of the administration of such laws.

7. Notwithstanding the other provisions of Articles 1714 through 1718, where a Party is sued with respect to an infringement of an intellectual property right as a result of its use of that right or use on its behalf, that Party may limit the remedies available against it to the payment to the right holder of adequate remuneration in the circumstances of each case, taking into account the economic value of the use.

8. Each Party shall provide that, where a civil remedy can be ordered as a result of administrative procedures on the merits of a case, such procedures shall conform to principles equivalent in substance to those set out in this Article.

Article 1716: Provisional Measures

1. Each Party shall provide that its judicial authorities shall have the authority to order prompt and effective provisional measures:
    (a) to prevent an infringement of any intellectual property right, and in particular to prevent the entry into the channels of commerce in their jurisdiction of allegedly infringing goods, including measures to prevent the entry of imported goods at least immediately after customs clearance; and
    (b) to preserve relevant evidence in regard to the alleged infringement.

2. Each Party shall provide that its judicial authorities shall have the authority to require any applicant for provisional measures to provide to the judicial authorities any evidence reasonably available to that applicant that the judicial authorities consider necessary to enable them to determine with a sufficient degree of certainty whether:
    (a) the applicant is the right holder;
    (b) the applicant's right is being infringed or such infringement is imminent; and
    (c) any delay in the issuance of such measures is likely to cause irreparable harm to the right holder, or there is a demonstrable risk of evidence being destroyed.

    Each Party shall provide that its judicial authorities shall have the authority to require the applicant to provide a security or equivalent assurance sufficient to protect the interests of the defendant and to prevent abuse.

3. Each Party shall provide that its judicial authorities shall have the authority to require an applicant for provisional measures to provide other information necessary for the identification of the relevant goods by the authority that will execute the provisional measures.

4. Each Party shall provide that its judicial authorities shall have the authority to order provisional measures on an *ex parte basis* , in particular where any delay is likely to cause irreparable harm to the right holder, or where there is a demonstrable risk of evidence being destroyed.

5. Each Party shall provide that where provisional measures are adopted by that Party's judicial authorities on an *ex parte basis* :
    (a) a person affected shall be given notice of those measures without delay but in any event no later than immediately after the execution of the measures;

(b) a defendant shall, on request, have those measures reviewed by that Party's judicial authorities for the purpose of deciding, within a reasonable period after notice of those measures is given, whether the measures shall be modified, revoked or confirmed, and shall be given an opportunity to be heard in the review proceedings.

6. Without prejudice to paragraph 5, each Party shall provide that, on the request of the defendant, the Party's judicial authorities shall revoke or otherwise cease to apply the provisional measures taken on the basis of paragraphs 1 and 4 if proceedings leading to a decision on the merits are not initiated:

(a) within a reasonable period as determined by the judicial authority ordering the measures where the Party's domestic law so permits; or

(b) in the absence of such a determination, within a period of no more than 20 working days or 31 calendar days, whichever is longer.

7. Each Party shall provide that, where the provisional measures are revoked or where they lapse due to any act or omission by the applicant, or where the judicial authorities subsequently find that there has been no infringement or threat of infringement of an intellectual property right, the judicial authorities shall have the authority to order the applicant, on request of the defendant, to provide the defendant appropriate compensation for any injury caused by these measures.

8. Each Party shall provide that, where a provisional measure can be ordered as a result of administrative procedures, such procedures shall conform to principles equivalent in substance to those set out in this Article.

Article 1717: Criminal Procedures and Penalties

1. Each Party shall provide criminal procedures and penalties to be applied at least in cases of willful trademark counterfeiting or copyright piracy on a commercial scale. Each Party shall provide that penalties available include imprisonment or monetary fines, or both, sufficient to provide a deterrent, consistent with the level of penalties applied for crimes of a corresponding gravity.

2. Each Party shall provide that, in appropriate cases, its judicial authorities may order the seizure, forfeiture and destruction of infringing goods and of any materials and implements the predominant use of which has been in the commission of the offense.

3. A Party may provide criminal procedures and penalties to be applied in cases of infringement of intellectual property rights, other than those in paragraph 1, where they are committed wilfully and on a commercial scale.

Article 1718: Enforcement of Intellectual Property Rights at the Border

1. Each Party shall, in conformity with this Article, adopt procedures to enable a right holder, who has valid grounds for suspecting that the importation of counterfeit trademark goods or pirated copyright goods may take place, to lodge an application in writing with its competent authorities, whether administrative or judicial, for the

suspension by the customs administration of the release of such goods into free circulation. No Party shall be obligated to apply such procedures to goods in transit. A Party may permit such an application to be made in respect of goods that involve other infringements of intellectual property rights, provided that the requirements of this Article are met. A Party may also provide for corresponding procedures concerning the suspension by the customs administration of the release of infringing goods destined for exportation from its territory.

2. Each Party shall require any applicant who initiates procedures under paragraph 1 to provide adequate evidence:

    (a) to satisfy that Party's competent authorities that, under the domestic laws of the country of importation, there is *prima facie* an infringement of its intellectual property right; and

    (b) to supply a sufficiently detailed description of the goods to make them readily recognizable by the customs administration.

    The competent authorities shall inform the applicant within a reasonable period whether they have accepted the application and, if so, the period for which the customs administration will take action.

3. Each Party shall provide that its competent authorities shall have the authority to require an applicant under paragraph 1 to provide a security or equivalent assurance sufficient to protect the defendant and the competent authorities and to prevent abuse. Such security or equivalent assurance shall not unreasonably deter recourse to these procedures.

4. Each Party shall provide that, where pursuant to an application under procedures adopted pursuant to this Article, its customs administration suspends the release of goods involving industrial designs, patents, integrated circuits or trade secrets into free circulation on the basis of a decision other than by a judicial or other independent authority, and the period provided for in paragraphs 6 through 8 has expired without the granting of provisional relief by the duly empowered authority, and provided that all other conditions for importation have been complied with, the owner, importer or consignee of such goods shall be entitled to their release on the posting of a security in an amount sufficient to protect the right holder against any infringement. Payment of such security shall not prejudice any other remedy available to the right holder, it being understood that the security shall be released if the right holder fails to pursue its right of action within a reasonable period of time.

5. Each Party shall provide that its customs administration shall promptly notify the importer and the applicant when the customs administration suspends the release of goods pursuant to paragraph 1.

6. Each Party shall provide that its customs administration shall release goods from suspension if within a period not exceeding 10 working days after the applicant under paragraph 1 has been served notice of the suspension the customs administration has not been informed that:

    (a) a party other than the defendant has initiated proceedings leading to a decision on the merits of the case, or

    (b) a competent authority has taken provisional measures prolonging the suspension, provided that all other conditions for importation or exportation have been met. Each Party shall provide that, in appropriate cases, the customs administration may extend the suspension by another 10 working days.

7. Each Party shall provide that if proceedings leading to a decision on the merits of the case have been initiated, a review, including a right to be heard, shall take place on request of the defendant with a view to deciding, within a reasonable period, whether these measures shall be modified, revoked or confirmed.

8. Notwithstanding paragraphs 6 and 7, where the suspension of the release of goods is carried out or continued in accordance with a provisional judicial measure, Article 1716(6) shall apply.

9. Each Party shall provide that its competent authorities shall have the authority to order the applicant under paragraph 1 to pay the importer, the consignee and the owner of the goods appropriate compensation for any injury caused to them through the wrongful detention of goods or through the detention of goods released pursuant to paragraph 6.

10. Without prejudice to the protection of confidential information, each Party shall provide that its competent authorities shall have the authority to give the right holder sufficient opportunity to have any goods detained by the customs administration inspected in order to substantiate the right holder's claims. Each Party shall also provide that its competent authorities have the authority to give the importer an equivalent opportunity to have any such goods inspected. Where the competent authorities have made a positive determination on the merits of a case, a Party may provide the competent authorities the authority to inform the right holder of the names and addresses of the consignor, the importer and the consignee, and of the quantity of the goods in question.

11. Where a Party requires its competent authorities to act on their own initiative and to suspend the release of goods in respect of which they have acquired prima facie evidence that an intellectual property right is being infringed:

    (a) the competent authorities may at any time seek from the right holder any information that may assist them to exercise these powers;

    (b) the importer and the right holder shall be promptly notified of the suspension by the Party's competent authorities, and where the importer lodges an appeal against the suspension with competent authorities, the suspension shall be subject to the conditions, with such modifications as may be necessary, set out in paragraphs 6 through 8; and

    (c) the Party shall only exempt both public authorities and officials from liability to appropriate remedial measures where actions are taken or intended in good faith.

12. Without prejudice to other rights of action open to the right holder and subject to the defendant's right to seek judicial review, each Party shall provide that its competent authorities shall have the authority to order the destruction or disposal of infringing goods in accordance with the principles set out in Article 1715(5). In regard to counterfeit goods, the authorities shall not allow the re exportation of the infringing goods in an unaltered state or subject them to a different customs procedure, other than in exceptional circumstances.

13. A Party may exclude from the application of paragraphs 1 through 12 small quantities of goods of a non-commercial nature contained in travellers' personal luggage or sent in small consignments that are not repetitive.

14. Annex 1718.14 applies to the Parties specified in that Annex.

Article 1719: Cooperation and Technical Assistance

1. The Parties shall provide each other on mutually agreed terms with technical assistance and shall promote cooperation between their competent authorities. Such cooperation shall include the training of personnel.

2. The Parties shall cooperate with a view to eliminating trade in goods that infringe intellectual property rights. For this purpose, each Party shall establish and notify the other Parties by January 1, 1994 of contact points in its federal government and shall exchange information concerning trade in infringing goods.

Article 1720: Protection of Existing Subject Matter

1. Except as required under Article 1705(7), this Agreement does not give rise to obligations in respect of acts that occurred before the date of application of the relevant provisions of this Agreement for the Party in question.

2. Except as otherwise provided for in this Agreement, each Party shall apply this Agreement to all subject matter existing on the date of application of the relevant provisions of this Agreement for the Party in question and that is protected in a Party on such date, or that meets or subsequently meets the criteria for protection under the terms of this Chapter. In respect of this paragraph and paragraphs 3 and 4, a Party's obligations with respect to existing works shall be solely determined under Article 18 of the Berne Convention and with respect to the rights of producers of sound recordings in existing sound recordings shall be determined solely under Article 18 of that Convention, as made applicable under this Agreement.

3. Except as required under Article 1705(7), and notwithstanding the first sentence of paragraph 2, no Party may be required to restore protection to subject matter that, on the date of application of the relevant provisions of this Agreement for the Party in question, has fallen into the public domain in its territory.

4. In respect of any acts relating to specific objects embodying protected subject matter that become infringing under the terms of laws in conformity with this Agreement, and that were begun or in respect of which a significant investment was made, before the date of entry into force of this Agreement for that Party, any Party may provide for a limitation of the remedies available to the right holder as to the continued performance of such acts after the date of application of this Agreement for that Party. In such cases, the Party shall, however, at least provide for payment of equitable remuneration.

5. No Party shall be obliged to apply Article 1705(2)(d) or 1706(1)(d) with respect to originals or copies purchased prior to the date of application of the relevant provisions of this Agreement for that Party.
6. No Party shall be required to apply Article 1709(10), or the requirement in Article 1709(7) that patent rights shall be enjoyable without discrimination as to the field of technology, to use without the authorization of the right holder where authorization for such use was granted by the government before the text of the Draft Final Act Embodying the Results of the Uruguay Round of Multilateral Trade Negotiations became known.
7. In the case of intellectual property rights for which protection is conditional on registration, applications for protection that are pending on the date of application of the relevant provisions of this Agreement for the Party in question shall be permitted to be amended to claim any enhanced protection provided under this Agreement. Such amendments shall not include new matter.

Article 1721: Definitions

1. For purposes of this Chapter:
    confidential information includes trade secrets, privileged information and other materials exempted from disclosure under the Party's domestic law.
2. For purposes of this Agreement:
    encrypted program-carrying satellite signal means a program-carrying satellite signal that is transmitted in a form whereby the aural or visual characteristics, or both, are modified or altered for the purpose of preventing the unauthorized reception, by persons without the authorized equipment that is designed to eliminate the effects of such modification or alteration, of a program carried in that signal;
    geographical indication means any indication that identifies a good as originating in the territory of a Party, or a region or locality in that territory, where a particular quality, reputation or other characteristic of the good is essentially attributable to its geographical origin;
    in a manner contrary to honest commercial practices means at least practices such as breach of contract, breach of confidence and inducement to breach, and includes the acquisition of undisclosed information by other persons who knew, or were grossly negligent in failing to know, that such practices were involved in the acquisition;
    intellectual property rights refers to copyright and related rights, trademark rights, patent rights, rights in layout designs of semiconductor integrated circuits, trade secret rights, plant breeders' rights, rights in geographical indications and industrial design rights;
    nationals of another Party means, in respect of the relevant intellectual property right, persons who would meet the criteria for eligibility for protection provided for in the Paris Convention (1967), the Berne Convention (1971), the Geneva Convention (1971), the International Convention for the Protection of Performers, Producers of Phonograms and Broadcasting Organizations (1961), the UPOV

Convention (1978), the UPOV Convention (1991) or the *Treaty on Intellectual Property in Respect of Integrated Circuits* , as if each Party were a party to those Conventions, and with respect to intellectual property rights that are not the subject of these Conventions, "nationals of another Party" shall be understood to be at least individuals who are citizens or permanent residents of that Party and also includes any other natural person referred to in Annex 201.1 (CountrySpecific Definitions);

public includes, with respect to rights of communication and performance of works provided for under Articles 11, 11bis(1) and 14(1)(ii) of the Berne Convention, with respect to dramatic, dramatico-musical, musical and cinematographic works, at least, any aggregation of individuals intended to be the object of, and capable of perceiving, communications or performances of works, regardless of whether they can do so at the same or different times or in the same or different places, provided that such an aggregation is larger than a family and its immediate circle of acquaintances or is not a group comprising a limited number of individuals having similarly close ties that has not been formed for the principal purpose of receiving such performances and communications of works; and

secondary uses of sound recordings means the use directly for broadcasting or for any other public communication of a sound recording.

ANNEX 1701.3. INTELLECTUAL PROPERTY CONVENTIONS

1. Mexico shall:
    (a) make every effort to comply with the substantive provisions of the 1978 or 1991 UPOV Convention as soon as possible and shall do so no later than two years after the date of signature of this Agreement; and
    (b) accept from the date of entry into force of this Agreement applications from plant breeders for varieties in all plant genera and species and grant protection, in accordance with such substantive provisions, promptly after complying with subparagraph (a).
2. Notwithstanding Article 1701(2)(b), this Agreement confers no rights and imposes no obligations on the United States with respect to Article 6bis of the Berne Convention, or the rights derived from that Article.

ANNEX 1705.7. COPYRIGHT

The United States shall provide protection to motion pictures produced in another Party's territory that have been declared to be in the public domain pursuant to 17 U.S.C. section 405. This obligation shall apply to the extent that it is consistent with the Constitution of the United States, and is subject to budgetary considerations.

ANNEX 1710.9. LAYOUT DESIGNS

Mexico shall make every effort to implement the requirements of Article 1710 as soon as possible, and shall do so no later than four years after the date of entry into force of this Agreement.

ANNEX 1718.14. ENFORCEMENT OF INTELLECTUAL PROPERTY RIGHTS

Mexico shall make every effort to comply with the requirements of Article 1718 as soon as possible and shall do so no later than three years after the date of signature of this Agreement.

PART SEVEN: ADMINISTRATIVE AND INSTITUTIONAL PROVISIONS

18. PUBLICATION, NOTIFICATION AND ADMINISTRATION OF LAWS

Article 1801: Contact Points

Each Party shall designate a contact point to facilitate communications between the Parties on any matter covered by this Agreement. On the request of another Party, the contact point shall identify the office or official responsible for the matter and assist, as necessary, in facilitating communication with the requesting Party.

Article 1802: Publication

1. Each Party shall ensure that its laws, regulations, procedures and administrative rulings of general application respecting any matter covered by this Agreement are promptly published or otherwise made available in such a manner as to enable interested persons and Parties to become acquainted with them.
2. To the extent possible, each Party shall:
   (a) publish in advance any such measure that it proposes to adopt; and
   (b) provide interested persons and Parties a reasonable opportunity to comment on such proposed measures.

Article 1803: Notification and Provision of Information

1. To the maximum extent possible, each Party shall notify any other Party with an interest in the matter of any proposed or actual measure that the Party considers

might materially affect the operation of this Agreement or otherwise substantially affect that other Party's interests under this Agreement.

2. On request of another Party, a Party shall promptly provide information and respond to questions pertaining to any actual or proposed measure, whether or not that other Party has been previously notified of that measure.

3. Any notification or information provided under this Article shall be without prejudice as to whether the measure is consistent with this Agreement.

Article 1804: Administrative Proceedings

With a view to administering in a consistent, impartial and reasonable manner all measures of general application affecting matters covered by this Agreement, each Party shall ensure that in its administrative proceedings applying measures referred to in Article 1802 to particular persons, goods or services of another Party in specific cases that:

(a) wherever possible, persons of another Party that are directly affected by a proceeding are provided reasonable notice, in accordance with domestic procedures, when a proceeding is initiated, including a description of the nature of the proceeding, a statement of the legal authority under which the proceeding is initiated and a general description of any issues in controversy;

(b) such persons are afforded a reasonable opportunity to present facts and arguments in support of their positions prior to any final administrative action, when time, the nature of the proceeding and the public interest permit; and

(c) its procedures are in accordance with domestic law.

Article 1805: Review and Appeal

1. Each Party shall establish or maintain judicial, quasi-judicial or administrative tribunals or procedures for the purpose of the prompt review and, where warranted, correction of final administrative actions regarding matters covered by this Agreement. Such tribunals shall be impartial and independent of the office or authority entrusted with administrative enforcement and shall not have any substantial interest in the outcome of the matter.

2. Each Party shall ensure that, in any such tribunals or procedures, the parties to the proceeding are provided with the right to:
   (a) a reasonable opportunity to support or defend their respective positions; and
   (b) a decision based on the evidence and submissions of record or, where required by domestic law, the record compiled by the administrative authority.

3. Each Party shall ensure, subject to appeal or further review as provided in its domestic law, that such decisions shall be implemented by, and shall govern the practice of, the offices or authorities with respect to the administrative action at issue.

Article 1806: Definitions

For purposes of this Chapter:

administrative ruling of general application means an administrative ruling or interpretation that applies to all persons and fact situations that fall generally within its ambit and that establishes a norm of conduct but does not include:

(a) a determination or ruling made in an administrative or quasi-judicial proceeding that applies to a particular person, good or service of another Party in a specific case; or

(b) a ruling that adjudicates with respect to a particular act or practice.

19. REVIEW AND DISPUTE SETTLEMENT IN ANTIDUMPING/COUNTERVAILING DUTY MATTERS

Article 1901: General Provisions

1. Article 1904 applies only with respect to goods that the competent investigating authority of the importing Party, applying the importing Party's antidumping or countervailing duty law to the facts of a specific case, determines are goods of another Party.

2. For purposes of Articles 1903 and 1904, panels shall be established in accordance with the provisions of Annex 1901.2.

3. Except for Article 2203 (Entry into Force), no provision of any other Chapter of this Agreement shall be construed as imposing obligations on a Party with respect to the Party's antidumping law or countervailing duty law.

Article 1902: Retention of Domestic Antidumping Law and Countervailing Duty Law

1. Each Party reserves the right to apply its antidumping law and countervailing duty law to goods imported from the territory of any other Party. Antidumping law and countervailing duty law include, as appropriate for each Party, relevant statutes, legislative history, regulations, administrative practice and judicial precedents.

2. Each Party reserves the right to change or modify its antidumping law or countervailing duty law, provided that in the case of an amendment to a Party's antidumping or countervailing duty statute:

(a) such amendment shall apply to goods from another Party only if the amending statute specifies that it applies to goods from that Party or from the Parties to this Agreement;

(b) the amending Party notifies in writing the Parties to which the amendment applies of the amending statute as far in advance as possible of the date of enactment of such statute;

(c) following notification, the amending Party, on request of any Party to which the amendment applies, consults with that Party prior to the enactment of the amending statute; and

(d) such amendment, as applicable to that other Party, is not inconsistent with

    (i) the *General Agreement on Tariffs and Trade (GATT), the Agreement on Implementation of Article VI of the General Agreement on Tariffs and Trade (the Antidumping Code) or the Agreement on the Interpretation and Application of Articles VI, XVI and XXIII of the General Agreement on Tariffs and Trade* (the Subsidies Code), or any successor agreement to which all the original signatories to this Agreement are party, or

    (ii) the object and purpose of this Agreement and this Chapter, which is to establish fair and predictable conditions for the progressive liberalization of trade between the Parties to this Agreement while maintaining effective and fair disciplines on unfair trade practices, such object and purpose to be ascertained from the provisions of this Agreement, its preamble and objectives, and the practices of the Parties.

Article 1903: Review of Statutory Amendments

1. A Party to which an amendment of another Party's antidumping or countervailing duty statute applies may request in writing that such amendment be referred to a binational panel for a declaratory opinion as to whether:

(a) the amendment does not conform to the provisions of Article 1902(2)(d)(i) or (ii); or

(b) such amendment has the function and effect of overturning a prior decision of a panel made pursuant to Article 1904 and does not conform to the provisions of Article 1902(2)(d)(i) or (ii).

Such declaratory opinion shall have force or effect only as provided in this Article.

2. The panel shall conduct its review in accordance with the procedures of Annex 1903.2.

3. In the event that the panel recommends modifications to the amending statute to remedy a non-conformity that it has identified in its opinion:

(a) the two Parties shall immediately begin consultations and shall seek to achieve a mutually satisfactory solution to the matter within 90 days of the issuance of the panel's final declaratory opinion. Such solution may include seeking corrective legislation with respect to the statute of the amending Party;

(b) if corrective legislation is not enacted within nine months from the end of the 90day consultation period referred to in subparagraph (a) and no other mutually satisfactory solution has been reached, the Party that requested the panel may

    (i) take comparable legislative or equivalent executive action, or

    (ii) terminate this Agreement with regard to the amending Party on 60day written notice to that Party.

Article 1904: Review of Final Antidumping and Countervailing Duty Determinations

1. As provided in this Article, each Party shall replace judicial review of final antidumping and countervailing duty determinations with binational panel review.

2. An involved Party may request that a panel review, based on the administrative record, a final antidumping or countervailing duty determination of a competent investigating authority of an importing Party to determine whether such determination was in accordance with the antidumping or countervailing duty law of the importing Party. For this purpose, the antidumping or countervailing duty law consists of the relevant statutes, legislative history, regulations, administrative practice and judicial precedents to the extent that a court of the importing Party would rely on such materials in reviewing a final determination of the competent investigating authority. Solely for purposes of the panel review provided for in this Article, the antidumping and countervailing duty statutes of the Parties, as those statutes may be amended from time to time, are incorporated into and made a part of this Agreement.

3. The panel shall apply the standard of review set out in Annex 1911 and the general legal principles that a court of the importing Party otherwise would apply to a review of a determination of the competent investigating authority.

4. A request for a panel shall be made in writing to the other involved Party within 30 days following the date of publication of the final determination in question in the official journal of the importing Party. In the case of final determinations that are not published in the official journal of the importing Party, the importing Party shall immediately notify the other involved Party of such final determination where it involves goods from the other involved Party, and the other involved Party may request a panel within 30 days of receipt of such notice. Where the competent investigating authority of the importing Party has imposed provisional measures in an investigation, the other involved Party may provide notice of its intention to request a panel under this Article, and the Parties shall begin to establish a panel at that time. Failure to request a panel within the time specified in this paragraph shall preclude review by a panel.

5. An involved Party on its own initiative may request review of a final determination by a panel and shall, on request of a person who would otherwise be entitled under the law of the importing Party to commence domestic procedures for judicial review of that final determination, request such review.

6. The panel shall conduct its review in accordance with the procedures established by the Parties pursuant to paragraph 14. Where both involved Parties request a panel to review a final determination, a single panel shall review that determination.

7. The competent investigating authority that issued the final determination in question shall have the right to appear and be represented by counsel before the panel. Each Party shall provide that other persons who, pursuant to the law of the importing Party, otherwise would have had the right to appear and be represented in a domestic judicial review proceeding concerning the determination of the competent

investigating authority, shall have the right to appear and be represented by counsel before the panel.

8. The panel may uphold a final determination, or remand it for action not inconsistent with the panel's decision. Where the panel remands a final determination, the panel shall establish as brief a time as is reasonable for compliance with the remand, taking into account the complexity of the factual and legal issues involved and the nature of the panel's decision. In no event shall the time permitted for compliance with a remand exceed an amount of time equal to the maximum amount of time (counted from the date of the filing of a petition, complaint or application) permitted by statute for the competent investigating authority in question to make a final determination in an investigation. If review of the action taken by the competent investigating authority on remand is needed, such review shall be before the same panel, which shall normally issue a final decision within 90 days of the date on which such remand action is submitted to it.

9. The decision of a panel under this Article shall be binding on the involved Parties with respect to the particular matter between the Parties that is before the panel.

10. This Agreement shall not affect:
    (a) the judicial review procedures of any Party, or
    (b) cases appealed under those procedures,
    with respect to determinations other than final determinations.

11. A final determination shall not be reviewed under any judicial review procedures of the importing Party if an involved Party requests a panel with respect to that determination within the time limits set out in this Article. No Party may provide in its domestic legislation for an appeal from a panel decision to its domestic courts.

12. This Article shall not apply where:
    (a) neither involved Party seeks panel review of a final determination;
    (b) a revised final determination is issued as a direct result of judicial review of the original final determination by a court of the importing Party in cases where neither involved Party sought panel review of that original final determination; or
    (c) a final determination is issued as a direct result of judicial review that was commenced in a court of the importing Party before the date of entry into force of this Agreement.

13. Where, within a reasonable time after the panel decision is issued, an involved Party alleges that:
    (a) (i) a member of the panel was guilty of gross misconduct, bias, or a serious conflict of interest, or otherwise materially violated the rules of conduct,
    (ii) the panel seriously departed from a fundamental rule of procedure, or

    (iii) the panel manifestly exceeded its powers, authority or jurisdiction set out in this Article, for example by failing to apply the appropriate standard of review, and
    (b) any of the actions set out in subparagraph (a) has materially affected the panel's decision and threatens the integrity of the binational panel review process,
    that Party may avail itself of the extraordinary challenge procedure set out in Annex 1904.13.

14. To implement the provisions of this Article, the Parties shall adopt rules of procedure by January 1, 1994. Such rules shall be based, where appropriate, on judicial rules of appellate procedure, and shall include rules concerning: the content and service of requests for panels; a requirement that the competent investigating authority transmit to the panel the administrative record of the proceeding; the protection of business proprietary, government classified, and other privileged information (including sanctions against persons participating before panels for improper release of such information); participation by private persons; limitations on panel review to errors alleged by the Parties or private persons; filing and service; computation and extensions of time; the form and content of briefs and other papers; pre and posthearing conferences; motions; oral argument; requests for rehearing; and voluntary terminations of panel reviews. The rules shall be designed to result in final decisions within 315 days of the date on which a request for a panel is made, and shall allow:

    (a) 30 days for the filing of the complaint;

    (b) 30 days for designation or certification of the administrative record and its filing with the panel;

    (c) 60 days for the complainant to file its brief;

    (d) 60 days for the respondent to file its brief;

    (e) 15 days for the filing of reply briefs;

    (f) 15 to 30 days for the panel to convene and hear oral argument; and

    (g) 90 days for the panel to issue its written decision.

15. In order to achieve the objectives of this Article, the Parties shall amend their antidumping and countervailing duty statutes and regulations with respect to antidumping or countervailing duty proceedings involving goods of the other Parties, and other statutes and regulations to the extent that they apply to the operation of the antidumping and countervailing duty laws. In particular, without limiting the generality of the foregoing, each Party shall:

    (a) amend its statutes or regulations to ensure that existing procedures concerning the refund, with interest, of antidumping or countervailing duties operate to give effect to a final panel decision that a refund is due;

    (b) amend its statutes or regulations to ensure that its courts shall give full force and effect, with respect to any person within its jurisdiction, to all sanctions imposed pursuant to the laws of the other Parties to enforce provisions of any protective order or undertaking that such other Party has promulgated or accepted in order to permit access for purposes of panel review or of the extraordinary challenge procedure to confidential, personal, business proprietary or other privileged information;

    (c) amend its statutes or regulations to ensure that

        (i) domestic procedures for judicial review of a final determination may not be commenced until the time for requesting a panel under paragraph 4 has expired, and

        (ii) as a prerequisite to commencing domestic judicial review procedures to review a final determination, a Party or other person intending to commence such procedures shall provide notice of such intent to the Parties concerned and to other persons entitled to commence such review procedures of the same final determination no later than 10 days prior to the latest date on which a panel may be requested; and

(d) make the further amendments set out in its Schedule to Annex 1904.15.

Article 1905: Safeguarding the Panel Review System

1. Where a Party alleges that the application of another Party's domestic law:
   (a) has prevented the establishment of a panel requested by the complaining Party;
   (b) has prevented a panel requested by the complaining Party from rendering a final decision;
   (c) has prevented the implementation of the decision of a panel requested by the complaining Party or denied it binding force and effect with respect to the particular matter that was before the panel; or
   (d) has resulted in a failure to provide opportunity for review of a final determination by a panel or court of competent jurisdiction that is independent of the competent investigating authorities, that examines the basis for the competent investigating authority's determination and whether the competent investigating authority properly applied domestic antidumping and countervailing duty law in reaching the challenged determination, and that employs the relevant standard of review identified in Article 1911,

   the Party may request in writing consultations with the other Party regarding the allegations. The consultations shall begin within 15 days of the date of the request.

2. If the matter has not been resolved within 45 days of the request for consultations, or such other period as the consulting Parties may agree, the complaining Party may request the establishment of a special committee.

3. Unless otherwise agreed by the disputing Parties, the special committee shall be established within 15 days of a request and perform its functions in a manner consistent with this Chapter.

4. The roster for special committees shall be that established under Annex 1904.13.

5. The special committee shall comprise three members selected in accordance with the procedures set out in Annex 1904.13.

6. The Parties shall establish rules of procedure in accordance with the principles set out in Annex 1905.6.

7. Where the special committee makes an affirmative finding with respect to one of the grounds specified in paragraph 1, the complaining Party and the Party complained against shall begin consultations within 10 days thereafter and shall seek to achieve a mutually satisfactory solution within 60 days of the issuance of the committee's report.

8. If, within the 60day period, the Parties are unable to reach a mutually satisfactory solution to the matter, or the Party complained against has not demonstrated to the satisfaction of the special committee that it has corrected the problem or problems with respect to which the committee has made an affirmative finding, the complaining Party may suspend:
   (a) the operation of Article 1904 with respect to the Party complained against; or

(b) the application to the Party complained against of such benefits under this Agreement as may be appropriate under the circumstances.

If the complaining Party decides to take action under this paragraph, it shall do so within 30 days after the end of the 60day consultation period.

9.   In the event that a complaining Party suspends the operation of Article 1904 with respect to the Party complained against, the latter Party may reciprocally suspend the operation of Article 1904 within 30 days after the suspension of the operation of Article 1904 by the complaining Party. If either Party decides to suspend the operation of Article 1904, it shall provide written notice of such suspension to the other Party.

10. At the request of the Party complained against, the special committee shall reconvene to determine whether:

(a) the suspension of benefits by the complaining Party pursuant to paragraph 8(b) is manifestly excessive; or

(b) the Party complained against has corrected the problem or problems with respect to which the committee has made an affirmative finding.

The special committee shall, within 45 days of the request, present a report to both Parties containing its determination. Where the special committee determines that the Party complained against has corrected the problem or problems, any suspension effected by the complaining Party or the Party complained against, or both, pursuant to paragraph 8 or 9 shall be terminated.

11. If the special committee makes an affirmative finding with respect to one of the grounds specified in paragraph 1, then effective as of the day following the date of issuance of the special committee's report:

(a) binational panel or extraordinary challenge committee review under Article 1904 shall be stayed

(i) in the case of review of any final determination of the complaining Party requested by the Party complained against, if such review was requested after the date on which consultations were requested pursuant to paragraph 1, and in no case more than 150 days prior to an affirmative finding by the special committee, or

(ii) in the case of review of any final determination of the Party complained against requested by the complaining Party, at the request of the complaining Party; and

(b) the time set out in Article 1904(4) or Annex 1904.13 for requesting panel or committee review shall not run unless and until resumed in accordance with paragraph 12.

12. If either Party suspends the operation of Article 1904 pursuant to paragraph 8(a), the panel or committee review stayed under paragraph 11(a) shall be terminated and the challenge to the final determination shall be irrevocably referred to the appropriate domestic court for decision, as provided below:

(a) in the case of review of any final determination of the complaining Party requested by the Party complained against, at the request of either Party, or of a party to the panel review under Article 1904; or

(b) in the case of review of any final determination of the Party complained against requested by the complaining Party, at the request of the complaining Party, or of a person of the complaining Party that is a party to the panel review under Article 1904.

If either Party suspends the operation of Article 1904 pursuant to paragraph 8(a), any running of time suspended under paragraph 11(b) shall resume.

If the suspension of the operation of Article 1904 does not become effective, panel or committee review stayed under paragraph 11(a), and any running of time suspended under paragraph 11(b), shall resume.

13. If the complaining Party suspends the application to the Party complained against of such benefits under the Agreement as may be appropriate under the circumstances pursuant to paragraph 8(b), panel or committee review stayed under paragraph 11(a), and any running of time suspended under paragraph 11(b), shall resume.

14. Each Party shall provide in its domestic legislation that, in the event of an affirmative finding by the special committee, the time for requesting judicial review of a final antidumping or countervailing duty determination shall not run unless and until the Parties concerned have negotiated a mutually satisfactory solution under paragraph 7, have suspended the operation of Article 1904 or the application of other benefits under paragraph 8.

Article 1906: Prospective Application

This Chapter shall apply only prospectively to:

(a) final determinations of a competent investigating authority made after the date of entry into force of this Agreement; and

(b) with respect to declaratory opinions under Article 1903, amendments to antidumping or countervailing duty statutes enacted after the date of entry into force of this Agreement.

Article 1907: Consultations

1. The Parties shall consult annually, or on the request of any Party, to consider any problems that may arise with respect to the implementation or operation of this Chapter and recommend solutions, where appropriate. The Parties shall each designate one or more officials, including officials of the competent investigating authorities, to be responsible for ensuring that consultations occur, when required, so that the provisions of this Chapter are carried out expeditiously.

2. The Parties further agree to consult on:

   (a) the potential to develop more effective rules and disciplines concerning the use of government subsidies; and

   (b) the potential for reliance on a substitute system of rules for dealing with unfair transborder pricing practices and government subsidization.

3. The competent investigating authorities of the Parties shall consult annually, or on the request of any Party, and may submit reports to the Commission, where

appropriate. In the context of these consultations, the Parties agree that it is desirable in the administration of antidumping and countervailing duty laws to:

(a) publish notice of initiation of investigations in the importing Party's official journal, setting forth the nature of the proceeding, the legal authority under which the proceeding is initiated, and a description of the goods at issue;

(b) provide notice of the times for submissions of information and for decisions that the competent investigating authorities are expressly required by statute or regulations to make;

(c) provide explicit written notice and instructions as to the information required from interested parties and reasonable time to respond to requests for information;

(d) accord reasonable access to information, noting that in this context

   (i) "reasonable access" means access during the course of the investigation, to the extent practicable, so as to permit an opportunity to present facts and arguments as set out in paragraph (e); when it is not practicable to provide access to information during the investigation in such time as to permit an opportunity to present facts and arguments, reasonable access shall mean in time to permit the adversely affected party to make an informed decision as to whether to seek judicial or panel review, and

   (ii) "access to information" means access to representatives determined by the competent investigating authority to be qualified to have access to information received by that competent investigating authority, including access to confidential (business proprietary) information, but does not include information of such high degree of sensitivity that its release would lead to substantial and irreversible harm to the owner or which is required to be kept confidential in accordance with domestic law of a Party; any privileges arising under the domestic law of the importing Party relating to communications between the competent investigating authorities and a lawyer in the employ of, or providing advice to, those authorities may be maintained;

(e) provide an opportunity for interested parties to present facts and arguments, to the extent time permits, including an opportunity to comment on the preliminary determination of dumping or of subsidization;

(f) protect confidential (business proprietary) information received by the competent investigating authority to ensure that there is no disclosure except to representatives determined by the competent investigating authority to be qualified;

(g) prepare administrative records, including recommendations of official advisory bodies that may be required to be kept, and any record of *ex parte* meetings that may be required to be kept;

(h) provide disclosure of relevant information, including an explanation of the calculation or the methodology used to determine the margin of dumping or the amount of the subsidy, on which any preliminary or final determination of dumping or of subsidization is based, within a reasonable time after a request by interested parties;

(i) provide a statement of reasons concerning the final determination of dumping or subsidization; and

(j) provide a statement of reasons for final determinations concerning material injury to a domestic industry, threat of material injury to a domestic industry or material retardation of the establishment of such an industry.

Inclusion of an item in subparagraphs (a) through (j) is not intended to serve as guidance to a binational panel reviewing a final antidumping or countervailing duty determination pursuant to Article 1904 in determining whether such determination was in accordance with the antidumping or countervailing duty law of the importing Party.

Article 1908: Special Secretariat Provisions

1. Each Party shall establish a division within its section of the Secretariat established pursuant to Article 2002 to facilitate the operation of this Chapter, including the work of panels or committees that may be convened pursuant to this Chapter.

2. The Secretaries of the Secretariat shall act jointly to provide administrative assistance to all panels or committees established pursuant to this Chapter. The Secretary for the Section of the Party in which a panel or committee proceeding is held shall prepare a record thereof and shall preserve an authentic copy of the same in that Party's Section office. Such Secretary shall, on request, provide to the Secretary for the Section of any other Party a copy of such portion of the record as is requested, except that only public portions of the record shall be provided to the Secretary for the Section of any Party that is not an involved Party.

3. Each Secretary shall receive and file all requests, briefs and other papers properly presented to a panel or committee in any proceeding before it that is instituted pursuant to this Chapter and shall number in numerical order all requests for a panel or committee. The number given to a request shall be the file number for briefs and other papers relating to such request.

4. The Secretary for the Section of the Party in which a panel or committee proceeding is held shall forward to the Secretary for the Section of the other involved Party copies of all official letters, documents or other papers received or filed with that Party's Section office pertaining to any proceeding before a panel or committee, except for the administrative record, which shall be handled in accordance with paragraph 2. The Secretary for the Section of an involved Party shall provide on request to the Secretary for the Section of a Party that is not an involved Party in the proceeding a copy of such public documents as are requested.

Article 1909: Code of Conduct

The Parties shall, by the date of entry into force of this Agreement, exchange letters establishing a code of conduct for panelists and members of committees established pursuant to Articles 1903, 1904 and 1905.

Article 1910: Miscellaneous

On request of another Party, the competent investigating authority of a Party shall provide to the other Party copies of all public information submitted to it for purposes of an antidumping or countervailing duty investigation with respect to goods of that other Party.

Article 1911: Definitions

For purposes of this Chapter:

administrative record means, unless otherwise agreed by the Parties and the other persons appearing before a panel:

(a) all documentary or other information presented to or obtained by the competent investigating authority in the course of the administrative proceeding, including any governmental memoranda pertaining to the case, and including any record of *ex parte* meetings as may be required to be kept;

(b) a copy of the final determination of the competent investigating authority, including reasons for the determination;

(c) all transcripts or records of conferences or hearings before the competent investigating authority; and

(d) all notices published in the official journal of the importing Party in connection with the administrative proceeding;

antidumping statute as referred to in Articles 1902 and 1903 means "antidumping statute" of a Party as defined in Annex 1911;

competent investigating authority means "competent investigating authority" of a Party as defined in Annex 1911;

countervailing duty statute as referred to in Articles 1902 and 1903 means "countervailing duty statute" of a Party as defined in Annex 1911;

domestic law for purposes of Article 1905(1) means a Party's constitution, statutes, regulations and judicial decisions to the extent they are relevant to the antidumping and countervailing duty laws;

final determination means "final determination" of a Party as defined in Annex 1911;

foreign interests includes exporters or producers of the Party whose goods are the subject of the proceeding or, in the case of a countervailing duty proceeding, the government of the Party whose goods are the subject of the proceeding;

general legal principles includes principles such as standing, due process, rules of statutory construction, mootness and exhaustion of administrative remedies;

goods of a Party means domestic products as these are understood in the *General Agreement on Tariffs and Trade* ;

importing Party means the Party that issued the final determination;

interested parties includes foreign interests;

involved Party means:

(a) the importing Party; or
(b) a Party whose goods are the subject of the final determination;

remand means a referral back for a determination not inconsistent with the panel or committee decision; and

standard of review means the "standard of review" for each Party as defined in Annex 1911.

ANNEX 1901.2. ESTABLISHMENT OF BINATIONAL PANELS

1. On the date of entry into force of this Agreement, the Parties shall establish and thereafter maintain a roster of individuals to serve as panelists in disputes under this Chapter. The roster shall include judges or former judges to the fullest extent practicable. The Parties shall consult in developing the roster, which shall include at least 75 candidates. Each Party shall select at least 25 candidates, and all candidates shall be citizens of Canada, Mexico or the United States. Candidates shall be of good character, high standing and repute, and shall be chosen strictly on the basis of objectivity, reliability, sound judgment and general familiarity with international trade law. Candidates shall not be affiliated with a Party, and in no event shall a candidate take instructions from a Party. The Parties shall maintain the roster, and may amend it, when necessary, after consultations.

2. A majority of the panelists on each panel shall be lawyers in good standing. Within 30 days of a request for a panel, each involved Party shall appoint two panelists, in consultation with the other involved Party. The involved Parties normally shall appoint panelists from the roster. If a panelist is not selected from the roster, the panelist shall be chosen in accordance with and be subject to the criteria of paragraph 1. Each involved Party shall have the right to exercise four peremptory challenges, to be exercised simultaneously and in confidence, disqualifying from appointment to the panel up to four candidates proposed by the other involved Party. Peremptory challenges and the selection of alternative panelists shall occur within 45 days of the request for the panel. If an involved Party fails to appoint its members to a panel within 30 days or if a panelist is struck and no alternative panelist is selected within

45 days, such panelist shall be selected by lot on the 31st or 46th day, as the case may be, from that Party's candidates on the roster.

3. Within 55 days of the request for a panel, the involved Parties shall agree on the selection of a fifth panelist. If the involved Parties are unable to agree, they shall decide by lot which of them shall select, by the 61st day, the fifth panelist from the roster, excluding candidates eliminated by peremptory challenges.

4. On appointment of the fifth panelist, the panelists shall promptly appoint a chairman from among the lawyers on the panel by majority vote of the panelists. If there is no majority vote, the chairman shall be appointed by lot from among the lawyers on the panel.

5. Decisions of the panel shall be by majority vote and based on the votes of all members of the panel. The panel shall issue a written decision with reasons, together with any dissenting or concurring opinions of panelists.

6. Panelists shall be subject to the code of conduct established pursuant to Article 1909. If an involved Party believes that a panelist is in violation of the code of conduct, the involved Parties shall consult and if they agree, the panelist shall be removed and a new panelist shall be selected in accordance with the procedures of this Annex.

7. When a panel is convened pursuant to Article 1904 each panelist shall be required to sign:
    (a) an application for protective order for information supplied by the United States or its persons covering business proprietary and other privileged information;
    (b) an undertaking for information supplied by Canada or its persons covering confidential, personal, business proprietary and other privileged information; or
    (c) an undertaking for information supplied by Mexico or its persons covering confidential, business proprietary and other privileged information.

8. On a panelist's acceptance of the obligations and terms of an application for protective order or disclosure undertaking, the importing Party shall grant access to the information covered by such order or disclosure undertaking. Each Party shall establish appropriate sanctions for violations of protective orders or disclosure undertakings issued by or given to any Party. Each Party shall enforce such sanctions with respect to any person within its jurisdiction. Failure by a panelist to sign an application for a protective order or disclosure undertaking shall result in disqualification of the panelist.

9. If a panelist becomes unable to fulfill panel duties or is disqualified, proceedings of the panel shall be suspended pending the selection of a substitute panelist in accordance with the procedures of this Annex.

10. Subject to the code of conduct established pursuant to Article 1909, and provided that it does not interfere with the performance of the duties of such panelist, a panelist may engage in other business during the term of the panel.

11. While acting as a panelist, a panelist may not appear as counsel before another panel.

12. With the exception of violations of protective orders or disclosure undertakings, signed pursuant to paragraph 7, panelists shall be immune from suit and legal process relating to acts performed by them in their official capacity.

ANNEX 1903.2. PANEL PROCEDURES UNDER ARTICLE 1903

1. The panel shall establish its own rules of procedure unless the Parties otherwise agree prior to the establishment of that panel. The procedures shall ensure a right to at least one hearing before the panel, as well as the opportunity to provide written submissions and rebuttal arguments. The proceedings of the panel shall be confidential, unless the two Parties otherwise agree. The panel shall base its decisions solely on the arguments and submissions of the two Parties.

2. Unless the Parties to the dispute otherwise agree, the panel shall, within 90 days after its chairman is appointed, present to the two Parties an initial written declaratory opinion containing findings of fact and its determination pursuant to Article 1903.

3. If the findings of the panel are affirmative, the panel may include in its report its recommendations as to the means by which the amending statute could be brought into conformity with the provisions of Article 1902(2)(d). In determining what, if any, recommendations are appropriate, the panel shall consider the extent to which the amending statute affects interests under this Agreement. Individual panelists may provide separate opinions on matters not unanimously agreed. The initial opinion of the panel shall become the final declaratory opinion, unless a Party to the dispute requests a reconsideration of the initial opinion pursuant to paragraph 4.

4. Within 14 days of the issuance of the initial declaratory opinion, a Party to the dispute disagreeing in whole or in part with the opinion may present a written statement of its objections and the reasons for those objections to the panel. In such event, the panel shall request the views of both Parties and shall reconsider its initial opinion. The panel shall conduct any further examination that it deems appropriate, and shall issue a final written opinion, together with dissenting or concurring views of individual panelists, within 30 days of the request for reconsideration.

5. Unless the Parties to the dispute otherwise agree, the final declaratory opinion of the panel shall be made public, along with any separate opinions of individual panelists and any written views that either Party may wish to be published.

6. Unless the Parties to the dispute otherwise agree, meetings and hearings of the panel shall take place at the office of the amending Party's Section of the Secretariat.

ANNEX 1904.13. EXTRAORDINARY CHALLENGE PROCEDURE

1. The involved Parties shall establish an extraordinary challenge committee, composed of three members, within 15 days of a request pursuant to Article 1904(13). The members shall be selected from a 15-person roster comprised of judges or former judges of a federal judicial court of the United States or a judicial court of superior jurisdiction of Canada, or a federal judicial court of Mexico. Each Party shall name five persons to this roster. Each involved Party shall select one member from this roster and the involved Parties shall decide by lot which of them shall select the third member from the roster.

2. The Parties shall establish by the date of entry into force of the Agreement rules of procedure for committees. The rules shall provide for a decision of a committee within 90 days of its establishment.

3. Committee decisions shall be binding on the Parties with respect to the particular matter between the Parties that was before the panel. After examination of the legal and factual analysis underlying the findings and conclusions of the panel's decision in order to determine whether one of the grounds set out in Article 1904(13) has been established, and on finding that one of those grounds has been established, the committee shall vacate the original panel decision or remand it to the original panel for action not inconsistent with the committee's decision; if the grounds are not established, it shall deny the challenge and, therefore, the original panel decision shall stand affirmed. If the original decision is vacated, a new panel shall be established pursuant to Annex 1901.2.

ANNEX 1904.15. AMENDMENTS TO DOMESTIC LAWS

Schedule of Canada

1. Canada shall amend sections 56 and 58 of the *Special Import Measures Act* , as amended, to allow the United States with respect to goods of the United States or Mexico with respect to goods of Mexico or a United States or a Mexican manufacturer, producer, or exporter, without regard to payment of duties, to make a written request for a redetermination; and section 59 to require the Deputy Minister to make a ruling on a request for a redetermination within one year of a request to a designated officer or other customs officer.

2. Canada shall amend section 18.3(1) of the *Federal Court Act* , as amended, to render that section inapplicable to the United States and to Mexico; and shall provide in its statutes or regulations that persons (including producers of goods subject to an investigation) have standing to ask Canada to request a panel review where such persons would be entitled to commence domestic procedures for judicial review if the final determination were reviewable by the Federal Court pursuant to section 18.1(4).

3. Canada shall amend the *Special Import Measures Act* , as amended, and any other relevant provisions of law, to provide that the following actions of the Deputy Minister shall be deemed for the purposes of this Article to be final determinations subject to judicial review:

    (a) a determination by the Deputy Minister pursuant to section 41;

    (b) a redetermination by the Deputy Minister pursuant to section 59; and

    (c) a review by the Deputy Minister of an undertaking pursuant to section 53(1).

4. Canada shall amend Part II of the *Special Import Measures Act* , as amended, to provide for binational panel review respecting goods of Mexico and the United States.

5. Canada shall amend Part II of the *Special Import Measures Act* , as amended, to provide for definitions related to this Chapter, as may be required.

6. Canada shall amend Part II of the *Special Import Measures Act* , as amended, to permit the governments of Mexico and the United States to request binational panel review of final determinations respecting goods of Mexico and the United States.

7. Canada shall amend Part II of the *Special Import Measures Act* , as amended, to provide for the establishment of binational panels requested to review final determinations in respect of goods of Mexico and the United States.

8. Canada shall amend Part II of the *Special Import Measures Act* , as amended, to provide that binational panel review of a final determination shall be conducted in accordance with this Chapter.

9. Canada shall amend Part II of the *Special Import Measures Act* , as amended, to provide that an extraordinary challenge proceeding shall be requested and conducted in accordance with Article 1904 and Annex 1904.13.

10. Canada shall amend Part II of the *Special Import Measures Act* , as amended, to provide for a code of conduct, immunity for anything done or omitted to be done during the course of panel proceedings, the signing of and compliance with disclosure undertakings respecting confidential information, and remuneration for members of panels and committees established pursuant to this Chapter.

11. Canada shall make such amendments as are necessary to establish a Canadian Secretariat for this Agreement and generally to facilitate the operation of this Chapter and the work of the binational panels, extraordinary challenge committees and special committees convened under this Chapter.

Schedule of Mexico

Mexico shall amend its antidumping and countervailing duty statutes and regulations, and other statutes and regulations to the extent that they apply to the operation of the antidumping and countervailing duty laws, to provide the following:

(a) elimination of the possibility of imposing duties within the fiveday period after the acceptance of a petition;

(b) substitution of the term *Initial Resolution* ("Resolución de Inicio") for the term *Provisional Resolution* ("Resolución Provisional") and the term *Provisional Resolution* ("Resolución Provisional ") for the term *Resolution Reviewing the Provisional Resolution* ("Resolución que revisa a la Resolución Provisional");

(c) full participation in the administrative process for interested parties, as well as the right to administrative appeal and judicial review of final determinations of investigations, reviews, product coverage or other final decisions affecting them;

(d) elimination of the possibility of imposing provisional duties before the issuance of a preliminary determination;

(e) the right to immediate access to review of final determinations by binational panels for interested parties, without the need to exhaust first the administrative appeal;

(f) explicit and adequate timetables for determinations of the competent investigating authority and for the submission of questionnaires, evidence and comments by interested parties, as well as an opportunity for them to present facts and arguments in support of their positions prior to any final determination, to the extent time permits, including an opportunity to be adequately informed in a timely manner of and to comment on all aspects of preliminary determinations of dumping or subsidization;

(g) written notice to interested parties of any of the actions or resolutions rendered by the competent investigating authority, including initiation of an administrative review as well as its conclusion;

(h) disclosure meetings with interested parties by the competent investigating authority conducting its investigations and reviews, within seven calendar days after the date of publication in the *Federal Official Journal* ("Diario Oficial de la Federación") of preliminary and final determinations, to explain the margins of dumping and the amount of subsidies calculations and to provide the interested parties with copies of sample calculations and, if used, computer programs;

(i) timely access by eligible counsel of interested parties during the course of the proceeding (including disclosure meetings) and on appeal, either before a national tribunal or a panel, to all information contained in the administrative record of the proceeding, including confidential information, excepting proprietary information of such a high degree of sensitivity that its release would lead to substantial and irreversible harm to the owner as well as government classified information, subject to an undertaking for confidentiality that strictly forbids use of the information for personal benefit and its disclosure to persons who are not authorized to receive such information; and for sanctions that are specific to violations of undertakings in proceedings before national tribunals or panels;

(j) timely access by interested parties during the course of the proceeding, to all non-confidential information contained in the administrative record and access to such information by interested parties or their representatives in any proceeding after 90 days following the issuance of the final determination;

(k) a mechanism requiring that any person submitting documents to the competent investigating authority shall simultaneously serve on interested persons, including foreign interests, any submissions after the complaint;

(l) preparation of summaries of *ex parte* meetings held between the competent investigating authority and any interested party and the inclusion in the administrative record of such summaries, which shall be made available to parties to the proceeding; if such summaries contain business proprietary information, the documents must be disclosed to a party's representative under an undertaking to ensure confidentiality;

(m) maintenance by the competent investigating authority of an administrative record as defined in this Chapter and a requirement that the final determination be based solely on the administrative record;

(n) informing interested parties in writing of all data and information the administering authority requires them to submit for the investigation, review, product coverage proceeding, or other antidumping or countervailing duty proceeding;

(o) the right to an annual individual review on request by the interested parties through which they can obtain their own dumping margin or countervailing duty rate, or can change the margin or rate they received in the investigation or a previous review, reserving to the competent investigating authority the ability to initiate a review, at any time, on its own motion and requiring that the competent investigating authority issue a notice of initiation within a reasonable period of time after the request;

(p) application of determinations issued as a result of judicial, administrative, or panel review, to the extent they are relevant to interested parties in addition to the plaintiff, so that all interested parties will benefit;

(q) issuance of binding decisions by the competent investigating authority if an interested party seeks clarification outside the context of an antidumping or countervailing duty investigation or review with respect to whether a particular product is covered by an antidumping or countervailing duty order;

(r) a detailed statement of reasons and the legal basis for final determinations in a manner sufficient to permit interested parties to make an informed decision as to whether to seek judicial or panel review, including an explanation of methodological or policy issues raised in the calculation of dumping or subsidization;

(s) written notice to interested parties and publication in the *Federal Official Journal* ("Diario Oficial de la Federación") of initiation of investigations setting forth the nature of the proceeding, the legal authority under which the proceeding is initiated, and a description of the product at issue;

(t) documentation in writing of all advisory bodies' decisions or recommendations, including the basis for the decisions, and release of such written decisions to parties to the proceeding; all decisions or recommendations of any advisory body shall be placed in the administrative record and made available to parties to the proceeding; and

(u) a standard of review to be applied by binational panels as set out in subparagraph (c) of the definition of "standard of review" in Annex 1911.

Schedule of the United States

1. The United States shall amend section 301 of the *Customs Courts Act* of 1980, as amended, and any other relevant provisions of law, to eliminate the authority to issue declaratory judgments in any civil action involving an antidumping or countervailing duty proceeding regarding a class or kind of Canadian or Mexican merchandise.

2. The United States shall amend section 405(a) of the *United States-Canada Free-Trade Agreement Implementation Act of 1988* , to provide that the interagency group established under section 242 of the *Trade Expansion Act of 1962* shall prepare a list of individuals qualified to serve as members of binational panels, extraordinary challenge committees and special committees convened under this Chapter.

3. The United States shall amend section 405(b) of the *United States-Canada Free-Trade Agreement Implementation Act of 1988* , to provide that panelists selected to serve on panels or committees convened pursuant to this Chapter, and individuals designated to assist such appointed individuals, shall not be considered employees of the United States.

4. The United States shall amend section 405(c) of the *United States-Canada Free-Trade Agreement Implementation Act of 1988* , to provide that panelists selected to serve on panels or committees convened pursuant to this Chapter, and individuals

designated to assist the individuals serving on such panels or committees, shall be immune from suit and legal process relating to acts performed by such individuals in their official capacity and within the scope of their functions as such panelists or committee members, except with respect to the violation of protective orders described in section 777f(d)(3) of the *Tariff Act of 1930* , as amended.

5. The United States shall amend section 405(d) of the *United States-Canada Free-Trade Agreement Implementation Act of 1988* , to establish a United States Secretariat to facilitate the operation of this Chapter and the work of the binational panels, extraordinary challenge committees and special committees convened under this Chapter.

6. The United States shall amend section 407 of the *United States-Canada Free-Trade Agreement Implementation Act of 1988* , to provide that an extraordinary challenge committee convened pursuant to Article 1904 and Annex 1904.13 shall have authority to obtain information in the event of an allegation that a member of a binational panel was guilty of gross misconduct, bias, or a serious conflict of interest, or otherwise materially violated the rules of conduct, and for the committee to summon the attendance of witnesses, order the taking of depositions and obtain the assistance of any district or territorial court of the United States in aid of the committee's investigation.

7. The United States shall amend section 408 of the *United States-Canada Free-Trade Agreement Implementation Act of 1988* , to provide that, in the case of a final determination of a competent investigating authority of Mexico, as well as Canada, the filing with the United States Secretary of a request for binational panel review by a person described in Article 1904(5) shall be deemed, on receipt of the request by the Secretary, to be a request for binational panel review within the meaning of Article 1904(4).

8. The United States shall amend section 516A of the *Tariff Act of 1930* , as amended, to provide that judicial review of antidumping or countervailing duty cases regarding Mexican, as well as Canadian, merchandise shall not be commenced in the Court of International Trade if binational panel review is requested.

9. The United States shall amend section 516A(a) of the *Tariff Act of 1930* , as amended, to provide that the time limits for commencing an action in the Court of International Trade with regard to antidumping or countervailing duty proceedings involving Mexican or Canadian merchandise shall not begin to run until the 31st day after the date of publication in the *Federal Register* of notice of the final determination or the antidumping duty order.

10. The United States shall amend section 516A(g) of the *Tariff Act of 1930* , as amended, to provide, in accordance with the terms of this Chapter, for binational panel review of antidumping and countervailing duty cases involving Mexican or Canadian merchandise. Such amendment shall provide that if binational panel review is requested such review will be exclusive.

11. The United States shall amend section 516A(g) of the *Tariff Act of 1930* , as amended, to provide that the competent investigating authority shall, within the period specified by any panel formed to review a final determination regarding Mexican or Canadian merchandise, take action not inconsistent with the decision of the panel or committee.

12. The United States shall amend section 777 of the *Tariff Act of 1930* , as amended, to provide for the disclosure to authorized persons under protective order of proprietary information in the administrative record, if binational panel review of a final determination regarding Mexican or Canadian merchandise is requested.

13. The United States shall amend section 777 of the *Tariff Act of 1930* , as amended, to provide for the imposition of sanctions on any person who the competent investigating authority finds to have violated a protective order issued by the competent investigating authority of the United States or disclosure undertakings entered into with an authorized agency of Mexico or with a competent investigating authority of Canada to protect proprietary material during binational panel review.

ANNEX 1905.6. SPECIAL COMMITTEE PROCEDURES

The Parties shall establish rules of procedure by the date of entry into force of this Agreement in accordance with the following principles:

(a) the procedures shall assure a right to at least one hearing before the special committee as well as the opportunity to provide initial and rebuttal written submissions;

(b) the procedures shall assure that the special committee shall prepare an initial report typically within 60 days of the appointment of the last member, and shall afford the Parties 14 days to comment on that report prior to issuing a final report 30 days after presentation of the initial report;

(c) the special committee's hearings, deliberations, and initial report, and all written submissions to and communications with the special committee shall be confidential;

(d) unless the Parties to the dispute otherwise agree, the decision of the special committee shall be published 10 days after it is transmitted to the disputing Parties, along with any separate opinions of individual members and any written views that either Party may wish to be published; and

(e) unless the Parties to the dispute otherwise agree, meetings and hearings of the special committee shall take place at the office of the Section of the Secretariat of the Party complained against.

ANNEX 1911. COUNTRYSPECIFIC DEFINITIONS

For purposes of this Chapter:

antidumping statute means:

(a) in the case of Canada, the relevant provisions of the *Special Import Measures Act* , as amended, and any successor statutes;

(b) in the case of the United States, the relevant provisions of Title VII of the *Tariff Act of 1930* , as amended, and any successor statutes;

(c) in the case of Mexico, the relevant provisions of the *Foreign Trade Act Implementing Article 131 of the Constitution of the United Mexican States* ("Ley Reglamentaria del Artículo 131 de la Constitución Política de los Estados Unidos Mexicanos en Materia de Comercio Exterior"), as amended, and any successor statutes; and

(d) the provisions of any other statute that provides for judicial review of final determinations under subparagraph (a), (b) or (c), or indicates the standard of review to be applied to such determinations;

competent investigating authority means:

(a) in the case of Canada (i) the Canadian International Trade Tribunal, or its successor, or (ii) the Deputy Minister of National Revenue for Customs and Excise as defined in the *Special Import Measures Act* , as amended, or the Deputy Minister's successor;

(b) in the case of the United States
    (i) the International Trade Administration of the United States Department of Commerce, or its successor, or
    (ii) the United States International Trade Commission, or its successor; and

(c) in the case of Mexico, the designated authority within the Secretariat of Trade and Industrial Development ("Secretaría de Comercio y Fomento Industrial"), or its successor;

countervailing duty statute means:

(a) in the case of Canada, the relevant provisions of the *Special Import Measures Act* , as amended, and any successor statutes;

(b) in the case of the United States, section 303 and the relevant provisions of Title VII of the *Tariff Act of 1930* , as amended, and any successor statutes;

(c) in the case of Mexico, the relevant provisions of the *Foreign Trade Act Implementing Article 131 of the Constitution of the United Mexican States* ("Ley Reglamentaria del Artículo 131 de la Constitución Política de los Estados Unidos Mexicanos en Materia de Comercio Exterior"), as amended, and any successor statutes; and

(d) the provisions of any other statute that provides for judicial review of final determinations under subparagraph (a), (b) or (c), or indicates the standard of review to be applied to such determinations;

final determination means:

(a) in the case of Canada,
    (i) an order or finding of the Canadian International Trade Tribunal under subsection 43(1) of the Special Import Measures Act,
    (ii) an order by the Canadian International Trade Tribunal under subsection 76(4) of the *Special Import Measures Act* , as amended, continuing an order or finding made under subsection 43(1) of the Act with or without amendment,
    (iii) a determination by the Deputy Minister of National Revenue for Customs and Excise pursuant to section 41 of the *Special Import Measures Act* , as amended,

(iv) a redetermination by the Deputy Minister pursuant to section 59 of the *Special Import Measures Act* , as amended,

(v) a decision by the Canadian International Trade Tribunal pursuant to subsection 76(3) of the *Special Import Measures Act* , as amended, not to initiate a review,

(vi) a reconsideration by the Canadian International Trade Tribunal pursuant to subsection 91(3) of the *Special Import Measures Act* , as amended, and

(vii) a review by the Deputy Minister of an undertaking pursuant to subsection 53(1) of the *Special Import Measures Act* , as amended;

(b) in the case of the United States,

(i) a final affirmative determination by the International Trade Administration of the United States Department of Commerce or by the United States International Trade Commission under section 705 or 735 of the *Tariff Act of 1930* , as amended, including any negative part of such a determination,

(ii) a final negative determination by the International Trade Administration of the United States Department of Commerce or by the United States International Trade Commission under section 705 or 735 of the *Tariff Act of 1930* , as amended, including any affirmative part of such a determination,

(iii) a final determination, other than a determination in (iv), under section 751 of the *Tariff Act of 1930* , as amended,

(iv) a determination by the United States International Trade Commission under section 751(b) of the *Tariff Act of 1930* , as amended, not to review a determination based on changed circumstances, and

(v) a final determination by the International Trade Administration of the United States Department of Commerce as to whether a particular type of merchandise is within the class or kind of merchandise described in an existing finding of dumping or antidumping or countervailing duty order; and

(c) in the case of the Mexico,

(i) a final resolution regarding antidumping or countervailing duties investigations by the Secretar a de Comercio y Fomento Industrial ("Secretariat of Trade and Industrial Development"), pursuant to Article 13 of the Ley Reglamentaria del Artículo 131 de la Constitución Política de los Estados Unidos Mexicanos en Materia de Comercio Exterior (" *Foreign Trade Act Implementing Article 131 of the Constitution of the United Mexican States* "), as amended,

(ii) a final resolution regarding an annual administrative review of antidumping or countervailing duties by the *Secretariat of Trade and Industrial Development* ("Secretaría de Comercio y Fomento Industrial"), as described in paragraph (o) of its Schedule to Annex 1904.15, and

(iii) a final resolution by the *Secretariat of Trade and Industrial Development* ("Secretaría de Comercio y Fomento Industrial"), as to whether a particular type of merchandise is within the class or kind of merchandise described in an existing antidumping or countervailing duty resolution; and

standard of review means the following standards, as may be amended from time to time by the relevant Party:

(a) in the case of Canada, the grounds set out in subsection 18.1(4) of the *Federal Court Act* , as amended, with respect to all final determinations;

(b) in the case of the United States,

    (i) the standard set out in section 516A(b)(l)(B) of the *Tariff Act of 1930* , as amended, with the exception of a determination referred to in (ii), and

    (ii) the standard set out in section 516A(b)(l)(A) of the *Tariff Act of 1930* , as amended, with respect to a determination by the United States International Trade Commission not to initiate a review pursuant to section 751(b) of the *Tariff Act of 1930* , as amended; and

(c) in the case of the Mexico, the standard set out in Article 238 of the *Federal Fiscal Code* ("Código Fiscal de la Federación"), or any successor statutes, based solely on the administrative record.

PART SEVEN: ADMINISTRATIVE AND INSTITUTIONAL PROVISIONS

20. INSTITUTIONAL ARRANGEMENTS AND DISPUTE SETTLEMENT PROCEDURES

Section A - Institutions

Article 2001: The Free Trade Commission

1. The Parties hereby establish the Free Trade Commission, comprising cabinet-level representatives of the Parties or their designees.

2. The Commission shall:

    (a) supervise the implementation of this Agreement;

    (b) oversee its further elaboration;

    (c) resolve disputes that may arise regarding its interpretation or application;

    (d) supervise the work of all committees and working groups established under this Agreement, referred to in Annex 2001.2; and

    (e) consider any other matter that may affect the operation of this Agreement.

3. The Commission may:

    (a) establish, and delegate responsibilities to, ad hoc or standing committees, working groups or expert groups;

    (b) seek the advice of non-governmental persons or groups; and

    (c) take such other action in the exercise of its functions as the Parties may agree.

4. The Commission shall establish its rules and procedures. All decisions of the Commission shall be taken by consensus, except as the Commission may otherwise agree.

5. The Commission shall convene at least once a year in regular session. Regular sessions of the Commission shall be chaired successively by each Party.

Article 2002: The Secretariat

1. The Commission shall establish and oversee a Secretariat comprising national Sections.
2. Each Party shall:
   (a) establish a permanent office of its Section;
   (b) be responsible for
      (i) the operation and costs of its Section, and
      (ii) the remuneration and payment of expenses of panelists and members of committees and scientific review boards established under this Agreement, as set out in Annex 2002.2;
   (c) designate an individual to serve as Secretary for its Section, who shall be responsible for its administration and management; and
   (d) notify the Commission of the location of its Section's office.
3. The Secretariat shall:
   (a) provide assistance to the Commission;
   (b) provide administrative assistance to
      (i) panels and committees established under Chapter Nineteen (Review and Dispute Settlement in Antidumping and Countervailing Duty Matters), in accordance with the procedures established pursuant to Article 1908, and
      (ii) panels established under this Chapter, in accordance with procedures established pursuant to Article 2012; and
   (c) as the Commission may direct
      (i) support the work of other committees and groups established under this Agreement, and
      (ii) otherwise facilitate the operation of this Agreement.

Section B - Dispute Settlement

Article 2003: Cooperation

The Parties shall at all times endeavor to agree on the interpretation and application of this Agreement, and shall make every attempt through cooperation and consultations to arrive at a mutually satisfactory resolution of any matter that might affect its operation.

Article 2004: Recourse to Dispute Settlement Procedures

Except for the matters covered in Chapter Nineteen (Review and Dispute Settlement in Antidumping and Countervailing Duty Matters) and as otherwise provided in this Agreement, the dispute settlement provisions of this Chapter shall apply with respect to the avoidance or settlement of all disputes between the Parties regarding the interpretation or application of this Agreement or wherever a Party considers that an actual or proposed measure of another

Party is or would be inconsistent with the obligations of this Agreement or cause nullification or impairment in the sense of Annex 2004.

Article 2005: GATT Dispute Settlement

1. Subject to paragraphs 2, 3 and 4, disputes regarding any matter arising under both this Agreement and the *General Agreement on Tariffs and Trade* , any agreement negotiated thereunder, or any successor agreement (GATT), may be settled in either forum at the discretion of the complaining Party.

2. Before a Party initiates a dispute settlement proceeding in the GATT against another Party on grounds that are substantially equivalent to those available to that Party under this Agreement, that Party shall notify any third Party of its intention. If a third Party wishes to have recourse to dispute settlement procedures under this Agreement regarding the matter, it shall inform promptly the notifying Party and those Parties shall consult with a view to agreement on a single forum. If those Parties cannot agree, the dispute normally shall be settled under this Agreement.

3. In any dispute referred to in paragraph 1 where the responding Party claims that its action is subject to Article 104 (Relation to Environmental and Conservation Agreements) and requests in writing that the matter be considered under this Agreement, the complaining Party may, in respect of that matter, thereafter have recourse to dispute settlement procedures solely under this Agreement.

4. In any dispute referred to in paragraph 1 that arises under Section B of Chapter Seven (Sanitary and Phytosanitary Measures) or Chapter Nine (Standards-Related Measures):
   (a) concerning a measure adopted or maintained by a Party to protect its human, animal or plant life or health, or to protect its environment, and
   (b) that raises factual issues concerning the environment, health, safety or conservation, including directly related scientific matters,

   where the responding Party requests in writing that the matter be considered under this Agreement, the complaining Party may, in respect of that matter, thereafter have recourse to dispute settlement procedures solely under this Agreement.

5. The responding Party shall deliver a copy of a request made pursuant to paragraph 3 or 4 to the other Parties and to its Section of the Secretariat. Where the complaining Party has initiated dispute settlement proceedings regarding any matter subject to paragraph 3 or 4, the responding Party shall deliver its request no later than 15 days thereafter. On receipt of such request, the complaining Party shall promptly withdraw from participation in those proceedings and may initiate dispute settlement procedures under Article 2007.

6. Once dispute settlement procedures have been initiated under Article 2007 or dispute settlement proceedings have been initiated under the GATT, the forum selected shall be used to the exclusion of the other, unless a Party makes a request pursuant to paragraph 3 or 4.

7. For purposes of this Article, dispute settlement proceedings under the GATT are deemed to be initiated by a Party's request for a panel, such as under Article XXIII:2

of the *General Agreement on Tariffs and Trade 1947* , or for a committee investigation, such as under Article 20.1 of the Customs Valuation Code.

Article 2006: Consultations

1. Any Party may request in writing consultations with any other Party regarding any actual or proposed measure or any other matter that it considers might affect the operation of this Agreement.
2. The requesting Party shall deliver the request to the other Parties and to its Section of the Secretariat.
3. Unless the Commission otherwise provides in its rules and procedures established under Article 2001(4), a third Party that considers it has a substantial interest in the matter shall be entitled to participate in the consultations on delivery of written notice to the other Parties and to its Section of the Secretariat.
4. Consultations on matters regarding perishable agricultural goods shall commence within 15 days of the date of delivery of the request.
5. The consulting Parties shall make every attempt to arrive at a mutually satisfactory resolution of any matter through consultations under this Article or other consultative provisions of this Agreement. To this end, the consulting Parties shall:
   (a) provide sufficient information to enable a full examination of how the actual or proposed measure or other matter might affect the operation of this Agreement;
   (b) treat any confidential or proprietary information exchanged in the course of consultations on the same basis as the Party providing the information; and
   (c) seek to avoid any resolution that adversely affects the interests under this Agreement of any other Party.

Article 2007: Commission - Good Offices, Conciliation and Mediation

1. If the consulting Parties fail to resolve a matter pursuant to Article 2006 within:
   (a) 30 days of delivery of a request for consultations,
   (b) 45 days of delivery of such request if any other Party has subsequently requested or has participated in consultations regarding the same matter,
   (c) 15 days of delivery of a request for consultations in matters regarding perishable agricultural goods, or
   (d) such other period as they may agree,
   any such Party may request in writing a meeting of the Commission.
2. A Party may also request in writing a meeting of the Commission where:
   (a) it has initiated dispute settlement proceedings under the GATT regarding any matter subject to Article 2005(3) or (4), and has received a request pursuant to Article 2005(5) for recourse to dispute settlement procedures under this Chapter; or
   (b) consultations have been held pursuant to Article 513 (Working Group on Rules of Origin), Article 723 (Sanitary and Phytosanitary Measures Technical

Consultations) and Article 914 (Standards-Related Measures Technical Consultations).

3. The requesting Party shall state in the request the measure or other matter complained of and indicate the provisions of this Agreement that it considers relevant, and shall deliver the request to the other Parties and to its Section of the Secretariat.

4. Unless it decides otherwise, the Commission shall convene within 10 days of delivery of the request and shall endeavor to resolve the dispute promptly.

5. The Commission may:
   (a) call on such technical advisers or create such working groups or expert groups as it deems necessary,
   (b) have recourse to good offices, conciliation, mediation or such other dispute resolution procedures, or
   (c) make recommendations,

   as may assist the consulting Parties to reach a mutually satisfactory resolution of the dispute.

6. Unless it decides otherwise, the Commission shall consolidate two or more proceedings before it pursuant to this Article regarding the same measure. The Commission may consolidate two or more proceedings regarding other matters before it pursuant to this Article that it determines are appropriate to be considered jointly.

Article 2008: Request for an Arbitral Panel

1. If the Commission has convened pursuant to Article 2007(4), and the matter has not been resolved within:
   (a) 30 days thereafter,
   (b) 30 days after the Commission has convened in respect of the matter most recently referred to it, where proceedings have been consolidated pursuant to Article 2007(6), or
   (c) such other period as the consulting Parties may agree,

   any consulting Party may request in writing the establishment of an arbitral panel. The requesting Party shall deliver the request to the other Parties and to its Section of the Secretariat.

2. On delivery of the request, the Commission shall establish an arbitral panel.

3. A third Party that considers it has a substantial interest in the matter shall be entitled to join as a complaining Party on delivery of written notice of its intention to participate to the disputing Parties and its Section of the Secretariat. The notice shall be delivered at the earliest possible time, and in any event no later than seven days after the date of delivery of a request by a Party for the establishment of a panel.

4. If a third Party does not join as a complaining Party in accordance with paragraph 3, it normally shall refrain thereafter from initiating or continuing:
   (a) a dispute settlement procedure under this Agreement, or

(b) a dispute settlement proceeding in the GATT on grounds that are substantially equivalent to those available to that Party under this Agreement,

regarding the same matter in the absence of a significant change in economic or commercial circumstances.

5. Unless otherwise agreed by the disputing Parties, the panel shall be established and perform its functions in a manner consistent with the provisions of this Chapter.

Article 2009: Roster

1. The Parties shall establish by January 1, 1994 and maintain a roster of up to 30 individuals who are willing and able to serve as panelists. The roster members shall be appointed by consensus for terms of three years, and may be reappointed.

2. Roster members shall:
    (a) have expertise or experience in law, international trade, other matters covered by this Agreement or the resolution of disputes arising under international trade agreements, and shall be chosen strictly on the basis of objectivity, reliability and sound judgment;
    (b) be independent of, and not be affiliated with or take instructions from, any Party; and
    (c) comply with a code of conduct to be established by the Commission.

Article 2010: Qualifications of Panelists

1. All panelists shall meet the qualifications set out in Article 2009(2).
2. Individuals may not serve as panelists for a dispute in which they have participated pursuant to Article 2007(5).

Article 2011: Panel Selection

1. Where there are two disputing Parties, the following procedures shall apply:
    (a) The panel shall comprise five members.
    (b) The disputing Parties shall endeavor to agree on the chair of the panel within 15 days of the delivery of the request for the establishment of the panel. If the disputing Parties are unable to agree on the chair within this period, the disputing Party chosen by lot shall select within five days as chair an individual who is not a citizen of that Party.
    (c) Within 15 days of selection of the chair, each disputing Party shall select two panelists who are citizens of the other disputing Party.
    (d) If a disputing Party fails to select its panelists within such period, such panelists shall be selected by lot from among the roster members who are citizens of the other disputing Party.

2.   Where there are more than two disputing Parties, the following procedures shall apply:
     (a) The panel shall comprise five members.
     (b) The disputing Parties shall endeavor to agree on the chair of the panel within 15 days of the delivery of the request for the establishment of the panel. If the disputing Parties are unable to agree on the chair within this period, the Party or Parties on the side of the dispute chosen by lot shall select within 10 days a chair who is not a citizen of such Party or Parties.
     (c) Within 15 days of selection of the chair, the Party complained against shall select two panelists, one of whom is a citizen of a complaining Party, and the other of whom is a citizen of another complaining Party. The complaining Parties shall select two panelists who are citizens of the Party complained against.
     (d) If any disputing Party fails to select a panelist within such period, such panelist shall be selected by lot in accordance with the citizenship criteria of subparagraph (c).
3.   Panelists shall normally be selected from the roster. Any disputing Party may exercise a peremptory challenge against any individual not on the roster who is proposed as a panelist by a disputing Party within 15 days after the individual has been proposed.
4.   If a disputing Party believes that a panelist is in violation of the code of conduct, the disputing Parties shall consult and if they agree, the panelist shall be removed and a new panelist shall be selected in accordance with this Article.

Article 2012: Rules of Procedure

1.   The Commission shall establish by January 1, 1994 Model Rules of Procedure, in accordance with the following principles:
     (a) the procedures shall assure a right to at least one hearing before the panel as well as the opportunity to provide initial and rebuttal written submissions; and
     (b) the panel's hearings, deliberations and initial report, and all written submissions to and communications with the panel shall be confidential.
2.   Unless the disputing Parties otherwise agree, the panel shall conduct its proceedings in accordance with the Model Rules of Procedure.
3.   Unless the disputing Parties otherwise agree within 20 days from the date of the delivery of the request for the establishment of the panel, the terms of reference shall be:

"To examine, in the light of the relevant provisions of the Agreement, the matter referred to the Commission (as set out in the request for a Commission meeting) and to make findings, determinations and recommendations as provided in Article 2016(2)."

4.   If a complaining Party wishes to argue that a matter has nullified or impaired benefits, the terms of reference shall so indicate.
5.   If a disputing Party wishes the panel to make findings as to the degree of adverse trade effects on any Party of any measure found not to conform with the obligations

of the Agreement or to have caused nullification or impairment in the sense of Annex 2004, the terms of reference shall so indicate.

Article 2013: Third Party Participation

A Party that is not a disputing Party, on delivery of a written notice to the disputing Parties and to its Section of the Secretariat, shall be entitled to attend all hearings, to make written and oral submissions to the panel and to receive written submissions of the disputing Parties.

Article 2014: Role of Experts

On request of a disputing Party, or on its own initiative, the panel may seek information and technical advice from any person or body that it deems appropriate, provided that the disputing Parties so agree and subject to such terms and conditions as such Parties may agree.

Article 2015: Scientific Review Boards

1. On request of a disputing Party or, unless the disputing Parties disapprove, on its own initiative, the panel may request a written report of a scientific review board on any factual issue concerning environmental, health, safety or other scientific matters raised by a disputing Party in a proceeding, subject to such terms and conditions as such Parties may agree.
2. The board shall be selected by the panel from among highly qualified, independent experts in the scientific matters, after consultations with the disputing Parties and the scientific bodies set out in the Model Rules of Procedure established pursuant to Article 2012(1).
3. The participating Parties shall be provided:
    (a) advance notice of, and an opportunity to provide comments to the panel on, the proposed factual issues to be referred to the board; and
    (b) a copy of the board's report and an opportunity to provide comments on the report to the panel.
4. The panel shall take the board's report and any comments by the Parties on the report into account in the preparation of its report.

Article 2016: Initial Report

1. Unless the disputing Parties otherwise agree, the panel shall base its report on the submissions and arguments of the Parties and on any information before it pursuant to Article 2014 or 2015.

2. Unless the disputing Parties otherwise agree, the panel shall, within 90 days after the last panelist is selected or such other period as the Model Rules of Procedure established pursuant to Article 2012(1) may provide, present to the disputing Parties an initial report containing:
    (a) findings of fact, including any findings pursuant to a request under Article 2012(5);
    (b) its determination as to whether the measure at issue is or would be inconsistent with the obligations of this Agreement or cause nullification or impairment in the sense of Annex 2004, or any other determination requested in the terms of reference; and
    (c) its recommendations, if any, for resolution of the dispute.
3. Panelists may furnish separate opinions on matters not unanimously agreed.
4. A disputing Party may submit written comments to the panel on its initial report within 14 days of presentation of the report.
5. In such an event, and after considering such written comments, the panel, on its own initiative or on the request of any disputing Party, may:
    (a) request the views of any participating Party;
    (b) reconsider its report; and
    (c) make any further examination that it considers appropriate.

Article 2017: Final Report

1. The panel shall present to the disputing Parties a final report, including any separate opinions on matters not unanimously agreed, within 30 days of presentation of the initial report, unless the disputing Parties otherwise agree.
2. No panel may, either in its initial report or its final report, disclose which panelists are associated with majority or minority opinions.
3. The disputing Parties shall transmit to the Commission the final report of the panel, including any report of a scientific review board established under Article 2015, as well as any written views that a disputing Party desires to be appended, on a confidential basis within a reasonable period of time after it is presented to them.
4. Unless the Commission decides otherwise, the final report of the panel shall be published 15 days after it is transmitted to the Commission.

Article 2018: Implementation of Final Report

1. On receipt of the final report of a panel, the disputing Parties shall agree on the resolution of the dispute, which normally shall conform with the determinations and recommendations of the panel, and shall notify their Sections of the Secretariat of any agreed resolution of any dispute.
2. Wherever possible, the resolution shall be non-implementation or removal of a measure not conforming with this Agreement or causing nullification or impairment in the sense of Annex 2004 or, failing such a resolution, compensation.

Article 2019: Non-Implementation-Suspension of Benefits

1. If in its final report a panel has determined that a measure is inconsistent with the obligations of this Agreement or causes nullification or impairment in the sense of Annex 2004 and the Party complained against has not reached agreement with any complaining Party on a mutually satisfactory resolution pursuant to Article 2018(1) within 30 days of receiving the final report, such complaining Party may suspend the application to the Party complained against of benefits of equivalent effect until such time as they have reached agreement on a resolution of the dispute.

2. In considering what benefits to suspend pursuant to paragraph 1:
   (a) a complaining Party should first seek to suspend benefits in the same sector or sectors as that affected by the measure or other matter that the panel has found to be inconsistent with the obligations of this Agreement or to have caused nullification or impairment in the sense of Annex 2004; and
   (b) a complaining Party that considers it is not practicable or effective to suspend benefits in the same sector or sectors may suspend benefits in other sectors.

3. On the written request of any disputing Party delivered to the other Parties and its Section of the Secretariat, the Commission shall establish a panel to determine whether the level of benefits suspended by a Party pursuant to paragraph 1 is manifestly excessive.

4. The panel proceedings shall be conducted in accordance with the Model Rules of Procedure. The panel shall present its determination within 60 days after the last panelist is selected or such other period as the disputing Parties may agree.

Section C - Domestic Proceedings and Private Commercial Dispute Settlement

Article 2020: Referrals of Matters from Judicial or Administrative Proceedings

1. If an issue of interpretation or application of this Agreement arises in any domestic judicial or administrative proceeding of a Party that any Party considers would merit its intervention, or if a court or administrative body solicits the views of a Party, that Party shall notify the other Parties and its Section of the Secretariat. The Commission shall endeavor to agree on an appropriate response as expeditiously as possible.

2. The Party in whose territory the court or administrative body is located shall submit any agreed interpretation of the Commission to the court or administrative body in accordance with the rules of that forum.

3. If the Commission is unable to agree, any Party may submit its own views to the court or administrative body in accordance with the rules of that forum.

Article 2021: Private Rights

No Party may provide for a right of action under its domestic law against any other Party on the ground that a measure of another Party is inconsistent with this Agreement.

Article 2022: Alternative Dispute Resolution

1. Each Party shall, to the maximum extent possible, encourage and facilitate the use of arbitration and other means of alternative dispute resolution for the settlement of international commercial disputes between private parties in the free trade area.
2. To this end, each Party shall provide appropriate procedures to ensure observance of agreements to arbitrate and for the recognition and enforcement of arbitral awards in such disputes.
3. A Party shall be deemed to be in compliance with paragraph 2 if it is a party to and is in compliance with the 1958 *United Nations Convention on the Recognition and Enforcement of Foreign Arbitral Awards* or the 1975 *InterAmerican Convention on International Commercial Arbitration* .
4. The Commission shall establish an Advisory Committee on Private Commercial Disputes comprising persons with expertise or experience in the resolution of private international commercial disputes. The Committee shall report and provide recommendations to the Commission on general issues referred to it by the Commission respecting the availability, use and effectiveness of arbitration and other procedures for the resolution of such disputes in the free trade area.

ANNEX 2001.2. COMMITTEES AND WORKING GROUPS

A. Committees

1. Committee on Trade in Goods (Article 316)
2. Committee on Trade in Worn Clothing (Annex 300-B, Section 9.1)
3. Committee on Agricultural Trade (Article 706)
   • Advisory Committee on Private Commercial Disputes Regarding Agricultural Goods (Article 707)
4. Committee on Sanitary and Phytosanitary Measures (Article 722)
5. Committee on Standards-Related Measures (Article 913)
   • Land Transportation Standards Subcommittee (Article 913(5))
     Telecommunications Standards Subcommittee (Article 913(5))
     Automotive Standards Council (Article 913(5))
     Subcommittee on Labelling of Textile and Apparel Goods (Article 913(5))
6. Committee on Small Business (Article 1021)
7. Financial Services Committee (Article 1412)
8. Advisory Committee on Private Commercial Disputes (Article 2022(4))

B. Working Groups

1. Working Group on Rules of Origin (Article 513)
   - Customs Subgroup (Article 513(6))
2. Working Group on Agricultural Subsidies (Article 705(6))
3. Bilateral Working Group (Mexico United States) (Annex 703.2(A)(25))
4. Bilateral Working Group (Canada Mexico) (Annex 703.2(B)(13))
5. Working Group on Trade and Competition (Article 1504)
6. Temporary Entry Working Group (Article 1605)

C. Other Committees and Working Groups Established under this Agreement

ANNEX 2002.2. REMUNERATION AND PAYMENT OF EXPENSES

1. The Commission shall establish the amounts of remuneration and expenses that will be paid to the panelists, committee members and members of scientific review boards.
2. The remuneration of panelists or committee members and their assistants, members of scientific review boards, their travel and lodging expenses, and all general expenses of panels, committees or scientific review boards shall be borne equally by:
   (a) in the case of panels or committees established under Chapter Nineteen (Review and Dispute Settlement in Antidumping and Countervailing Duty Matters), the involved Parties, as they are defined in Article 1911; or
   (b) in the case of panels and scientific review boards established under this Chapter, the disputing Parties.
3. Each panelist or committee member shall keep a record and render a final account of the person's time and expenses, and the panel, committee or scientific review board shall keep a record and render a final account of all general expenses. The Commission shall establish amounts of remuneration and expenses that will be paid to panelists and committee members.

ANNEX 2004. NULLIFICATION AND IMPAIRMENT

1. If any Party considers that any benefit it could reasonably have expected to accrue to it under any provision of:
   (a) Part Two (Trade in Goods), except for those provisions of Annex 300-A (Automotive Sector) or Chapter Six (Energy) relating to investment,
   (b) Part Three (Technical Barriers to Trade),
   (c) Chapter Twelve (Cross-Border Trade in Services), or
   (d) Part Six (Intellectual Property),
   is being nullified or impaired as a result of the application of any measure that is not inconsistent with this Agreement, the Party may have recourse to dispute settlement under this Chapter.

2. A Party may not invoke:
    (a) paragraph 1(a) or (b), to the extent that the benefit arises from any crossborder trade in services provision of Part Two, or
    (b) paragraph 1(c) or (d),

    with respect to any measure subject to an exception under Article 2101 (General Exceptions).

PART EIGHT: OTHER PROVISIONS

21. EXCEPTIONS

Article 2101: General Exceptions

1. For purposes of:
    (a) Part Two (Trade in Goods), except to the extent that a provision of that Part applies to services or investment, and
    (b) Part Three (Technical Barriers to Trade), except to the extent that a provision of that Part applies to services,

    GATT Article XX and its interpretative notes, or any equivalent provision of a successor agreement to which all Parties are party, are incorporated into and made part of this Agreement.

    The Parties understand that the measures referred to in GATT Article XX(b) include environmental measures necessary to protect human, animal or plant life or health, and that GATT Article XX(g) applies to measures relating to the conservation of living and non-living exhaustible natural resources.

2. Provided that such measures are not applied in a manner that would constitute a means of arbitrary or unjustifiable discrimination between countries where the same conditions prevail or a disguised restriction on trade between the Parties, nothing in:
    (a) Part Two (Trade in Goods), to the extent that a provision of that Part applies to services,
    (b) Part Three (Technical Barriers to Trade), to the extent that a provision of that Part applies to services,
    (c) Chapter Twelve (Cross-Border Trade in Services), and
    (d) Chapter Thirteen (Telecommunications),

    shall be construed to prevent the adoption or enforcement by any Party of measures necessary to secure compliance with laws or regulations that are not inconsistent with the provisions of this Agreement, including those relating to health and safety and consumer protection.

Article 2102: National Security

1. Subject to Articles 607 (Energy - National Security Measures) and 1018 (Government Procurement Exceptions), nothing in this Agreement shall be construed:
    (a) to require any Party to furnish or allow access to any information the disclosure of which it determines to be contrary to its essential security interests;
    (b) to prevent any Party from taking any actions that it considers necessary for the protection of its essential security interests
        (i)   relating to the traffic in arms, ammunition and implements of war and to such traffic and transactions in other goods, materials, services and technology undertaken directly or indirectly for the purpose of supplying a military or other security establishment,
        (ii) taken in time of war or other emergency in international relations, or
        (iii) relating to the implementation of national policies or international agreements respecting the non-proliferation of nuclear weapons or other nuclear explosive devices; or
    (c) to prevent any Party from taking action in pursuance of its obligations under the United Nations Charter for the maintenance of international peace and security.

Article 2103: Taxation

1. Except as set out in this Article, nothing in this Agreement shall apply to taxation measures.
2. Nothing in this Agreement shall affect the rights and obligations of any Party under any tax convention. In the event of any inconsistency between this Agreement and any such convention, that convention shall prevail to the extent of the inconsistency.
3. Notwithstanding paragraph 2:
    (a) Article 301 (Market Access - National Treatment) and such other provisions of this Agreement as are necessary to give effect to that Article shall apply to taxation measures to the same extent as does Article III of the GATT; and
    (b) Article 314 (Market Access - Export Taxes) and Article 604 (Energy Export Taxes) shall apply to taxation measures.
4. Subject to paragraph 2:
    (a) Article 1202 (Cross-Border Trade in Services - National Treatment) and Article 1405 (Financial Services - National Treatment) shall apply to taxation measures on income, capital gains or on the taxable capital of corporations, and to those taxes listed in paragraph 1 of Annex 2103.4, that relate to the purchase or consumption of particular services, and
    (b) Articles 1102 and 1103 (Investment - National Treatment and Most-Favored Nation Treatment), Articles 1202 and 1203 (Cross-Border Trade in Services - National Treatment and Most-Favored Nation Treatment) and Articles 1405 and 1406 (Financial Services - National Treatment and Most-Favored Nation Treatment) shall apply to all taxation measures, other than those on income,

capital gains or on the taxable capital of corporations, taxes on estates, inheritances, gifts and generation-skipping transfers and those taxes listed in paragraph 1 of Annex 2103.4,

except that nothing in those Articles shall apply

(c) any most-favored-nation obligation with respect to an advantage accorded by a Party pursuant to a tax convention,

(d) to a non-conforming provision of any existing taxation measure,

(e) to the continuation or prompt renewal of a non-conforming provision of any existing taxation measure,

(f) to an amendment to a non-conforming provision of any existing taxation measure to the extent that the amendment does not decrease its conformity, at the time of the amendment, with any of those Articles,

(g) to any new taxation measure aimed at ensuring the equitable and effective imposition or collection of taxes and that does not arbitrarily discriminate between persons, goods or services of the Parties or arbitrarily nullify or impair benefits accorded under those Articles, in the sense of Annex 2004, or

(h) to the measures listed in paragraph 2 of Annex 2103.4.

5. Subject to paragraph 2 and without prejudice to the rights and obligations of the Parties under paragraph 3, Article 1106(3), (4) and (5) (Investment - Performance Requirements) shall apply to taxation measures.

6. Article 1110 (Expropriation and Compensation) shall apply to taxation measures except that no investor may invoke that Article as the basis for a claim under Article 1116 (Claim by an Investor of a Party on its Own Behalf) or 1117 (Claim by an Investor of a Party on Behalf of an Enterprise), where it has been determined pursuant to this paragraph that the measure is not an expropriation. The investor shall refer the issue of whether the measure is not an expropriation for a determination to the appropriate competent authorities set out in Annex 2103.6 at the time that it gives notice under Article 1119 (Notice of Intent to Submit a Claim to Arbitration). If the competent authorities do not agree to consider the issue or, having agreed to consider it, fail to agree that the measure is not an expropriation within a period of six months of such referral, the investor may submit its claim to arbitration under Article 1120 (Submission of a Claim to Arbitration).

Article 2104: Balance of Payments

1. Nothing in this Agreement shall be construed to prevent a Party from adopting or maintaining measures that restrict transfers where the Party experiences serious balance of payments difficulties, or the threat thereof, and such restrictions are consistent with paragraphs 2 through 4 and are:

(a) consistent with paragraph 5 to the extent they are imposed on transfers other than Cross-Border trade in financial services; or

(b) consistent with paragraphs 6 and 7 to the extent they are imposed on Cross-Border trade in financial services.

General Rules

2. As soon as practicable after a Party imposes a measure under this Article, the Party shall:
   (a) submit any current account exchange restrictions to the IMF for review under Article VIII of the Articles of Agreement of the IMF;
   (b) enter into good faith consultations with the IMF on economic adjustment measures to address the fundamental underlying economic problems causing the difficulties; and
   (c) adopt or maintain economic policies consistent with such consultations.
3. A measure adopted or maintained under this Article shall:
   (a) avoid unnecessary damage to the commercial, economic or financial interests of another Party;
   (b) not be more burdensome than necessary to deal with the balance of payments difficulties or threat thereof;
   (c) be temporary and be phased out progressively as the balance of payments situation improves;
   (d) be consistent with paragraph 2(c) and with the Articles of Agreement of the IMF; and
   (e) be applied on a national treatment or most-favored-nation treatment basis, whichever is better.
4. A Party may adopt or maintain a measure under this Article that gives priority to services that are essential to its economic program, provided that a Party may not impose a measure for the purpose of protecting a specific industry or sector unless the measure is consistent with paragraph 2(c) and with Article VIII(3) of the Articles of Agreement of the IMF.

Restrictions on Transfers other than Cross-Border Trade in Financial Services

5. Restrictions imposed on transfers, other than on cross border trade in financial services:
   (a) where imposed on payments for current international transactions, shall be consistent with Article VIII(3) of the Articles of Agreement of the IMF;
   (b) where imposed on international capital transactions, shall be consistent with Article VI of the Articles of Agreement of the IMF and be imposed only in conjunction with measures imposed on current international transactions under paragraph 2(a);
   (c) where imposed on transfers covered by Article 1109 (Investment - Transfers) and transfers related to trade in goods, may not substantially impede transfers from being made in a freely usable currency at a market rate of exchange; and
   (d) may not take the form of tariff surcharges, quotas, licenses or similar measures.

Restrictions on Cross-Border Trade in Financial Services

6. A Party imposing a restriction on Cross-Border trade in financial services:

(a) may not impose more than one measure on any transfer, unless consistent with paragraph 2(c) and with Article VIII(3) of the Articles of Agreement of the IMF; and

(b) shall promptly notify and consult with the other Parties to assess the balance of payments situation of the Party and the measures it has adopted, taking into account among other elements

(i) the nature and extent of the balance of payments difficulties of the Party,

(ii) the external economic and trading environment of the Party, and

(iii) alternative corrective measures that may be available.

7. In consultations under paragraph 6(b), the Parties shall:

(a) consider if measures adopted under this Article comply with paragraph 3, in particular paragraph 3(c); and

(b) accept all findings of statistical and other facts presented by the IMF relating to foreign exchange, monetary reserves and balance of payments, and shall base their conclusions on the assessment by the IMF of the balance of payments situation the Party adopting the measures.

Article 2105: Disclosure of Information

Nothing in this Agreement shall be construed to require a Party to furnish or allow access to information the disclosure of which would impede law enforcement or would be contrary to the Party's law protecting personal privacy or the financial affairs and accounts of individual customers of financial institutions.

Article 2106: Cultural Industries

Annex 2106 applies to the Parties specified in that Annex with respect to cultural industries.

Article 2107: Definitions

For purposes of this Chapter:

cultural industries means persons engaged in any of the following activities:

(a) the publication, distribution, or sale of books, magazines, periodicals or newspapers in print or machine readable form but not including the sole activity of printing or typesetting any of the foregoing;

(b) the production, distribution, sale or exhibition of film or video recordings;

(c) the production, distribution, sale or exhibition of audio or video music recordings;

(d) the publication, distribution or sale of music in print or machine readable form; or

(e) radiocommunications in which the transmissions are intended for direct reception by the general public, and all radio, television and cable broadcasting undertakings and all satellite programming and broadcast network services;

international capital transactions means "international capital transactions" as defined under the Articles of Agreement of the IMF;

IMF means the International Monetary Fund;

payments for current international transactions means "payments for current international transactions" as defined under the Articles of Agreement of the IMF;

tax convention means a convention for the avoidance of double taxation or other international taxation agreement or arrangement;

taxes and **taxation measures** do not include:

(a) a "customs duty" as defined in Article 318 (Market Access Definitions); or
(b) the measures listed in exceptions (b),(c), (d) and (e) of that definition; and
    transfers means international transactions and related international transfers and payments.

ANNEX 2103.4. SPECIFIC TAXATION MEASURES

1. For purposes of Article 2103(4)(a) and (b), the listed tax is the asset tax under the *Asset Tax Law* ("Ley del Impuesto al Activo") of Mexico.
2. For purposes of Article 2103(4)(h), the listed tax is any excise tax on insurance premiums adopted by Mexico to the extent that such tax would, if levied by Canada or the United States, be covered by Article 2103(4)(d), (e) or (f).

ANNEX 2103.6. COMPETENT AUTHORITIES

For purposes of this Chapter:

competent authority means

(a) in the case of Canada, the Assistant Deputy Minister for Tax Policy, Department of Finance;
(b) in the case of Mexico, the Deputy Minister of Revenue of the Ministry of Finance and Public Credit ("Secretaría de Hacienda y Crédito Público");
(c) in the case of the United States, the Assistant Secretary of the Treasury (Tax Policy), Department of the Treasury.

ANNEX 2106. CULTURAL INDUSTRIES

Notwithstanding any other provision of this Agreement, as between Canada and the United States, any measure adopted or maintained with respect to cultural industries, except as specifically provided in Article 302 (Market Access - Tariff Elimination), and any measure of equivalent commercial effect taken in response, shall be governed under this Agreement exclusively in accordance with the provisions of the *Canada - United States Free Trade Agreement* . The rights and obligations between Canada and any other Party with respect to such measures shall be identical to those applying between Canada and the United States.

22. FINAL PROVISIONS

Article 2201: Annexes

The Annexes to this Agreement constitute an integral part of this Agreement.

Article 2202: Amendments

1. The Parties may agree on any modification of or addition to this Agreement.
2. When so agreed, and approved in accordance with the applicable legal procedures of each Party, a modification or addition shall constitute an integral part of this Agreement.

Article 2203: Entry into Force

This Agreement shall enter into force on January 1, 1994, on an exchange of written notifications certifying the completion of necessary legal procedures.

Article 2204: Accession

1. Any country or group of countries may accede to this Agreement subject to such terms and conditions as may be agreed between such country or countries and the Commission and following approval in accordance with the applicable legal procedures of each country.
2. This Agreement shall not apply as between any Party and any acceding country or group of countries if, at the time of accession, either does not consent to such application.

Article 2205: Withdrawal

A Party may withdraw from this Agreement six months after it provides written notice of withdrawal to the other Parties. If a Party withdraws, the Agreement shall remain in force for the remaining Parties.

Article 2206: Authentic Texts

The English, French and Spanish texts of this Agreement are equally authentic.

IN WITNESS WHEREOF, the undersigned, being duly authorized by their respective Governments, have signed this Agreement.

Notes

1. **Article 201 (Definitions of General Application):** A good of a Party may include materials of other countries.
2. **Article 301 (Market Access - National Treatment):** "goods of the Party" as used in paragraph 2 includes goods produced in the state or province of that Party.
3. **Article 302(1) (Tariff Elimination):** this paragraph is not intended to prevent any Party from modifying its non-NAFTA tariffs on originating goods for which no NAFTA tariff preference is claimed.
4. **Article 302(1):** this paragraph does not prohibit a Party from raising a tariff back to an agreed level in accordance with the NAFTA's phase-out schedule following a unilateral reduction.
5. **Article 302(1) and (2):** paragraphs 1 and 2 are not intended to prevent a Party from maintaining or increasing a customs duty as may be authorized by any dispute settlement provision of the GATT or any agreement negotiated under the GATT.
6. **Article 303 (Restriction on Drawback and Duty Deferral):** in applying the definition of "used" in Article 415 to this Article, the definition of "consumed" in Article 318 shall not apply.
7. **Article 305(2) (d) (Temporary Admission of Goods):** where another form of monetary security is used, it shall not be more burdensome than the bonding requirement referred to in this subparagraph. Where a Party uses a non-monetary form of security, it shall not be more burdensome than existing forms of security used by that Party.
8. **Article 307(1) (Goods Re-Entered after Repair or Alteration):** this paragraph does not cover goods imported in bond, into foreign-trade zones or in similar status, that are exported for repairs and are not re-imported in bond, into foreign-trade zones or in similar status.
9. **Article 307(1):** for purposes of this paragraph, alteration includes laundering used textile and apparel goods and sterilizing previously sterilized textile and apparel goods.

10. **Article 318 (Market Access - Definitions):** 10-digit items set out in the Tariff Schedule of Canada are included for statistical purposes only.

11. **Article 318:** with respect to the definition of "repair or alteration", an operation or process that is part of the production or assembly of an unfinished good into a finished good is not a repair or alteration of the unfinished good; a component of a good is a good that may be subject to repair or alteration.

12. **Annex 300-A (Trade and Investment in the Automotive Sector) , Appendix 300-A.1 - Canada:** paragraphs 1 and 2 shall not be construed to modify the rights and obligations set out in Chapter Ten of the *Canada - United States Free Trade Agreement* , except that the NAFTA rules of origin shall replace the *Canada - United States Free Trade Agreement* rules of origin for purposes of Article 1005(1).

13. **Annex 300-A , Appendix 300-A.2 - Mexico:** citations to the Auto Decree and the Auto Decree Implementing Regulations included in parentheses are provided for purposes of reference only.

14. **Annex 300-B (Textile and Apparel Goods) , Section 1 (Scope and Coverage):** the general provisions of Chapter Two (Definitions), Chapter Three (Market Access), Chapter Four (Rules of Origin) and Chapter Eight (Emergency Action) are subject to the specific rules for textiles and apparel goods set out in the Annex.

15. **Annex 300-B , Section 2 (Tariff Elimination):** with respect to paragraph 1, "as otherwise provided in this Agreement" refers to such provisions as Section 4, Article 802 (Global Actions) and Chapter 22 (General Exceptions).

16. **Annex 300-B, Sections 4 (Bilateral Emergency Actions (Tariff Actions)) and 5 (Bilateral Emergency Actions (Quantitative Restrictions)):** for purposes of Sections 4 and 5:

    (a) "increased quantities" is intended to be interpreted more broadly than the standard provided in Article 801(1), which considers imports "in absolute terms" only. For purposes of these Sections, "increased quantities" is intended to be interpreted in the same manner as this standard is interpreted in the draft Agreement on Textiles and Clothing, contained in the *Draft Final Act Embodying the Results of the Uruguay Round of Multilateral Trade Negotiations* (GATT document MTN.TNC/W/FA) issued by the Director-General of the GATT on December 20, 1991 ("Draft Uruguay Round Agreement on Textiles and Clothing"); and

    (b) "serious damage" is intended as a less stringent standard than "serious injury" under Article 801(1).The "serious damage" standard is drawn from the Draft Uruguay Round Agreement on Textiles and Clothing. The factors to be considered in determining whether the standard has been met are set out in Section 4.2 and are also drawn from that Draft. "Seriousdamage" is to be interpreted in the light of its meaning in Annex A of the Multifiber Arrangement or any successor agreement.

17. **Annex 300-B , Section 5:** in paragraph 5(c), the term "equitable treatment" is intended to have the same meaning as it has in customary practice under the Multifiber Arrangement.

18. **Annex 300-B , Section 7, paragraph 1(c) (Review and Revision of Rules of Origin):** for subheading 6212.10, the rule and paragraph 1 shall not be applied if the Parties agree, prior to entry into force of this Agreement, on measures to ease the

administrative burden and reduce costs associated with the application of the rule for headings 62.06 through 62.11 to the apparel in subheading 6212.10.

19. **Annex 300-B, Section 7, paragraph (2) (d) (ii):** with respect to provisions (a) through (i) of the rule for subheadings 6205.20 through 6205.30, prior to the entry into force of this Agreement the Parties will extend cooperation as necessary in an effort to encourage production in the free trade area of shirting fabrics specifically identified in the rule.

20. **Annex 300-B, Appendix 3.1, paragraph 17 (Administration of Import and Export Prohibitions, Restrictions and Consultation Levels):** for purposes of applying paragraph 17, the determination of the component that determines the tariff classification of the good shall be based on GRI 3(b) of the Harmonized System, and if the component cannot be determined on the basis of GRI 3(b), then the determination will be based on GRI 3(c) or, if GRI 3(c) is inapplicable, GRI 4.When the component that determines the tariff classification is a blend of two or more yarns or fibers, all yarns and, where applicable, fibers, in that component are to be considered.

21. **Annex 300-B, Schedule 3.1.3.   (Conversion Factors):** the conversion factors in this Schedule are those used for imports into the United States.   Canada   and Mexico may by mutual agreement develop their own conversion factors for trade between them.

22. **Article 401 (Originating Goods):** the phrase "specifically describes" is intended solely to prevent Article 401(d) from being used to qualify a part of another part, where the heading or subheading covers the final good, the part made from the other part and the other part.

23. **Article 402 (Regional Value Content):**

    (a) Article 402(4) applies to intermediate materials, and VNM in paragraphs 2 and 3 does not include

        (i) the value of any non-originating materials used by another producer to produce an originating material that is subsequently acquired and used in the production of the good by the producer of the good, and

        (ii) the value of non-originating materials used by the producer to produce an originating self-produced material that is designated by the producer as an intermediate material pursuant to Article 402(10) ;

    (b) with respect to paragraph 4, where an originating intermediate material is subsequently used by the producer with non-originating materials (whether or not produced by the producer) to produce the good, the value of such non-originating materials shall be included in the VNM of the good;

    (c) with respect to paragraph 8, sales promotion, marketing and after-sales service costs, royalties, shipping and packing costs, and non-allowable interest costs included in the value of materials used in the production of the good are not subtracted out of the net cost in the calculation under Article 402(3) ;

    (d) with respect to paragraph 10, an intermediate material used by another producer in the production of a material that is subsequently acquired and used by the producer of the good shall not be taken into account in applying the proviso set out in that paragraph, except where two or more producers accumulate their production under Article 404;

(e) with respect to paragraph 10, if a producer designates a self-produced material as an originating intermediate material and the Customs Administration of the importing Party subsequently determines that the intermediate material is not originating, the producer may rescind the designation and recalculate the value content of the good accordingly; in such a case, the producer shall retain its rights of appeal or review with regard to the determination of the origin of the intermediate material; and

(f) under paragraph 4, with respect to any self-produced material that is not designated as an intermediate material, only the value of non-originating materials used to produce the self-produced material shall be included in VNM of the good.

24. **Article 403 (Automotive Goods):**

(a) for purposes of paragraph 1, "first person in the territory of a Party" means the first person who uses the imported good in production or resells the imported good; and

(b) for purposes of paragraph 2,

(i) a producer may not designate as an intermediate material any assembly, including a component identified in Annex 403.2, containing one or more of the materials listed in Annex 403.2, and

(ii) a producer of a material listed in Annex 403.2 may designate a self-produced material used in the production of that material as an intermediate material, in accordance with the provisions of Article 402(10).

25. **Article 405(6) (De Minimis):** for purposes of applying paragraph 6, the determination of the component that determines the tariff classification of the good shall be based on GRI 3(b) of the Harmonized System.   If the component cannot be determined on the basis of GRI 3(b), then the determination will be based on GRI 3(c) or, if GRI 3(c) is inapplicable, GRI 4. When the component that determines the tariff classification is a blend of two or more yarns or fibers, all yarns and, where applicable, fibers, in that component are to be taken into account.

26. **Article 413 (Interpretation and Application):** the rules of origin under Chapter Four are based on the 1992 Harmonized System, amended by the new tariff items created for rules of origin purposes.

27. **Article 415 (Rules of Origin - Definitions):** the phrase "except for the application of Article 403(1) or 403(2) (a) " in the definition of "transaction value" is intended solely to ensure that the determination of transaction value in the context of Article 403(1) or (2) (a) shall not be limited to the transaction of the producer of the good.

28. **Article 514 (Customs Procedures - Definitions):** the Uniform Regulations will clarify that "determination of origin" includes a denial of preferential tariff treatment under Article 506(4), and that such denial is subject to review and appeal.

29. **Article 603, paragraphs 1 through 5 (Energy - Import and Export Restrictions):** these paragraphs shall be interpreted consistently with Article 309 (Import and Export Restrictions).

30. **Article 703 (Agriculture - Market Access):** the most-favored-nation rate as of July 1, 1991 is the over-quota tariff rate specified in Annex 302.2.

31. **Annex 703.2, Section A (Mexico and the United States):** this quota replaces Mexico's current access under the "first tier" of the U.S.   tariff   rate   quota   as

described in Additional Note 3(b)(i) of Chapter 17 of the Harmonized Tariff Schedule of the United States prior to the date of entry into force of this Agreement.

32. **Annex 703.2 , Section A (Mexico and the United States):** the United States operates a re-export program under Additional U.S. Note 3 to Chapter 17 of the U.S. Harmonized Tariff Schedule and under 7 C.F.R. Part 1530 (subparts A and B).

33. **Annex 703.2 , Section B (Canada and Mexico):** the incorporation in paragraph 6 is not intended to override the exceptions to Articles 301 and 309 set out in Canada's and Mexico's respective Schedules to Annex 301.3.

34. **Article 906(4) and (6) (Compatibility and Equivalence):** these paragraphs are not intended to restrict the right of the importing Party to revise its measures.

35. **Article 908(2) (Conformity Assessment):** this paragraph does not treat the issue of membership in the Parties' respective conformity assessment bodies.

36. **Article 915 (Standards-Related Measures - Definitions):** the definition of "standard" shall be interpreted to mean --
    (a) characteristics for a good or a service,
    (b) characteristics, rules or guidelines for
        (i) processes or production methods relating to such good, or
        (ii) operating methods relating to such service, and
    (c) provisions specifying terminology, symbols, packaging, marking or labelling for
        (i) a good or its related process or production method, or
        (ii) a service or its related operating method,
    for common and repeated use, including explanatory and other related provisions, set out in a document approved by a standardizing body, with which compliance is not mandatory.

37. **Article 915:** the definition of "technical regulation" shall be interpreted to mean --
    (a) characteristics or their related processes and production methods for a good,
    (b) characteristics for a service or its related operating methods, or
    (c) provisions specifying terminology, symbols, packaging, marking, or labelling for
        (i) a good or its related process or production method, or
        (ii) a service or its related operating method,
    set out in a document, including applicable administrative, explanatory and other related provisions, with which compliance is mandatory.

38. **Annex 1001.2c (Country Specific Thresholds):** Canada and the United States will consult regarding this Annex before the entry into force of this Agreement.

39. **Article 1101 (Investment - Scope and Coverage):** this Chapter covers investments existing on the date of entry into force of this Agreement as well as investments made or acquired thereafter.

40. **Article 1101(2) and Annex 602.3:** to the extent that a Party allows an investment to be made in an activity set out in Annex III or Annex 602.3, the investment shall be entitled to the protection of Chapter Eleven (Investment).

41. **Article 1106 (Performance Requirements):** Article 1106 does not preclude enforcement of any commitment, undertaking or requirement between private parties.

42. **Article 1305 (Monopolies):** for purposes of this Article, "monopoly" means an entity, including a consortium or government agency, that in any relevant market in

the territory of a Party is maintained or designated as the sole provider of public telecommunications transport networks or services.

43. **Article 1501 (Competition Law):** no investor may have recourse to investor-state arbitration under the Investment Chapter for any matter arising under this Article.

44. **Article 1502 (Monopolies and State Enterprises):** nothing in this Article shall be construed to prevent a monopoly from charging different prices in different geographic markets, where such differences are based on normal commercial considerations, such as taking account of supply and demand conditions in those markets.

45. **Article 1502(3):** a "delegation" includes a legislative grant, and a government order, directive or other act transferring to the monopoly, or authorizing the exercise by the monopoly of, governmental authority.

46. **Article 1502(3) (b):** differences in pricing between classes of customers, between affiliated and non-affiliated firms, and cross-subsidization are not in themselves inconsistent with this provision; rather, they are subject to this subparagraph when they are used as instruments of anticompetitive behavior by the monopoly firm.

47. **Article 2005(2) (GATT Dispute Settlement):** this obligation is not intended to be subject to dispute settlement under this Chapter.

CHAPTER SOURCES

The following chapters have been previously published:

Chapter 1 – This is an edited, reformatted and augmented version of a Congressional
    Research Service publication, report R40784, dated August 27, 2009.
Chapter 2 – This website information has been edited, reformatted and augmented from
    www.sice.oas.org/trade/nafta/naftatce.asp

INDEX

C

D

G

H

I

S